COLUMBIA UNIVERSITY GERMANIC STUDIES
EDITED BY ROBERT HERNDON FIFE
NEW SERIES
———
NUMBER FIVE

THE TREATMENT OF ANCIENT LEGEND AND HISTORY IN BODMER

THE TREATMENT OF
ANCIENT LEGEND AND HISTORY
IN BODMER

BY

ANTHONY SCENNA

AMS PRESS, INC.
NEW YORK
1966

74759

Reprinted with the permission of the
Original Publisher, 1966

AMS PRESS, INC.
New York, N.Y. 10003
1966

Manufactured in the United States of America

To the Memory of My Father

PREFACE

It is my pleasant duty to express my deep gratitude to all those who have aided me in the preparation of this study. I am indebted to the libraries of Amherst College and the Universities of Chicago, Columbia, and Harvard for the use of their collections. The Preußische Staatsbibliothek in Berlin and the university library in Leipsic have kindly furnished me with photostatic material. I wish to thank the authorities of the Staatsarchiv in Zurich for the use of its facilities. To the Zentralbibliothek in Zurich I am especially indebted for placing at my disposal the manuscripts and unpublished correspondence of Bodmer, which I have used extensively. Thanks are due Professor Clinton W. Keyes of Columbia University for numerous helpful suggestions and Mr. F. H. Wagman for aid in reading the page proof. Above all I am grateful to Professor Robert Herndon Fife, whose encouragement, helpful suggestions, and invaluable guidance have contributed very materially to the completion of the work in its present form.

A. S.

CONTENTS

I

AIMS AND MATERIALS

The aim of the following work is to study Bodmer's treatment of ancient historical and legendary material, particularly in his ethical and political dramas.

Among the Swiss scholars and authors of the Eighteenth Century Bodmer is outstanding for his wide reading in the history and literature of other countries. The vast store of information that he gathered appears throughout his work. His relation to English literature has been treated adequately by Vetter,[1] to Italian literature by Donati,[2] and to French literature by Betz.[3] A field of Bodmer's knowledge of foreign authors which has as yet received no comprehensive treatment is that of Greece and Rome. His relation to antiquity may be approached from three angles: his attitude toward the literary theories of antiquity,[4] the technique and quality of his translations from classical authors,[5] and the treatment of ancient historical and legendary material in his dramas. It is to the aspect last mentioned that the present study proposes to devote itself especially. An investigation of this hitherto neglected phase of Bodmer's literary activity would, however, be incomplete if it did not also explore the development of the author's interest in the classics and the ideas and theories that gave a peculiar direction to his treatment of ancient sources. It must be conceded that his political dramas have little claim to merit as works of literature

[1] Theodor Vetter, "J. J. Bodmer und die englische Litteratur," *Johann Jakob Bodmer. Denkschrift zum CC. Geburtstag,* hrsg. von der Stiftung von Schnyder von Wartensee (Zürich: Alb. Müller, 1900), pp. 313-86.

[2] L. Donati, "J. J. Bodmer und die italienische Litteratur," *Denkschrift,* pp. 241-312.

[3] Louis P. Betz, "J. J. Bodmer und die französische Litteratur," *Denkschrift,* pp. 163-239.

[4] Cf. Friedrich Braitmaier, *Geschichte der poetischen Theorie und Kritik* (Frauenfeld: J. Hubers Verlag, 1888), Part I, 203-14. The present author wishes to call attention also to a forthcoming work by Max Wehrli of Zurich on the subject of Bodmer as a literary critic, in which this aspect of Bodmer and antiquity may possibly receive some attention.

[5] For the bibliographical material on Bodmer's translation of Homer, cf. Jakob Baechtold, *Geschichte der deutschen Literatur in der Schweiz,* anastatic reprint of 1892 ed. (Frauenfeld: J. Huber & Co., 1919), notes, pp. 200 f.

or as contributions to theatrical history. But they were the expression of a national and political soul-experience that is significant for an understanding of Bodmer and his Swiss contemporaries. The impact of the world of antiquity on Northern and Western Europe in the Eighteenth Century and its echoes in literature and art have been studied long and intensively for the light they shed on the ideas and aspirations of the period. An examination of Bodmer's selection and presentation of ancient sources should make some contribution, not only to literary biography, but also to the history of ideas. From this viewpoint it is particularly significant that most of the material treated here centers in Bodmer's vocation as a teacher of history to Swiss youth. For fifty years, from 1725 to 1775, Bodmer taught this subject at the Carolinum, a higher school in Zurich, took an active part in current historical research,[6] and had as his pupils a number of boys who later rose to considerable prominence.[7] Bodmer's dramatic works are to be viewed as a result of this activity.

Our work begins with an examination of the background which young Bodmer created at school and elsewhere by studies in the literature and history of antiquity. It then proceeds to show the extent to which he drew upon ancient authors to develop and illustrate his critical ideas. The main part of the investigation is concerned with an analysis of the individual themes on ancient subjects. The works fall naturally into three groups and within these groups they are treated in the order in which Bodmer wrote them. A uniform method of approach is used for each of the plays. The available material on the composition and reception of each drama is examined and an attempt is made to show the extent and sources of Bodmer's borrowings. In many cases he has translated or paraphrased closely ancient authors. Such passages are indicated by exact references to the sources, with an occasional quotation from Bodmer's text and often from the original, when clarity

[6] Cf. Gustav Tobler, *J. J. Bodmer als Geschichtschreiber.* "Neujahrsblatt herausgegeben von der Stadtbibliothek in Zürich auf das Jahr 1891" (Zürich: Orell Füßli & Co.), 1891.

[7] Among these may be mentioned Joh. Heinrich Füßli (1741-1825), who achieved an enviable reputation as a painter; Joh. Caspar Hirzel (1725-1803), a friend of Ewald von Kleist in Berlin; Joh. Caspar Lavater (1741-1801); and Heinrich Pestalozzi (1746-1827).

of presentation demands. Unless otherwise stated, references to Greek and Roman writers are to the edition in the "Loeb Classical Library," since it is assumed that these texts are generally accessible to an American public.[8] Unless otherwise stated references to Plutarch are to the biographies in the *Lives*. References to Bodmer's works are to act, scene, and page in the published text. Finally an attempt is made for each play to determine the changes made by Bodmer in his adaptations. In addition to the dramas, a brief treatment of certain poems based on ancient themes is included.

For biographical facts and for Bodmer's ideas and intentions the study draws on unpublished works and letters by Bodmer now in the Zentralbibliothek in Zurich. This rich collection includes approximately 2,000 letters by Bodmer and some 3,800 letters to Bodmer. The bulk of this correspondence is still unpublished. Unfortunately Bodmer's hand is difficult to read and this has been largely responsible for the fact that these letters have not been fully exploited.[9] In preparing this study, a considerable part of the correspondence has been examined, and two groups of the letters have been found especially helpful, those from Bodmer to J. G. Sulzer, the German aesthetic philosopher, and to Hans Heinrich Schinz (1726-1788), who was a pastor in the town of Altstetten near Zurich from 1754 until his death in 1788. The correspondence with Sulzer is interesting because he was Bodmer's unofficial literary representative in Germany and aided the Swiss writer in the publication of some of his works by German firms. The collection in Zurich contains 257 letters from Bodmer to Sulzer. The correspondence with Schinz is indispensable for any study of Bodmer's activity after 1752. It extends from May of that year to December, 1782. In those thirty years Bodmer wrote Schinz 975 letters, together with more than a hundred odd sheets. This is the largest number of letters from Bodmer to one individual. All these letters are in Zurich and are, for the most part, unpublished. They cover completely the period in which Bodmer

[8] These will not be listed in the bibliography.

[9] Almost every one who has worked with these letters has spoken of their illegibility, a characteristic which Bodmer realized keenly. He complained to Sulzer in 1775: "Meine Briefe haben das Princip der Vernichtung in sich selbst, weil sie so schwer zu entziffern sind. Sie sind schon lebendig todt." Baechtold, *op. cit.*, p. 524.

wrote the works which form the major part of this study, 1759-1782. It is not only their great range that makes them necessary for the study of Bodmer during this period; more important is their intimate and personal character. They are letters, as Bodmer said, "in which I wrote about the poetic, political, and personal thoughts which were going through my mind—as it were, a diary."[10] Schinz was, in effect, Bodmer's literary secretary and the latter concealed nothing from him;[11] he transcribed many of Bodmer's manuscripts and helped him with corrections and suggestions. The letters to him may therefore be said to furnish a fairly complete account of Bodmer's views and activities during the period which is of importance to us. An examination of these letters of Bodmer shows that he was in the habit of repeating the same observation in almost the same words to several correspondents to whom he wrote at approximately the same time. It was felt, therefore, that since a selection amid the vast mass of correspondence was necessary, the purpose of our investigation would be met adequately by concentrating upon the letters to the two friends who were his personal intimates and literary helpers and whom, especially Pastor Schinz, he made the recipients of continuous and informal communication of his ideas and feelings.[12]

A further word should be said in explanation of the treatment of the unpublished letters. Parts of the originals will be found quoted in the footnotes when such extracts seem to have special pertinence or interest. References to these letters are followed by the abbreviation *MS ZBZ*.[13] These excerpts are reproduced as in the original manuscripts; since this work is, however, in no sense a critical

[10] Jakob Baechtold, "Bodmer's Tagebuch (1752 bis 1782)," *Turicensia. Beiträge zur zürcherischen Geschichte* (Zürich: S. Höhr, 1891), p. 206.

[11] *Ibid.*, p. 209.

[12] The letters to both Sulzer and Schinz have been examined in their entirety with the purpose of extracting the references and observations bearing directly upon the dramas in this study. Occasionally a quotation from the letters *to* Bodmer has been used, but no claim is made to completeness in the use of these letters.

[13] The letters are filed chronologically according to addressees in pasteboard boxes under the heading "Bodmer Nachlaß." They contain the following letters: Bodmer to Schinz, nos. 1-367 (May 3, 1752 to Dec. 31, 1775) in box XIV; nos. 368-722 (Jan. 7, 1776 to Dec. 31, 1779) in box XV; nos. 723-975 (Jan. 5, 1780 to the end of 1782) in box XVI; 103 odd sheets in box XVI. Bodmer to Sulzer: these run from Feb. 14, 1745 to Dec., 1778; those before July, 1774, are bound in two volumes, 12a and 12b; the others are in box XX. Transcriptions of some of the letters are in Zurich.

edition of the letters, certain orthographic changes have been made for the sake of uniformity and intelligibility. Capitalization and punctuation are normalized to conform with current usage; final inflexional endings, often indicated in the manuscripts by a nasal curve, are resolved in all cases. Double consonants are written when the original has a single consonant with a superimposed mark of length; the consonant combinations ß, ck, tz are normalized throughout. In these minor orthographic changes the author follows the practice of Baechtold, who made similar changes in his fragmentary extracts from the letters.[14]

The classification of the dramas requires some explanation. The first group contains those plays which are based primarily on legendary material. This does not necessarily mean that some of the other works do not also draw upon such material. *Ulysses, Electra,* and *Oedipus* are merely versions of ancient legends and have no tendentious aim. Chronologically they are the first works on ancient themes by Bodmer and are to be considered as experimental. Both *Die Rettung in den Mauern von Holz* and *Die Tegeaten* are plays whose plots are concerned mainly with the development and fulfillment of prophecies. *Patroclus* must be viewed as a treatment of legendary material in preparation for Bodmer's translation of Homer. All of these works seem to fall together into a unified group. The second class contains those plays in which the ethical import seems to dominate Bodmer's interest and treatment. In the case of *Octavius Cäsar* and *Cato* Bodmer has chosen to study the morality of ancient Rome and he seeks to show the degrading effect of power, wealth, and luxury on Roman society. In *Brittannicus* the author attacks the weakness and instability of Nero. *Aristomenes* is more personal in its theme, which may be characterized as the betrayal of Aristomenes' personal faith in Aristocrates by the latter's treachery. Each of these plays seems to have some ethical content.

The political dramas are most important because they exemplify the most significant attitude of Bodmer toward antiquity. They fall into three sub-groups. *Cicero, Thrasea Pätus, Cajus Gracchus,* and *Brutus und Kassius Tod* stand together; in each one the death

[14] Baechtold, *Gesch. d. d. Lit. i. d. Schweiz.* Probably no person since the Eighteenth Century has done more work with Bodmer's correspondence than Baechtold.

of its hero is the climax of the action. According to Bodmer's point of view they are "great souls," who are martyrs to the cause of freedom and democracy. Differing from these in one essential are the dramas which may be called patriotic plays. In these the heroes do not die, but are responsible for the assassination of the tyrants and exemplify the triumph of democratic ideals over despotism. This is true in *Marcus Brutus, Timoleon,* and *Pelopidas. Karl von Burgund* is classified in this group, despite the fact that its figures are taken from medieval Swiss history, because it praises the bravery of the Swiss by the use of an ancient garb in both form and expression. *Julius Cäsar* and *Tarquinius Superbus,* as well as *Nero,* belong together as dramas in which the attack on these autocratic rulers, on their ambitions and faults, is the most important element in Bodmer's treatment.

It is not claimed, of course, that the classification outlined above is the only one applicable to these dramas. It is quite possible to arrange them in other groups and examine them from other standpoints. No one group excludes necessarily the characteristics of another completely. For instance, *Marcus Brutus* and *Julius Cäsar* treat the same theme. They are, however, differentiated by the fact that in the former the patriotic action of the conspirators assumes more significance than in the latter, in which Caesar's ambitions and greed for power are stressed as the more important elements in the theme. The present arrangement seems to have more merit than any other logical classification and must be considered only an attempt to classify each play according to that interest in the material which seemed to be uppermost in Bodmer's mind.

In treating the individual works, the order followed in each group is chronological according to the time of composition. For our purpose this is more important than the date of publication.

Finally the limits of the study exclude the treatment of some of Bodmer's unimportant works. Thus no consideration is given to his translations from the Greek and Latin, except to list them in the appendix. Bodmer's prose version of the Pygmalion fable (1747) is omitted, because, as Betz has pointed out, its source was the French version by Saint Hyacinthe (1684-1746).[15] An-

---

[15] Betz, *op. cit.,* p. 212.

other work which does not properly belong to our study is a series of dialogues published between 1763 and 1766, entitled *Gespräche im Elysium und am Acheron*.[16] While such characters from the ancient world as Octavia, Brutus, Vergil, Cicero, Cato, Homer, etc., appear here, the dialogues are in large measure imitations of George Lyttleton's *Dialogues of the Dead* (1760) and they cannot be included among the expressions of Bodmer's conception of antiquity.[17]

Two other themes are mentioned briefly here rather than in the main text, because they do not present any characteristic attitude of Bodmer toward the ancient world and also because they have already been treated adequately. They are the two parodies *Polytimet* and *Atreus und Thyest*, directed against Lessing and Weisse. *Polytimet* was written in June, 1759, and was published in the next year.[18] Bodmer intended it as a parody on Lessing and characterized it as "the most gentle criticism that one can make of Lessing's *Philotas*."[19] He sent it to Laurenz Zellweger with the statement that Lessing's work had led him to write it.[20] This work has been treated quite adequately by Meissner, and it is hardly necessary to deal with it again.[21] Bodmer's satire has not, of course, influenced critical opinion of the *Philotas* as a striking experiment in the field of the classical tragedy. The Swiss author's reprint, with interpolations, of Christian Felix Weisse's *Atreus und Thyest* has also been treated fully from the standpoint of a parody by Meissner.[22] He has covered in detail the prose additions in the Zurich version and has pointed out that Bodmer's

[16] Cf. Baechtold, *op. cit.*, notes, p. 192; also Theod. Vetter, "Bibliographie der Schriften J. J. Bodmers und der von ihm besorgten Ausgaben," *Denkschrift*, pp. 395 f.

[17] Cf. Th. Vetter, *Bodmer und die englische Litteratur*, pp. 345 f.

[18] Baechtold, *Tagebuch*, p. 196.

[19] J. J. Bodmer, *Polytimet* (Zürich: Conrad Orell und Comp., 1760), p. iii.

[20] Bodmer to Zellweger, Jan. 31, 1760, MS ZBZ.: "Ich schicke Ihnen den Polytimet. Er ist meine Arbeit. Ich habe ihn aber einem andern untergeschoben. Lessings Philotas hat ihn verursacht." This letter seems to be incorrectly recorded as addressed to Sulzer by Baechtold. *Gesch. d. d. Lit. i. d. Schweiz*, p. 657. It may possibly be another letter.

[21] Erich Meissner, *Bodmer als Parodist* (Naumburg a. S.: H. Sieling, 1904), pp. 43 ff.

[22] *Ibid.*, pp. 68 ff.: Meissner describes (p. 71) Bodmer's method as follows: "The element of parody depends upon numerous prose interpolations, by means of which the actors give a comical turn to their own words or to those of others."

attack was directed against Weisse's pompous language, his out-landish figures of speech, the introduction of physical and psychical impossibilities, the rapid and inconsistent changes of feeling in the characters, as well as the unnatural and stilted expressions, monologues, and asides. Meissner has reproduced extensively Bodmer's additions, and it is hardly necessary to reconsider them here, for they show no original treatment of the theme. How trivial Bodmer's occupation with Weisse was can be gathered from a remark addressed by the former to Sulzer: "If I continue to write *Antiatreus* pieces in the apathy of my years, they are only *débauches d'esprit* and one must allow me these because they keep my mind in a state of continuous activity."[23] Concerning Bodmer's work on the theme, he wrote Schinz in 1767 that he had a copy of Weisse's play and could not see why the critics had found it worthy of praise.[24] So he set about attacking it. By early April, 1768, the parody was partly finished and he hoped that it would appear soon. At this time he called the work "a critical farce, a mere whim and unworthy of the name of Bodmer."[25] Later he sought to defend his venture and wrote Schinz that he had done Weisse no injustice; his *Atreus* was not a parody on Weisse, but merely a revision of the theme, a fact which the latter had failed to appreciate fully.[26] No literary importance can be attached to the Swiss version of this theme, and the only explanation of its appearance is to be found in Bodmer's personal antagonism to Weisse.

[23] Bodmer to Sulzer, Mar. 6, 1769, J. Baechtold, *Gesch. d. d. Lit. i. d. Schweiz*, p. 651.

[24] Bodmer to Schinz, Oct. 6, 1767, MS ZBZ. Weisse's play appeared in 1766.

[25] Bodmer to Schinz, Apr. 19, 1768, MS ZBZ.: "welcher doch nur eine critische Farce ist, unwürdig des Bodmerischen Nahmens und nur Laune." The play appeared in Bodmer's *Neue theatralische Werke* (Lindau: Jakob Otto, 1768), pp. 137-311.

[26] Bodmer to Schinz, July 29, 1771, MS ZBZ.: "Let them show me that Weisse has had this knowledge and I am willing to confess that I have done him an injustice in the new *Atreus* and the *Liberation of Thebes*. . . . These pieces are neither parodies nor disguises. They are rather revisions and one must almost deny that Weisse and his friends possess the attribute of a sound mother-wit, if we are expected to believe that they have not perceived the justness of these revisions, although they make themselves so very obnoxious over them." The reference to the *Lib. of Thebes* is to Bodmer's *Eindrücke der Befreyung von Theben,* published in his *Neue theat. Werke*, pp. 313-32. It is a satire in which a certain Nicander attends an imaginary performance of Weisse's *Thebes* (1764) and makes disparaging remarks about the play. Cf. Meissner, *op. cit.*, pp. 77 ff.

II

THE DEVELOPMENT OF BODMER'S INTEREST
IN THE ANCIENTS

Johann Jakob Bodmer was born on July 19, 1698, in the hamlet of Greifensee near Zurich, the son of the pastor Hans Jakob Bodmer and Ester Orell, both of whom came from long established, middle-class Zurich families.[1]

After rudimentary instruction in Greifensee by his father, in which the subject of Latin was most important,[2] young Bodmer was sent for his formal education to Zurich. Here he was enrolled at first in the Collegium Humanitatis and later in the Carolinum, both schools which undoubtedly cultivated the narrow classical program of the day as well as any in Switzerland. Previous to this formal study in Zurich, Bodmer's training in Latin had been limited to grammar and his progress had been very slow.[3] In the Collegium his horizon in Latin was widened and he began to read material from classical authors.[4] He received from his godmother, Katharina Werdmüller, Ovid's *Metamorphoses* in the version made by Jörg Wickram from the medieval form of Albrecht von Halberstadt.[5] He devoured its contents and found in it a stimulus for his further interest in books.[6] His knowledge of the mythology in Ovid gave him a position of respect among his classmates.[7] The translation led him to study the original.[8]

---

[1] Cf. Hans und Hermann Bodmer, "J. J. Bodmer. Sein Leben und seine Werke," *Denkschrift,* p. 3. For the genealogy of the Bodmer family cf. Anton Largiardèr, "Die Ahnentafel Joh. Jakob Bodmers," *Schweizer Archiv für Heraldik,* XLII (1928), 145-59.

[2] H. und H. Bodmer, *op. cit.,* p. 4: at the age of twelve Bodmer wrote Latin and Greek verses. Cf. L. Meister, *Über Bodmern. Nebst Fragmenten aus seinen Briefen* (Zürich: Orell Geßner, Füßli und Compagn., 1783), p. 19.

[3] Theodor Vetter, "Bodmer's persönliche Anekdoten," *Zürcher Taschenbuch,* XV (1892), p. 96.

[4] *Ibid.,* p. 97.

[5] *Ibid.,* p. 95. Wickram's version appeared in 1545.

[6] As an old man Bodmer recalled: "und gewiß hat Wickrams Ovid . . . die Liebe zu Büchern bey mir unauslöschlich aufgefacht." Bodmer to Schinz, June 24, 1778, MS ZBZ.

[7] Vetter, *Pers. Anek.,* p. 97.

[8] *Ibid.,* p. 123.

He read Catullus with the commentary of Isaac Vossius and became especially interested in the poem on the nuptials of Peleus and Thetis, which he later translated.[9] From this time dates also his study of the *Aeneid* and the *Odyssey*. He occupied himself with Cicero, reading the *Offices, On Old Age,* and *On Friendship;* Horace became his constant companion, as he wrote.[10] Much of his pocket money was used to purchase Latin works of the Sixteenth and Seventeenth Centuries, such as those of Marcus Vida.[11] He mastered the Latin language and seemed quite proficient in the usual Latin school-exercises. As he remembered in later years, however, he was not attracted by formal linguistic study and notes, but absorbed from these authors "the morals of men and of states."[12] This interest in the cultural and moral aspects of antiquity he kept throughout his whole life.

The intense theological emphasis which characterized the Carolinum was uncongenial to him and made the son more and more dissatisfied with the father's intention of making a pastor out of young Bodmer. Then came the step which turned Bodmer's thoughts to a literary career, the trip to Geneva. During this journey he kept in touch with two classmates, J. J. Breitinger and Johann Caspar Hagenbuch, who were striving to outdo each other in zeal for the classics.[13] To them Bodmer wrote letters in Latin during his stay in Geneva and Lyons (1718) and in Lugano (1719).[14] To Heinrich Meister and Jakob Ulrich he addressed from Geneva some verses in Latin, among them the following iambs of his youthful muse:

> Superba me tenent, amice, moenia
> Quae Rhodanus alluit frequens;
> Lacus Lemani postquam ereptus vinculis
> Movit pedes in Galliam.[15]

[9] *Ibid.,* p. 124.
[10] *Ibid.,* p. 100.
[11] *Ibid.,* p. 124.
[12] *Ibid.,* p. 102.
[13] *Ibid.,* p. 100.
[14] E.g., Bodmer to Meister, June 21, 1718, and Oct. 29, 1718. L. Meister, *op. cit.,* pp. 63-65.
[15] J. H. Füßli, "Bodmer," *Schweitzersches Museum,* I (July, 1783), 17; in a letter addressed to Meister dated June 18, 1718.

His interest led him to ask Meister to purchase a set of Lucretius for him, "a clean edition and without the addition of notes."[16] His library at this time contained a copy of Ovid's *Tristia,* Cicero's *Offices,* and a drama entitled *Antigone* by an unknown Italian author.[17] It is fair to assume that Bodmer read these works and that they had some share in the process of literary fermentation that was going on within him.

In the summer of 1719 Bodmer returned to the vicarage in Greifensee, and other authors began to appear in his readings from the ancients. He planned to publish a collection of imitations of passages from French and classical authors, with notes and parallel passages; however, this project was never executed.[18] The first mention of Plutarch appears now in the form of a request, addressed to young Breitinger, for a copy of the *Lives* in the French translation by Amyot.[19] Bodmer may well have known the original Greek. It was to become his favorite reading in the field of ancient biographical history. The letters to Breitinger at this time contain also the first mention of Aristotle, although a thorough knowledge of the latter's literary canons seems, at this date, improbable. The two friends were planning the *Discourse der Mahlern,* and Breitinger raised objections to the use of the Greek author as a possible source of material.[20] Bodmer was incensed at his friend's objections and accused him of condemning Aristotle without having read him.[21] In reply Breitinger acknowledged this accusation as essentially true, for he confessed that he had read no more in Aristotle's works than in the *Koran* or in the writings of Confucius.[22] It is impossible to say how well Bodmer knew Aristotle at this time.

It is clear from the foregoing that Bodmer enjoyed the usual

[16] *Ibid.,* p. 33; in a letter dated Mar. 7 and 14, 1719.
[17] *Ibid.,* p. 33.
[18] Bodmer to Meister, May 5, 1720, L. Meister, *op. cit.,* p. 80.
[19] Bodmer to Breitinger, May 30, 1720, J. Zehnder-Stadlin, *Pestalozzi. Idee und Macht der menschlichen Entwicklung* (Gotha: Thienemann, 1875), p. 206: Breitinger was requested to procure a copy from Hagenbuch.
[20] Breitinger to Bodmer, Feb. 13, 1720, MS ZBZ.
[21] Bodmer to Breitinger, Feb. 23, 1720, MS ZBZ.: "Ihr seyd verwegen, daß Ihr einen Author verurtheilt, den Ihr nicht gelesen habt. Ich kann mir nicht einbilden, daß Ihr das geringste Buch dieses berühmten Mannes gelesen habt."
[22] Breitinger to Bodmer, Feb. 23, 1720, MS ZBZ.

grounding in the technical aspects of Latin and Greek, that he was acquainted with a few representative works of antiquity, and that his readings in these works aided materially in moulding his plastic mind. It is interesting to note that Bodmer's acquaintance with Homer thus antedates his enthusiasm for Milton.[23]

In 1725, after five years in the Zurich cantonal chancery, Bodmer succeeded Balthasar Bullinger as teacher of history at the Carolinum. During his long term of service, until 1775,[24] he had a marked influence in broadening the field of historical research. He felt little sympathy with the type of history represented by pure chronicle, for he was convinced that continuity in history was based on a chain of cause and effect. These had their explanation not only in political and military events, but also in the natural and cultural environment of the people, conditions of physical geography, climate, cultural and intellectual developments, as well as individual peculiarities. He was one of the first to be aware of the concept of historical pragmatism, and he regretted that he was anticipated in expressing this point of view by Montesquieu in his *Considérations sur les causes de la grandeur des Romains et de leur décadence* (1734).[25] He regarded Sallust and Plutarch as exemplifying better than other historians of antiquity this type of approach to the material.[26] The customs and morals of the people, as he found them treated in Plutarch, interested him. Above all, he concerned himself with the importance of characters, of the great men who had an influence on the development of history.

As early as 1721 Bodmer devoted a chapter in the *Discourse der Mahlern* to the subject of historical writing.[27] Historians he divides into three groups: those who copy records and documents, those who criticize these, and those who write from personal experience.

[23] Bodmer's serious concern with *Paradise Lost* falls in the year 1723. Cf. Jakob Schmitter, *J. J. Bodmers Übersetzungen von J. Miltons Verlorenem Paradies* (Zürich: Gebr. Leemann & Co., 1913), p. 5.

[24] Bodmer was made professor of Politics and Swiss History in 1731; in 1775 he was succeeded by Joh. Heinrich Füssli (1745-1832).

[25] Tobler, *Bodmer als Geschichtschreiber,* p. 6.

[26] *Ibid.,* p. 2.

[27] Bodmer, *Die Discourse der Mahlern* (4 Theile. Zürich: Joseph Lindinner, Bodmerische Druckerey, 1721-23), Part I, Disc. 5. Part I is also available in a reprint edited by Theodor Vetter (Frauenfeld: J. Huber, 1891). Cf. Tobler, *op. cit.,* pp. 2 ff.

The first group writes chronicles and compiles data from official records. The requisite qualities for success in such work are the ability to read and write, the patience to sit diligently over records, and a certain amount of curiosity. The second group, the critical historians, is composed of those who work over the material recorded by the first one. These critics must be endowed with considerable understanding and wisdom in order to separate the true from the false and thus to formulate a truthful picture of the nature and politics of a people or of a person. The third group, the originals, is composed of those who have actually participated in the events recorded by them. Such historians must have balanced and keen minds in order to make their writings both truthfully proportionate and deeply penetrating. It is this last group that has the best equipment to deal with the most proper subject in history, namely characters. For Bodmer characters consist of "the subtle and orderly descriptions of all those qualities by means of which a whole nation or a person can be distinguished."[28] The conception of characters in this sense is very important for Bodmer's idea of history. Although the historian of the second group can reconstruct such characters, his dependence upon material that is not acquired by personal observation gives him less claim to accuracy and truth than in the case of those in the third group.[29] Bodmer considered it regrettable that the historians of his day should have neglected the importance of character, whereas the Roman and Greek historians excelled in this approach to history.[30] The study of differences in characters gives the historian a basis for judging the fundamental goodness or badness of historical figures, from which qualities their actions spring. It is difficult to escape Bodmer's moral implication. Sallust is chosen to illustrate this type of historian, and a long passage is quoted from his treatment of Catiline. Sallust points out that the key to Catiline's actions lies in the statement that "his passions were wicked and corrupt."[31] When, in 1746, Bodmer reëdited the *Discourse der Mah-*

[28] *Discourse der Mahlern,* Vetter ed., p. 26.
[29] *Idem.*
[30] *Ibid.*, pp. 26 f.
[31] *Ibid.*, p. 27. Bodmer returns to praise Sallust in his *Critische Betrachtungen*, p. 395.

lern under the title of *Der Mahler der Sitten,* he stressed more emphatically the importance of characters and declared that history is the more useful in proportion to the extent and exactness with which it reveals the hearts of men.[32] The best historians are those who write about events with which they have had some personal contact and who can portray in their treatment of people the moral essence of their character.

It is not our purpose here to attempt an analysis of Bodmer's national historical writings in order to see how closely he followed the conception of history outlined above. It is to be noted, however, that he took Livy as his model when he began to edit in 1735 the *Helvetische Bibliothek,* a collection of historical articles. This work was intended as a treatment of both events and their causes. Bodmer explains this further by quoting the statement in which the Roman historian defines the purpose of his work: to study life and morals, the men and policies which established and enlarged the empire, to investigate the relaxing of discipline and the decline of morals as the cause of national decadence.[33] A year before the publication of the *Helvetische Bibliothek* Bodmer planned to include in the work "biographies, reviews, rare printed and unprinted historical works, political opinions, etc."[34] In form, however, this work differs from that of Livy; it is not a consecutive account by one author of the history of Switzerland, but a collection of articles by several authors in the style of an historical journal.

Bodmer's early conception of history, especially ancient history, may be characterized as one having little interest in military events as such and embodying a strong interest in the ethical and moral implication of events as determined by human figures. He found history best represented in the great characters and figures who were active in politics. As will be seen later, he championed the supporters of democracy and republicanism.

Let us now turn to a brief consideration of the illustrative ma-

[32] Tobler, *op. cit.*, p. 7.

[33] J. J. Bodmer, *Helvetische Bibliothek* (Zürich: Conrad Orell und Comp., 1735-41. 6 Stücke), preface, p. 6, verso. Cf. Livy *Hist.* I. preface. 9.

[34] Bodmer to Zellweger, Feb. 24, 1734, Tobler, *op. cit.*, p. 13: "vitae, recensiones, gedruckte rare und ungedruckte historische pièces, politische Gutachten, ec."

terial from the ancients used by Bodmer in his critical works through the year 1741. This material is literary rather than historical, but it forms part of the background for his treatment of ancient themes. No attempt will be made to show Bodmer's indebtedness to ancient theories of literary criticism, rather this illustrative material is presented to show the vitality and range of Bodmer's interest in antiquity.

Die Discourse der Mahlern show little classical influence and that which appears is hardly more than superficial. Many of the chapters are headed with Latin quotations from such authors as Ovid, Lucretius, Vergil, Sallust, Juvenal, or Horace. At the beginning of the twentieth chapter, Part I, appear Horace's famous words: "Ut pictura poesis erit." Bodmer makes no distinction between the aims of painting and poetry; both seek to imitate nature and differ only in their media. Whatever is not found in the range of natural events must be disallowed as proper subject-matter for poetry, sculpture, and painting, because the effect of a portrayal of the unnatural on the reader or the observer would afford no pleasure. Bodmer praises Ovid for his apt selection of material and his use of figures. In the fifteenth chapter, Part IV, Bodmer recommends a list of readings for women, in which he includes the following: Xenophon's *Denkwirdigen Reden des Socrates* in the German translation by Thomase, *Les caractères de Theophraste* in the translation by Jean de la Bruyère, the works of Lucian in the French rendering of d'Ablancourt, Segrais' French version of the *Aeneid*, the comedies of Terence in the translation by Anne Lefebre d'Acier, and R. P. Tateron's translation of Horace's works, also in French.[35]

In 1727 Bodmer and Breitinger published the *Einfluß und Gebrauch der Einbildungskraft.*[36] Bodmer quotes a long passage from Quintilian.[37] In another passage Theophrastus is set up as a master of description, especially moral, a skill which is attributed partly to his education in the school of Aristotelian morals and

---

[35] *Discourse der Mahlern*, Pt. IV, pp. 103 f.
[36] *Von dem Einfluß und Gebrauche der Einbildungs-Krafft.* Franckfurt und Leipzig, 1727.
[37] *Ibid.*, pp. 120-23. Quintilian *Instit. Orat.* VI. iii.

partly to his long experience in observing the character and actions of men.[38] Particularly interesting is a description of the actions of a miser, which Bodmer renders into German from Theophrastus.[39]

At this time Bodmer was corresponding with J. U. König in an attempt to form a literary society which was to be dedicated to the memory of Opitz. It was to be called the *Boberfeldische Gesellschaft* and was to publish a periodical under the title of *Der Phantast*. The plan did not advance beyond the embryonic state, but Bodmer executed a lyrical drama, probably intending it as a contribution to this periodical.[40] The play was called *Marc Anton und Kleopatra Verliebung* and was written in 1725. Only one scene in blank verse has been preserved in a letter from Bodmer to Johann Michael von Löen, dated January 12, 1729. It is a love scene in which the author intended to refute the notion "that women should on account of an innate sense of modesty offer opposition and resistance before yielding to men's love."[41]

In Bodmer's *Brief-Wechsel von der Natur des poetischen Geschmackes*, several references to ancient literature are found.[42] Bodmer praises Euripides' treatment of the Iphigenia theme as one of the most apt examples of pity, from which all pleasure in tragedy comes.[43] He is attracted by the effect that the grief of the mother and the wailing of the daughter produce. For Bodmer, not only pity and terror, but also the sublime is necessary in tragedy in order to effect a catharsis, which must aim at some moral improvement. Sophocles' tragedies are good examples. *Antigone* is calculated to reform disobedience to royalty; *Ajax*, ambition; the

---

[38] *Einfluß und Gebrauche*, pp. 151 f.

[39] *Ibid.*, pp. 157 f.

[40] Cf. Baechtold, *Ges. d. d. Lit. i. d. Schweiz*, p. 537. Bodmer sent the work to König, who hoped to use it as an operetta. He rejected it, however, and wrote Bodmer that it did not suit his purpose, because the recitatives were too long and the arias too few; in fact the whole work could not be mended to fit the stage. J. U. König to Bodmer, May 15, 1725, Alois Brandl, *Berthold H. Brockes* (Innsbruck: Wagner, 1878), p. 141.

[41] A. von Löen, "Eine Reliquie von Johann Jakob Bodmer," *Blätter für literarische Unterhaltung*, 1 (1856), 32-35: the quotation is on p. 33.

[42] *Brief-Wechsel von der Natur des poetischen Geschmackes*. Zürich: Conrad Orell, und Comp., 1736.

[43] *Ibid.*, p. 33.

Trachinians, desires of the flesh; *Oedipus,* violent anger arising from insult.[44]

It is interesting to note that in his *Critische Abhandlung von dem Wunderbaren*[45] Bodmer compares the mythology of Milton's angels with that of Homer's deities and heroes. He raises the question as to whether Milton has not followed Homer in this.[46]

In 1741 came the *Critische Betrachtungen.*[47] This is Bodmer's most important critical work and is replete with illustrations from classical authors. In seeking to define the sphere of activity in which the poetic imagination should hold sway, Bodmer looked to antiquity for his material. He praises once again personal experience as the best source for enriching the imagination, as, for instance, in the case of Homer, who gained his great knowledge from his extensive travels.[48] This kind of experience develops the powers of judgment, "the guiding star of the imagination." In the comparison of poetry with painting and sculpture Bodmer stresses their common aim, the imitation of whatever is in accordance with nature. He does not deny that painting and poetry can influence and stir the imagination through their respective media. Color, expression, position, and symmetry are capable of producing many thoughts and sensations in the human mind. A good example in point is for Bodmer the work of Michelangelo.[49] But for the Swiss critic, painting and sculpture, in their effect upon the observer, are "roundabout, slow, and incomplete," and therefore they must yield first place to writing in the matter of reproducing nature perfectly. Poetic descriptions are, in Bodmer's mind, analogous to paintings. Excellent examples of artistic perfection in poetic description are Ovid's version of the Pygmalion fable,[50] and the passage in which he praises the carvings on the goblet of Hylean Alcon, depicting certain funeral rites.[51] Bodmer quotes

[44] *Ibid.,* p. 101.
[45] *Critische Abhandlung von dem Wunderbaren in der Poesie und dessen Verbindung mit dem Wahrscheinlichen.* Zürich: Conrad Orell und Comp., 1740.
[46] *Ibid.,* pp. 25 f.
[47] *Critische Betrachtungen über die poetischen Gemählde der Dichter.* Zürich: Conrad Orell und Comp., 1741.
[48] *Ibid.,* p. 17.
[49] *Ibid.,* p. 36.
[50] *Ibid.,* p. 42. Ovid *Metam.* X. 247-60.
[51] *Crit. Betracht.,* pp. 44 f. *Metam.* XIII. 681-99.

both passages from Ovid's *Metamorphoses*. In the second of these it is pointed out that the poetic technique is more expressive and more instructive, because it can describe the historical setting and the action as depicted.[52] The fourth chapter of Bodmer's work is devoted to an analysis of the relation of the poetic description to the subject matter, of the creation to reality. Again Ovid provides illustrations of apt descriptions; Bodmer admires that of the drunken man who supports himself on his staff and clings to his misshapen ass,[53] or the vividness with which Ovid portrays the brutal excision of Philomela's tongue by the Thracian king Tereus.[54] From the same author is selected the passage which narrates the ensnarement of Mars and Venus in the bronze net of Vulcan and the exposing of the two trapped lovers to the sight of the gods; a painting of this incident could never surpass poetry in producing the illusion of reality.[55] In Ovid's story of Proserpina's abduction by Pluto, in the loss of the flowers gathered by her and the grief aroused in her behalf, the reader is made to feel the deep emotion which is in her heart, a feeling which no painting, Bodmer says, could reproduce adequately in an observer.[56] Most of the material from the ancients to illustrate vividness of description is taken from Ovid.

The fifth chapter of the *Critische Betrachtungen* is a study of the relation between the poetic image and its expression. Clarity is the first virtue of skillful expression, and Bodmer supports this statement by the authority of Quintilian, who insists that any passage should be intelligible to a person who is giving only half of his attention to the text.[57] The use of unusual words or common words with unusual meanings is allowed on the authority of Aristotle, from whom Bodmer quotes.[58] Such words make for both clarity and elegance, and if they occur in figurative or metaphorical expressions they avoid the banality of platitude. The language must be not only clear but also perceptible to the senses and force-

---

[52] *Crit. Betracht.*, p. 47.
[53] *Ibid.*, p. 74. *Metam.* IV. 26 f.
[54] *Crit. Betracht.*, pp. 74 f. *Metam.* VI. 551-60.
[55] *Crit. Betracht.*, p. 75. *Metam.* IV. 184-88.
[56] *Crit. Betracht.*, p. 76. *Metam.* V. 398-401.
[57] *Crit. Betracht.*, p. 87. *Institut. Orat.* VIII. ii. 23.
[58] *Crit. Betracht.*, pp. 94-96. *Poet.* XXII.

ful, that is, it must be expressed in metaphors which are exact in their meaning. Bodmer acknowledges as his authority Longinus,[59] and points out that the latter mentions such good examples as the descriptions by Xenophon[60] and by Plato[61] of parts of the human body. He translates Plato's passage as it is quoted in Longinus. The reader is reminded on the authority of both Quintilian and Aristotle that the poet must exercise his critical faculties with regard to the aptness of the metaphors and must maintain a decent limit to their number.[62] The use of metaphors should be restricted to those situations in which ordinary words are flat, as for example in the metaphor used by Vergil when he describes the Trojans setting up their cooking utensils and eating their food on the shores of Libya.[63] In speaking of the purpose of poetry as "das sinnliche Ergetzen der Phantasie zu verschaffen," Bodmer follows Longinus;[64] that the cause of this pleasure proceeds from imitation Bodmer takes on the authority of Aristotle.[65]

The poet's material, as it appears in Bodmer's system of poetics, is classified into three groups: the beautiful, the great, and the gigantic. Beauty is "das Übereinstimmende in dem Mannigfaltigen."[66] Illustrations from the ancients of passages representing this beauty are found in comparisons taken from the world of every-day occurrences, such as Ovid's description of the new-born Adonis,[67] or of Atalanta,[68] and Vergil's description of Lavinia.[69] A good example of the beauty of the human face is that of Aeneas in Vergil.[70] Expressions designating the time of day gain in effectiveness by the use of poetic circumlocutions, as is shown by many illustrations from Ovid and Vergil.[71] The power of song is shown

[59] *Treatise concerning the Sublime.* XXXII.
[60] *Memorabilia* I. iv. 5 f.
[61] *Timaeus* 69 Df.
[62] *Crit. Betracht.*, pp. 102 f. Quint. *Institut. Orat.* VIII. vi. 14. Arist. *Poet.* XXII.
[63] *Crit. Betracht.*, pp. 103 f. *Aen.* I. 177-78, 213-15.
[64] *Crit. Betracht.*, p. 127. Long. *Sublime* XV.
[65] *Crit. Betracht.*, pp. 131 ff.
[66] *Ibid.*, p. 153.
[67] *Ibid.*, p. 166. *Metam.* X. 515-17.
[68] *Crit. Betracht.*, p. 167. *Metam.* X. 594-96.
[69] *Crit. Betracht.*, p. 167. *Aen.* XII. 65-69.
[70] *Crit. Betracht.*, p. 171. *Aen.* I. 588-93.
[71] *Crit. Betracht.*, pp. 176-78. *Metam.* XIV. 53-54. XI. 451, 453, 353-58, 96-98. X. 446. *Aeneid* XII. 113-15, 76-77. XI. 210, 182-83. VIII. 369, 97. VII. 148-49, 25-26. III. 588-89.

by the example of Demodocus in the *Odyssey*[72] and that of Orpheus in the *Metamorphoses*.[73] The second group of the poet's material Bodmer calls "the great," and he means by this objects or concepts which seem almost too large to be comprehended as a whole by the human senses or mind. Ancient authors contribute no illustrations to this category. The third group is that of "the gigantic or the violent," by which Bodmer means the clash of natural forces and its influence on man's mind or fate. Some of the best and most moving descriptions of violent natural phenomena are found in the works of classical authors. Vergil's account of the storm on the Tyrrhenian Sea is one of the best,[74] and is modelled upon a similar one from Homer.[75] The purpose of both descriptions is to impress the reader with the titanic character of the gigantic danger in which the heroes find themselves. Bodmer compares two other descriptions of storms in Homer and Vergil[76] and notes that Ovid and Vergil have excellent treatments of shipwreck.[77] The flood in the first book of the *Metamorphoses* is an especially striking illustration of the wondrous and the rare.[78] Now Bodmer lists the treatments of Aetna among such ancient authors as Pindar, Pliny, Gellius, Macrobius, Ovid, Seneca, Vergil, Lucretius, and Lucian.[79]

In the chapter on expressing human feelings in mien and action Bodmer uses Cicero to illustrate gesture as a means of expression for the dumb.[80] From Ovid he quotes the story of Myrrha's forbidden love and the expression of her sense of shame.[81] The numerous examples to illustrate horror are taken from Vergil,[82] while those to show anger and rage come mostly from Seneca and Vergil; those for sadness from Ovid and Homer. In the chapter on personal characters Bodmer returns once again to the praise

[72] *Crit. Betracht.*, pp. 179-80. *Ody.* VIII. 62, 487.
[73] *Crit. Betracht.*, p. 181. *Metam.* XI. 41-43.
[74] *Crit. Betracht.*, pp. 240 f. *Aen.* I. 81-91, 102-07.
[75] *Crit. Betracht.*, p. 241. *Ody.* V. 291-96, 313-30.
[76] *Crit. Betracht.*, p. 253. *Ody.* XII. 105 ff. *Aen.* III. 191-99.
[77] *Crit. Betracht.*, pp. 258 f. *Metam.* XI. 490-506. *Georg.* I. 318-34.
[78] *Crit. Betracht.*, p. 261. *Metam.* I. 264-69.
[79] *Crit. Betracht.*, pp. 263-73.
[80] *Ibid.*, p. 285.
[81] *Crit. Betracht.*, pp. 292-94. *Metam.* X. 357-67, 402-03, 414-15, 423-25, 457-59.
[82] *Crit. Betracht.*, pp. 296-98. *Aen.* II. 378. XII. 447-48, 665-68. VII. 446-47, 458-59. III. 29-30, 47-48. XI. 120-21.

of Greek and Roman historical biographies in matters of character portrayal. He warns the reader not to look for a slavish order of events in Plutarch, who is often not concerned with his hero's most outstanding military victories. Plutarch's aim is to reveal the motivating forces of an historical character.[83] Sallust is another expert in this type of writing,[84] and he receives particular praise for his account of the Catiline conspiracy and his use of character portrayal.[85]

The foregoing will serve to give a representative picture of the ancient authors whom Bodmer studied in the years from 1721 to 1741 and to show that they were not read without having exerted an influence upon his critical ideas. Although this body of illustrations from classical authors does not exhaust the list of authors or works used by Bodmer during this period, it is important for us to note that his literary ideas cannot be understood without recourse to the ancients, whom he accepted as patterns in genre and style. It is further significant for Bodmer's treatment of ancient historical themes to note that his attitude towards character portrayal is already established in these critical works, some twenty years before he set his pen to his dramas.

We have seen that during his formative years Bodmer acquired a good working knowledge of ancient authors and that he displayed considerable interest in certain historians of antiquity. We have established further the body of material from the ancients that he had at his command in order to illustrate his ideas in the critical works down to the early 1740's. Before proceeding to analyze the plays themselves, it will be of some interest to mention the steps in Bodmer's writings which led him to this form. By 1750 he had turned from literary criticism to the field of biblical poetry. In that year the first two cantos of *Noah* appeared.[86] In rapid succession other biblical epics followed: *Jacob und Joseph* (1752), *Jacob und Rachel* (1752), *Die Syndflut* (1753), *Joseph*

---

[83] *Crit. Betracht.*, pp. 394 f.
[84] *Ibid.*, pp. 395-400.
[85] *Ibid.*, pp. 480-88.
[86] The first completed version of *Noah* appeared in 1752; three revised editions were published in 1765, 1772, and 1781, each bearing the title *Die Noachide*.

und Zulika (1753), *Iacobs Wiederkunft von Haran* (1753), *Der erkannte Joseph und der keusche Joseph* (1754). As the last work appeared, he had turned his attention to classical themes. In 1753 he completed *Die geraubte Helena,* a translation from Coluthus, and probably about this time two poems with the title *Die geraubte Europa,* one a translation from Moschus and the other from Nonnus.[87] These are Bodmer's first translations from the Greek that were published at that time. In 1755 he published some long passages which were rendered into German from the *Odyssey,*[88] and in 1760 came a complete version in hexameters of the fourth and sixth cantos of the *Iliad.*[89] He was thus directing his attention to antiquity, and before the end of this decade, 1750-60, he had begun to write dramas on ancient themes, an activity that filled the years from 1759 to 1770.

[87] These two poems appeared without date. Cf. Vetter, "Bibliographie," p. 394.

[88] J. J. Bodmer, *Fragmente in der erzälenden Dichtart* (Zürich: Conrad Orell und Comp., 1755), pp. 1-38. Cf. appendix.

[89] J. J. Bodmer, *Vierter Gesang; und Sechster Gesang der Ilias.* Zürich: Conrad Orell, und Comp., 1760.

III

DRAMAS OF LEGEND AND PROPHECY

In 1759, when Bodmer turned to the classical world for subjects for the series of dramas that was to occupy him during the decade that followed, he had already tried his hand at this form.[1] As early as 1725 he had, as we have seen, written a play in pentameter under the title of *Marc Anton und Kleopatra Verliebung*, only one scene of which has been preserved.[2] In 1746 he had sent J. G. Sulzer a pastoral play in prose entitled *Cimon*, which was published in 1773. In 1754 he recast two of his biblical poems in dramatic form, using the hexameter: *Der erkannte Joseph* and *Der keusche Joseph*. Never again did Bodmer return to this or any other meter in the drama, but confined himself thereafter to prose. None of the plays just mentioned bears any relation, as regards language and form of treatment, to his later efforts in this field.

In comparison with the earlier efforts, the dramatic interest that began in the late 1750's was active and sustained for a considerable period of years. For themes Bodmer turned first to the history of Switzerland. Between December, 1756, and July, 1757, he wrote *Friederich von Tokenburg* (Toggenburg), which was published in 1761. Another play, *Die Schweizer über dir, Zürich* or *Stüssi*, was begun in October, 1757 and revised in March, 1770, but was never published. A third, *Rudolf Brun*, was begun in March, 1758, but likewise remained unpublished. *Friederich von Tokenburg* deals with a family anecdote from Swiss national history and treats of the fratricide committed by Diethelm V of Toggenburg, who killed his brother Friedrich I in 1226.[3] *Stüssi* is based upon the political relations of Zurich to Lucerne and Schwyz between the years 1437 and 1443.[4] Stüssi, burgomaster of Zurich, opposes his adversary Reding, attacks the short-sightedness of Swiss diplomats in the Fifteenth Century, laments the insignificant influence of the

[1] Cf. Baechtold, *Ges. d. d. Lit. i. d. Schweiz*, pp. 639 f.
[2] Cf. *supra* Chap. II, note 41.
[3] Gustav Tobler, "Bodmers politische Schauspiele," *Denkschrift*, pp. 121-24.
[4] *Ibid.*, pp. 124-33.

people at large on affairs of state, and extols the virtues of democracy. The play is a worthy forerunner of Bodmer's political dramas.
Rudolf Brun is also a political play, dealing with an historical incident in the history of Zurich. In 1336 a group of citizens under
the leadership of Brun charged the municipal councillors with dis-
honesty and incompetency, and demanded of them a complete
accounting of their official acts.[5] Against this background Bodmer
has treated a favorite theme, the rights and sovereignty of the
people as opposed to the privileges of a vested group. It is with
the experience gained by writing these dramas that Bodmer approached his ancient material.

When Bodmer turned to the ancients for themes, his interest
was attracted by certain Greek legends in which prophecy is an
important motive. In each of these works the story is concerned
more directly with the fulfillment of a prophetic utterance than is
the case with the dramas to be considered later. This chapter deals
with those plays in which this type of material appears. *Ulysses,*
Electra, and *Oedipus* are works in which Bodmer has undertaken
to give his version of these legends, and our problem is to analyze
these plays to see what new interpretation, if any, has been given
to the material. The plays were written in 1759 and thus are
Bodmer's earliest dramatic attempts with ancient themes, with the
exception of the work on Antony and Cleopatra referred to above,
only one scene of which has been preserved. They show less
originality than the later dramas and may be looked upon as experimental. The next two, *Die Tegeaten* and *Die Rettung in den*
Mauern von Holz, are works in which the action is entirely dependent upon the interpretation and fulfillment of prophecy. Here
Bodmer has taken an oracular statement, from Plutarch and
Herodotus respectively, and built a play around it. In *Patroclus,*
Homer has furnished the details for the play, in which the heroic
death of the main character brings home to the reader the intense interest of the author in the great epic of antiquity. The
conception of legend as it existed in Bodmer's mind may be characterized as one in which the fate of heroic figures is controlled by
outside forces; but, as we shall see, the action of these forces is
humanized by Bodmer, that is, he favors the attitude that the

[5] *Ibid.,* pp. 134-37.

judgments of the gods of antiquity were influenced by human priests who presided over the oracles. These works have little political import.

ULYSSES

Early in 1759 Bodmer was working on his *Ulysses*,[6] and it appeared in the following year.[7] He had been acquainted with the theme in an Italian version as early as 1735, when he wrote Gottsched that Lazzarini's *Ulisse il giovane* had come to his attention.[8] In the preface to his play Bodmer acknowledges that it is based on that of Lazzarini, who, he says, invented the story without the use of history or legend.[9] The preface continues with a German quotation from the dedicatory letter in the Italian preface; in the latter Lazzarini defends his tragedy as a truthful action, taken "from the same secret story from which Sophocles took his," that is his *Euryalus*.[10] There is no indication that Bodmer went beyond Lazzarini in treating this theme, so our problem is limited to an examination of the relation of the German and the Italian versions.

Bodmer's friends in Zurich did not like the play.[11] Sulzer in Berlin was somewhat displeased to have a false oracle prophesy events of the future.[12] Later in that year, 1760, Sulzer reported that the critics in Berlin had not received the play favorably.[13] Its author was disappointed and complained to Schinz that it seemed impossible for him to win the approbation of the Germans with his plays.[14]

[6] Baechtold, *Tagebuch*, p. 196.

[7] *Ulysses, Telemachs Sohn. Ein Trauerspiel.* Zürich: Geßner, 1760.

[8] Bodmer to Gottsched, March 28, 1735, T. W. Danzel, *Gottsched und seine Zeit*, 2d ed. (Leipzig: Dyk'sche Buchhandlung, 1855), p. 192. For the complete correspondence between Bodmer and Gottsched, cf. Eugen Wolff, "Briefwechsel Gottscheds mit Bodmer und Breitinger," *Zeitschrift f. deut. Unterricht*, XI (1897), 353-81. The play is Domenico di Morro Lazzarini's (1668-1734) *Ulisse il Giovane*. Padua, 1720. I quote from a reprint in *Raccolta di tragedie scritte nel secolo XVIII*. Milano, 1825, I, 321-428.

[9] Bodmer, *Ulysses*, p. 3.

[10] *Ibid.*, pp. 3 f.

[11] Wieland to Zimmermann, April 6, 1759, C. M. Wieland, *Ausgewählte Briefe von C. M. Wieland an verschiedene Freunde in den Jahren 1751-1810 geschrieben*, hrsg. von H. Geßner (Zürich: Geßnersche Buchhandlung, 1815-16), I, 354.

[12] Sulzer to Bodmer, May 27, 1760, Zehnder-Stadlin, *op. cit.*, p. 395.

[13] Sulzer to Bodmer, Dec. 17, 1760, MS ZBZ.

[14] Bodmer to Schinz, Dec. 1, 1760, MS ZBZ.: "Es scheint mir nicht möglich, den Beyfall der muntern Deutschen zu erhalten."

In the opening scene, between Eurynome, wife of Ulysses, and Evippe, the background of the action is presented. Ulysses has always looked upon his wife as the daughter of the king of Phocis, and hence of noble birth, but she herself does not know the history of her family and is aware of a deception in not disclosing this state of ignorance to her husband. The reason for her silence lies in an oath of secrecy exacted by her supposed father Polymnius. Evippe persuades Eurynome to maintain this silence at least until an heir shall be born. According to Polymnius, Eurynome was purchased, under the name of Nicandra, from a pirate at the festival of Neptune. The union between Eurynome and Ulysses is a very lukewarm one. With this background the action proceeds from Ulysses' announcement that Theodotus, his arch enemy and king of Samus, has been made prisoner. According to the utterance of the Delphian oracle Theodotus must be sacrificed before an heir can be born. Eurynome objects to the sacrifice and intercedes on behalf of the victim. The priest Samgar is sceptical about the oracle's statement, for he thinks it comes from that part of Olympus which is hostile to the house of Ulysses. He recalls an older prophecy that Ulysses would murder his own son and be guilty of incest in a union with his daughter.[15] Ulysses remains obdurate in his intention to kill Theodotus, despite the strong pleas presented to him by the chorus of priests, by Eumaeus, and by others. Theodotus is reconciled to death as the command of the gods, and contemplates life after death with a sense of satisfaction. In the midst of the preparations for the sacrifice, Asteria, the former nurse of Theodotus, enters and alleges on oath that the latter is not the son of Pisander, but she refuses to disclose his real identity. Ulysses remains still unmoved and Theodotus is executed. At this point Ctesippus returns from a confinement of twenty years in Pisander's prison. The story which he tells reveals that Ulysses has killed his own son in Theodotus and is wedded to his own daughter in Eurynome. Corroboration of the details comes from

[15] Bodmer, *Ulysses,* I, 3, pp. 25 f.:

Was für unglückliche Tage hat dir das Schicksal bereitet!
Deine Gemahlin wird dir zwar Kinder gebähren, doch mußt du
Einmal den Sohn mit eigener Hand ermorden, dein Ehbett
Durch ein verfluchtes Band mit der Tochter bluthschänderisch theilen.

Asteria and Evippe. The realization of his crime brings Ulysses to the brink of suicide; he blinds himself with a glowing brand. News arrives from Samus that the city has overthrown its tyrant and wishes to place itself under the rule of Ulysses, but the latter refuses this offer. The play ends with the voice of an invisible angel imposing upon Ulysses the duty of resigning himself to his suffering.

In many details Bodmer has followed his Italian model closely, but it is hardly a "translation" of Lazzarini's work.[16] The story of Eurynome's life corresponds in both versions; the secrecy concerning her real birth, Polymnius' purchase of the babe from the pirate, and her adoption by him are only a few instances in which the two stories agree.[17] The secret of Eurynome's birth must be kept until an heir to Ulysses is born; with Bodmer the secrecy is imposed by an oath taken by Eurynome's father, while with the Italian author it is ordered by the oracle at Delphi. When later Asteria is summoned to confirm the facts of the queen's life, Bodmer paraphrases closely the report of Lazzarini's Asteria, especially in such details as the child's name and the pirate's part in her life.[18] In another scene Asteria appears in order to report, similarly in both versions, the facts of Theodotus' life, especially that she received him from a Corinthian stranger and that the boy so pleased the queen as to be adopted by her.[19] The oracle's prophecy that Ulysses would murder his own son and commit incest with his daughter is translated literally by Bodmer from the Italian.[20] Samgar and Agelao plead in vain with Ulysses to spare Theodotus; although their pleas are similar, Agelao, in Lazzarini's play, uses a dream to support his intercession, while Samgar emphasizes the fact that the sacrifice of the victim cannot logically affect the situation.[21] In both plays representatives of the city of Samus arrive to offer Ulysses the leadership of their city.[22] These are some of the parallels in which Bodmer has followed his model.

[16] Cf. L. Donati, *Bod. u. d. ital. Lit.*, p. 264.
[17] Bodmer, *Ulysses*, I, 1, pp. 6, 10. Lazzarini, *Ulisse*, pp. 351-53.
[18] Bod., IV, 2, pp. 82 ff. Lazzarini, pp. 412-14.
[19] Bod., III, 2, pp. 61 f. Laz., pp. 385-87.
[20] Bod., I, 2, p. 17 and I, 3, pp. 25 f. Laz., pp. 345, 343.
[21] Bod., I, 3, pp. 19-22. Laz., pp. 367-72.
[22] Bod., V, 5, p. 125. Laz., pp. 400-02.

In some other respects the plays do not agree. Bodmer does
not employ a dream motif in the character of Ulysses, whereas the
Italian Ulysses dreams that his two children are killed during an
attack on Ithaca by Pisander.[23] Bodmer has introduced his own
invention in the use of a chorus of priests, men, and children.[24]
Eurynome's death is much less violent in the German version, in
which she "emitted sighs from the depths of her heart, and with
one of these expired her beautiful soul into the air." In the Italian
play she plunges from a cliff into the sea.[25] Lazzarini's hero puts
out his eyes with his daughter's girdle, whereas Bodmer's Ulysses
blinds himself with a brand from the fire on the altar.[26] The character of Samgar has a counterpart in the Italian Agelao, although
the former has quite an original point of view; as Bodmer explained, he is to Ulysses what Pylades was to Orestes.[27] He appears
as an enlightened person, and insists upon a total and complete
denial of the power of divine oracle when Ulysses heaps the blame
for his misfortune upon the gods and their prophecies. He maintains that ambiguous statements of oracles come from some evil
spirit, "which has led and continues to lead the priests astray."[28]
He characterizes the anger of the gods as nothing more than a
series of actions which arise from the freedom of the human
will.[29] In fact the attitude of Samgar seems quite Christian as
formulated in Ulysses' echo of the former's belief in a god "who
indeed stands above the gods of the Greeks."[30] His god is one of
forgiveness and Bodmer introduces this divinity through Samgar
in order to bring consolation and strength to Ulysses. This is clear
in the words of the invisible angel who speaks to Ulysses at the
close of the play with an echo of Scriptural phraseology: "The
spirit which trieth the reins has seen the uprightness of the heart."[31]

[23] Laz., pp. 341-42.

[24] Bod., II, 3.

[25] Bod., IV, 4, p. 95. Laz., p. 423.

[26] Bod., V, 1, p. 100. Laz., p. 419.

[27] Bodmer to Sulzer, May 5, 1759, MS ZBZ.: "Er ist Ulysses das, was Pylades dem
Orestes war."

[28] Bod., V, 4, p. 119.

[29] Bod., V, 4, p. 120.

[30] Bod., V, 4, p. 121.

[31] Bod., V, 5, p. 127: "Der Geist, der die Nieren erforscht, hat die Aufrichtigkeit
deines Herzens gesehn."

The final admonition in the play sets up an ideal of hope, endurance, and humility:

God will reveal to thee on another planet a course of life in which thou shalt proceed from one virtue to another, from the good to the better, and shalt see heroes in thy company who are more than worthy of thy emulation. Place thy trust in His provident guidance! Be true to that light which, inspired by eternal truth, shines in your innermost soul and endure the suffering of this world in patience![32]

In Samgar Bodmer has departed from Lazzarini. These changes by Bodmer signify an attempt to temper the idea of inexorable fate by introducing an ameliorating and a Christian attitude.

Compared with Lazzarini, Bodmer's version of this theme has a more liberal attitude toward fate. It is characterized further by the introduction of a significant Christian element in the words of Samgar and in the voice of the invisible angel at the end of the play. Even in Theodotus a spirit of resignation is felt that is not in Lazzarini. In *Ulysses* the influence of Bodmer's work with biblical themes asserts itself as the most important change made by him. In most of the details of the story, however, the Swiss author has felt no inspiration to give his own interpretation. Had Bodmer treated this theme several years later, when he was looking at antiquity through the eyes of a political observer, he would undoubtedly have developed more fully the overthrow of the despotic government of Samus, as reported by the ambassadors of that city, and would have given the theme more political emphasis.

ELECTRA

In 1746 Bodmer came directly into contact with the theme of Electra as material which could be adapted for modern treatment. J. E. Schlegel wrote him that he had been working for four years on a project which was to include parallels from the versions of Electra by Euripides, Aeschylus, and Sophocles,[33] and later

---

[32] Bod., V, 5, pp. 127 f.: "Gott will in einem andern Stern eine Laufbahn vor dir eröffnen, auf welcher du von Tugend zu Tugend, vom Guten zum Bessern wetteilaufen sollst, und Helden in deine Gesellschaft sehen sollst, die deiner Nacheiferung mehr als würdig sind. Verlasse dich auf seine vorsehende Leitung. Sey dem Lichte, das, von der ewigen Wahrheit entflammt, in deinem innersten leuchtet, getreu und leide das Leiden dieser Welt geduldig."

[33] J. E. Schlegel to Bodmer, April 19, 1746, G. F. Stäudlin, *Briefe berühmter und edler Deutschen an Bodmer* (Stuttgart: Gebrüder Mäntler, 1794), p. 37.

announced the publication of the work as imminent.[34] The theme did not interest Bodmer personally until May, 1759. Then he set about writing a version of it,[35] which was published in the following year.[36]

While the play received no public reviews, it found an unfavorable reception from private writers. Bodmer wrote J. G. Zimmermann that he had read the play in manuscript to his friends, who received it coldly, holding that it had an excess of design, calm, and caution. Bodmer's answer was that the public of the time was wrong in demanding "tumult, storm, and extravagance."[37] One particular experience with the work must have been very painful to Bodmer; eighteen years after the event he recalled that he had ventured to read the play one June evening in 1759 to a group of his friends in a garden near the Lindentor in Zurich. One by one his listeners fled to the refreshment table in an adjoining room, until only Gessner remained.[38] Others, however, praised it, such as Wieland, who wrote that the plan of the work pleased him immensely and that he regretted it could not be judged on its own merits, without inviting the inevitable and belittling comparisons with the versions of Sophocles and Euripides.[39] Schinz thought well of the work when he received the fourth and fifth acts to copy for Bodmer.[40] Strangely enough, Zimmermann thought the play was that of Euripides.[41]

Perhaps the dominant note in Bodmer's work is the hostile attitude of the mother to her daughter, Clytemnestra to Electra. The latter receives a tablet, informing her that Orestes still lives and

[34] J. E. Schlegel to Bodmer, Oct. 8, 1746, *ibid.*, p. 43. Schlegel published a translation of Sophocles' *Electra* in his *Theatralische Werke* (1747).

[35] Baechtold, *Tagebuch*, p. 196.

[36] *Electra, oder die gerechte Übelthat. Ein Trauerspiel.* Zürich: Conrad Orell, und Comp., 1760.

[37] Bodmer to Zimmermann, March 23, 1760, Ed. Bodemann, *J. G. Zimmermann. Sein Leben und bisher ungedruckte Briefe* (Hannover: Hahn'sche Buchhandlung, 1878), p. 177.

[38] Bodmer to Schinz, Feb. 10, no year (the internal evidence dates the letter about 1777), MS ZBZ.: "Einer flüchtete nach dem andern in das Nebenzimmer zu dem Schenktische. Der einzige Geßner blieb bey mir sitzen."

[39] Wieland to J. Hess, Aug. 7, 1759, C. M. Wieland, *Ausgew. Briefe*, II, 70.

[40] Bodmer to Schinz, Sept. 6, 1759, MS ZBZ.

[41] Bodmer to Laurenz Zellweger, April 17, 1760, MS ZBZ.

has been commanded by an oracle to avenge his father's death. This news gives her courage to speak more defiantly than ever to her overbearing mother. Unfortunately the spies of Aegisthus have reported the arrival of the tablet, and Electra has to surrender it under threat of violence. Aegisthus reads its contents and prepares to deal with Orestes. The latter and Pylades arrive at the palace in disguise, allege that they have murdered Orestes, and claim the reward that Aegisthus has offered for this deed. As proof of the murder they produce a gem with the figure of Pelops, son of Tantalus, which they claim to have taken from the body of their victim. Electra is present at this scene and begins to lose hope of seeing her brother again. She attempts in vain to persuade her slave Deiphobides to kill the real Orestes, in whom she sees the self-acknowledged murderer, and then she plans to carry out the deed herself. In a scene where Orestes and Pylades receive a scepter and a goblet as the reward for their supposed crime, Electra wounds the former with an arrow, but not mortally. In punishment for this attempt on Orestes' life Clytemnestra orders her daughter to be given to her own slave Deiphobides as his wife. Orestes intercedes in behalf of his sister and the punishment is stayed. By means of a shawl, dating from Electra's childhood, recognition between brother and sister is effected. They plan to carry out the oracle's order while Aegisthus is away and they are still within the palace walls. Only the fear of the curse that will fall upon him for killing his own mother restrains Orestes at first, but this is shortly swept aside. Just as the return of Aegisthus is announced, Orestes commands Deiphobides to kill Clytemnestra and the body is covered. When he enters the palace, Aegisthus is shown his dead wife and then slain by Orestes. The latter orders both bodies to be burned and goes to wash his hands in the pure waters of the river Inachus.

In his treatment of this ancient legend Bodmer followed the subject-matter of antiquity, but "according to a new outline."[42]

---

[42] It would appear from the following that Bodmer proceeded from the versions of Euripides and probably of Sophocles: "If my *Yarico* was a struggle, then I have won many struggles. My *Electra* and *Oedipus*, my *Ulysses*, my *Gray*, *Polytimet*, *Pelopidas*, *Romeo* were struggles. . . . The opponents were Euripides, Sopho-

He cast the work in acts and scenes, wrote in prose, and omitted the chorus, in these respects departing from the ancient form of the tragedy. He locates the scene of action in the palace of Aegisthus on the banks of the Inachus in Argos, while Euripides locates his play before a peasant's cottage on the borders of Argolis and Sophocles uses Agamemnon's palace at Mycenae as the scene of his play. During the play Bodmer changes the scene from the outside to the inside of the palace, the last act taking place "in the ivory room." The unity of time is maintained and some attempt is made to keep the unity of action. In a short preface Bodmer informs the reader that Electra has received a tablet at the grave of Agamemnon. This tablet and the oracle's command to Orestes to kill his mother and Aegisthus play a very important part in the German play as well as in the legend of antiquity. Bodmer delays the recognition of brother and sister for some time, but when Electra learns who stands before her, she breaks down: "ein Tränenbach fließt." Orestes holds a shawl, the token of recognition, to catch these tears.[43] It is the shawl with which Electra had bound his head when she gave him into the custody of Melisander, and she recognizes it immediately.[44] Orestes and Pylades gain the confidence of Clytemnestra by claiming to be the murderers of Orestes; this claim is an innovation of Bodmer. The false identity used by the Swiss author is found in Aeschylus, in whose *Choëphoroe* Orestes appears before Clytemnestra as a traveller with the report that Orestes is dead.[45] This news plunges Electra into a state of anger, which soon gives way to a desire to slay the self-acknowledged murderer of her brother; this motif is new in the German play. Clytemnestra gives her daughter to her own slave as his wife. This may have been suggested to Bodmer

cles, Lazzarini, Wieland, Lessing, Weisse." Bodmer to Schinz, Oct. 17, 1774, MS ZBZ.: "Wenn meine Yarico ein Kampf war, so habe ich viele Kämpfe bestanden. Meine Electra und Ödipus, mein Ulysses, meine Graya, Polytimet, Pelopidas, Romeo waren Kämpfe . . . Die andern Gegner waren Euripides, Sophokles, Lazzarini, Wieland, Lessing, Weiße."

[43] Bodmer, *Electra*, IV, 3, p. 116.

[44] Euripides effects recognition through an old man who sees a scar on Orestes' brow (573); Aeschylus uses a cloth also; Sophocles uses Agamemnon's ring, which Orestes shows to Electra and thus establishes his identity.

[45] *Choëphoroe* 682: the manner of Orestes' death is not related.

by the humiliating scene in the Euripidean version, where Electra appears as the untouched wife of a peasant. Bodmer's ending follows closely that of Sophocles. Such changes as Bodmer has made have a tendency to a greater realism of motivation.

Further it must be noted that Bodmer has made some modifications in the *dramatis personae* of the play. The most striking of these is the introduction of Deiphobides as the slave of Electra. He is presented as the son of Deiphobus, eldest son of Priam, and thus of noble birth. With the intention of exciting him to murder the supposed slayer of her brother, Electra exalts his noble ancestry with extravagant praise. She recites the great deeds of his father, material which Bodmer probably took from the *Iliad:* that Deiphobus had stopped and shattered with his shield Meriones' spear,[46] and that he had killed Hypsenor, son of Hippasus, to avenge the death of his comrade Asius.[47] She exhorts Deiphobides to rise to the greatness of his ancestry with the words: "Cease to be a slave."[48] But he refuses to be an accomplice in such a deed, since he has no injustice to avenge against this stranger and since he fears the pursuit of the Furies. Another interesting addition to the details of *Electra* is the reference to Menelaus. Aegisthus announces that this hero has arrived at the port of Nauplia with his wife Helen; Bodmer has taken this report from Euripides' *Orestes.*[49] Clytemnestra suggests that Menelaus be invited to a banquet and orders an ambush of thirty men to slay him without warning. Aegisthus orders presents to be prepared for the new arrivals and asks his wife to add for Helen "the alabaster swan."[50] This swan, Aegisthus explains, had been given to Clytemnestra's mother, Leda, by Zeus when he visited her one night in human form;[51] Bodmer was, of course, acquainted with the swan motif in the Greek legend.[52] However, the plan to murder Menelaus and Helen is not developed further. In the German play Aegisthus and

[46] *Iliad* XIII. 156 ff.
[47] *Iliad* XIII. 410 ff. Bod., *Electra*, III, 1, p. 71.
[48] Bod., *Elec.*, III, 1, p. 73.
[49] Bod., *Elec.*, I, 3, p. 21. *Orestes* 52 ff., 241 f.
[50] Bod., *Elec.*, I, 3, pp. 22 ff.
[51] Bod., *Elec.*, I, 3, p. 24. Cf. Euripides *Helen* 16 ff. *Orestes* 1385 ff.
[52] Cf. Pauly, *Real-Encyclopädie der class. Altertumswissenschaft*, XXIII, 1117.

Clytemnestra wish to kill Menelaus because they fear that he will attempt to avenge the murder of Agamemnon. In Euripides it is Orestes who resists Menelaus in his attempt to free his wife Helen. There is no good reason for Bodmer's use of Menelaus and Helen in his story, for the scene in which they are mentioned has no direct connection with the rest of the plot.[53]

Bodmer's purpose in treating this theme was to place before his readers a modern version of this ancient legend in dramatic form. The play is much weaker than those of antiquity and lacks great pathos or passion. His characters seem colorless and the plot is lacking in dramatic merit.

OEDIPUS

Oedipus was written between March, 1759, and November, 1760.[54] Bodmer reported to Schinz that his friends in Zurich did not like it.[55] It appeared in 1761[56] and was immediately subjected to a critical review by Gerstenberg,[57] to which Bodmer wrote an answer.[58]

The play opens with the following "contents" in the place of the prologue, characteristic of the ancient drama.

A ghost frightens Oedipus away from the embraces of Jocasta. He is now recognized as that one who had slain Laius. To punish his crime he condemns himself to exile. Then it is revealed that he is the son of the slain Laius and Jocasta is the woman who had borne him to Laius. He punishes his unwitting crime by voluntary blindness.[59]

The version of this theme in antiquity which has the greatest similarity to that of Bodmer is Sophocles' *Oedipus Rex*. Bodmer does not use the priest of Zeus, nor the daughter Ismene, who is a mute character in Sophocles. All other persons of the play are common to both authors. To be sure the shepherd from Corinth, unnamed in Sophocles, is given the name of Lycas, son of Poseidon,

---

[53] I, 3.

[54] Baechtold, *Tagebuch,* pp. 196 f.

[55] Bodmer to Schinz, Aug. 10, 1759, MS ZBZ.

[56] J. J. Bodmer, *Drey neue Trauerspiele* (Zürich: Heidegger und Compagnie, 1761), pp. 205-320.

[57] *Bibliothek der schönen Wissenschaften und der freyen Künste,* VII (1762), 318-33.

[58] *Freymüthige Nachrichten,* XIX (1762), 236 ff.

[59] Bod., *Drey neue Trauerspiele,* p. 206.

who appears in Theban mythology as a ruler of the city. To Sophocles' second messenger Bodmer gives the name of Nessus, which was probably suggested to him by that of Nessos, the centaur-son of Ixion and Nephele. He employs him as the ferryman who is dispatched to take Oedipus down the river Asopus. Antigone appears as the daughter of Oedipus and takes an active part in the play. Bodmer uses the chorus.

The play opens with a dream scene. Jocasta, arising much earlier than usual, tells Creon of the presence of an evil spirit, who appears with a scepter in his hand whenever Oedipus attempts to enter her bed. It is manifest to her as a shining shade, but to Oedipus as a ghost, with features closely resembling those of Laius. Oedipus tries to attack it with a knife, but it proves invulnerable. It speaks no word, but makes threatening gestures that Oedipus should leave the room. While Jocasta is relating this to Creon, Oedipus manages to catch a short sleep, during which the spirit again appears to him in the company of a second similar one. While Oedipus has no fear at this time of these ghosts, he is concerned with the ambiguous utterance of the Pythian oracle at Delphi; it had said that his own mother would bear him children and that he would slay his own father.[60] Creon refers him to the blind seer Teiresias for an interpretation of the apparition; Creon looks upon it as an omen of some impending disaster. Bodmer's source for the ghost motif is unknown. As in Sophocles, the prophet Teiresias identifies the spirit as that of Laius and accuses Oedipus of having slain him. The latter determines to sacrifice a black lamb at the grave of Laius and to place upon the altar wreaths and locks of hair from Jocasta. The sacrifice is not found in Sophocles, but Seneca includes the sacrifice of a bull and a heifer in his version, which may possibly have served Bodmer as a model in this detail.[61] The ceremony itself is disturbed by the appearance of a black owl, which flies out of a grove dedicated to the Furies and makes off with the sacrificial flowers and the hair.[62] The omen does not upset Oedipus, not even when he relates

---

[60] Bod., I, 2, p. 219.

[61] Seneca *Oedipus* 299 ff.

[62] Bod., II, 1, p. 234. Birds formed an important part of the augury services of Teiresias. Cf. Roscher, *Ausführliches Lexikon der griechischen und römischen Mythologie,* V, 188.

the incident of Laius' death, for he is as yet unaware of Laius'
identity. Bodmer's version of the deed differs only slightly from
that of Sophocles. Oedipus meets a carriage carrying an elderly
man, who strikes Oedipus. The latter loses his patience, throws a
stone at this man, later identified as Laius, and knocks him from
the carriage. The son notices some resemblance of the man to himself, but gives it no further thought.[63] The instrument used by
Oedipus in Sophocles is a staff; Bodmer has changed this into a
stone.[64] Confirmation of the oracle's prophecy in both versions is
effected through the testimony of two messengers, Lycas and
Nessus. Jocasta commits suicide because of their message, her
death being reported by a fisherman; she drowns herself in the
Asopus, which flows behind the palace. Here again Bodmer has
his own version. He introduces also Antigone, daughter of Oedipus,
as an active person. When the father must unfold to her the
ghastly fate that has overtaken the family, we have an attempt at
real tragic pathos: "The gods thought you should learn by the
example of your father that fate has not united happiness and
virtue."[65] She begs to be permitted to accompany him into exile
and is allowed to do so only after considerable supplication. The
decision of Oedipus to leave Thebes has already been made in the
fourth act, where he appears "mit der Reisetasche."[66] This occurs
before Lycas reveals that Oedipus is the son of Jocasta and Laius;
Oedipus makes the decision voluntarily. In the version of Sophocles
this course of action is not finally determined until the last lines.

Bodmer continues the use of the chorus, but in all its utterances
he uses it either to attempt to minimize the guilt of Oedipus or to
show the people's love for him. The former is the case when the
leader of the chorus upbraids the Thebans for unjustly accusing
a man of murder committed in self-defense.[67] He opposes flight,
for the loss of Oedipus would be a punishment for the whole city

---

[63] Bod., II, 2, pp. 247 f.
[64] Sophocles *Oedipus Rex* 810 ff.
[65] Bod., IV, 1, p. 274: "Die Götter meinten, du solltest bey dem Beyspiele deines
Vaters lernen, daß das Schicksal das Glück nicht mit der Tugend verbunden hat."
[66] Bod., IV, 1, p. 273.
[67] Bod., III, 1, p. 256.

and a greater misfortune than the death of Laius.[68] When Oedipus wishes to leave Creon reigning in his stead, the chorus will not hear a word of it; this is unlike Sophocles, in whose version Oedipus is forced to surrender the rule to Creon. Later the chorus returns to comfort Oedipus, who is now blind. One does not have the feeling that the chorus is an integral part of Bodmer's treatment.

At the end of the play the author has introduced a very religious note. Oedipus is very sceptical of the greatness of the gods; the prophet Teiresias tries to console him in a long speech on the harmony of the world. In place of a number of deities, he sets up a state of monolatry and asserts that the presence of good and evil, beauty and ugliness in the world is so well apportioned by the power of God that these opposite qualities result in harmony, truth, and right.[69] The attitude reflected in these observations is more Christian than heathen. When Oedipus interrogates Teiresias about the obedience required by the priests and about life after death, he is admonished not to obey them, but to hearken to his own reason, which takes account of one's virtue, innocence, and piety. Bodmer, in the spirit of the ancients, uses extensively the religious conventions of antiquity, such as oracles, prophecies, and omens. But he is at heart a product of the Eighteenth Century and speaking through Teiresias, distrusts the obscurantism and arbitrary power of the priests as spokesmen for the gods. "The gods of Olympus and of Orcus," he tells Oedipus, "are nothing more than the forces and endowments which are innate in the very nature of divine, mortal, and human creatures."[70] Further, he commands Oedipus not to listen to the priests, but to hearken to his own reason. In a letter to Schinz Bodmer expresses this distrust very clearly:

How easily the mysteries of the hierophants could have been traduced. . . . I must in addition point out that the mysteries of the Greeks were nothing more than meetings of particular brotherhoods, assemblies by night of ignorant, uneducated people who were directed by priests. They

[68] Bod., III, 2, p. 260.
[69] Bod., V, 4, p. 312.
[70] Bod., V, 4, p. 312: "Die Götter des Olympus und des Orcus sind nichts anders als Kräfte und Gaben, die in der Natur der himmlischen, der irdischen, und der menschlichen Wesen liegen."

were impostures, such as those of the freemasons, in which, to be sure, great men were enrolled for very ambitious and self-interested aims.[71]

Teiresias is an enlightened priest, the opposite of these imposters. He shows Oedipus that his prophetic powers do not come from Apollo, but are the endowment of his soul, which he has received from the "king of souls."[72] This note is an invention of Bodmer.

DIE RETTUNG IN DEN MAUERN VON HOLZ

Die Rettung in den Mauern von Holz appeared in 1769,[73] having been written in March of the preceding year.[74] Bodmer had no model for this play; he found in Herodotus the few data about which he built the plot.

Its background is the evacuation of Athens shortly before the naval engagement between the Greeks and the Persians at Salamis in the year 480 B.C., and may be summarized as follows. The last of the Greek ships are ready to take the Athenians to Troezen, safe from the attacking Persians. Euphorion, father of three sons, Theonoe, Amynias, and Aeschylus, who has just returned from exile, does not wish to leave Athens. He is old and would rather die, as long as he cannot fight. Aeschylus dwells at some length on the sad plight of the city and interprets the following prophecy of Apollo as referring not to the ships but to the wooden walls of the citadel:

> Yet shall a wood-built wall by Zeus all-seeing be granted
> Unto the Trito-born, a stronghold for thee and thy children.[75]

He refutes his sister Cynegire in her support of the priestess' prophecy that whatever lies within the boundaries of Cecrops and

---

[71] Bodmer to Schinz, undated, MS ZBZ. (The letter is arranged after that dated Feb. 12, 1772): "Wie leicht haben die Mysterien der Hierophanten verleumdet werden können . . . Noch muß ich zu bemerken geben, daß die Mysterien der Griechen nichts anders als conventicula von particularen Brüderschaften waren, nächtliche Zusammenkünfte von unwissenden, ungelehrten Personen, die von Hierophanten dirigiert wurden; Gaukeleyen, wie der Freymäurer, in welche freilich auch große Männer aus herrschsüchtigen und interessierten Absichten sich einschreiben ließen."

[72] Bod., V, 4, p. 313.

[73] J. J. Bodmer, Politische Schauspiele. Drittes Bändgen. Von Griechischem Innhalt (Lindau und Chur: typographische Gesellschaft, 1769), pp. 113-86.

[74] Baechtold, Tagebuch, p. 201.

[75] Bod., Rettung, I, 3, p. 132. Herodotus Hist. VII. 141. (The translation is that of A. D. Godley in the "Loeb Classical Library.")

Cithaeron will fall into the hands of the Persians.[76] Flight seems to him the only means of rescue; Aristides, son of Lysimachus, supports him in this view. A small group of warriors under the leadership of Timogenidas wishes to remain behind and defend the citadel. Euphorion tries to prevent the sacrifice of Dosithea, daughter of Copreus; she, together with her daughter Proserpina, wishes to win glory by dying on the altar of Ceres. The Persians appear in the distance and Euphorion orders his slave Sitacles to clothe him in his garments of state, and then he ascends the throne. As he prays for the salvation of his people, some Persians enter the room. Euphorion is murdered in the last scene by Patizetes.

In this material Bodmer drew from the *History* of Herodotus. The latter mentions the fact that a great number, but not all, of the Athenians went to Troezen.[77] A proclamation ordered all to abandon their homes and take to the ships. Bodmer uses the prophecy of the oracle as the cause for the exodus from Athens. He translates two lines of Herodotus' text into German, and the rest of the Greek is paraphrased very closely in a speech by Cynegire.[78] The interpretation of the ambiguity in the words "wooden walls" appears in Bodmer's play when Timogenidas plans to remain behind with a force in order to defend the Acropolis, for he has taken an oath to do this.[79] According to Herodotus this opinion was held by some of the old men,[80] although Timogenidas remains unmentioned in this connection.[81] Cynegire tells briefly of the destruction of the Persian fleet by a storm on the coast of Euboea.[82]

The characters of Bodmer show some originality of treatment. Euphorion figures conspicuously as the symbol of Athenian weakness. There is no trace of greatness in him, merely the realization that he has outlived his usefulness and that he prefers to die in Athens, so that his ashes may find burial among the graves of his

[76] Bod., I, 3, p. 133. Herodotus, VII. 141.
[77] *Hist.* VIII. 41.
[78] Bod., I, 3, pp. 133 f. Herod., VII. 141.
[79] Bod., II, 1, p. 140.
[80] *Hist.* VII. 142.
[81] Herodotus mentions a certain Theban Temagenidas, son of Herpys, in connection with the control of the passes of Cithaeron (IX. 38 f.) and again during the siege of Thebes by the Greeks (IX. 86 f.).
[82] Bod., I, 3, p. 131. Herod., VIII. 12 f.

ancestors.[83] He is killed by Patizetes when he resents the latter's sacrilegious desire to destroy the images of the gods.[84] Concerning his death Bodmer wrote: "Bowed by his old age he chose his death-bed in his native Athens, when the Athenians entrusted their lives in wooden ships to the stormy elements."[85] In a long monologue Euphorion reviews the sad state of the city.[86] This picture of him is quite unhistorical. Aristides is represented as having returned from his banishment by the Athenians, which was ordered out of fear that he would go over to the Persians.[87] Mention is also made of Aristides' capitulation to Miltiades at the battle of Marathon and his reconciliation with his opponent Themistocles at the battle of Salamis.[88] He even defends Themistocles as the savior of Greece, when he says of him: "The gods have chosen this man so that they may through him make the preparations which will save Athens. . . . If Themistocles does not rescue the city by his skill, then not only Athens but Greece and the whole Peloponnesus are lost."[89] The first brother, Aeschylus, is also represented as returning to the city. Bodmer motivates his return from a desire to help his fatherland, for Aeschylus has heard such sad news as Epialtes' treacherous betrayal to the Persians of the secret pass through the Oetan mountains, and also of the death of Leonidas.[90] The German play introduces a fictive character in Diotima, the betrothed of Aeschylus. The second brother, Amynias, has little connection with the action. Bodmer found him in Herodotus, who mentions a certain Ameinias of Pallene, an Athenian captain, who distinguished himself in the naval engagement

[83] Bod., I, 1, p. 123.

[84] Bod., III, 6, pp. 183 f. Herodotus (III. 61) mentions a certain Patizeithes as one of the magi implicated in the assumption of power by Smerdis.

[85] Bodmer, *Anekdoten von dem traurigen Ende gewisser politischer Dramen*, MS ZBZ., p. 15: "Euphorion ist es, der mit der Gemüthsruhe der festlichen Tage stirbt. Von hohem Alter gebeugt, wählte er das Sterbebett in seiner Vaterstadt, als die Athener sich in den Mauern von Holz dem stürmischen Elemente vertrauten."

[86] Bod., III, 5, pp. 180 ff.

[87] Bod., I, 3, pp. 135 f.

[88] Bod., II, 4, pp. 149 f. Herod., VIII. 79.

[89] Bod., II, 5, pp. 159-60: "Die Götter haben diesen Mann ausersehn, daß sie durch ihn die Veranstaltungen treffen, die Athen retten sollen."

[90] Bod., I, 3, pp. 129 f. Cf. Herod., VII. 214, 224.

at Salamis.[91] A third brother, Theonoe, is an invention of Bodmer, although his name in history may have suggested to the Swiss author that of Euphorion's daughter Cynegire.[92] To her is attached the oracle's prophecy and the attempt to persuade her father to accompany the other fugitives to Troezen. Euphorion's slave, Sitacles, appears as a Persian captive. As he dresses his master he is encouraged to assume the armor of a Persian, mix with the invading soldiers, and thus save his own life.[93] Herodotus mentions the Thracian king Sitacles in connection with the betrayal of certain ambassadors.[94]

The story of this play centers about the interpretation of a prophecy and Bodmer has woven skillfully around it the historical exodus of the Athenians as reported by Herodotus. His most important contribution to the material is found in the character of Euphorion, who represents in his person the sad plight of Athens and at the same time shows such an attachment to it on account of its former greatness as to be unwilling to forsake it in time of despair. The passive nature of the characters, however, and in fact, of the whole play, leaves the reader in some doubt as to Bodmer's purpose in sketching so boldly the defeatism of Euphorion. More significant is the patriotism of Themistocles and Timogenidas, although this has hardly been accorded a position of sufficient importance to rank the play among the political dramas. Had Bodmer introduced the battle of Salamis as part of the story, he would undoubtedly have given the material more emphasis with regard to the themes of patriotism and bravery.

DIE TEGEATEN

This play was written in May, 1768,[95] and was published in the following year.[96] Bodmer found the theme in Plutarch,[97] as he wrote Schinz: "Plutarch has the anecdote of the Tegeans, but in

[91] Herod., VIII. 84, 93.
[92] Herod., VI. 114.
[93] Bod., III, 2, p. 169.
[94] Herod., VII. 137.
[95] Baechtold, Tagebuch, p. 201.
[96] Pol. Schauspiele, III, 8-110.
[97] Moralia, "Parallela graecha et romana" 16.

fragments which are of very slight authority; however, the affair has still every semblance of probability, even if the fragments were by another."[98]

The background of the play is given by Democritus, one of the characters. The Tegeans and the Pheneans are drawn up on the battlefield ready for a combat which has been brought about by a most unfortunate incident. Timopolis, king of the Tegeans, has captured a beautiful slave, who is at the same time the concubine of Eupolis, king of the Pheneans. Timopolis refuses to surrender her and the issue has developed into a defense of national honor. The Tegean Critolaus is in love with Legiska, sister of the Phenean Demoticus, and the latter is in love with the former's sister Demodice. With this background the play opens in a period of armistice, as each of the armies awaits a reply to its respective appeal to the oracle. Both sides pledge themselves to abide by its decision. Demodice is being visited by her lover Democritus. In the presence of the latter, King Ctesimachus delivers the report of the oracle, which orders each side to select three sons, children of one mother, and to let these settle the issue by combat. Both the Tegeans and the Pheneans receive the same command:

If the steers fall, then Phenea shall serve and Tegea shall rule;
If the boars fall, then Phenea shall rule and Tegea shall serve.[99]

Ctesimachus objects to the light-hearted ease with which the gods play with the fate of men. The pronouncement is received with general dissatisfaction by the soldiers, but they agree to abide by it and prepare for the combat. As in Plutarch, the two sons of Reximachus are slain, but the third Tegean, Critolaus, kills by stratagem the three sons of Demostratus. When Demodice hears of the death of her beloved at the hands of her own brother, she is unstrung and contemplates suicide; she rages against her brother Critolaus until he loses his self-control and kills her in a fit of

[98] Bodmer to Schinz, Aug. 9, 1777, MS ZBZ.: "Die Anecdote von den Tegeaten hat Plutarchus, aber in Fragmenten, die sehr sublestae fidei sind. Aber die Sache selbst hat doch alle Wahrscheinlichkeit, wenn die Fragmente gleich von einem andern wären."

[99] Bod., *Tegeaten*, I, 3, p. 23:
Fallen die Stiere, so dient Pheneone, und Tegea herrschet,
Fallen die Eber, so herrscht Pheneone, und Tegea dient ihr.

rage.[100] He justifies his act on the basis of patriotism and duty, but his father Ctesimachus maintains that his son has offended the state in thus taking the law into his own hands. Critolaus will submit to the judgment of the people.

In dealing with this anecdote Bodmer was confronted with the task of expanding the cryptic statements of Plutarch. He made certain changes. A cause for the feud between the two cities is introduced in Timopolis' capture of the slave of Eupolis and his refusal to give her up. In developing this phase of the incident Bodmer points the speeches to the fact that the matter has become "an affair of the nation" and a defense of national honor; they are no longer fighting for the possession of the slave, as Critolaus says, "but to avenge their fellow-citizens, friends, and relatives, whose blood has dyed the enemy spears."[101] The intervention of the oracle at Delphi is unknown to Plutarch, but Bodmer makes a great deal of it. Its utterance is at once veiled and ambiguous in meaning, and Bodmer introduces a prophet Eumolpus to interpret it. The latter appears between the two armies and charges them with disobedience to Apollo.[102] He interprets the words "three sons of the boar and three of the warlike steer" in the prophecy as meaning that the former refer to the three sons of Ctesimachus, whose shields are adorned with engraved figures of boars, while the latter are the three sons of Demostratus, whose shields have figures of steers.[103] At the end of the play Bodmer sets up the sovereignty of the state when Ctesimachus brands Critolaus' murder of his sister Demodice as an unwarranted presumption of authority. "You were not her judge," Ctesimachus says, "the state, the people, the regent at its head should have passed judgment on her. You wanted to avenge the state and you have committed an act of presumption against it. When a particular person sets himself up as a judge, that means the destruc-

---

[100] Cf. Bodmer to Gleim, Sept. 21, 1775, Wilhelm Körte, *Briefe der Schweizer Bodmer, Sulzer, Geßner* (Zürich: Heinrich Geßner, 1804), pp. 433 f.: "Man erlaubt mir doch, daß ich . . . die D e m o d i c a Aufruhr . . . reden lasse?"

[101] Bod., I, 1, p. 15: "sondern die Mitbürger, die Freunde und die Verwandten zu rächen, deren Blut die Lanzen des Feindes gefärbt hat."

[102] Bod., II, 1, p. 41.

[103] Bod., II, 1, pp. 42 f.

tion of the state."[104] He advises his son to journey to Athens and
to ward off the avenging Furies by purifying himself before the
statue of Pallas. The relation of Ctesimachus to his son and daughter is explained by Bodmer in a letter to Schinz; in this he says
that the father's attitude toward the daughter is not supposed to
be one of passionate condemnation, but one of sympathy with her
distressed condition. Critolaus' anger is aroused slowly and re-
luctantly until he commits the deed in a fit of blind passion. The
deed dispels his passion and brings him back to the sober realization that he has offended the people and the state,[105] and at the
end of the play he submits to this higher authority in the words:
"My judge shall be the people of Tegea."[106]

In the matter of feeling Bodmer has introduced a new element
into his treatment. When Demoticus visits Demodice during the
armistice, the latter expresses the greatest concern for his safety;
she beseeches him not to be brave and not to place himself in the
front ranks of the army. Critolaus is slightly vexed by this and
answers: "You show too much concern for the life of your beloved,
but too little for our glory."[107] Later when Demodice learns of her
lover's death she gives way to a burst of rage and lamentation
which is governed by strong feeling, as for instance in her words:
"O cruel brother! He has not only laid Phenea low, he has killed
his relative, friend, and the bridegroom of his sister. He has at
the same time murdered in him the bride of Demoticus."[108] To her

[104] Bod., III, 4, p. 97: "Du warest nicht ihr Richter, der Staat, das Volk und
der Regent an seinem Haupt sollten sie gerichtet haben. Du hast den Staat rächen
wollen, und hast dich selbst an ihm vergriffen. Es ist eine Zerstörung des Staates,
wenn eine besondere Person sich zum Richter aufwirft."

[105] Bodmer to Schinz, Oct. 5, 1768, MS ZBZ.: "Ctesimachus soll niemals gegen
seine Tochter in hitzigem Affekt und aufgebracht gewesen seyn. Er soll mit ihrem
Unglück Mitleiden gehabt und sie zur Geduld gewiesen haben. Seine Vorstellungen von
dem Glück und den Siegen der Tegeaten soll er nur brauchen, ihr Unglück zu zer-
streuen. So gar soll er sie mit der Macht ihrer Liebe entschuldigen ... Kritolaus hat
sich lange gefasst, bis er aufs äußerste getrieben ward und die That im Schwindel
der Gedanken gethan hat. Und durch die That hat seine Hitze verdampfet, nur
so verdampfet, daß er die Vorstellungen seines Vaters überdacht, und sich wieder
gefaßt hat."

[106] Bod., III, 5, p. 107: "Mein Richter ist das Volk von Tegea."

[107] Bod., I, 2, p. 20.

[108] Bod., II, 6, p. 72: "Der grausame Bruder! Er hat nicht Pheneone allein in den
Staub gelegt, er hat den Verwandten, den Freund, den Bräutigam seiner Schwester
umgebracht; er hat in ihm zugleich Demotikus Braut hingerichtet."

father's admonition to restrain her emotions, she replies: "You command me to restrain my tears; order me not to bleed when my heart has been pierced."[109] The meeting of Critolaus and Demodice after the combat is marked by unrestrained emotion. She rushes in shouting: "Where is he, where is he, who with fraternal hand has dissolved, rent asunder, destroyed the most beautiful tie with which love has ever joined two tender souls?"[110] As a woman in love she is quite incapable of understanding why the oracle's command should be executed. Gorgophone, sister of Demostratus and wife of Ctesimachus, appears in several scenes to give voice to her feelings and sentiments as a mother and sister.[111] In these two women, Demodice and Gorgophone, Bodmer has emphasized the part played by feeling and sentiment more than appears in Plutarch. He makes no mention of the latter's report that it was the mother who prosecuted the son for his sister's murder, a serious loss to the dramatic possibilities in the material.

The changes made by Bodmer tend to give the material dramatic unity and force. The introduction of the state's sovereignty as the arbiter over the individual's actions shows his interest in the political side of the theme, but the emphasis of the play is largely on the prophecy and its fulfillment. The distinctive contribution to the theme lies in the introduction of the human emotion and passion of Demodice and Critolaus, by means of which Bodmer has attempted to offset the rigid demand of fate. Though undeveloped by Bodmer, the theme presents an interesting conflict between Critolaus' loyalty to the order of the oracle and his love for Legiska, sister of his opponents in battle.

PATROCLUS

In January, 1772, Bodmer composed his drama *Patroclus*,[112] but did not publish it until 1778.[113] At the earlier of these two dates

---

[109] Bod., II, 6, p. 73: "Du befiehlst mir die Thränen zu mäßigen; befiehl mir nicht zu bluten, wenn mein Herz durchstochen ist."

[110] Bod., III, 3, p. 81: "Wo ist er, wo ist er, der mit brüderlicher Hand das schönste Band, womit die Liebe zwo zärtliche Seelen verknüpfte, aufgelöst, zerrissen, zerstört hat?"

[111] Bod., II, 1, pp. 37-39. III, 2, pp. 78-80. III, 5, p. 102.

[112] Baechtold, *Tagebuch*, p. 203.

[113] *Patroclus, Ein Trauerspiel; nach dem griechischen Homers.* Augsburg: Johann Jakob Mauracher, 1778.

he was working on his translation of the *Iliad,* although at that
time he had little hope of finishing it, as he wrote.[114] The play remained in his hands until 1774, when he sent it to Schinz; he
wished him to have it, he said, "because otherwise I must regard it
as lost."[115] The manuscript reached Schinz in due time, and Bodmer reported his joy that his friend had the work.[116] He sent the
unpublished manuscript also to Gottlob David Hartmann (1752-
75), the Swabian poet and friend of Bodmer and Lavater, who
had spent several weeks in the late fall of 1773 visiting Lavater in
Zurich.[117] About the middle of 1776 Bodmer complained that the
drama was moldering away in his desk.[118] He hoped through this
work to direct his readers to Homer, for "the characters, sentiments, and language" were those of the Greek epic writer and
one could not, Bodmer wrote, censure his German play without
also criticizing Homer.[119] But when the play appeared, it was
neglected by the literary world. Bodmer was disappointed that he
could not compete with the writers who were then in favor, and in
1781 he wrote that he had expended all his efforts to give *Patroclus*
"die sanftesten und mildesten Sitten," but it had not made such
an impression as Leisewitz' *Julius von Tarent.*[120]

The play has been described as the story of the death of Patroclus in dialogue, with strict observance of the unities.[121] Achilles,
Patroclus, and Phoenix appear in a scene which describes the sad
plight of their leader Achilles, in anger because Agamemnon has
taken his mistress Briseis. The words of comfort spoken to Achilles
by both Patroclus and Phoenix do not help him forget his hatred

[114] Bodmer to Schinz, April 12, 1777, MS ZBZ.: "Im Jahr 1772 durfte ich nicht
hoffen, daß ich die I l i a s vollenden würde."
[115] Bodmer to Schinz, Jan. 27, 1774, MS ZBZ.: "Ich wünsche sehr, daß Sie den
Patroclus haben, weil ich ihn sonst für verlohren halten muß."
[116] Bodmer to Schinz, Feb. 11, 1774, MS ZBZ.
[117] Th. Vetter, *Pers. Anekdoten,* p. 116.
[118] Bodmer to Gleim, July, 1776, W. Körte, *op. cit.,* p. 439.
[119] Bodmer to Schinz, Sept. 17, 1777, MS ZBZ.: "Mein Patroclus sollte die Leser
zu Homer führen. Character, Sentimens, Sprache sind Homers. Man wird mich
nicht tadeln können, daß man nicht zugleich ihn tadle."
[120] Bodmer to Schinz, June 7, 1781, MS ZBZ.: "Ich habe an meinem Patroclus
alle Mühe angewandt, ihm die sanftesten und mildesten Sitten zu geben. Wenn ich
es gethan, so ist mir leid, daß er den Eindruck nicht gemacht hat, den Julius von
Tarent . . . machet."
[121] G. Finsler, *Homer in der Neuzeit* (Berlin: B. G. Teubner, 1912), p. 409.

of Agamemnon, nor do they succeed in stirring him to participate in the combat, although the Greeks are hard pressed by the Trojans. This occupies two long scenes. Achilles is first moved by the sight of Nestor's chariot, returning from the battlefield with the wounded warrior Machon, and by the heroic efforts of Patroclus, who rescues from death Eurypylus, son of Euaemon. Achilles remains steadfast in his refusal to fight. Moved by the pleas of Patroclus, and especially by the wounds of Eurypylus, Achilles finally allows Patroclus to don his armor, but commands him expressly to avoid a personal combat with Hector. Achilles offers a sacrifice to the gods. Diomede, daughter of Phorcas, sings the praises of Achilles; Iphis sings those of Patroclus. The victorious fighting of the latter is reported. Then Briseis returns to the camp of Achilles and begs him not to turn her out; he orders her to withdraw to the women's tent. Now Antilochus brings the news of the tragic death of Patroclus. The last scenes of the play are filled with the description of the recovery of his body and the laments of Briseis, Iphis, and Diomede. Achilles' wrath is stirred up at the sight of his dead comrade and he decides to avenge this deed on Hector.

Bodmer's source is quite clearly Homer's *Iliad*. Paraphrase, translation, and use of isolated events are the devices employed in adapting the material. The passage in which Patroclus describes the care of the wounded warrior Eurypylus is a good example of a paraphrase of the original.[122] Another is the scene in which Achilles, having granted Patroclus permission to enter the battle in his armor,[123] orders preparations for battle to be made. These include the yoking of the swift horses Xanthus and Balius,[124] the gathering of the Myrmidon soldiers,[125] and the cleansing and preparation of the beautiful cup for the sacrifice by Achilles to Zeus.[126] Bodmer follows Homer in the prayer of Achilles to Zeus.[127] So also the details of Patroclus' combat are reproduced faithfully,

[122] Bodmer, *Patroclus*, II, 2, p. 21. Homer *Iliad* XI. 842-48.
[123] Bod., II, 3, p. 27. Homer, XVI. 64 f., 128.
[124] Bod., II, 4, p. 28. Homer, XVI. 145 ff.
[125] Bod., II, 4, p. 28. Homer, XVI. 193 ff.
[126] Bod., II, 4, p. 29. Homer, XVI. 220 ff.
[127] Bod., II, 8, pp. 36 f. Homer, XVI. 230 ff.

as for instance the latter's pursuit of the disordered Trojans,[128] the speed of Hector's horse, which saves him from the spear of Patroclus,[129] Sarpedon's resistance to Patroclus, and his death at the latter's hands, as well as the futile attempt of the Trojans to recover the body.[130] Nor has Bodmer omitted the prophecy that Patroclus would meet his death at the hands of a Trojan.[131] He has also introduced in a modified form the laments of the women, especially that of Briseis over the dead body of Patroclus.[132] In other instances the material has been taken from Homer, but the examples noted above are perhaps sufficient to show how extensively Bodmer used the *Iliad* as a source for this play.

An important modification made by Bodmer is the emphasis on the part played by the women Iphis, Diomede, and Briseis. These figures are characterized by an intense devotion to their lovers, as for instance when Iphis says: "Es ist eine Seligkeit in der Liebe des liebenswürdigen Patroclus zu leben."[133] Bodmer introduces the return of Briseis to Achilles, his stout refusal to take her back, and his final order of dismissal. At first he does not wish to take her back because he looks upon her as a cast-off, but she pleads: "Agamemnon has not incurred this guilt; I stood by him untouched and come chastely from him."[134] The laments of the women at the end of the play add to the emotional content of the theme. Achilles' wrath is very intense, and although Homer, as well as Bodmer, motivates Achilles' refusal to aid Agamemnon because of this feeling, the Swiss author gives it his own expression in such a passage as the following:

My resolution stands as immovable as that of Jove, to deny the proud man everything, to deny everything to him whom Jupiter has robbed of every feeling of justice and abandoned to his madness. His gold, his silver, his daughter, all that he can offer me, Electra adorned with the

---

[128] Bod., III, 1, p. 38. Homer, XVI. 291 ff.

[129] Bod., III, 1, p. 39. Homer, XVI. 380 ff.

[130] Bod., III, 1, pp. 39 f. Homer, XVI. 462 ff., 563 ff.

[131] Bod., III, 4, p. 46. Homer, XVIII. 8 ff.

[132] Bod., III, 10, p. 53. III, 6, p. 47. Homer, XIX. 282 ff.

[133] Bod., II, 6, p. 31.

[134] Bod., III, 2, p. 43: "Agamemnon hat diese Schuld nicht auf sich geladen, ich bin unberührt bey ihm gestanden und komme rein aus seiner Hand."

charms of Venus, his cities, all that comes from him is hateful to me and I despise it as I despise hell.[135]

Bodmer has adapted the material to his form by reporting briefly events which are narrated by definite persons in the *Iliad* and thus has given more unity to his treatment.[136]

In general, *Patroclus* is to be regarded as a work that was part of Bodmer's preparation for the translation of the *Iliad*. This is true especially of the battle scenes, the descriptions of which occupy a place of prominence in the range of Bodmer's selection.

SUMMARY

In summarizing Bodmer's attitude toward the material in these plays, certain aspects stand out prominently. The author follows closely the accounts in antiquity. The few liberties that he takes with them are such as are necessary for dramatic purposes, as in the introduction of new characters or in the giving of names to figures unnamed in the sources. In *Ulysses, Electra,* and *Oedipus* Bodmer is experimenting with this type of material and allows himself less latitude for personal interpretation than is the case in some of his later plays. In both *Die Tegeaten* and *Die Rettung in den Mauern von Holz,* he is forced to expand the brief accounts of Plutarch and Herodotus and he injects more of himself into these treatments. But in *Patroclus* he tries again to follow the original closely. The legends and prophecies of the ancient world are accepted as valid determinants of the events in the lives of the people of that time, but with certain reservations for the Germans of the Eighteenth Century. The theological background of Bodmer's early life and his interest in biblical epics are reflected in two ancient priests, Samgar in *Ulysses* and Teiresias in *Oedipus,* both of whom exhibit a strong tendency to question the efficacy of

[135] Bod., I, 1, p. 8: "Mein Vorsatz steht feste, so unbeweglich wie des Jovis, alles dem stolzen Manne, alles zu versagen, ihm, den Jupiter jedes gerechten Gefühls beraubt, und in den Unsinn dahin gegeben hat. Sein Gold, sein Silber, seine Tochter, alles was er mir anbieten kann, Electra mit den Reizungen der Venus geschmückt, seine Städte, alles, was von ihm kommt, ist mir verhaßt, und ich verabscheue es wie die Hölle." Cf. *Iliad* IX. 385 ff.

[136] E.g., Eurypylus in II, 3; Polites in III, 1; Pylaemon in III, 3; Antilochus in III, 5.

ancient oracles to control human destiny, and both of whom find consolation in a Christian philosophy for the unfortunate victims of fate, Ulysses and Oedipus. Such an aspiration of Bodmer to liberalize the iron-bound demands of ancient fate is in keeping with the spirit of his century. Concomitant with this liberalizing force of fate is what may be called a humanizing tendency, which is followed by Bodmer when he stresses the parts of the women in the plays with the purpose of increasing their emotional content. This is evident in the hatred existing between Clytemnestra and her daughter in *Electra,* in the sympathy shown Oedipus in the play of that name, in the actions and language of Demodice in *Die Tegeaten* or of Briseis in *Patroclus.* In other words, the feelings and personal side of the characters have attracted Bodmer as being more important than the restricting influence of fate as found in the sources. Except in *Die Tegeaten,* where Bodmer has established the state as the final court of appeal in limiting the individual's power, these dramas are lacking in the political tone which characterizes some of the other plays.

IV

DRAMAS OF ETHICAL IMPORT

The plays in this chapter are all taken from historical accounts and emphasize some ethical aspect of the material as most important. By the word "ethical" Bodmer would imply an attack on some weakness or moral characteristic that so detracts from the character as to exclude him from a group of heroic figures. This applies to the main character in each play. The attack is in part directed against moral shortcomings. Thus in *Octavius Cäsar* the accusation made against Augustus, the libertine, is emphasized when he attempts to punish his daughter and granddaughter for the same sins of which he himself is accused, and in fact more grievously than in the case of these women. In *Brittannicus* Bodmer seeks to give a picture of a man who is so taken with fear and indecision as to abandon the religious faith of his fathers, and even to commit murder. In *Cato* the attack is directed against luxury as a symptom of decadence. In *Aristomenes* the conflict with moral law comes through a breach of personal trust, when Aristomenes is betrayed by Aristocrates. The former differs from the characters of the other plays in this group through superior moral quality, but is beguiled by an evil character. The dramas in this chapter do not exclude prophecies from their action, witness for instance that uttered by Locusta in *Brittannicus* and that of Maniclus in *Aristomenes*. But unlike the treatment of such material in the plays of the previous group, these prophecies are subordinate elements in the plot. Likewise the political significance of *Octavius Cäsar* and *Brittannicus*, in so far as these plays may be considered attacks on despotism, or the praise of Aristomenes' patriotism by Evergetidas, is not Bodmer's main interest in these themes. The ethical and moral aspects of ancient society, as we have seen above, appealed to Bodmer as a significant chapter in ancient history. This interest is the expression of a personal attitude which must have shown itself also in Bodmer's teaching.

OCTAVIUS CÄSAR

The idea of treating the figure of the Roman emperor Augustus in a play was an old one with Bodmer. In 1747 he had observed with a feeling of regret that the militarists of Roman times had been esteemed much more highly than the writers, whose patronage, dependant as it was upon imperial favor, was filled with much obvious, but often insincere, flattery.[1] He had the Augustan Age in mind and wrote: "If I should ever feel strong enough to write a tragedy, then I would write it about Augustus, whom I would portray in a light quite different from that in which he has been presented by Vergil, Horace, and a thousand others."[2] He objected to this praise of the emperor because the latter persecuted and killed the defenders of freedom.[3] When Bodmer began to write plays on ancient themes, he carried out in June, 1764, the work which he had projected more than seventeen years before[4] and published it in 1769.[5]

In the preface to this drama Bodmer reports a change in his approach to the subject so as to include not only the political aspect of the material, as contemplated in 1747, but more especially an attack on the moral character of Augustus, the man. He points out that the accusations of immorality which the two Julias, mother and daughter, made against the emperor were supported by the facts of history,[6] and he asks the reader to make his own decision on the question of "whether he [Augustus] was the happy man the world thought he was" after they had read his account of the imperial indiscretions and liberties.[7] To illustrate these Bodmer quotes examples from Suetonius.[8]

[1] Bodmer to Sulzer, March 15, 1747, Zehnder-Stadlin, *op. cit.*, p. 390.

[2] *Idem.*

[3] *Ibid.*, p. 390: he quotes two passages to illustrate this "lästerliche Schmeichelei," as he terms it:

O Meliboee, Deus nobis haec otia fecit.	Sive mutata iuvenem figura
Namque erit ille mihi semper Deus.	Ales in terris imitaris almae
Vergil *Eclogues* I. 6 f.	filium Majae, patiens vocari
	Caesaris ultor.
	Horace *Odes* I. ii. 41 ff.

[4] Baechtold, *Tagebuch*, p. 199.

[5] *Politische Schauspiele. 2. Bändgen. Aus den Zeiten der Cäsare* (Lindau und Chur: typographische Gesellschaft, 1769), pp. 2-72.

[6] *Ibid.*, pp. 4 f.

[7] *Ibid.*, p. 4.

[8] *Ibid.*, p. 6: these include the emperor's relations to Aulus Hirtius in Spain,

The criticism of the drama by Klotz[9] set out to divide the work into a series of quotations, selected largely with the intention of showing how absurd Bodmer's play was and how unwarranted its claim to be included in a volume of political dramas. More stinging, however, was the critic's attack on the language and actions of Augustus' daughter Julia. Klotz found fault first with her passion for Julius Antony, son of Marc Antony, and second with her abusive criticism of her father's immoral actions, when she herself was under fire for grievous misconduct. Bodmer took note of these criticisms at once in a letter to Schinz. After accusing Klotz of ignorance in matters Latin, he defended Julia's burst of affection for Antony as natural for such an emotional temperament. In explanation of her invective against her father, Bodmer says that Julia had been too long and too intimately acquainted with him to be expected to practice restraint, especially considering her fiery temper.[10] Klotz also criticized the stilted and pedantic language of Bodmer's characters, among whom Julia distinguishes herself by the readiness with which she cites Roman history. Five years later, in 1774, Bodmer referred scornfully to these strictures: "Did not Klotz say that they speak a language which one does not hear every day? . . . Julia speaks as eruditely as if she had attended university lectures. (For she knew what all women in Rome at that time knew, and what our professors must still learn.)"[11]

As the play opens the emperor appears in conversation with Fabius Maximus lamenting the fact that, though he heads the world's largest empire, he must tolerate a dissolute daughter and granddaughter, both Julia by name. Julius Antony, one of the elder Julia's lovers, is called into the presence of Augustus and

---

and his habit of singeing the hair from his legs by means of red-hot nutshells, Suet. *Aug.* XVIII; Antony's taunts to Octavius for his relations to Drusilla, Tertulla, etc., Suet. *Aug.* LXIX. 2; the immorality at the private dinner of Augustus, called the banquet of the "twelve gods," Suet. *Aug.* LXX. 1.

[9] *Deutsche Bibliothek,* III (1769), 397-403.

[10] Bodmer to Schinz, Aug. 21, 1769, MS ZBZ.: "Aber Julia war auch zu lang und zu enge mit ihrem Vater bekannt, als daß sie sich sehr hätte hinterhalten sollen, und man muß ihr feuriges Temperament denken." Klotz had spoken of Julia, "die keinen Augenblick ohne ihr Herzblatt bleiben kann." *Op. cit.,* p. 398.

[11] Bodmer to Schinz, June 3, 1774, MS ZBZ.: "Hat nicht Klotz gesagt . . . Julia rede so gelehrt, als wenn sie Collegien gehört hätte. (Denn sie wußte, was alle Frauen in ihrem Rom wußten, und unsere Professoren lernen müssen.)"

ordered to sever further relations with her under penalty of death. Antony attempts to defend Julia as a beautiful creature who is governed entirely by her emotions, but the father cuts him off with autocratic severity: "You have broken the laws, and to violate them is an insult to the ruler who is their guardian. Realize that your life is under my thumb!"[12] At this moment Julia arrives and, throwing her arms about Antony, covers him with kisses. A violent scene between father and daughter follows, in which Julia insists that Venus has given her "a heart that never tires of love and is never satiated with it" and so excites her father that he brands her an "advocate of disgrace." Since Julia remains obdurate to all pleas and exhortations, he orders both her and her lover to be locked up in prison. Livia, Julia's mother, attempts to defend her daughter's conduct as no worse than the normal behavior in profligate Rome; but Augustus does not heed her plea and orders Antony to be decapitated. Aroused by this, Livia suggests to Tiberius, Julia's husband, the possibility of gaining the crown by crime. When Julia is confronted with her lover's head, she clings more firmly to him dead than when he was alive. Octavius admits that the removal of the lover has not had the desired effect on his daughter, and is greatly disturbed by the domestic situation. He resolves to send Julia into exile. Things take a turn for the worse when the granddaughter Julia arrives. When Augustus offers to allow her to accompany her mother into banishment, she breaks into a tirade on his moral shortcomings and calls particular attention to the occasion when "he took the wife of a consul before his very eyes into a chamber and brought her back with her ears glowing and her hair dishevelled."[13] Octavius is alarmed that his indiscreet conduct is known even to his granddaughter and denounces all women. Fabius tries to comfort him in his dejection, and the play ends lamely with Tiberius casting greedy eyes on the throne.

[12] Bod., *Oct. Cäs.,* I, 2, p. 20: "Du hast die Gesetze gebrochen; und sie zu brechen ist Beleidigung des Herrschers, der ihr Schützer ist. Wisse, daß dein Leben an einem Faden hängt!"

[13] Bod., III, 2, p. 54: "Rom hat nicht vergessen, daß er die Frau eines Consularen vor dem Angesichte ihres Gemahls in ein Closet gezogen, und sie mit röthenden Ohren und zerrauften Haaren zurückgebracht hat."

Bodmer has incorporated into this work material from the Latin historians Suetonius and Tacitus. Julius Antony, in defending Julia, accuses her husband Tiberius of loose conduct during his stay in Rhodes. Tacitus had mentioned this,[14] also that Julius Antony was one of Julia's lovers and was executed by Augustus.[15] In attempting a defense of her conduct, Bodmer's Julia enumerates other family precedents for her profligacy, such as those of Caesar's wife Pompeia; she recalls particularly the incident during the festival called *Bona Dea,* when Clodius took liberties with her in the very presence of Augustus. Both passages go back to Suetonius and Plutarch.[16] From the same authorities Bodmer draws the conduct of Cato's sister Servilia, her indiscreet association with Caesar, and especially the rumor that Brutus was the son of Caesar.[17] Suetonius supplies a number of motives and incidents of importance for characterizing Augustus which are selected with discrimination from the *Lives* of Tiberius and Augustus. Thus Julia accuses Octavius of consorting with the wives of the senators in order to gain secret information.[18] When Livia cannot restrain Augustus in his anger, she attempts to excite Tiberius to aspire to the rule of Rome.[19] After Julia has seen Antony's head and still refuses to reform her life, the emperor thinks of killing her. This is suggested to him by the report of the suicide of Phoebe, one of Julia's confidants, a passage which Bodmer has taken directly from Suetonius. Speaking to his daughter, the emperor says: "Hat man dir gesagt, daß ihre Kupplerinn, die Phöbe, wegen einiger Winke von mir, sich selbst erwürget habe? Ich wünschte, daß ich der Phöbe Vater wäre."[20] As we have seen, when the granddaughter Julia is permitted to accompany her mother into exile, the profligate girl flaunts in Augustus' face the

[14] Bod., *Oct. Cäs.*, I, 2, p. 19. Tacitus *Annals* I. iv. 4.
[15] Tac., IV. xliv. 5. Death by decapitation is an innovation of Bodmer.
[16] Bod., I, 3, p. 24. Suet. *Julius* VI. 2. Plut. *Cicero* XXVIII.
[17] Bod., I, 3, p. 24. Suet. *Julius* L. 2. Plut. *Brutus* V. 2.
[18] Bod., I, 3, p. 25. Suet. *Augustus* LXIX. 1.
[19] Bod., II, 1, pp. 32 f. Cf. Suet. *Tiberius* XXI. 2: here Augustus listens to his wife's entreaties to adopt Tiberius.
[20] Bod., II, 2, pp. 35 f. Suet. *Augustus* LXV. 2: "Certe cum sub idem tempus una ex consciis liberta Phoebe suspendio vitam finisset, maluisse se ait Phoebes patrem fuisse."

public scandal arising from his immorality with a certain consul's wife at a banquet; this incident is reported in a paraphrase from Suetonius.[21] Octavius is so incensed at the notoriety of his misdeeds that he characterizes the women as "ulcers in my soul, boils in my heart," using here the words of Suetonius, as well as in expressing his disgust with his marriage: "Would that I ne'er had wedded and would I had died without offspring."[22] All this material was selected by Bodmer with the purpose of showing the immoral side of Augustus' life and of demonstrating the reason for his domestic tragedy. He stands quite clearly under the influence of the moralist Tacitus in this use of the material from both Suetonius and Tacitus. The selection of the motives and incidents explains the text of the play as Bodmer probably borrowed it from Tacitus: "Great as had been the good fortune of the Divine Augustus in public matters, he had been unhappy in his domestic relations because of the profligate conduct of his daughter and granddaughter."[23]

But certain liberties have been taken with the sources. Thus Bodmer pays little attention to the chronology of the events, nor is he concerned with the historical exactness of the material. For instance, Tiberius is represented as being in Rome when Augustus banished Julia. The latter event took place in 2 B.C., whereas Tiberius had gone to Rhodes in 6 B.C. and did not return to Rome for eight years.[24] Nor is there any evidence that Tiberius was ordered by Augustus to go to Rhodes in exile, as indicated in the words of Livia.[25] Julia was banished to the island of Pandateria and not to Planasia, as Bodmer states.[26] The Swiss author makes no mention of the numerous lovers besides Antony; and the scene

[21] Bod., III, 2. p. 54. Suet. *Aug.* LXIX. 1.

[22] Bod., III, 4, p. 62. Suet. *Aug.* LXV. 4: the verse is quoted by Suetonius in the Greek; it is found in the *Iliad* (III. 40), where Hector addresses the words to Paris, but with the verbs in the second person.

[23] Tac. *Ann.* III. xxiv. 2.

[24] Cf. V. Gardthausen, *Augustus und seine Zeit* (Leipzig: B. G. Teubner, 1891), I, 1115 f. Cf. also Suet. *Tiberius* XIV. 1.

[25] Bod., II, 2, p. 33. Cf. Tac. *Ann.* I. liii. 2: he gives Julia's conduct as the "real reason for his retirement to Rhodes." Suetonius assigns still other reasons for his retirement, but in no event was it forced upon him by Augustus. *Tiberius* X. Gardthausen says this event was very embarrassing to Octavius. *Op. cit.*, I, 1106 f.

[26] Bod., II, 4, p. 46 and III, 2, p. 51. Tac. *Ann.* I. liii. 1.

in which Julius Antony defends his conduct toward Julia has no historical basis. Likewise the important part played by Fabius Maximus as confidant to Augustus in this matter has been invented by Bodmer. In a sense the strong emphasis on Augustus' disgust with the immorality of his daughter may be considered unhistorical in so far as the exaggerated emphasis of this view is disproportionate to the facts. Nor can the vigor of the emperor in his condemnation of the two Julias and in them the morality of the age be considered an accurate version of the man's attitude as a whole.

One further interesting borrowing should be noted here. On reading the play Sulzer wrote Bodmer that the description from Winckelmann had not displeased him,[27] referring to a description of Julius Antony spoken by Julia, after the former has been executed by Augustus. To be sure Sulzer considered it unnatural that Julia should speak the words used by Winckelmann, because she lacked the latter's spirit.[28] The passage in question is quoted almost verbatim by Bodmer from Winckelmann's description of the Belvedere statue of Apollo, e.g.:

Barbarischer als ein Scythe wüthtest du gegen das weiche Haar, und hattest keine Empfindung für seine Reitze, wenn es wie die zarten und flüßigen Schlingen edler Weinreben, von einer sanften Luft bewegt, um das göttliche Haupt spielte, mit dem Öle der Götter gesalbet, und von den Grazien mit holder Pracht auf den Scheitel gebunden.[29]

Its eloquent and poetic phrases seem little suited to the profligate Julia.

DER TOD DES BRITTANNICUS

Among Bodmer's papers in Zurich is an unpublished manuscript entitled *Der Tod des Brittannicus. Ein Trauerspiel.* The play is written on thirty-two sheets of Bodmer's letter paper in his own hand, together with several sheets of additions. A copy, minus these additions, is also found there. The work is in prose and is divided into three acts, the second of which contains five scenes

---

[27] Sulzer to Bodmer, Nov. 19, 1774, W. Körte, *op. cit.*, p. 417.
[28] *Idem.*
[29] Bod., II, 3, p. 38: the footnote to this passage acknowledges Winckelmann's description of the statue as the model for Bodmer. J. J. Winckelmann, *Geschichte der Kunst des Alterthums*, XI, 3, 11.

and the others two each. The characters are Nero, Seneca, Otho, Britannicus, Agrippina, Octavia, and Locusta. It was written in 1764, for Bodmer told Sulzer in August of that year: "I have written the *Death of Britannicus,* in which I put Nero into a state of agitation and doubt which is quite similar to that of Solomon but also fits Nero's character."[30] Furthermore the *Salomo* of which Bodmer speaks is Klopstock's play and was published in that year. Bodmer acknowledges in the preface to the play the influence of Klopstock, saying that he wished "to show the inhuman character of Solomon, whom Klopstock has investigated, but to portray him in his true light, namely in the person of Nero."[31]

After the death of Claudius in 54 A.D., Nero was elevated to the throne as *Imperator* of Rome. According to Tacitus in the *Annals,* a weak plea was made at the time of the election in favor of the legitimate heir, Tiberius Claudius Britannicus, but Nero prevailed.[32] The relation between these two had never been cordial, for Nero entertained the fear that the youth, born in 41 A.D., might one day challenge his right to rule. This seemed imminent in 55 A.D. when Agrippina, Nero's mother, became enraged at the loss of her influence over Nero and at his passion for the freed-woman Acte and threatened to befriend Britannicus, to enlist the army in his support, and to place him in power. Alarmed and jealous, Nero caused Britannicus to be murdered at a banquet by poison that was administered by a criminal, Locusta by name. These are the facts recorded by history.

In his dramatization Bodmer has given this account an entirely different aspect. Seneca and Otho appear discussing Nero's perturbation and fear. The latter enters in the second scene, cursing life and apprehensive of a prophecy that he would some day murder his mother and his wife. His old tutor Seneca tries to convince him that this fear is a figment of the imagination, that he cannot

[30] Bodmer to Sulzer, in August, 1764, MS ZBZ.: "Ich habe den Tod des Brittannicus geschrieben, in welchem ich den Nero in Unruhe und Zweifel setze, die des Salomo seinem ganz ähnlich sind, aber die des Nero Charakter nicht übel anstehn."

[31] *Tod des Brittannicus,* preface, MS ZBZ.: "Er wollte den unmenschlichen . . . Salomo, den Klopstock aufgesucht hat, in seinem wahren Licht, unter Neros Person zeigen."

[32] Tac. *Annals* XII. lxix. 1 f. References are to the edition of Henry Furneaux (Oxford: Clarendon Press, 1891), Vol. II.

be guilty of a crime through mere prophecy. But Nero insists that fate is inexorable, explaining that this prophecy comes from the god of the Chaldeans. Seneca's attempt to show that this deity is antiquated falls upon deaf ears. The emperor wishes to make away with himself, but Seneca and Otho flatter him with the plea that his death would be an irreparable loss to Rome. The philosopher promises to find a solution of this difficulty and takes his leave. Meanwhile Nero continues to pour out his heart to Otho, emphasizing that his fear of punishment after death is greater than his fear of life: "If I thought that these tormenting thoughts would leave me on my departure from this life, how quickly I would flee from this world, in order to seek the peace I cannot find here. But if the peace that I seek were to double my present anxiety and pile agony on agony—that is what restrains my hand from seizing the dagger."[33] Otho suggests a life of activity and pleasure to make him forget his fears. He asks permission to summon Locusta, who is acquainted with the bloody rites that can dispel Nero's fears. When she is brought in, Locusta exhorts Nero to find peace with Moloch by the sacrifice of a boy. Unwilling to accede to this at first, the emperor dismisses her and calls for Acte to soothe his soul with her music: "You plunge me into doubts, that like a violent storm drive me about in confusion as to my course. Must I not fear that they will dash me against the rocks? Leave me Locusta!"[34]

The second act opens with a scene between Seneca and Nero, in which the philosopher tries to dissuade his ruler from placing his trust in a foreign god. But Nero is now resolved on the sacrifice and recalls Locusta. She announces that the boy who first enters the room must be the sacrificial victim, but Nero objects to this manner of selection, for they are in his palace, into which "only the sons of important senators come." Seneca suggests that Locusta

---

[33] Bod., *Brittannicus*, I, 3, p. 6: "Dächte ich, daß mich mit dem Leben auch diese qualvollen Gedanken verlassen würden, wie schnell wollte ich aus dieser Welt fliehen, die Ruhe zu suchen, die ich hier nicht finde. Aber wenn die Ruhe, die ich suche, verdoppelte Unruhe, Pein mit Pein gehäuft wäre,—das ist das, was mir die Hand zurückbindet, daß ich nicht nach dem Dolche greife."

[34] Bod., I, 4, p. 10: "Du stürzest mich in Zweifel, die mit stürmerischer Gewalt mich in der Irre herumtreiben. Muß ich nicht fürchten, daß sie mich an Klippen schmettern? Verlaß mich Locusta!"

be the victim. As Britannicus arrives in the company of Octavia, Nero's wife, Locusta designates him as the victim, while Octavia is enraged at the choice and objects in no uncertain terms. Her attitude, supported by the objections of Seneca, serves only to throw the emperor into a state of greater agitation, especially when Locusta portrays more vividly the revengeful nature of Moloch. Britannicus clings to Octavia, who offers herself if the victim must come from the royal family. Nero appeals to Locusta to obtain a pledge of a lesser sacrifice from Moloch, and declares that he will die rather than sacrifice the boy. As the emperor departs to walk through his garden and to reflect on the situation, Agrippina appears. When the matter becomes clear to her, she sees Nero's evil nature revealed fully and, after reviewing his career of treachery, resolves to call upon the army to support the cause of Britannicus. At Seneca's request she agrees to attempt to bring Nero back to his composure of mind, but warns him that she will champion Britannicus' right to the throne if she finds Nero "hardened in his melancholy superstition or in the madness of his tyrannical jealousy."

In the third act the emperor reports that Moloch has relented and will be satisfied with the sacrifice of an ordinary boy. By this ceremony Locusta promises also to conjure up a spirit that will disclose the future of the empire. Nero is anxious to know this, for he feels his safety jeopardized by his mother and Britannicus and he gives a sinister interpretation to Octavia's love for the boy: "the zeal with which she is concerned for the life of Britannicus is not love for the boy. She loves in him the means of frightening me, and this makes him more hateful to me than anything that might give me reason to fear him."[35] Locusta reports that the sacrifice has been performed. From the description of the spirit, Nero recognizes the emperor Claudius. The wraith exalts Nero as the master of the world and of the arts; it promises him eternal life if he can reach without mishap his seventy-third birthday. Nero is happy, but Seneca is disdainful of the prophecy. Suddenly a noise

[35] Bod., III, 1, p. 23: "Der Eifer, mit welchem sie für des Brittannicus Leben besorgt ist., ist nicht Liebe zu dem Knaben. Sie liebt in ihm das Werkzeug mir Furcht einzujagen, und dieses macht mir ihn verhaßter als alles, was ich von ihm selbst Ursache zu fürchten haben möchte."

is heard outside and Octavia rushes in with the news that Britannicus is dying. She accuses Locusta of the crime, but Agrippina knows that Nero is responsible for it and foretells that he will spill her blood and in the end will take his own life. As the emperor leaves the scene in the company of Seneca, she warns the latter that his life is also in danger.

The play thus follows, as we have seen, the historical account, and Bodmer has taken the events from both Tacitus and Suetonius. He has, however, taken certain liberties with his material, a procedure which he states and defends in his unpublished preface: "In this play license has been taken with history, but no freer license than tragedians in general are accustomed to take with historical subjects."[36] The prophecy that Nero would murder his mother is taken from Tacitus,[37] as well as the fact that it was revealed to Agrippina.[38] It is presented as a saying of the Chaldeans. In the drama it plays an important part in Nero's state of mind, for it explains the fear that he will be pursued by the Furies; Bodmer found this motive in Suetonius, who reports that the emperor was hounded by the Furies.[39] When Agrippina learns that Nero has yielded to the demand of Locusta and her god, she breaks into a bitter accusation of his character and his ambition: "It is the seed of evil, over which he is no longer master and can no longer disguise. Hitherto my admonitions and my authority have kept his vice in check . . . the good deeds which he owes to my influence are his strongest yoke."[40] Part of her arraignment is based upon the account of Tacitus, especially such statements as that describing Nero's desire to weaken his mother's influence in matters of state, her threat to appeal to the legions for aid, and the passion of Nero for Acte that is responsible for Agrippina's

---

[36] Bod., "N.B." (preface to *Brittannicus*): "In diesem Schauspiele sind gegen die Geschichte Licenzen, doch nicht größere als die Tragiker insgemein mit den historischen Sujets zu nehmen gewohnt sind."

[37] Bod., I, 2, p. 2. *Annals* XIV. ix. 5.

[38] Bod., III, 4, p. 29.

[39] Bod., I, 4, p. 8. Suet. *Nero* XXXIV. 4.

[40] Bod., II, 5, p. 18: "Es ist die Saat der Bosheit, der er nicht mehr Meister ist, die er nicht mehr in Verstellung verhüllen kann. Bisher hatten meine Vermahnungen, mein Ansehen seine Laster noch in Zaum gefasset . . . Die Gutthaten, die er mir zu danken hat, sind sein schwerstes Joch."

loss of influence over him.[41] Bodmer includes in his attack, as does Tacitus, an accusation against Otho and Aenaeus Serenus for serving as screens for Nero's affair with the freedwoman,[42] as well as Agrippina's censure of the emperor for allowing Seneca and Burrus to arrogate to themselves the power that belonged to her and for dismissing Pallas, the treasurer of the royal household, because he was loyal to her.[43] From Suetonius come certain characteristics, such as the recognition of Claudius in the spirit that appears to Locusta; Bodmer mentions specifically the trembling limbs and tottering gait of Nero's predecessor.[44] The warning against a crisis in the seventy-third year of the ruler's life is found in Suetonius.[45] Bodmer follows Tacitus in describing how the emperor receives the news of Britannicus' death; he remains unconcerned and with an air of innocence, seeks to explain the boy's unconscious state as an epileptic fit.[46] In general the selection of these facts and characteristics tends to emphasize Nero's evil nature, the same approach used, as we shall see, in Bodmer's *Nero*. Here in *Brittannicus* it is the moral and ethical aspects of history that interest the author.

The influence of Klopstock's *Salomo* upon this play is clearest in matters pertaining to the sacrifice required by Moloch. Bodmer's Locusta corresponds to Moloch's priestess Darda in Klopstock and Nero corresponds to Solomon. There are numerous examples to illustrate Bodmer's borrowings from Klopstock. Nero repeats Darda's words when he shrinks at first from consenting to the sacrifice.[47] In dismissing Locusta and ordering Acte to appear with her music, Nero paraphrases Solomon's order. Thus Klopstock's resounding verse,

> Bringt mir die Sänger
> Mit ihren Harfen her, daß meiner Seele
> Diese Bilder entfliehen, und sich zur Stille
> Mein Herz besänftige,

[41] Bod., II, 5, p. 18. Tac., XIII. xii-xiv.
[42] Bod., II, 5, pp. 18 f. Tac., XIII. xii. 1, xiii. 1.
[43] Bod., III, 1, p. 22. Tac., XIII. xiv. 5, 1.
[44] Bod., III, 2, p. 26. Suet. *Claudius* XXX.
[45] Bod., III, 2, p. 27. Suet. *Nero* XL. 3.
[46] Bod., III, 3, pp. 28 f.; III, 4, p. 30. Tac., XIII. xvi. 5.
[47] Bod., I, 4, p. 9. Klopstock, *Salomo*, I, 6, p. 34. References to Klopstock are to the following edition: *Klopstocks Werke* (Leipzig: Göschen, 1806), Vol. IX.

appears in Bodmer's somewhat bombastic prose: "Laß die Sängerin kommen. Acte soll mit ihren windschnellen Fingern die Saiten rühren, und sanfte Töne darein singen, meine empörten Geister in Ordnung zu wiegen."[48] In the description of the rites of the human sacrifice Bodmer has been influenced by Klopstock when the Swiss author speaks of placing the child in the fiery arms of Moloch: "Gebeute, Cäsar, und die Glut soll in Moloch entflammen, dem Opferknaben in seine Arme aufzunehmen."[49] Again the Klopstockian style appears when Locusta describes the hissing of the blood and brains as they fall into the fire: "wenn ich mir . . . sein schwarzes Blut und Hirn zischend und im Feuer herabfließend vorstelle!"[50] A sacrificial wreath is required in both versions of the ceremony and in both it is necessary for the mothers of the children to witness the gruesome performance.[51] When it is over, both Locusta and Semira use the same expression in their reports.[52] Moloch must see the blood and ashes of the children in the urns before he will allow the spirit to appear to Locusta.[53] Through similarity in the treatment of the sacrifice, Bodmer has been influenced by Klopstock to associate Nero with the belief in the heathen god Moloch.

In considering the influence of the Latin historians Tacitus and Suetonius, as well as of Klopstock, it is necessary to bear in mind that Bodmer is trying to portray in Nero a man who is filled with doubt and indecision. This interpretation of the man is hardly the complete picture as drawn by the historians. Quite unhistorical is, of course, the motive which brings the emperor under the spell of Moloch. In Bodmer's play Nero's fears exist only in his imagination. They are two: first that he will commit matricide, and second,

[48] Klopstock, III, 6, p. 87. Bod., I, 4, p. 10.
[49] Bod., II, 2, p. 12. Klop., III, 5, pp. 80 f.:
"So werden denn
In dem glühenden Arm die Opferknaben
Zerflossen seyn."
[50] Bod., II, 4, p. 16. Klop., III, 6, p. 86:
"Schnell zischt' und floß vom Glühenden
Ihr schwarzes Blut und Hirn herab."
[51] Bod., III, 2, p. 24. Klop., III, 3, p. 79.
[52] Bod., III, 2, p. 24. Klop., III, 10, p. 96.
[53] Bod., III, 2, p. 25. Klop., IV, 2, p. 104. Suetonius records that Nero tried to summon the shade of his mother. *Nero* XXXIV. 4.

that the wrath of Moloch will be poured out upon him unless he complies with Locusta's demand for a sacrifice. The extensive discussions of these two fears never find any sympathy in Otho or Seneca. When Octavia and Agrippina object to Nero's compliance with the priestess' command, Nero is thrown more and more into uncertainty, which is banished only by the favorable prophecy of Locusta. In all this Bodmer has failed to show any logical or dramatic connection between the death of Britannicus and the fears of Nero. In fact the latter appears in sympathy with the boy and even demands that other victims be substituted for him. When without further motivation, the death of Britannicus is reported, the emperor shows no interest in the news. Only when his mother accuses him of wishing to hinder the rightful assumption of power by Britannicus, is he concerned for his own safety. From the standpoint of Nero's fears the play is poorly motivated. Furthermore, the title is poorly chosen, for Britannicus plays an insignificant part in the plot, appearing only once and making only two short speeches.

The ethical import of the play lies in the effort, as stated by the author, to portray Nero's fear. This is presented as a characteristic that is unworthy of a ruler. In Nero it is the more to be condemned because it is linked with selfish capriciousness and with the murder of Britannicus. The boy is, in Bodmer's mind, entirely innocent of any ambition for the throne. His two speeches are pleas for his life and do not betray the slightest threat to Nero's political security. In essence the piece is a condemnation of the emperor's depravity as manifest in his fear and the resulting murder, and in this light ranks with Bodmer's portrayal of Augustus as a condemnation of autocracy in ancient Rome.

CATO

Written in October, 1764,[54] Bodmer published in 1768 *Cato der Ältere, oder der Aufstand der römischen Frauen.*[55] Little is known about the origin of the play beyond the mention by Bodmer in

[54] Baechtold, *Tagebuch*, p. 199.
[55] Bodmer, *Neue theatralische Werke* (Lindau: Jakob Otto, 1768), pp. 81-134.

a letter to J. C. Hess.[56] Baechtold has criticized the play as weak and has given its contents briefly.[57]

Concerning the source of the material there can be no doubt that Bodmer used Livy's *History of Rome,* to which he has added only a few petty details. In treating the historical account he has taken over from Livy a number of passages by translating them into his text as speeches of various characters. The theme deals with the repeal of the Oppian Law in Rome in the year 195 B.C. and the strong opposition against its repeal offered by Marcus Porcius Cato, who was then consul. The decree had been issued twenty years before and contained the prohibition "that no woman should possess more than half an ounce of gold or wear a parti-colored garment."[58] Bodmer is concerned particularly with this part of the Law.

A comparison in parallel form of the passages which have been taken from Livy would show the complete lack of originality of the German play. The selection is Bodmer's, but the text, as has been said, Livy's. Thus Fulvia, one of the women in the play, points out that wives are forbidden the use of gold ornaments, although their husbands are lavish with the gold embroidered upon their garments, those of the priests, and even upon the ornate trappings of the horses. Paulla maintains that the gold used in garments is never lost, but constitutes a reserve upon which both family and state can draw in time of need. Word for word the speeches of these two women come from the Latin historian, who puts these words in the mouth of Lucius Valerius.[59] When Titus Junius objects that no husband could control his wife's desires if limits were not set by law to the splendor of feminine attire, he is following the words of his prototype in Livy.[60] Paulla and Fulvia acknowledge the right of family control by father and husband, but they object to the restrictions of a master whose authority is imposed by law; they will tolerate the patriarchal

[56] Bodmer to Joh. Casp. Hess, Feb. 28, 1765, MS ZBZ.
[57] *Gesch. d. d. Lit. i. d. Schweiz,* p. 644.
[58] Livy *Hist.* XXXIV. i. 3.
[59] Bodmer, *Cato,* I, 3, pp. 92 f. Livy *Hist.* XXXIV. vii. 2 ff.
[60] Bod., I, 3, p. 93. Livy, XXXIV. iv. 18.

ruler, but not the legal despot. They repeat here the speech of Lucius Valerius recorded in Livy as an answer to Cato and an appeal to do away with the Law.[61] That the women of the provinces should be permitted unrestricted display of their wealth makes Fundavia and Fulvia, as it makes Valerius in Livy, wonder whether the Romans or the provincials are the masters of the empire.[62] Cato attacks the assembly of Roman women in a public demonstration against the Law as a violation of private modesty and public decorum. Bodmer's translation is more verbose than his original.[63] In a long speech Valerius, speaking as in the *History*, defends the women's spirited assertion of their demands, and calls attention to the brave participation of the women in the defense of the Capitoline Hill against the Sabines, against the Volscian legions in their attack on Rome after the expulsion of the Tarquin kings, and to the willing sacrifice of the women's gold to ransom the city from the Gauls.[64] Other instances of direct translation could be given,[65] but those mentioned are typical. A characteristic example of Bodmer's German version in comparison with the Latin original will illustrate his method of reproduction. It is Cato who speaks as follows:

Das Gesetz ist neu, es ist wahr, warum ist es nicht früher errichtet worden? weil noch keine Hoffart war, die man hätte im Zaum halten müssen. Cyneas hatte nicht nur unsern Anherren, sondern auch unsern Anfrauen reiche Geschenke angeboten, es war damals noch kein Gesetz gegen den übertriebenen Schmuck der Frauen, dennoch widerstunden sie der Versuchung: darum hatte man nicht nöthig, ein solches Gesetz zu machen. Würde in diesen Tagen Cyneas mit seinen Geschenken herumgegangen seyn, o! er hätte [Frauen] auf den öffentlichen Plätzen angetroffen, die beyde Hände darnach ausgestreckt hätten.[66]

[61] Bod., I, 3, pp. 94 f. Livy, XXXIV. vii. 11 ff.
[62] Bod., I, 4, pp. 95 f. Livy, XXXIV. vii. 5 f.
[63] Bod., II, 2, pp. 104, 106. Livy, XXXIV. ii. 9 f., iii. 8.
[64] Bod., II, 3, pp. 107 ff. Livy, XXXIV. v. 3, 7-10.
[65] E.g., Bod., II, 3, p. 110: Cato's speech beginning "Bedenke Valerius." Livy, XXXIV. iii. 1 ff. Bod., II, 3, pp. 113 f.: Cato's speech beginning "Ich weiß es." Livy, XXXIV. iv. 1 ff. Bod., II, 3, pp. 111 f.: Valerius' speech beginning "Nimmer werde ich." Livy, XXXIV. vi. 4-10.
[66] Bod., II, 3, pp. 112 f. Livy, XXXIV. iv. 6 f., 10 f.: "Patrum nostrorum memoria per legatum Cineam Pyrrhus non virorum modo sed etiam mulierum animos donis temptavit. Nondum lex Oppia ad coercendam luxuriam muliebrem lata erat; tamen nulla accepit. Quam causam fuisse censetis? Eadem fuit quae maioribus nostris nihil de hac re lege sanciundi; nulla erat luxuria quae coerceretur . . . Itaque minime

It will be noted that Bodmer reproduces the ideas of the Roman historian in paraphrases which at times seem close to verbal renderings.

He has, however, added several elements to the play. Most prominent among these is the appearance of the Latin poet Quintus Ennius, who supports the Oppian Law and is in sympathy with Cato.[67] The scene in which he figures is composed largely of a plea by Fulvia to enlist the poet in the cause for repeal. He denies this request and is answered with certain disparaging remarks from Paulla. His rejoinder is a repetition in verse of Cato's text that luxury has been the ruin of other great nations and will bring about the decline of Rome also:

Look with fear upon wealth and the idleness of peace; arrogance has ruined states which Mars has not laid low. Never has Rome been so exposed to the dangers of vice as it has been since indigence has disappeared from its boundaries and Tarentum, Corinth, and Rhodes, with flowing robes and temples wreathed in roses, have banished poverty from the land.[68]

In these original verses Bodmer has used the hexameter, a meter which claims Ennius as one of its first exponents in Latin literature. The Swiss author must have been a bit sceptical about these verses, for Paulla, although she admires them, is careful to add the words: "wiewol er einigemal stolpert."[69] Another amusing scene, and one of the very few in Bodmer's plays, is that in which the tribune Titus Junius Brutus is bribed to advocate the repeal of the Oppian Law. Paulla promises her daughter to Titus' son in return for his efforts. To this he answers ironically: "an irresistible

---

mirum est nec Oppiam nec aliam ullam tum legem desideratam esse quae modum sumptibus mulierum faceret, cum aurum et purpuram data et oblata ultro non accipiebant. Si nunc cum illis donis Cineas urbem circumiret, stantes in publico invenisset quae acciperent."

[67] Ennius' admiration for Cato is well attested; cf. Cicero Pro Archia IX.

[68] Bod., II, 1, p. 102:

Fürchtet euch vor dem Reichthum, und vor dem müßigen Frieden;
Hoffart hat Staaten zerstört, die Mars nicht niedergelegt hat.
Niemals ist Rom dem Anfall des Lasters so nahe gewesen,
Als seit dem sich der Mangel von ihren Grenzen gewandt hat,
Und Tarent und Corinth und Rhodus in schwimmenden Kleidern,
Und mit Rosen die Schläfe bekränzt, die Armuth vertrieben.

[69] Bod., II, 1, p. 103.

temptation."[70] There is no historical basis for such an incident. Fantastic and humorously conceived is the appearance of an Egyptian merchant after the Law has been repealed. He brings exotic wares, such as rare pieces of cloth from Assyria and Arabia, Phrygian tiaras, artfully wrought anklets, golden nets, and trinkets from the city of Crotona. Paulla orders him to bring them to the palace. She refuses to heed Opimia's suggestion to turn the merchant away and thus to uphold the women's sense of pride and virtue of self-denial.

The characters are rather uninteresting. The men, Cato, Titus Junius Brutus, and Lucius Valerius, are found in Livy's account, where also two tribunes, Marcus and Publius Brutus, are mentioned as supporters of the Oppian Law. The women, Paulla, Fulvia, Opimia, Fundavia, Tarpeia, and Florana, are probably invented by Bodmer, for Livy mentions the names of no women in connection with the repeal of the Law. Tarpeia may have been suggested to Bodmer by the daughter of Tarpeius, governor of the Roman citadel on the Saturnian Hill; Livy records that she was bribed by a reward of gold bracelets to open the gates of the stronghold to the Sabines. Perhaps Bodmer wished to symbolize in her the greed of women.[71] But in general the figures in the play have no individual stamp.

Cato is significant among Bodmer's plays for its attack on luxury and wealth as breeders of corruption and laxity of public morals. In the first part of the play this attitude is presented by Cato and is to be interpreted as Bodmer's personal point of view. The humorous actions in the latter scenes are his way of introducing a bit of mild satire on their vanity and are unique in the plays treated in this study. The personal experience of Bodmer's readings in Livy is illustrated in those passages where he draws extensively on the Latin historian. Here he shows little originality in the treatment of the source.

[70] Bod., II, 4, p. 116: "eine unwiderstehliche Versuchung!"

[71] Livy *Hist.* I. xi. 6. Cf. also Bodmer's unpublished manuscript, *Zufällige Gedanken über das Pracht- und Aufwandsmandat,* which was probably read before the "Helvetisch-vaterländische Gesellschaft." It is a plea for the curbing of luxury by means of high taxes, the proceeds of which were to be distributed to the less fortunate peasant class. G. Tobler, *Bod. als Geschichtschreiber,* p. 29.

ARISTOMENES VON MESSENIEN

In the spring of 1768 Bodmer reported to Schinz that he had completed two of the three acts of *Aristomenes,* adding: "It is Aristomenes of Messenia, whom you probably know from Pausanias. But it has the defect that, although it is quite historical, it will seem incredible to our cowardly, weak-hearted men, and too natural and too simple to our unnatural mode of thought."[72] It was completed in May, 1768,[73] and published in that year.[74]

The play is in three acts, and shows little dramatic quality, being rather a series of descriptions and pictures based upon the story of the Spartans' capture of Eira at the end of the second Messenian War. It opens with the fugitive Messenians lamenting the capture of their city. Each character, as he enters, contributes a part of the story of the attack, defense, and capitulation of Eira. The prophecy of a certain seer, Maniclus, that the fall of the city was at hand, has been fulfilled. It is at this time of discouragement that Damithales arrives with a message from the king of Arcadia inviting the exiled people to settle in his land. The invitation is not accepted, for revenge on the Spartans is uppermost in the minds of the Messenians. Now, too, the treacherous King Aristocrates arrives with an army from the Peloponnesus. Aristomenes, leader of the Messenians, refuses to accept the help of this army, since he has planned a bold undertaking; he will attempt the capture of Sparta while the Spartans are engaged in sacking Eira. The plan and its details are revealed in the presence of Aristocrates, who sends a messenger with tablets addressed to the Spartan leader Anaxander and revealing the plan of Aristomenes. Damithales, a staunch Messenian patriot, is mistrustful of Aristocrates, for he had observed that the latter paled thrice when he heard the plan against Sparta. So he sets a watch on Aristocrates and intercepts the messenger as he returns with Anaxander's answer. The Arcadian soldiers are present and demand that the tablets be opened.

[72] Bodmer to Schinz, May 6, 1768, MS ZBZ.: "Es ist Aristomenes von Messenien, den Sie aus Pausanias kennen können. Es hat doch den Fehler, wiewol es ganz historisch ist, daß es unsern feigen und weichen Männern unglaublich und unserer unnatürlich, vielfachen Denkungsart zu einfältig und zu natürlich vorkommen wird."

[73] Baechtold, *Tagebuch*, p. 201.

[74] *Politische Schauspiele*, III, 187-256.

The treachery of Aristocrates is thus revealed and he is stoned to death. Aristomenes is moved to tears by this betrayal of his faith. At the end of the play he decides to sail across the Aegean and found a colony, hoping eventually to enlist the aid of Ardys, king of Lydia, in another campaign against the Spartans.

The relation of Bodmer to his source in Pausanias is a close one.[75] From him Bodmer took the length of the siege of Eira, eleven summers.[76] One motive is expanded significantly. Whereas Pausanias only mentions the fact that the women took up arms, the German play embodies the bravery of the women in the figure of Hagnagora, who encourages the other women to bear their adversity as a temporary stage on the path to ultimate victory and extols to them the virtues and greatness of Aristomenes as a fighter. She urges her daughter to take comfort in the fact "that you are sprung from Aristomenes, who has followed in the footsteps of Hercules and Epeitus, his great ancestors."[77] Agila, the wife of Gorgus, praises Aristomenes also, when attempting to convince the latter's daughters that his fate is in the hands of Jupiter. This god had sent her a dream conveying clearly a divine command to free Aristomenes from the Cretan archers who had once captured him during a truce between the Lacedaemonians and the men of Eira. This she had accomplished by plying the Cretans with wine, stealing a dagger from one of them, and cutting the bonds of Aristomenes. Both the dream and the story of this brave deed are taken directly from Pausanias, although the Greek historian does not give Agila a name.[78] The capture of the acropolis of Eira was brought about through the treachery of a dissolute woman of the city, and Bodmer has compressed the long account of Pausanias into a few lines.[79] Evergetidas describes at some length the death of the seer Theoclus and his lofty patriotism, which led him to sacrifice his life as fate had decreed; he died "so that he should

---

[75] In his *Description of Greece* IV. "Messenia."

[76] Bodmer, *Aristomenes*, I, 1, p. 190. Pausanias *Greece* IV. xvii. 11.

[77] Bod., I, 2, p. 211: "Doch alle Noth . . . sollte der Gedanke versüßen, daß ihr von Aristomenes entsprossen seyd, der in die Fußstapfen des Herkules und des Epytus, seiner großen Ahnen, getreten ist."

[78] Bod., I, 3, pp. 214 f. Paus., IV. xix. 5 f.

[79] Bod., I, 3, p. 220. Paus., IV. xx. 5-10. (In Bodmer's printed text there is an error in the pagination of scenes 2, 3, and 4; I quote as in the printed version.)

live to reëstablish the city of Eira under a more fortunate star in other regions."[80] Bodmer's model here is Pausanias, who emphasizes the force of fate.[81] This is embodied in a prophecy of the oracle at Delphi, which had predicted the fall of Messenia, "whensoever a he-goat drinks of Neda's winding stream." The Swiss author reproduces the prophecy in the following German translation:

> Wenn der Feigenbaum dürstend sich neigt den Nedes zu trinken
> Dann verlaßen die Götter Messen', und sie fällt in den Staub hin.[82]

But he omits Pausanias' explanation that the Greek word *tragos*, "he-goat," meant in the language of the Messenians a wild fig-tree also.[83] This is important, for Theoclus has seen a fig-tree whose leaves were touching the waters of the stream; he pointed this out to Aristomenes and informed him that the prophecy was fulfilled, that the destruction of Eira was at hand, and that he, Theoclus, must also die. Bodmer simply translates *tragos* with the German *Feigenbaum*. Otherwise he has taken over the material of the whole incident.[84] As in the source, the Messenians plan to sail away from Eira; the Arcadians offer their country as a safe haven.[85] Gorgus favors settlement in Zacynthos near Cephallenia and Maniclus suggests Sicily (Sardinia in Pausanias).[86] From Pausanias comes the plan to capture Sparta while its warriors are despoiling Eira.[87] The execution of the plan is delayed because of the unfavorable omens of a sacrifice; Stymphalus, in Bodmer's play, minimizes the importance of these signs, but attaches more weight to the excellence of Aristomenes' leadership.[88] Aristocrates had aided the Messenians in the third year of the war against the Spartans. Bodmer's character Damithales recalls the facts of the battle as recorded by Pausanias; Aristocrates had ordered his men to retreat at the first

---

[80] Bod., I, 5, p. 215: "daß er leben solle, Ira unter glücklichern Zeichen in andern Gegenden wieder aufzurichten."
[81] Bod., I, 5, pp. 213-15. Paus., IV. xxi. 11.
[82] Bod., I, 6 p. 216. Paus., IV. xx. 1.
[83] Paus., IV. xx. 2.
[84] Bod., I, 6, pp. 216 f. Paus., IV. xx. 1-3, xxi. 10.
[85] Bod., II, 1, p. 218. Paus., IV. xxii. 2.
[86] Bod., II, 3, p. 226. Paus., IV. xxiii. 5.
[87] Bod., II, 4, p. 233. Paus., IV. xxii. 4.
[88] Bod., III, 1, p. 237. Paus., IV. xxii. 5.

attack, thus leaving the center and left wings of the Messenian forces exposed to the victorious Spartans.[89] Suspicion falls upon Aristocrates, when he again offers the Messenians his aid. Bodmer follows his source closely in the incident of the capture of Aristocrates' messenger and the tablets, which reveal the treachery of the Arcadian king.[90] The message from Anaxander is the same in both versions; he thanks Aristocrates for retreating at the battle of the "Great Trench," for informing him of the present plan against Sparta, and he promises him rewards.[91] Such a succession of parallels shows how extensively Bodmer has exploited the account of Pausanias.

Bodmer's treatment of the characters represents his own peculiar interpretation. Women figure prominently in the first act, usually relating the terrible plight of the people, but they retain a firm faith in the gods and their concern for the fate of the people. A moral tendency is felt in their attitude. Hagnagora, in conversation with her two daughters, Erastithea and Polycharis, shows a strong faith in her husband. The adversity of the women, Bodmer stresses, is excellent character training, comparable to such a test as only Hercules was obliged to undergo. The two daughters assume that Jupiter has abandoned the people, and the mother feels it encumbent upon her to correct this erroneous idea. Agila is called upon to assist Hagnagora by reciting the brave deeds of Aristomenes. It is probable that Bodmer has introduced these female characters to enhance the heroism of Aristomenes as a representative of a heroic people. Damithales differs from his prototype in Pausanias by displaying greater emotion, especially in connection with the discovery of Aristocrates' treachery. This betrayal of personal faith moves Aristomenes deeply, and his moral goodness is set off all the more sharply by this crushing blow. In the ending of the play, the Messenians propose to found a new colony under the direction of Aristomenes. According to Pausanias, the king had no share in this venture, but died on a journey to Sardis.[92] The fortitude of the Messenians stands in bold relief as

[89] Bod., III, 2, pp. 241 f. Paus., IV. xvii. 7.
[90] Bod., III, 3, p. 245. Paus., IV. xxii. 6.
[91] Bod., III, 6, p. 249. Paus., IV. xxii. 6.
[92] Paus., IV. xxiv. 2 f.

an ethical virtue, which is best exemplified in their leader Aristomenes.

SUMMARY

In summarizing Bodmer's treatment of this historical material, it is evident that within the narrow limits of his selection he has had most success with the figure of Augustus in the fulfillment of his program, that is, the portrayal of the moral aspect of his character. The ethical interpretation which he has given to this side of the ruler's life and the domestic tragedy resulting from the lack of both personal and family discipline contain a warning to Bodmer's readers that the greatness of the Augustan Age should not blind them to the fact that it was characterized by a lack of public decency and decorum. This is the spirit of Tacitus as Bodmer interprets it. If it seems unusual to place so much stress on this defect in an otherwise impressive character, still Bodmer's attitude is consistent with his own puritanical nature, his sheltered and austere mode of life, and his views on public morality. A similar interpretation of the degrading effect of luxury in the play on the Oppian Law is in keeping with the cloistered and parsimonius life of the Swiss writer, although in *Cato* Bodmer has not been as successful in keeping the unity of his theme throughout the piece. That the repeal of the Law is not in accord with the author's own desire is to be seen in the concern with the greed of the woman for the wares of the Egyptian merchant toward the end of the play. The main emphasis in this play falls, not upon the interpretation of the characters, but rather upon luxury as a breeding ground of vice in public life and as destructive to the simple virtues of the citizen. Here the use of Livy's material is in accord with Bodmer's notion of the Latin historian's aim, which he had stated as early as 1735 in the preface to the *Helvetische Bibliothek*. In *Brittannicus* Nero's evil nature is portrayed by means of the crimes which were the effect of fear on his crazed mind. In his treatment of this theme, the author is most successful when he is dealing with the historical data of Suetonius and Tacitus. The tragic fate of an individual rather than moral rectitude is brought out in *Aristomenes*. Here the fire of the brave leader is dimmed by the discovery of Aristocrates' treachery. Equally important is the praise of the fortitude of the Messenians. This is emphasized vigorously in the character of the women, especially in Hagnagora, who extols Aristomenes as the best representative of this national virtue and regards the hardships of her people as the proper training for her daughters.

Within the limits of the material selected by Bodmer, he has followed closely the spirit of his sources. The ethical side of his classical experience is a vital part of his notion of the ancient world. The plays in this chapter exemplify his earlier observation on the value of history for revealing the hearts of men, and on the importance of personal morality as an element in determining the actions of historical figures.

V

POLITICAL DRAMAS

It is quite generally conceded that Bodmer's venture into the field of the drama was a failure from the standpoint of aesthetic attainment and that he possessed little literary talent for such work.[1] On the other hand, it is true that he presented a wealth of material to the German public of his time, and it is important for its content, if not for its form. His ideas on the theory of the drama were never organized into a comprehensive treatment, but numerous observations in his works and letters give a good picture of his attitude toward this kind of writing. The following is an attempt to sum up these statements as applied particularly to the political drama.

Bodmer's use of this form of expression for the material from the ancient world is based upon two assumptions: that characters are more important than action in the drama, and that this type of writing should aim to educate and improve the popular mind through the example of the characters employed in it. In 1746 he had taken exception to Aristotle's emphasis on action as the most important element of the tragedy when he pointed out that the poet's main purpose should be to portray a character in his best aspect. The action is only a means to this end.[2] Characters who exemplify the virtues of liberty and republicanism or those who oppose these ideals are proper figures for the dramatic form. Also in that year Bodmer had made the second of these assumptions when he set forth the purpose of tragedy as the cultivation of mo-

---

[1] Cf. Tobler, "Bod. pol. Schauspiele," *loc. cit.*, p. 157: Tobler deals only with the dramas based on Swiss history. Cf. also J. Baechtold, "Litterarische Bilder aus Zürichs Vergangenheit," in his *Kleine Schriften,* hrsg. von Theodor Vetter (Frauenfeld: J. Huber & Co., 1889), p. 116. Cf. also J. Baechtold, "Von und über Bodmer," *Archiv für Litteraturgeschichte,* VI (1877), 90.

[2] J. J. Bodmer, *Critische Briefe* (Zürich: Heidegger und Comp., 1746), pp. 71 f. (with Breitinger). Cf. also Bodmer to J. E. Schlegel, Sept. 2, 1747, in Hofrath von Morgenstern, "Briefe deutscher Dichter und Gelehrte aus den Jahren 1740 bis 1771," *Morgenblatt für gebildete Stände,* IV (Aug. 3, 1810), 738: "Doch ist gewiß, daß er aus den Charaktern zu wenig, aus der Fabel, das ist, der Handlung oder Intrige, zu viel gemacht hat."

rality, virtue, and usefulness. The effect of the drama was to be achieved through the emotions rather than through the reason. Its ideas should be, in addition to poetic, political in nature and should bring about such attitudes as hatred of tyranny, love of peace, bravery in the defense of one's country, and praise of justice. These are fundamental to the well-being of the state and the middle class.[3] In 1774 Bodmer wrote Schinz that the task of educating young people was passing out of the hands of fathers, teachers, and legislators, and he indicated that the dramatist would have to attempt to rectify this unfortunate situation.[4]

He had been trying to accomplish this in his dramas, and this pedagogical aim has, in fact, a definite basis in the biography of the Swiss author. In July, 1762, Bodmer organized a society under the name of the "Helvetische-politische Gesellschaft zu Schumachern," which was changed in 1765 to the "Helvetische-vaterländische Gesellschaft."[5] It was a political club, meeting weekly, and was supposed to train the youth of Zurich in the fundamentals of political thinking, to investigate the advantages and disadvantages of different types of government, and to inculcate in its members noble and patriotic ideals.[6] During the first year of its existence such topics as natural and civil freedom, the importance of morality in politics, republicanism, despotism, and history in general were discussed.[7] Bodmer led the discussions, and his interest in political matters at this time explains why he chose to treat this side of ancient history in so many of his plays. They are largely the outgrowth of this activity, which was concerned with the improvement of political consciousness in the people and follows democratic lines.

[3] Bodmer, *Crit. Betrachtungen*, p. 432.
[4] Bodmer to Schinz, June 3, 1774, MS ZBZ.: "Ich soll ihnen [den Deutschen] Dichter geben, wie die Griechen hatten, und die Nation und den Patriotism derselben fühlen. So sagen sie. Ich dachte sonst, daß die Väter durch die Erziehung, die Professoren und Prediger, die Gesetzgeber, die Söhne des Staates zu Menschen, Gesellschaftern, Christen bilden sollten . . . Erkennen sie, daß der Staat, das Lehramt, die Erziehung so übel beschaffen sind, daß die Schaubühne helfen muß, daß der dramatische Poet [nicht] nur erwecken, unterhalten, erhöhen, sondern empfindsam machen, pflanzen, aufbauen müsse?"
[5] Cf. Tobler, *Bod. als Geschichtschreiber*, pp. 27 ff.
[6] *Ibid.*, p. 39.
[7] *Ibid.*, p. 45.

Bodmer's clearest statement of his conception of the political drama is to be found in an article entitled *Politisches Trauerspiel,* written, probably in 1770, for Johann Georg Sulzer.[8] A partiality for the drama of the ancients appears in it. Great praise is accorded the educational value of the Greek stage in exemplifying democratic principles and rights; this was essential in a state where the people participated so directly in the government.[9] But the political systems of most European countries in the middle of the Eighteenth Century concentrated the ruling power in the hands of a few, so that the discussion of a people's rights was a dangerous theme. However, Bodmer contended, a drama dealing with matters of state and popular rights could still perform the same service as had been achieved by the ancient drama. Even if discussions on patriotism, natural rights, or matters of state might be too advanced for the majority of a theatrical audience, still they would exert their influence upon thinking people who might read these plays at home.[10] Bodmer was frankly concerned with the writing of armchair dramas, not pieces for the stage. He discounted scenery, the mechanics of the stage, and the simulation of actors as detractions from the serious intent of the works. Above all he resented the conscious effort of the dramatist to strive after the favor of the public, for to seek the plaudits of the pit meant the imposition of certain restraints upon the author's freedom.[11] He did not concern himself with the unities as unconditional necessities of the drama, nor did he hold that the action could not be interrupted while a character developed an idea at some length.[12] The protagonists in the political drama should be "strong souls"; as examples he mentions such figures from history as Aristides, Epaminondas, Timoleon, Gracchus, or Stoics and fanatics little

[8] J. G. Sulzer, *Allgemeine Theorie der schönen Künste,* 2d ed. (Leipzig: M. G. Weidemanns Erben & Reich, 1786-87), Part III, 593 ff. That Bodmer is the author of this article is proved by his acknowledgment of the authorship in the notes to his *Arnold von Brescia in Zürich* (Frankfurt, 1775), p. 47. Cf. also Sulzer's statement: "Ihr Aufsatz über das politische Drama ist fürtrefflich und soll mit Ihrer Erlaubnis ganz eingerückt werden." Sulzer to Bodmer, June 1, 1771, MS ZBZ.

[9] Sulzer, *op. cit.,* Pt. III, 593.

[10] *Ibid.,* p. 594.

[11] *Ibid.,* p. 595.

[12] *Idem.*

appreciated by the audience in the pit,[13] or oppressors of the state, such as Sulla, Caesar, or Catiline. It was not expected that a modern audience would be capable of understanding dialogues which were full of ratiocination, argumentation, and moralization. In Athens the people would have taken such passages to heart, but this could hardly be expected of an Eighteenth Century audience.[14]

The ideas contained in the article *Politisches Trauerspiel* occur again in Bodmer's letters to Schinz. The Swiss author boasted that he was reproducing the spirit of ancient writers in an attempt to awaken in his readers an interest in Sophocles and Euripides. But he felt that his dramas were too full of patriotism, natural impulses, serene grandeur, and simplicity.[15] Dramas in the spirit of Sophocles and Euripides were, for him, those "which have a distinguished relation to our state, our law, our history."[16] He entertained a great admiration for the understanding spirit of the ancients in matters of politics and morality.[17] He pointed out that the Eighteenth Century had no great dramas of a political nature; secondly, that the ruling princes would never allow such plays on the stage, even if they did exist;[18] and thirdly, if played, they would have no effect on the audience because the feeling for them had been dulled completely or had become atrophied, as he wrote.[19]

Little stress is placed on a clear cut form of the drama or upon a balanced structure. When, therefore, his works were attacked on

[13] *Ibid.*, p. 596.

[14] *Ibid.*, p. 597.

[15] Bodmer to Schinz, Dec. 7, 1767, MS ZBZ.: "Sie sind ihnen zu voll von Vaterland, Naturtrieben, stiller Größe, verschafter Einfalt."

[16] Bodmer to Schinz, Jan. 26, 1775, MS ZBZ.: "Ich verstehe durch Schauspiele von Sophokles und Euripides Geist solche, die eine ausgezeichnete Beziehung auf unsrem Staat, unsrem Rechte, unsrer Geschichte haben."

[17] Bodmer to Schinz, June 29, 1768, MS ZBZ.: "Es ist gewiß, wenn die Athener nicht politische und moralische Kenntnisse gehabt . . . daß sie Euripides und Sophokles und Aeschylus tragischen und moralischen und politischen Ernst nicht ohne Langweile und Verdruß gehört hätten."

[18] Bodmer to Schinz, Jan. 26, 1775, MS ZBZ.: "Wir haben dergleichen Dramen nicht, und unsere Fürsten würden sie nicht auf den Schauplatz bringen lassen. Würden sie doch aufgeführt, so thäten sie keine Würkung, weil sie nicht zu den Passionen gehorsam, den die Deutschen zu einem Grundsatze machen, passeten."

[19] Bodmer to Schinz, Feb. 17, 1775, MS ZBZ.: "Weil das Gefühl dafür ganz abgeschliffen ist, oder in einer andren Metapher abgetrocknet."

the basis of existing ideas of criticism, Bodmer defended his loose-
ness in matters of form and based his arguments on his intention,
in that he neither wrote for, nor sought the approbation of, the
stage and its critics. The disregard of the traditional unities in his
works he acknowledged freely and he called them trifles.[20] Political
emphasis was to take precedence over poetic ideas.[21] He directed
a spirited and extended defense of his works against the accusation
that traditional action was lacking, and he observed that action
and dramatic intrigues needed to be present only in a sketchy, undeveloped state.[22] In reply to a hostile review in the *Journal
helvétique* in 1769, Bodmer denied the critics the right to judge
his dramas according to the usual rules of the stage.[23] The sharp-
ness of the criticism on all sides led him to insist that he had
observed enough of the external devices of the drama to insure
understanding. For each of his plays he claimed a sequence of
action, an exposition, and a catastrophe.[24] Action included those
measures which are taken by characters to ward off some impending disaster or to hasten the fulfillment of some piece of good
fortune.[25] Bodmer refused to be bound by any set of dramaturgical
conventions, but felt that the coherence of his pieces lay in their
content. They were distinctly dramas to be read rather than to be
acted.

A thorough disregard of the stage and the favor of its audience
appears in almost every statement made by Bodmer concerning
his dramas. After emphasizing this in some unpublished notes of
1778 he continues: "I know too well that the noble and ignoble do
not assemble to feel in common, and therefore more intensely, the

[20] Bodmer to Sulzer, end of June, 1759, MS ZBZ.
[21] Bodmer to Schinz, Dec. 10, 1764, MS ZBZ.: "Es sind vielmehr politische als
poetische dramata, wiewol ich die Situationen, die sich zu poetischen und pathetischen
Vorstellungen anerbothen, nicht unbearbeitet vorbeigegangen bin, oder verabsäumt
habe."
[22] Bodmer to Schinz, June 29, 1768, MS ZBZ.: "Wahr ist, viel Handlung, Intrigues
sind nicht darinn, doch sind auch dieselben da, wiewol sehr simpel."
[23] Bodmer to Schinz, Oct. 24, 1769, MS ZBZ.: the reference is to a review of
Bodmer's *Neue theatralische Werke* published in the *Nouveau Journal Helvétique*,
1769, 295 f.
[24] Bodmer to Schinz, Nov., 1769, MS ZBZ.: "In jedem ist auch eine Gradation,
eine Verwickelung, Exposition . . . Catastrophe."
[25] Bodmer to Schinz, Aug. 1, 1770, MS ZBZ.: "Ich denke aber, zur Action gehören
auch die Maßregeln, die von den Personen genommen worden, ein Unglück abzu-
wenden, oder ein vornehmes auszuführen."

dignity and the rights of humanity."[26] The Germans, he had declared a decade earlier, were incapable of understanding the *genus orationis deliberativum* in a drama, and the actors, being unable to convey to their audiences such abstract ideas, excluded them from the stage.[27] In his opinion the liveliness of the players and the spectators of the parterre did not allow enough time for an adequate understanding of the content of his dramas,[28] and the development of such an audience was the result of a decline in national spirit.[29] While Bodmer's dramas cannot be judged fairly by recourse to regular rules, it is also true that they did not, by their example, establish a new set of dramaturgical principles. Certainly few accept Sulzer's opinion, expressed in a letter to Bodmer in 1761, that the latter had created a new type of drama in his political pieces.[30]

In his conception of character Bodmer maintains in his *Critische Betrachtungen* that to be worthy of literary treatment, people drawn from history should conform to a type. In historical discussions, he holds, a special truth is to be selected and a general truth is to be derived from the special one. The poet treats the historical figures inductively in order to find in them the heroic virtue which can become a general ideal.[31] As a result of this subjective attitude toward the past, Bodmer idealized the men of the

---

[26] *Anekdoten von meinen politischen Dramen. An Schinz, Prediger. 1778,* MS ZBZ., p. 4: "Ich weiß zu wohl, daß die Edeln und die Unedeln sich nicht versammeln, um gemeinschaftlich, und darum desto stärker die Würde und die Rechte der Menschheit zu empfinden." The manuscript mentioned here is composed largely of excerpts made by Bodmer from his own letters; cf. Baechtold, *Gesch. d. d. Lit. i. d. Schweiz,* pp. 652 f. The passage quoted in this note occurs almost verbatim in a letter from Bodmer to Gleim, July, 1776, Wilhelm Körte, *op. cit.,* p. 438. In this connection cf. also T. Vetter, *Pers. Anek.,* p. 114.

[27] Bodmer to Schinz, Aug. 16, 1768, MS ZBZ.: "Die Deutschen können das genus orationis deliberativum in Schauspielen nicht leiden . . . und ihre Acteurs können die Action nicht, die dazu gehört. Darum machen sie selbst die Regel, daß alles deliberative müsse verworfen werden."

[28] Bodmer to Schinz, Nov., 1769, MS ZBZ.: "In diesen Schauspielen . . . darf man auch längere Perioden machen, als die Lebhaftigkeit des Acteurs und der Zuseher im Parterre gestattete."

[29] Bodmer to Schinz, Dec. 27, 1774, MS ZBZ.: "Das Wort Publicum ist entstanden seitdem man die Idee und den Gegenstand des Wortes Nation verlohren hat."

[30] Sulzer to Bodmer, June 1, 1761, Wilhelm Körte, *op. cit.,* p. 340.

[31] *Crit. Betrachtungen,* p. 413. Cf. also Franz Servaes, *Die Poetik Gottscheds und der Schweizer.* "Quellen und Forschungen," Nr. 60 (Strassburg: Karl J. Trübner, 1887), p. 140.

ancient world about whom he constructed his dramas, seeing in them either the positive or the negative side of a political ideal. The ancient republics were for him the protectors of political virtues, and their fall could not be understood correctly without taking into consideration the disappearance of democracy from their political society. Bodmer presented the positive side of his own political creed in the figures who stood for democracy, as for example Cicero or Thrasea Paetus; the negative side he portrayed in those who stood for despotism, such as Julius Caesar or Nero. He felt that he deserved praise for exposing the erroneous character of the political principles embodied in the rule of the latter type.[32] He was well aware that the strong republican sentiments in the plays barred them from the stage, and Bodmer was in agreement with this, for he felt that an acquaintance with these political characters of Rome or Greece might fan the embers of republicanism, which lay dormant in the people, into the fire of revolution.[33] As a teacher of history and politics in a rather reactionary city he felt that he was especially liable to official censure. In 1765, at the time when he was busily occupied with his dramas, he wrote Schinz that he was not *en odeur de sainteté politique,* and that he had to consider any complaints about the misuse of freedom as applying directly to him.[34] It was for this reason, perhaps, that he sought ancient rather than contemporary figures and that the political ideas in his dramas are rather general than specific. His figures are, however, the reflection of his political convictions and their portrayal is based on a Rousseau-like conception of broad social liberty. They are based on "political truths" which were hateful to existing governments and are antipathetical to despotism in any of its manifestations.[35] He hoped secretly that his

[32] Bodmer to Schinz, July 21, 1770, MS ZBZ.: "Wenn sie sehen würden, wie Demosthenes und Cicero die Könige der Erden, und die Consule von Rom, die Könige gemacht, behandelt haben, so würden sie mich nicht so ausstellen, daß ich auf den Tarquinius, den Cäsar, den Octavius, den Nero, so heftig losziehe. Sie würden mich lieber loben."

[33] Bodmer, *Anekdoten von dem traurigen Ende gewisser politischer Dramen,* n.d., MS ZBZ., p. 25: "Aber sie sind auch gefährlich. Durch das Anschauen dieser römischen und griechischen Seelen möchten in die Seele des Volkes Funken fallen, die Feuer darinn auffachen könnten, das itzt schläft."

[34] Bodmer to Schinz, Jan. 17, 1765, Zehnder-Stadlin, *op. cit.,* p. 462.

[35] T. Vetter, *Bod. pers. Anekdoten,* pp. 113 f.

plays would create the serious interest which he believed marked the ancient audience. In this he failed.

The plays included in the group "political dramas" are those in which the political implications of the themes are more important than the legendary motives, such as prophecy, or the ethical thesis. These works are based upon historical material in the accounts of ancient historians. There is, as we have seen, one exception, *Karl von Burgund,* which treats a chapter from Swiss history, but in the form of the ancient drama. This explains its inclusion in our study. The characters which Bodmer has chosen for his central figures may be classified as "martyrs of freedom," "patriots," and "despots," and this grouping has been followed in our analysis. The first includes the plays in which the hero dies as a champion of republicanism and freedom. In them the main character stands in a glorifying light of heroism. The second group contains works in which the hero murders the despotic opponent of republicanism and in which the emphasis falls rather upon the patriotic action of the assassin than upon the tyrannical character of his victim. Here *Karl von Burgund* is an exception. The third class includes the plays in which both theme and action seem to stress the despotic nature and deserved death of the tyrant rather than the patriotic endeavor of the champions of republicanism. The distinction between "patriots" and "despots" may seem to be an arbitrary one, but is sufficiently clear to justify such a grouping. In any case, the end is either the death or exile of the despot. Our analysis follows the chronological order of composition within each group.

MARTYRS OF FREEDOM
MARCUS TULLIUS CICERO

The first mention of a work on Cicero occurs in 1761, when Bodmer wrote Schinz that he was planning a story of the orator's death and that it might develop into a tragedy if he only had time to work on it.[36] After pondering over the theme for some time,

---

[36] Bodmer to Schinz, Oct. 9, 1761, MS ZBZ.: "Ich trage in meinem Kopf einen Plan des Ciceros Todt herum, der ein Trauerspiel werden könnte, wenn ich Muße genug hätte."

he set about the actual composition in April, 1762.[37] He wished to preserve the anonymity of the author and to publish it as the work of another.[38] To Schinz he expressed a certain satisfaction that he had planned the work at the same age as that of Cicero at the time of his death. He added that only four people had seen the work up to that time.[39] By November, 1763, the publication of the play was imminent, and Bodmer issued an advance notice of its appearance in the *Freymüthige Nachrichten* of Zurich.[40] The only publicity received by the play was a brief comment in the *Wöchentliche Anzeigen* of Zurich. The unknown author of this notice spoke of the play as an historical dialogue and emphasized Cicero's lack of decision as being in accord with history, but objected to Bodmer's occasional use of French endings, as in the words "formie, solecisme, stoicisme."[41] The immediate oblivion into which the play slipped caused its author some anxiety. He wrote Sulzer that his readers, accustomed to judge the external side of Cicero from his orations, had missed the real inner meaning of the Latin writer; they had not read his *Letters to Atticus* and therefore could not see that the play had "more historical truth than fiction."[42] Four years later, in 1768, he took the public to task for its ignorant attitude toward the play, for he wrote: "The speeches and thoughts are not really mine, but Cicero's own, from whom I have taken them."[43]

The play deals with the death of the great Roman in 43 B.C.

[37] Baechtold, *Tagebuch*, p. 197.

[38] Bodmer to L. Zellweger, May 2, 1762, MS ZBZ.: "Den Cicero habe ich aus den Spänen gehauen, aber ich mache daraus vor jedermann ein Geheimnis. Ich wollte dieses Stück gern für die Arbeit eines unbekannten geben."

[39] Bodmer to Schinz, July 24, 1762, MS ZBZ.

[40] Bodmer to Schinz, Nov. 28, 1763, MS ZBZ. The notice appeared in *Freymüthige Nachrichten von neuen Büchern, und andern zur Gelehrtheit gehörigen Sachen*, XX (1763), 388. Bodmer's play appeared in 1764: *Marcus Tullius Cicero. Ein Trauerspiel*. Zürich: Orell, Geßner und Comp., 1764.

[41] *Wöchentliche Anzeigen zum Vortheil der Liebhaber der Wissenschaft*, II (1765), 408.

[42] Bodmer to Sulzer, March 27, 1764, MS ZBZ.: "Man hat nicht bemerkt, daß in meinem Cicero mehr historische Wahrheit als Erdichtung ist, weil man die Epistoles ad Atticum nicht gelesen hat."

[43] Bodmer to Schinz, May 24, 1768, MS ZBZ.: "Denn die Reden und Gedanken darinnen sind eben nicht meine, sondern Ciceros selbst, bey welchem ich sie genommen habe."

Cicero appears in refuge at his estate at Formiae, where, at first alone and then with his freedman Tiro, he contemplates the fall of the republic and his own approaching death. The plot against his life is revealed by Popilius, when the latter attempts to win the aid of Cicero's servant Philologus. Popilius has been commissioned by Octavius to murder Cicero and to bring his head to Rome. The writer becomes suspicious of Popilius when he offers a false truce from Octavius, Lepidus, and Antony. He makes an abortive attempt on Cicero's life, which is frustrated by the appearance of blackbirds in the orator's sleeping chamber. Quintus Tullius, brother of Marcus, arrives from Rome with a proscription list, which includes both Ciceros. Quintus suggests flight to Brutus in Macedonia; Marcus has already attempted to flee but was forced to turn back because of storms and unfavorable winds. He is weary of life and sees death as the only end to his worries, but finally gives a reluctant answer in the affirmative. They decide to await Quintus' son, who is coming from Rome. Meanwhile a slave reports the presence of Roman troops, among them Popilius, who are surrounding the house. The slaves form a bodyguard to escort Cicero to the ship, but the sight of the soldiers causes him to disband them, and he meets his death at the hands of Herennius. Fulvia, wife of Antony, now appears and reports that Quintus' son had revealed, under torture, the whereabouts of Cicero. Popilius lays at her feet the head of the dead writer. She reviles it and pierces its tongue with a hair pin. The play ends with a speech on immortality by Tiro.

Bodmer declares that Cicero's ideas are important in the tragedy. From the standpoint of the source material, the play may be divided into two parts: the facts concerning Cicero's death and the ideas and thoughts of the hero. In neither case does Bodmer's presentation show a very stimulating approach, for the play lacks tensity and is rather an epic portrayal of a steadfast, stoical spirit.[44]

As his source for the events surrounding Cicero's death Bodmer follows most closely the account in Plutarch.[45] From him he took

---

[44] Cf. Bodmer, *Cicero*, p. ii: "Sie sind zu sanft, zu gelassen, zu gottergeben, zu heilig, als daß die unordentlichen Regungen, an welchem der stürmerische Geist einen Gefallen hat, in ihren Reden und Handlungen vielen Plaz bekommen könnte."

[45] *Cicero* XLVII f.

the proposed flight to Macedonia and the first, frustrated attempt to leave Italy. Plutarch's incident of the crows appears in a close paraphrase in Bodmer in the scene where Popilius secretes himself in Cicero's chamber.[46] Other material from the ancient biographer includes the description of the transportation of Cicero's litter to the sea by the slaves,[47] the betrayal of this move to the Romans by Philologus,[48] Cicero's refusal to let his slaves fight for his life, and the actual murder by Herennius.[49]

For the part of Fulvia we must look for another source. This is found in Dio, who reports the incident of the head as occurring in Rome.[50] Bodmer copies this account faithfully.[51] Probably Bodmer's invention, however, is Fulvia's order to Herennius to quarter Cicero's body and to throw it into the street.[52] There is no record that Fulvia appeared at Formiae at this time, nor that she reported the torture of the younger Quintus in an attempt to extract from him the hiding place of his uncle.[53] Furthermore, Bodmer adds an interesting motivation of Popilius, who desires to win the favor of Fulvia by bringing Cicero's head to her. In return for this he hopes to receive some of the orator's confiscated possessions.[54]

Bodmer made further innovations in the theme. In the first scene of the second act, Popilius promises Philologus his freedom and thus wins his help for the plot against Cicero's life; this is found in no previous source. New is also the report of the elder Quintus on the proscriptions.[55] Bodmer represents Quintus as captured during the attempted flight and bound at the order of Fulvia.[56] One of Cicero's secretaries is introduced to report the maltreatment of the writer's head at the hands of Fulvia.[57] The orator's chief secretary, Tiro, appears as his master's confidant and the

---

[46] Bodmer, *Cicero*, III, 1, p. 29. Plutarch *Cicero* XLVII. 6.
[47] Bod., IV, 4, p. 56. Plut., XLVII. 6.
[48] Bod., V, 1, p. 60. Plut., XLVIII. 2.
[49] Bod., V, 2, pp. 64 f. Plut., XLVIII. 3 f.
[50] Dio *Roman History* XLVII. viii. 4.
[51] Bod., V, 6, p. 72.
[52] Bod., V, 6, p. 73.
[53] Dio says Quintus was tortured but revealed nothing. *Hist.* XLVII. x. 7.
[54] Bod., II, 1, p. 18; V, 4, p. 68.
[55] Bod., III, 3, pp. 33 f.
[56] Bod., V, 3, pp. 67 f.
[57] Bod., V, 6, pp. 72 f.

reporter of his death. Near the end of the play he speaks a lengthy eulogy of his master's greatness and emphasizes especially Cicero's efforts "to establish the great truth that the fate of man does not end with his physical existence, that the spirit . . . continues to live on in order to receive its reward or punishment."[58]

More difficult is the examination of the Ciceronian ideas in the play. They may be grouped under two heads: first, Cicero's well known belief in immortality and his readiness to die, and second, his admiration for Plato. They are not always clearly differentiated.

The idea of immortality as found in the play does not pretend to be definite. At the beginning Cicero makes a long speech on the subject of cosmology. He praises the order and arrangement of the sun and the earth, the processes of growth, the celestial bodies, which surpass the earth in riches; he points out that it is natural for the soul, when its work is over on this planet, to ascend to its place of origin, the heavens. Death presents no fears if the soul's prospect of such a home is assured.[59] His spirit does not think of the earth as its natural abode despite the world's orderliness, and it is filled with a desire "to leave the home of vice and the realm of tyrants."[60] Except for the political implication in the last phrase, this first scene suggests strongly the language of Cicero in his treatise *On the Nature of Gods*.[61] The second scene is devoted to a conversation between Cicero and his freedman Tiro, in which the former expresses his fears that he has not expended his best effort for the preservation of the republic. Tiro assures him at every turn that this is untrue. At the end of the scene, Cicero expresses his resignation to death in words which are taken from his essay *On Old Age:* "Socrates and Plato preached the doctrine of the soul's immortality, and what they taught is more certain than what the Pythian Apollo has pronounced from the tripod. My death may come now or at any time; it will not be untimely

---

[58] Bod., V, 6, p. 74: "die große Wahrheit zu befestigen, daß das Schicksal der Menschen mit diesem sichtbaren Leben nicht aufhöret, daß der Geist . . . immerfort lebet, die Belohnungen oder die Strafen zu empfangen."

[59] Bod., I, 1, pp. 3 ff.

[60] Bod., I, 1, p. 6.

[61] I. xx: here Velleius uses similar expressions in his attack on Stoicism.

even if it is a violent one."[62] After listening to his master contrast the nature of the soul's joys before and after death, Tiro replies in the words of Cicero: "You have lamented it sufficiently in your work *On Consolation*."[63] When Tiro pays his last respects to his master and praises the writer's faith in immortality and the soul's rewards and punishment, he uses a close paraphrase of Cicero in the *Tusculan Disputations*. Here the Latin writer describes "the two roads taken by souls after death. The bad ones are driven to the left away from the gods, while the good ascend to their original home with the gods."[64] In such passages as these Bodmer has introduced Cicero's concern with immortality.

The admiration for Plato is best set forth in a long speech by Cicero in praise of the Greek thinker.[65] He addresses his thanks to Plato for his inspiration, praises him as a source of consolation in such turbulent times, and esteems him highly as a teacher. He calls upon Plato to give him courage and fortitude to die rather than to live as a slave under political tyranny. He launches into an attack against the stifling effect of despotism upon freedom of thought and upon the search for truth, and ends with a final plea for Plato's works, which deserve to live as long as the universe exists. One of the most characteristic passages in this long speech is the complaint that the neglect of Plato will have disastrous consequences for civilization:

Wild barbaric hands will desecrate the sanctuary of knowledge and finally drag the works of freedom and wisdom down into the abyss of an all-consuming darkness. Vice will misuse for its execrable purpose the beautiful gifts of art, will turn its philosophical glance from the rights of humanity, and, with a mockery devoid of all good taste, will ridicule patriotism and divest it of its charm.[66]

[62] Bod., I, 2, p. 15: "Socrates und Plato haben die Unsterblichkeit der Seele gelehrt; und was sie lehrten, ist gewisser, als was Apollo Pythius von dem Dreyfusse ausgesprochen hat. Jetzt mag mein Tod kommen, wenn er will, er wird nicht unzeitig seyn, wenn er gleich gewaltsam ist." Cicero *De senectute* XXI.

[63] Bod., IV, 3, p. 50. *Tusc. Disp.* I. 31.

[64] Bod., V, 6, p. 74: "Es sind zween Wege, sagte er, zween Steige, welche die Geister gehen . . . [die Schlechten] werden von den Furien nach der Linken getrieben . . . [die Guten] steigen auf zu den Göttern." *Tusc. Disp.* I. 30.

[65] Bod., IV, 3, pp. 51-53.

[66] Bod., IV, 3, p. 54: "Wilde, barbarische Hände werden das Heiligthum der Erkenntniß entweihen, und zuletzt die Werke der Freyheit und der Weisheit in den Abgrund des alles verzehrenden Nacht schleppen. Das Laster wird die lieblichen

Bodmer's enthusiasm for Plato represents an attitude which is not based on a thorough examination of Plato's writings or their influence on Cicero.

Bodmer's heroic admiration of Cicero's idealism and conception of immortality is deeply felt and reproduced convincingly in this play. Only occasionally does the emphasis fall directly on the political aspect of the material, but the strong tone of Cicero's dissatisfaction with the political situation in Rome and his longing for the company of his heroes in the next world impress the reader with Bodmer's own aspirations as reflected in the death of the great Roman. The play exemplifies most clearly what Bodmer called the "abstract thoughts" which made his plays unsuitable for the stage, but characterize best the author's inner experience and vital interest in the thought of antiquity.

THRASEA PÄTUS

Little is known about *Thrasea Pätus* before its publication in 1769.[67] It was written in September, 1764;[68] and early in the following year Bodmer informed Schinz that he had found a publisher for this and several other plays, but that he was afraid to submit the work to the judgment of a "duly appointed" censor. He continues: "I fear that not only the emphatically political declaration in them but even the themes will have the character of reprobation."[69] This attempt to publish the plays failed, however, and Bodmer put them away until 1769. Klotz reviewed the play briefly when it appeared, giving a sketch of its contents and criticizing the language as extravagant and declamatory.[70] He called the discussions on the subject of death trivial, and referred to Demetrius' observations on this topic as "a most delightful play upon words."[71]

Gaben der Kunst zu fluchwürdigen Absichten mißbrauchen, das philosophische Auge von den Rechten der Menschlichkeit abzuziehen, und den Patriotisme mit abgeschmackten Gespötte von seinem Reize herunterzulachen."

[67] Bod., *Pol. Schauspiele*, II, 158-237.

[68] Baechtold, *Tagebuch*, p. 199.

[69] Bodmer to Schinz, Jan. 24, 1765, MS ZBZ.: "Aber ich fürchte, daß nicht nur die starken politischen Sätze darinnen, sondern die Sujets selbst den Charakter der Reprobation haben, wenn sie durch das Urtheil eines bestellten Censors gehen müssen."

[70] *Deutsche Bibliothek*, III (1769), 407-09.

[71] *Ibid.*, 408.

Bodmer defended his treatment of the subject by saying that he was merely copying from a source without trying to be particularly original.[72]

Thrasea Pätus deals with the trial and execution of that patriot by Nero through decree of the senate in the year 69 A.D. It is divided into three acts, which take place in the home of Paetus. When the play opens, the latter's supporters, Helvidius Priscus, his son-in-law, and Rusticus Aurelenus, are gathered to object to the assembly of the senate by Nero, to the insidious and false testimony of Cossutianus against Paetus, and to Nero's intimidation of the senators by a display of armed troops. Both Priscus and Aurelenus are ready to share the lot of Paetus and advise him to defy the imperial summons to appear before the senate. His presence, they maintain, cannot help his cause and will only result in a scene of public ridicule and scorn, in which he will be embarrassed and defenseless. Paetus, however, considers it his duty to appear at the trial and replies: "Let me meet slander undauntedly and let fate treat me as it will."[73] The second act opens with a scene between Arria, wife of Paetus, and her daughter Fannia, in which they are ready to suffer death with their husbands, while Servilia, daughter of Barea Soranus, who is also under trial, discourses on the innocence of her father. Demetrius arrives from the assembly and reports its proceedings: the strong accusation of Cossutianus, the timidity of the senators, the indictment of Barea Soranus by a certain Ostorius, and the attack on Servilia for consulting the priests of magic. But no decision as to their fate has yet been reached. At the beginning of the last act Arria and Paetus express their fearlessness of death. The latter, however, seeks to convince his wife that it would be more expedient for her to live for her daughter Fannia than to die with him. Rusticus Aurelenus attacks despotism, lamenting that "we must be poor members of the state in order that we may become good slaves. The despot who

[72] Bodmer to Schinz, Aug. 21, 1769, MS ZBZ.: "Der Demetrius in Thrasea Seite 218 will sagen, daß Leben sollte Tod genannt werden. Dieser Nahme gebühre ihm mit mehr Recht . . . Es ist dann ein Spiel. Wenn es doch eines wäre, so ist es des Demetrius, nicht des Dichters."

[73] Bod., I, 3, p. 180: "Laß mich der Verleumdung unerschrocken entgegen treten, und meinem Schiksale stille halten."

wishes to wield power without law is forced to enervate the spirit and courage of his subjects."[74] Demetrius and Paetus engage in a long discussion on immortality, during which Helvidius Priscus brings the verdict of the senate. He himself is exiled, while Paetus, Soranus, and his daughter Servilia are condemned to die in a manner of their own choosing. At the close of the play they are ready to carry out their sentences, while Paetus prepares to sacrifice himself to Jupiter.[75]

The source for the material in this drama is Tacitus in the *Annals,* where the most authentic account of the death of Paetus is found. In many instances Bodmer has taken details and even whole passages from the Latin. The accusations directed by Cossutianus against Paetus are the same with Bodmer as those recorded by Tacitus: Paetus' refusal to offer sacrifices for Nero's health and voice, and his refusal publicly to acknowledge the divinity of Poppaea.[76] That Soranus was tried along with Paetus is also found in the Latin historian. Bodmer introduces, as we have seen, the intimidation of the senators, who were obliged, as Tacitus reports, to file into the meeting between groups of armed soldiers with threatening faces. Bodmer borrows from the *Annals* the further accusation against Paetus that he was the leader of an opposition party, as dangerous as the Tuberones and Favonii of old.[77] The Latin historian is also the authority for Aurelenus' attempt to dissuade Paetus from attending the trial and thus exposing himself to unjust insults,[78] as well as Nero's cruelty to Paetus' wife and daughter.[79] The story of the trial is developed by Bodmer as in his source. Servilia laments the impeachment of her father

[74] Bod., III, 2, p. 214: "Wir müssen böse Staatsglieder seyn, damit wir gute Sklaven werden. Der Despot, der die gesezlose Macht haben will, ist genöthiget, den Geist und den Muth der Untergebenen zu entnerven."

[75] On the title page of the play Bodmer quotes the words which Paetus prays to Jupiter at the end of the *Annals* as the blood pours out of his veins: "Libamus Jovi liberatori" etc. *Ann.* XVI. xxxv. 3.

[76] Bodmer, *Thrasea Pätus,* I, 2, pp. 167 f. Tacitus *Annals* XVI. xxii. 1, 5. References are to the edition of Henry Furneaux (Oxford: Clarendon Press, 1891), Vol. II.

[77] Bod., I, 3, p. 173. Tac., XVI. xxii. 7: the reference is to Q. Aelius Tubero and M. Favonius, who were both severe Stoics, the former in the time of the Gracchi and the latter in that of Cicero.

[78] Bod., I, 3, pp. 173 f. Tac., XVI. xxvi. 1.

[79] Bod., I, 3, p. 176. Tac., XVI. xxvi. 4.

Barea Soranus, who had refused to punish Acratus for the sack of Pergamum.[80] Specifically mentioned by the Swiss author is the terror of the senators as Marcellus, with visible anger, makes his spirited attack on Paetus.[81] Among the other charges against Soranus are his personal ambition in Asia and the indictment of his daughter because she had given money to the Chaldeans in return for prophecies about the future. These, as well as her plea before the senate in behalf of her father, come directly from Tacitus.[82] The judgment which is rendered against them is also found in the *Annals;* Helvidius Priscus is banished from Rome, while Soranus and his daughter are condemned to die in a manner of their own choosing.[83] Following his source, Bodmer emphasizes Arria's wish to die with Paetus and the latter's earnest and successful request that she continue to live for her daughter's sake.[84] Tacitus reports that, just before the end, Paetus engaged Demetrius in a discussion of the immortality of the soul; this led Bodmer to invent such a discussion for his play.[85] In these selections Bodmer has followed Tacitus closely.

In three respects the author has expanded certain ideas in the sources according to his special interests. First, he emphasizes his deep hatred of tyranny and arbitrary violence as exemplified in Nero. Helvidius Priscus and Rusticus Aurelenus are selected as spokesmen against the authority of despotism. In the opening scene the former attacks Nero's regime for destroying the security of respectable citizens.[86] As the condemned await their fate, Aurelenus bursts into a lamentation of their predicament under the tyranny of Nero and of the inability of the laws to protect them against such despotism.[87] More vehement still is his outburst against Augustus and his successor for perversion of the laws:

[80] Bod., II, 2, pp. 189 f. Tac., XVI. xxiii. 1.
[81] Bod., II, 3, pp. 192 f.: "Schwarze Flammen der Wuth brannten in Marcellus Gesichte, Augen und Stimme. Die Senatoren waren nicht nur für ihr Mitglied bekümmert; sie zitterten für ihre eigenen Personen." Tac., XVI. xxix. 1.
[82] Bod., II, 3, pp. 193 f. and II, 5, pp. 202 f. Tac., XVI. xxx. 1 ff., xxxi.
[83] Bod., III, 5, pp. 225 f. Tac., XVI. xxxiii. 3.
[84] Bod., III, 1, pp. 209 ff. Tac., XVI. xxxiv. 3.
[85] Bod., III, 4, pp. 220 ff. Tac., XVI. xxxiv. 2.
[86] Bod., I, 1, p. 163.
[87] Bod., I, 2, pp. 166 f.

Cursed, eternally cursed be impious Augustus, who, by perverted interpretation, was the first to extend the old law of the republic protecting
the ruler from insult so as to make it apply to satirical verses and libels.
And what curses are strong enough for that man [Nero], who is not
satisfied with that and has assumed unto himself the rights and privileges
of the gods, in order that the number of his crimes and his own power
might be increased still further.[88]

Both Priscus and Aurelenus are impetuous, heedless men of action,
over against whom Bodmer has set the more stable Paetus. The
latter and Demetrius represent the second of Bodmer's interests
in the theme, fearlessness of death. Paetus' resignation to his fate
is based on the conviction that he is a martyr and should offer no
resistance. As he faces death, he is very calm, almost expectant:
"I have preferred to await death without resistance than to postpone it through resistance."[89] He shows the same feeling when
he insists upon going to the senate meeting despite his friends'
advice to the contrary. Bodmer intended Paetus, as he wrote
Gleim, to be a representative of Stoicism.[90] Demetrius considers
this life also as inferior to life after death and hence has no fear
of death. To Schinz Bodmer declares: "What Demetrius the philosopher says on page 218 is from Epictetus. I understand that he
looks on our mortal life as death, when compared with heavenly
life, and that such a name fits this life better."[91] Paetus maintains

---

[88] Bod., I, 2, p. 168: "Verflucht sey, ewig verflucht, der gottlose Augustus, der
zuerst das alte Gesetz der Republik von der verlezten Majestät durch eine verkehrte
Auslegung auf satyrische Verse und Libelle erstrecket hat! Und welche Flüche sind
schwer genug für den Mann, der, damit nicht zufrieden, sich selbst die Rechte und
Vorzüge der Götter zugeleget hat, damit die Anzahl der Verbrechen und seine Gewalt
noch mehr vergrößert würden."

[89] Bod., III, 8, p. 234.

[90] Bodmer to Gleim, Sept. 21, 1775, W. Körte, *op. cit.*, pp. 433 f.: "Man erlaubt
mir doch, daß ich den T h r a s e a Stoicismus . . . reden lasse?"

[91] Bodmer to Schinz, July 30, 1777, MS ZBZ.: "Was Demetrius der Philosoph,
S. 218 sagt, ist aus Epictet, und ich verstehe ihn, daß er das i r d i s c h e L e b e n
mit dem göttlichen verglichen für einen Tod hält, und daß d i e s e r N a h m e n ihm
zukomme." Klotz (*op. cit.*, p. 408) had quoted as follows from Bodmer's play:
"Was er im Leben thut, ist, daß er dem Tode arbeitet. Indem er lebet, ist er im
Tode, dann wenn er nicht mehr lebt, ist er nach dem Tode, oder man wolle sagen,
man sey todt nach dem Leben und im Leben sterbend." This refers to the following
in Epictetus (*Discourses* III. xxiv. 93 f.), which was probably in Bodmer's mind:
"This is the meaning of death, a greater change of that which is now, not into what
is not, but into what is not *now*. . . . You will not be, but something else will be,
something different from that which the universe now needs."

that the soul is dependent for its existence on the body, that death brings the dissolution of both, and that speculation about life after death is purposeless. But he does believe that there is a force of the greatest wisdom which is responsible for order in the universe. His faith in this force transcends all fear, even that of death, for it recognizes man's good heart and his pure intentions and it cannot let him go to ruin.[92] This gives him the courage to face death with composure and equanimity, and without concern for the future. Thirdly, Bodmer has emphasized the part played by the women Arria and Fannia, who appear always to identify themselves with their husbands. The typical expression of this relation is contained in the words of Arria: "His life is my life. I live in him and my spirit flies with his out of my body."[93] This attitude recurs in several scenes,[94] and because of its repetition is of some importance in showing Bodmer's interest in their unconditional resignation to their fate. In these three aspects, an intense hatred of tyranny, fearlessness of death, and the heroism of the women, Bodmer has given his own interpretation to the theme.

In *Thrasea Paetus* patriotism and the attack on despotism are presented in one of Bodmer's best dramatic efforts. Here is the ideal patriot who embodies political freedom, but who is so resigned to fate as to offer no active resistance. This is the picture as drawn by Tacitus and selected by Bodmer to set forth his own ideals. In the passive surrender to death and his noble martyrdom to the cause of freedom, Paetus reflects Bodmer's interest in the heroic aspect of the material.

CAJUS GRACCHUS

In November, 1769, Bodmer began work on his *Cajus Gracchus*.[95] Late in October he had written Schinz that he was planning a play on that subject.[96] He was careful to point out that the play

---

[92] Bod., III, 4, p. 223: "Kennt er mein gutes Herz und meinen reinen Willen, so muß er einen Gefallen daran haben. Und das, woran er Gefallen hat, wird er nicht untergehen lassen."

[93] Bod., II, 1, p. 184.

[94] E.g., II, 1; III, 1; III, 7.

[95] Baechtold, *Tagebuch*, p. 202.

[96] Bodmer to Schinz, Oct. 25, 1769, MS ZBZ.: "Ich habe das Sujet von Cajus Gracchus im Kopf, in welchem ich Politik und Pathetik genug voraussehe."

was to be read and not acted.[97] By the middle of November the second act was finished. "It has the fault," the author wrote, "that it will excite no passion except hatred of oppression."[98] By the middle of December the play was completed, and Bodmer prophesied that in the eyes of the Eighteenth Century politicians Gracchus would appear as the hero of a novel.[99] In sending the manuscript to Schinz to copy he commented briefly on the treatment of the figure in Nepos and Plutarch.[100] Three years elapsed before its publication in 1773.[101] Its appearance went unnoticed, as Bodmer complained to Schinz three years later.[102]

The drama treats the struggle and death of Caius Gracchus in 121 B.C., when he supported the people's cause against the power of the senate. It opens with the report of the murder of a lictor, Antyllius, by Fulvius, consul and supporter of Gracchus. The deed becomes the immediate provocation for an attack on Caius' party by Opimius, consul and partisan of the senate. Caius reproaches Fulvius for his lack of self-control in committing the deed and learns from the latter's reply of the hatred which the senate bears toward him; Fulvius points out to Gracchus his dangerous position in trying to be a friend of the people and yet not an enemy of the senate. A fortunate downpour of rain prevents immediate action against Caius, and Bodmer uses this opportunity to introduce Cornelia, mother of Caius, and his wife Licinia. The former exerts a restraining influence upon him and urges him to attempt an amicable settlement. Licinia fears for her husband's life. In a long scene between Caius and the consul Fannius, the latter criticizes severely the consul's policy as one which will eventually lead to civil war, for the two parties concerned, the populace and the nobles, can never be placed on an equal footing. Caius defends his own democratic attitude. Meanwhile the streets are filling with people and the senate is in session to take action. A certain

[97] Bodmer to Schinz, St. Martin's day, 1769, MS ZBZ.

[98] Bodmer to Schinz, Nov. 15, 1769, MS ZBZ.: "Die zweyte Handlung im Cajus Gracchus ist aus den Spänen gehauen. Sie hat den Fehler, daß sie keine Passion als Haß der Unterdrückung erreget."

[99] Bodmer to Schinz, Dec. 15, 1769, MS ZBZ.: "Dieser Cajus ist in dem Gedanken unserer Politiker ein Romanheld."

[100] Bodmer to Schinz, Jan. 17, 1770, MS ZBZ.

[101] *Cajus Gracchus, ein politisches Schauspiel.* Zürich: David Bürgklj, 1773.

[102] Bodmer to Schinz, Nov. 5, 1776, MS ZBZ.

Virbius brings Antyllius' body into the gathering and tries to arouse sympathy for the cause of the senators. It is reported that the senate has given Opimius authority to put the city under martial law, and Fulvius and Caius decide to collect their forces for open opposition; they are now urged to do this by Cornelia. On the next day, after taking leave of his wife and mother, Caius appears before the restless populace and makes a speech designed to retain the people's support in the impending struggle. In its beginning it follows Shakespeare's well known words: "Römer, Mitbürger, Freunde der Freyheit, und Cajus Freunde, ihr habet mich oft in den Gefahren, so dem Recht und dem Staat droheten, gehört; schenkt mir auch jetzo euer Ohr."[103] But its theme is contained in the one sentence, referring to the senators: "In reality they are opposing in my person the people and its rights."[104] As a last gesture of reconciliation Flaccus, son of Fulvius, is sent to Opimius to effect a truce. The latter refuses the offer and demands that Caius and Fulvius surrender to justice. They refuse, whereupon the troops of Opimius attack the supporters of Gracchus on the Aventine Hill and drive them into retreat. Caius does not participate in the fighting, but takes refuge in the temple of Diana and later escapes to a grove dedicated to the Furies. His servant, Philocrates, refuses to obey Caius' order to kill him and the play ends with the words: "they go further into the grove."

The chief source for the events of the play is Plutarch's account of the life of Gracchus; Bodmer knew that of Cornelius Nepos also. After completing the work, Bodmer wrote Schinz that in the latter part he had followed Plutarch, whom he had read in Amyot's French translation, and adds: "Plutarch was not a slave like Nepos."[105] The first incident in the open revolt led by Caius is taken directly from Plutarch; it describes the murder of Quintus Antyllius during a sacrifice.[106] Opimius accuses Caius of complicity in the death of Scipio Africanus; Plutarch reports that some

---

[103] Bod., III, 7, p. 67.

[104] Bod., III, 7, p. 69: "Aber eigentlich bekriegen sie in meiner Person das Volk und seine Rechte."

[105] Bodmer to Schinz, Jan. 17, 1770, MS ZBZ.: "Ich folge in dem letzten historischen Theile Plutarchen völlig . . . Ich habe Plutarch in Amiots Übersetzung. Plutarch war kein S c l a v e , wie Nepos."

[106] Bodmer, Cajus Gracchus, I, 1, pp. 4 f. Plut. Caius Gracchus XIII. 3-XIV. 1.

suspicion of this deed fell upon Caius.[107] The ancient biographer records that Caius proposed three laws to gratify the demands of the people; the first of these provided that land grants should be made to the people without interest payments, the second that public distribution of grain should be made and financed by the state, and the third that suffrage rights should be granted to the provinces. In Bodmer's play these laws are enumerated, and Fannius attacks them because they will inevitably bring about the ruin of the state.[108] From his source Bodmer borrowed the forum scene, in which the body of Antyllius is brought into the throng of people. Virbius, rather than the senators as in Plutarch, harangues the people in order to stir up feeling against Caius.[109] The attempt is unsuccessful, for the people, among other things, are mindful of the unavenged death of Tiberius Gracchus, who, we are told in Plutarch, had won popular favor by distributing among the people the estate of King Attalus of Pergamum.[110] In order to handle the situation, Opimius receives the power of a dictator, as in Bodmer's source; the people's party is ordered to take up arms.[111] The Swiss author was attracted by the speech of Licinia when she takes leave of her husband and has used a lengthy paraphrase of the passage in the original.[112] Meanwhile the senators receive orders to appear in arms on the next day and this causes the opposition much concern, as in the ancient biography.[113] Flaccus is introduced into the German play and is sent to the senate (in Plutarch to the forum) to plead for reconciliation and the avoidance of bloodshed.[114] The message is delivered, but the offer is spurned, especially by Opimius, who demands that Caius and his supporters should come as petitioners and stand proper trial.[115] Their refusal to comply with this demand is the signal for the attack. Bodmer follows closely his source in

[107] Bod., I, 3, p. 9. Plut., X. 4.
[108] Bod., II, 1, pp. 29, 35. Plut., V. 1 f.
[109] Bod., II, 4, p. 41. Plut., XIV. 2.
[110] Bod., II, 5, p. 48. Plutarch *Tiberius Gracchus* XIV. 1.
[111] Bod., II, 6, pp. 49 f. Plutarch *Caius Gracchus* XIV. 3 f., XVIII. 1.
[112] Bod., III, 3, pp. 56 f. Plut., XV. 2.
[113] Bod., III, 5, p. 63. Plut., XIV. 4, 6.
[114] Bod., III, 8, pp. 72 f. Plut., XVI. 1.
[115] Bod., III, 10, pp. 81, 82 f. Plut., XVI, 1 f.

reporting the fighting and the complete rout of the rebels by the archers of Opimius. Caius, seeing this, withdraws into the temple of Diana, where he laments the ingratitude of the people in abandoning him and his cause.[116] As in Plutarch, so in Bodmer, Caius retreats further into the sacred grove.[117] In all of these events the German play has borrowed its material from the ancient biography, often using paraphrases of the original.

In several instances, however, Bodmer has made interpretations of Plutarch when he reports varying accounts. Thus Cornelia represents two attitudes toward Caius' use of armed force. Early in the play she begs him to make his peace with the senate through the mediation of Fannius, because she is interested in the preservation of civil order.[118] Later, however, she urges her son to use violence to suppress his enemies, reminding him that she gave him life in order to use it in the cause of freedom: "Oppose with violence the violence which the laws cannot restrain."[119] Even here the Swiss author has in mind the report of the ancient biographer that two differing opinions were held regarding Cornelia's attitude toward her son's conflict with the senate.[120] In Bodmer's source Fulvius' son Flaccus appears twice before Opimius to plead for truce; for the sake of dramatic coherence our work combines these two appearances into one.[121] So in the ending of the play Bodmer seems undecided as to which of Plutarch's two reports about Caius' end he should use, and leaves the matter unsettled by allowing the hero to escape into a grove with his manumitted slave.[122]

In treating this theme Bodmer wanted to place special emphasis on the figure of Cornelia, stressing both the maternal as well as the heroic element in her character. After commenting on her letters as reported in Nepos, Bodmer adds in a letter to his friend

[116] Bod., III, 12, pp. 88 f. Plut., XVI. 3 ff.
[117] Bod., III, 13, pp. 92 f. Plut., XVII. 1 f.
[118] Bod., I, 4, p. 18.
[119] Bod., II, 5, p. 52: "Setze der Gewalt, welche die Gesetze nicht in Schranken fassen, Gewalt entgegen."
[120] Plut., XIII. 2: "Here, we are told, his mother also took active part in his seditious measures" and "others, however, say that Cornelia was very much displeased with these activities of her son."
[121] Bod., III, 10. Plut., XVI. 1 ff.
[122] Bod., III, 13, p. 95.

Schinz: "Thus I preferred to represent her as a greater person than she was. *Mater Gracchorum* alone gives me the greatest conception of her."[123] This is particularly the case in the scene invented by him, in which the slave Menecrates brings her the report of her son's doom and in which she praises him and laments his death.[124] She tries to comfort Licinia in her fear for her husband's life[125] and extols his devotion to the state as an ideal which transcends his love for his wife.[126] When Caius describes his work and destiny as being supernatural in character, she replies: "By these words do I recognize my Caius, the pride of his mother."[127] Her part in the play is an important one and Bodmer has handled her in convincing fashion.

What attracted Bodmer to the figure of Caius Gracchus was his uprightness and his devotion to the rights of the people. In commenting to Schinz on the election of a tribune, in which Caius' majority of votes was reported fraudently as a minority, Bodmer says: "This vexed him, but did not mislead him into evil paths."[128] He had in mind Caius' abhorrence of bloodshed and civil war, which take their greatest toll from the lower classes. The faith of Gracchus in the people and their support is expressed often. In the early part of the play, when he is still hoping to reconcile the senate and the people, he says: "I intend to defend the rights of the people, but to protect them without using any force except that which the rights of the tribuneship grant me. . . . Least of all should I like to win for the people even the most useful of laws by bloodshed and revolution."[129] But when he has broken with

---

[123] Bodmer to Schinz, Jan. 17, 1770, MS ZBZ.: "So wollte ich sie lieber größer, als sie war, vorstellen. Mater Gracchorum allein macht mir die größte Idee von ihr." The letters mentioned by Bodmer are two fragments from the book of Cornelius Nepos on the Latin historians, *Fragmenta* 1. Bodmer was not attracted by Nepos and in this same letter calls him "ein kleiner Schmeichler der Patricier."

[124] Bod., III, 12.

[125] Bod., I, 5, p. 24.

[126] *Idem.*

[127] Bod., I, 5, p. 26: "An dieser Rede erkenne ich meinen Cajus, den Stolz seiner Mutter."

[128] Bodmer to Schinz, Jan. 17, 1770, MS ZBZ.: "Dieses habe ihn verdrossen, aber nicht verführt, ungerade Wege zu gehen."

[129] Bod., I, 3, p. 10: "Ich will die Rechte des Volckes beschützen, aber sie zu beschützen keine Gewalt brauchen, als die, welche mir die Rechte des Tribunates

Opimius and the senate, he places his trust solely in the people: "I am lost if my confidence in the constancy of the people to whom I have dedicated my life fails me."[130] He is the champion of their rights and interprets the senate's attack on him as really a drive against the lower classes.[131] The tragedy of Gracchus lies in an excess of confidence on his part in the people's gratitude for his efforts in their behalf and their complete abandonment of him in the last crisis.

Cajus Gracchus is the expression of Bodmer's interest in popular rights. He has glorified these in the figure of its hero and the death of this patriot for this cause; Caius' heroism stands out as significant in the author's classical experience. The tragedy of the play is not that Gracchus dies, but that the defeat of his party is due to lack of support from the people for whom he sacrifices his life. In this play Bodmer has given considerable attention to the influence of the women, as exemplified in Cornelia. The spirit of the drama is perhaps more heroic than that of Plutarch's account, and Bodmer's treatment of the material as an outstanding instance of political sacrifice has given it a deeper meaning.

BRUTUS UND KASSIUS TOD

Bodmer continued the story of Caesar's murderers in his *Brutus und Kassius Tod*, which was written in the summer of 1781.[132] In September he promised the manuscript to Schinz.[133] Late in that month he reported to the same correspondent that the play was in the hands of Heidegger, the Zurich publisher, adding the fervent hope that it would be suitable for publication.[134] Heidegger had some misgivings about the play; "he fears no doubt," Bodmer writes, "that the *Negatifen* and the royalists will bear me ill

---

geben. . . . Am wenigsten wollte ich dem Volcke die nützlichsten Gesetze selbst durch Aufstand und Blut erwerben."

[130] Bod., II, 2, p. 39: "Bin ich verlohren, wenn mein Vertrauen auf die Standhaftigkeit des Volkes, dem ich mich geweihet habe, mich betriegt."

[131] Bod., III, 7, p. 69.

[132] Baechtold, *Tagebuch*, p. 213.

[133] Bodmer to Schinz, Sept. 15, 1781, MS ZBZ.

[134] Bodmer to Schinz, Sept. 21, 1781, MS ZBZ. The Heidegger mentioned here is probably Johann Heinrich Heidegger (1738-1823), who was one of the proprietors of the publishing house Orell, Füssli and Co. in Zurich from 1756 to 1798.

will on account of *Brutus and Cassius*."[135] The author looked upon
Brutus as the upholder of the republic and maintained that he
would have restored the republic if he had been victorious at
Philippi; "then his principles would have been vindicated by his
example."[136] In this composition Bodmer declared that he took
great pleasure in branding the tyrants once again.[137] Apparently
his friends did not like his treatment of the theme because it was
written in a dramatic and not a didactic form.[138] By the middle of
December, 1781, the manuscript had gone, not to the Zurich firm,
but to a publisher in Basel,[139] and appeared in the following year.[140]

The historical events of the play center about the defeat of
Brutus and Cassius on the plains of Philippi in 42 B.C. The two
champions of the republic meet after devious wanderings and decide upon an attack against the opposing forces led by Octavius
and Antony. Both contemplate suicide if the outcome is defeat.
That night an apparition, presumably Caesar, comes to Brutus.
The course of the battle is reported in the second act. Titinius
arrives with the intelligence that Cassius, despairing of victory,
has committed suicide. Brutus orders Titinius to reassemble the
scattered legions for a second battle. Incidental is the news that
Portia has also committed suicide. The third act opens with a
description of Brutus' forces, which are in retreat before the
victorious troops of Octavius and Antony. Brutus gives up all hope
of winning and refuses Messala's suggestion to take flight by sea.
He wishes death, because "all good Roman blood has been spilled
and only the poisoned blood remains." After ordering Strato
to plant his sword in the ground, he falls upon it. The play ends

[135] Bodmer to Schinz, Sept. 25, 1781, MS ZBZ.: "Heidegger fürchtet ohne Zweifel,
daß die Negatifen und Royalisten mich wegen Brutus und Cassius anfeinden werden."
The *Negatifen* were members of a political party in Geneva who were opposed
to the views of Rousseau.

[136] Bodmer to Schinz, Oct. 12, 1781, MS ZBZ.: "Von Brutus hatte man recht zu
erwarten, daß er die Republik hergestellt hätte, wenn er zu Philippi das Feld erhalten,
und dann hätten seine Grundsätze durch sein Beyspiel Unterstützung gefunden."

[137] Bodmer to Schinz, May, 1782, MS ZBZ.: "die Unterdrücker noch einmal zu
brandmachen."

[138] Bodmer to Schinz, Nov. 23, 1781, MS ZBZ.: "Man verwirft meinen Brutus
und Cassius, weil sie dramatisch und nicht didaktisch geschrieben sind."

[139] Bodmer to Schinz, Dec. 14, 1781, MS ZBZ.

[140] *Brutus und Kassius Tod.* Von dem Verfasser der Noachide. Basel: Carl August Serini, 1782.

with the complete capitulation of Brutus' officers and the capture
of the men and equipment. These events are put together loosely
into three acts, unbroken by scenes, with little dramatic quality,
no attempt at motivation, and no effective effort at character
delineation.

Plutarch is Bodmer's source for the events and characterization.
Following the biographer's interpretation, Brutus is compared
with the gods for great benevolence, justice, and nobleness of soul,
while Cassius is described as a somewhat rough and harsh person,
who wishes to be feared.[141] Their meeting at the beginning of the
play is the first since they parted at Piraeus to go their respective
ways to Macedonia and Syria.[142] Their attitude toward the approaching battle differs at first, as in Plutarch; Brutus favors immediate engagement with the enemy.[143] In defending his stand,
Bodmer's Brutus uses the same speech as in the biography; he
confesses that, following the example of Cato, he is willing to die
for his ideal of liberty, if fate has determined that his forces
should be defeated.[144] Cassius favors delay, but it is finally agreed,
as in Plutarch, to engage Antony's forces on the next day.[145]
The details of the battle correspond in both versions. Among these
may be mentioned the victory of Brutus' troops,[146] the capture of
the two jesters, Voluminius and Seculio,[147] the report that Messala's legions have attacked the enemy without orders and dashed
into the camp of Octavius,[148] and the annihilating defeat of the
Lacedaemonian troops.[149] Bodmer interrupts the report of the
battle by introducing, as does his source, the appearance of a
ghost to Brutus. The reality of such apparitions is denied by
Cassius in Plutarch and by Horace in Bodmer.[150] Cassius' attitude
in the battle follows Plutarch in all essential details, e.g., the

[141] Bodmer, *Brutus und Kassius Tod*, I, p. 3. Plutarch *Brutus* XXIX. 1 f. References to Bodmer's play are to act and page.
[142] Bod., I, pp. 7 f. Plut., XXVIII. 4.
[143] Bod., I, p. 11. Plut., XXXIX. 4.
[144] Bod., I, pp. 13 f. Plut., XL. 4 f.
[145] Bod., I, p. 14. Plut., XXXIX. 6.
[146] Bod., II, p. 16. Plut., XLII. 3.
[147] Bod., II, p. 18. Plut., XLV. 4.
[148] Bod., II, p. 18. Plut., XLI. 3.
[149] Bod., II, p. 18. Plut., XLI. 4.
[150] Bod., II, pp. 19 f. Plut., XXXVI. 3-XXXVII. 1, XLVIII. 1.

anger aroused in him when he sees the victorious troops of Brutus
engaged in taking spoils rather than in the envelopment of the
enemy,[151] or Cassius' futile attempt to rally his men when they
break ranks in an effort to avoid encirclement by the enemy's
right wing.[152] Nor does Bodmer omit the mission of Titinius to
reconnoitre the situation and the joyous shouts which greet
him from a distant part of the army; Cassius thinks the shouts
are occasioned by the enemy's joy in capturing his men and withdraws to his tent, where his head is later found severed from the
body.[153] Another interruption in the battle is introduced at the
end of the second act when Brutus receives the news of Portia's
death. From Plutarch Bodmer draws the comparison of the separation of Brutus from Portia and Andromache from Hector, using, as in his source, verses from the *Iliad;* but he substitutes the
name of Brutus for that of Hector:

Brutus, Brutus, du bist mir Vater, Mutter und Bruder,
Denn du bist, den mit mir die zärtlichsten Bande verknüpfen.[154]

The words describing Portia's death by swallowing live coals are
paraphrased from the original.[155] Certain events preceding the
death of Brutus come also from Plutarch; these include Brutus
awaiting the return of the messenger Statyllius from the battlefield,[156] the report of Marcus Cato's death,[157] that of Statyllius'
death,[158] and the decision of Brutus to commit suicide, although
Messala (in Plutarch, someone) advised him to flee.[159] The manner of death is the same in both versions of the incident; Brutus
falls upon the point of a sword held by Strato.[160] The Swiss author
has also the reported ruse of Licilius, who is captured for Brutus
by the enemy and is brought before Octavius, rather than before

[151] Bod., II, p. 24. Plut., XLIII. 1.
[152] Bod., II, p. 25. Plut., XLIII. 2.
[153] Bod., II, pp. 25 f. Plut., XLIII. 3 ff.
[154] Bod., II, p. 29. Plut., XXIII. 2 f.: The separation in Plutarch occurs when
Brutus fled from Italy because he feared Antony. The verses are from the *Iliad*
VI. 429 f.
[155] Bod., II, p. 31. Plut., LIII. 4.
[156] Bod., III, p. 32. Plut., LI. 4.
[157] Bod., III, p. 34. Plut., XLIX. 5.
[158] Bod., III, p. 35. Plut., LI. 4.
[159] Bod., III, pp. 36 f. Plut., LI. 2 f.
[160] Bod., III, p. 38. Cf. Plut., LII. 5.

Antony as in Plutarch.[161] In many of the passages referred to above the German text paraphrases the original closely, the selection of events being Bodmer's contribution. He makes them bear directly on the character of Brutus and stresses more than in Plutarch the inevitability of the hero's death, as one calamity after another befalls him. His resignation to death for the ideal of liberty makes him a passive character. Bodmer has summed up his conception of Brutus in the words of Octavius, translated freely from Shakespeare's *Julius Caesar:*

Brutus war der edelstè in der Zusammenschwörung; es war nicht Neid, nicht Herrschsucht, was ihn bewog, den Dolch in dem Busen seines Wohlthäters umzuwälzen. Es war katonischer Fanatisme, der übertriebene Begriff von dem Worte Freyheit und dem Namen Rom. Sein Leben war Ernst, sein Charakter zu dem schönen und guten gestimmt, daß die Natur laut rufen durfte: sie habe einen M e n s c h e n gebildet.[162]

Although Bodmer adheres closely to his source in treating this theme, he has introduced minor changes in the narrative of Plutarch. Most interesting is that of the poet Horace into the battle scene. It is he who brings in the two captives, Voluminius and Seculio,[163] and who reports to Strato the progress of the fighting. He refuses to believe that an apparition really came to Brutus in his tent and seeks to explain this as an hallucination, induced by the excited imagination of Brutus.[164] The participation of Horace in the battle at Philippi is historical, but not in the manner represented by Bodmer.[165] The author has joined into one the two meetings of Brutus and Cassius which are mentioned by Plutarch.[166] So too the latter's several references to Brutus' dreams are brought together into one dream by the simple expedient of omitting the spirit's answer to Brutus' question asking who he is.[167] Titinius brings Brutus the news of the death of Cassius, and re-

---

[161] Bod., III, pp. 40 f. Plut., L. 1 ff.

[162] Bod., III, p. 43. Shakespeare, V, 5, ll. 68-75. References to Shakespeare are to the edition of W. G. Clark and W. A. Wright (Cambridge and London: Macmillan & Co., 1865), Vol. VII.

[163] Bod., II, p. 18.

[164] Bod., II, p. 20.

[165] Cf. Horace *Odes* II. vii. 9 f. *Epistles* II. ii. 49. Horace refers with pride to his presence at Philippi.

[166] Plut., XXVIII. 4 (at Smyrna), XXXIV. 1 (at Sardis).

[167] Bod., II, p. 19.

lates that he found Pindar, a freedman who had attended Cassius at his suicide, dead near his master.[168] This varies from Plutarch's version, in which Pindar is never seen again after the death of Cassius.[169] The letter brought by Cleitus to Brutus from Portia is an invention of Bodmer; possibly its use was suggested by Plutarch, who mentions a letter from Brutus to his friends in which he laments the fate of his wife.[170] In the German play Portia's death occurs before that of Brutus and is caused by the arrival of a false report that his ship has been wrecked. Portia does not wish to outlive him.[171] These changes tend to add unity to Bodmer's treatment.

The heroism which Bodmer ascribes to Brutus stands out in the play in the glorification of his character and assumes more importance than the political aspect of the theme. Twenty years separated Bodmer's treatment of the active, political conspirator in *Marcus Brutus* and this picture of Brutus as a man who is resigned to his end, and it may well be that a similar change had come over the eighty-three-year old Swiss patriarch. But Brutus is still a martyr to his political ideal, and Bodmer has conceived the personal character of his hero in the spirit of Shakespeare, although the action and events of the play follow more closely the account of the ancient biographer.

PATRIOTS

MARCUS BRUTUS

Marcus Brutus was written in April, 1761.[172] In November of that year Bodmer sent the manuscript to Sulzer in Berlin and requested him to pass judgment on it. If he liked it, he was to try to have Philipp Reich in Leipsic publish it. Bodmer desired that the author should remain unknown and gave Sulzer *carte blanche* to make changes and improvements.[173] But difficulties were en-

---

[168] Bod., II, p. 26.
[169] Cf. Plut., XLIII. 6 f.
[170] Plut., LIII. 5.
[171] Bod., II, p. 31.
[172] Baechtold, *Tagebuch*, p. 197.
[173] Bodmer to Sulzer, "first weeks of November," 1761, MS ZBZ.: "Da ist mein Marcus Brutus. Ich mache Sie, wehrtester Freund, zum Arbitre über sein Leben und seinen Tod. . . . Aber lassen Sie ihn leben, so wollte ich gern, daß Sie ihn Herrn

countered, for Reich returned the manuscript. It was refused a
second time, and in 1764 Sulzer became discouraged. He wrote
Bodmer that he was now too proud to beg for publication and
would not "entrust *Brutus* or anything else to Reich."[174] During
the next three years the author, as he wrote, made two unsuccessful attempts to find a publisher, one with Mezler in Stuttgart and
another with Macklot in Karlsruhe. The theme and the treatment
seemed so bold that he had to take precautions for secrecy. "Here
I must keep it under lock and key," he wrote Schinz, "so that I
do not seem to be preaching rebellion and regicide."[175] He feared
that it was neither adapted for the stage nor for the press and
did not dare to come out into the open with it.[176] The refusal of
the publishers to accept the manuscript was attributed to their
fears "vor der Weißischen Cabale und den Lessingischen Busch-
klopfern."[177] After these disappointing attempts, the play finally
found its way into a volume of Bodmer's dramas.[178]

The "cabal" in Germany raised its voice very soon in a scath-
ing review of the whole collection, including *Brutus*.[179] Its author,
Klotz, directed his criticism against the play's lack of dramatic
quality. The characters were accused of being impotent, declamatory figures, all cast in the same weak mold. Brutus was branded
as the image of a swaggering officer,[180] Cassius as a school-boy
orator, with a slightly greater poetic tendency than the others,

---

Reich in Leipzig gäben, wofern Sie mit ihm noch immer gut stehen. . . . Ich gebe
Ihnen überhaupt carte blanche nach Ihren Einsichten, zu verändern, zu verbessern."
Whether Sulzer made any changes in the text is unknown. He spent the months
of January and February, 1763, in Bodmer's house; quite possibly changes were
made in the manuscript at this time.

[174] Sulzer to Bodmer, May 8, 1764, MS ZBZ.: "Eben so empfindlich war es mir,
daß derselbe Mann auch schon vor mehr als einem Jahr den B r u t u s nicht
annehmen wollte. . . . Ich bin zu stolz, eines Buchhändlers Gunst zu betteln . . .
so kann ich es mit mir selbst schlechterdings nicht mehr dahin bringen, daß ich
dem R e i c h den B r u t u s oder etwas anders antrage."

[175] Bodmer to Schinz, Feb. 12, 1767, MS ZBZ.: "Hier muß ich ihn unter dem
Schlüssel verwahren, damit ich nicht Rebellion und Königsmord zu predigen scheine."

[176] Bodmer to Schinz, Feb. 19, 1767, MS ZBZ.

[177] Bodmer to Hess, n. d., Mörikofer, *op. cit.*, pp. 219 f. Cf. also Bodmer to Hess,
July 31, 1767, Zehnder-Stadlin, *op. cit.*, p. 527.

[178] Bodmer, *Politische Schauspiele* (Zürich: Orell, Geßner und Comp., 1768), pp.
1-103.

[179] *Deutsche Bibliothek der schönen Wissenschaften*, II (1768), 209-224.

[180] *Ibid.*, p. 211.

and Marc Antony as a very simple flatterer; Caesar was an illogical person and a mocker of religious formulae, traits which
made him artificial.[181] The dialogue was stamped as strange, and
especially in the scene between Caesar and Cicero, as lacking in
good taste.[182] Quotations were introduced with the purpose of
showing how unnatural and illogical Bodmer's language was. The
author of the play did not attempt a public defense, but seven
years later he criticized the review in a letter to Schinz.[183] Here
he defended his use of "unnatural" expressions, citing two which
Klotz had attacked in his review: "Let us prepare Caesar as a
meal for the gods" and "the republic sticks like a fishbone in
Brutus' heart."[184] Bodmer continued that Shakespeare was full
of such metaphors and that many of those used had been taken
over from the British dramatist, while the poetic congratulations
which Cinna offers Brutus at the end of the play he had borrowed
from Vergil's *Georgics*.

Marcus Brutus is the first work which Bodmer wrote on the
death of Julius Caesar, a theme about which several plays center.
It is concerned mainly with the plot against Caesar's life and its
development. Portia tries to arouse Brutus to the deed as the
only salvation for Rome, but Brutus feels that the spirit of tyranny
rather than the tyrant should be destroyed. Cassius reports that
Caesar's experiment with public feeling by assuming the royal
diadem and allowing himself to be declared king has not met with
the approval of the populace. The two conspirators discuss the
overthrow of the dictator, but Cicero is not admitted to their confidence. Caesar appears and boasts of his dictatorial powers and
his ambition to become king. In two long drawn-out scenes, as in
the later play *Julius Cäsar,* he attempts unsuccessfully to win
Brutus and Cassius to aid him in his ambition. The plot develops
and Caesar becomes suspicious of Brutus and Cassius. The evil
omens in his own and Calpurnia's dreams, the warning against the

[181] *Ibid.*, p. 212.
[182] *Ibid.*, p. 213.
[183] Bodmer to Schinz, April 5, 1775, MS ZBZ.: "Shakespear ist voll von dergleichen Metaphern, und viele habe ich aus ihm genommen. Der poetische Glück-
wunsch, den Cinna, der Poet, dem Brutus zu Ende des Trauerspiels von diesem
Nahmen machet, ist aus Virgils Georgicis genommen, und ich lasse Brutus ihn
belachen."
[184] *Deutsche Bibliothek,* II, 214, 213.

Ides of March, the inauspicious report of the priest's sacrifice worry him, and he wishes to absent himself from the senate meeting; but he is unable to resist the taunts of Decimus Brutus that this would be interpreted as a sign of weakness, and hence goes to the senate. The last act is taken up with the report of his murder, as it is brought to Portia. The actions of the conspirators are praised and the prospects for restoring the republic are discussed; in these discussions Cinna figures prominently.

Bodmer has taken much of his material from Plutarch's biographies of Caesar and Brutus. In speaking against Caesar, Brutus contends that he owes no more to the dictator than had the first Brutus, who killed his own sons for their attempt to restore the Tarquin line of kings.[185] Bodmer mentions also ancestors of Brutus, calling them "Brutos" and "Ahalas," and probably took these from Plutarch, who traces Brutus' ancestry back to Servilius Ahala.[186] The German play paraphrases freely Plutarch's account of the Lupercalian festival, where Antony held the diadem out to Caesar, the people applauding when it was refused, for they did not want a king.[187] Cassius then quotes from the Sibylline books the statement of Plutarch and Suetonius that Parthia could be taken only by Romans who were under the leadership of a king.[188] Brutus and Cassius are now reconciled,[189] and the latter is no longer angry because Caesar had given Brutus the office of praetor, although he had been more deserving. Likewise Bodmer follows his source in emphasizing the importance of Brutus' leadership in the conspiracy, because this would give the plot a semblance of justice.[190] In both authors the reason for not including Cicero in the undertaking is that the conspirators fear his calculating caution and his timidity.[191] The refusal of Caesar to maintain a bodyguard is mentioned by Bodmer,[192] who has not failed also to introduce Caesar's love for Servilia, mother of Brutus;

[185] Bodmer, *Marcus Brutus,* I, 1, p. 8. Plutarch *Brutus* I, 1 f. *Publicola* III. 4, VI. 1 ff.
[186] Bod., I, 2, p. 10. Plut. *Caesar* LXI. 5. *Brutus* I. 3.
[187] Bod., I, 3, pp. 14 f. Plut. *Caesar* LXI. 3 f.
[188] Bod., I, 3, p. 15. Plut., LX. 1. Suet. *Julius* LXXIX. 3.
[189] Bod., I, 4, p. 17. Plut. *Brutus* X. 4.
[190] Bod., I, 4, p. 18. Plut. *Brutus* X. 1.
[191] Bod., I, 4, p. 19. Plut. *Brutus* XII. 2.
[192] Bod., II, 1, p. 24. Plut. *Caesar* LVII. 4. Suet. *Julius* LXXXVI. 1.

Caesar speaks of an unknown force which attracts him to Brutus. This is probably a reference to Plutarch's statement that Caesar had some grounds for believing Brutus to be his son.[193] This affection for Brutus appears in a desire to see him succeed to power, as mentioned in the biographies.[194] At first the dictator seems to be satisfied if he may wear the diadem in the provinces, but not in Rome; Plutarch says that the senate was willing to grant this.[195]

In the third act, dealing with the meeting of the senate and the murder of Caesar, Bodmer is quite close to his source. The presence of Pompey's statue in the senate chamber gives a divine sanction to the deed.[196] Antony's report that the praetors were conducting their routine trials as if nothing unusual were about to happen, is again a paraphrase of the original.[197] The warning against the Ides of March and the failure to find a heart in the sacrificial victim are also mentioned.[198] As in Plutarch, Bodmer's Caesar heeds Calpurnia's plea not to go to the senate,[199] until Decimus, using a paraphrase of the original, ridicules this as a sign of weakness.[200] As Caesar approaches the meeting, Asinius Pollio addresses much the same speech to Decimus which is spoken to Casca in Bodmer's source. This is one of the best passages to illustrate Bodmer's use of Plutarch; Asinius says: "Bey Jupiter, Decimus, du hast mir den Geheimniß gar zu sorgfältig verborgen, aber Cimber hat mir alles entdeckt. . . . Mich wundert, wie du in kurzer Zeit so reich geworden seyst, daß du dir hast in den Sinn kommen lassen, dich um die Würde des Aedilis zu bewerben."[201] The Swiss author has taken over almost completely the incident in which Popilius Laenas congratulates the conspirators, and then engages Caesar in a conversation; this causes the con-

---

[193] Bod., II, 1, p. 25. Plut. *Brutus* V. 2.
[194] Bod., II, 2, p. 33. Plut. *Caesar* LXII. 3. *Brutus* VIII. 2.
[195] Bod., II, 2, p. 33. Plut. *Caesar* LXIV. 2.
[196] Bod., III, 3, p. 56. Plut. *Caesar* LXVI. 1.
[197] Bod., IV, 1, pp. 63 f. Plut. *Brutus* XIV. 4 f.
[198] Bod., IV, 2, p. 67; 3, p. 70. Plut. *Caesar* LXIII. 3, 2.
[199] Bod., IV, 3, p. 73. Plut. *Caesar* LXIII. 7.
[200] Bod., IV, 5, p. 76. Plut. *Caesar* LXIV. 3.
[201] Bod., IV, 8, p. 79. Plut. *Brutus* XV. 2: "Some one came up to Casca . . . and said: 'You hid the secret from us, Casca, but Brutus has told me everything. . . . How did you get so rich on a sudden, my good fellow, as to stand for the aedileship?' "

spirators such great concern that they strike almost prematurely.[202] Bodmer has also included from Plutarch a description of the nervous state and Bacchic frenzy of Portia while waiting at home for the report of the murder.[203] These examples of Bodmer's borrowings from Plutarch leave no doubt as to the source of his material. In many cases he has paraphrased the original. The sequence and setting do not always correspond, nor are the passages spoken by the same persons in all cases.

In no other of these Swiss plays are passages taken from Shakespeare's *Julius Caesar* so easily recognized as in *Marcus Brutus*. Bodmer acknowledged this influence when he wrote: "Shakespeare is full of such metaphors and I have taken many from him." Baechtold has indicated and quoted some of these passages; Vetter has reprinted some of them also.[204] From Shakespeare Bodmer takes the passage which describes Brutus as a deeply brooding person, who scorns play, music, laughter, and is never at his heart's ease. Antony says of him: "Brutus hält nichts auf einigem Spiele, nichts auf Musik; er lachet selten, und wenn er lachet, geschiehet es mit so verdrießlichen Zügen in seiner Mine, als ob er mit sich selbst unzufrieden wäre, daß er sich so hat erniedrigen können."[205] Caesar's report of Calpurnia's disturbing dream,[206] as well as her own version of it,[207] is translated from the English.[208] The German Caesar's interpretation of his own dream is a close paraphrase of that by Decimus in Shakespeare.[209] Instead of Calpurnia, as in the English, it is here a priest who describes further strange phenomena in the German play, such as the fierce battle of the warriors in the clouds, the blood on the Capitol, the groaning of the men, and the shrieking of the ghosts; but again Bodmer has translated from the English.[210] The following example may be

[202] Bod., IV, 8, p. 80. Plut. *Brutus* XV. 3, XVI. 1 ff.
[203] Bod., IV, 10, p. 81. Plut. *Brutus* XV. 4 f.
[204] Baechtold, *Gesch. d. d. Lit. i. d. Schweiz*, pp. 641, 644; Vetter, "Bod. u.d. eng. Lit.," *loc. cit.*, pp. 369 f.
[205] Bod., II, 1, pp. 24 f. Shakespeare, *Julius Caesar*, I, 2, ll. 203-10.
[206] Bod., IV, 1, p. 64. Shakes., II, 2, ll. 1-3.
[207] Bod., IV, 2, p. 66. Shakes., II, 2, ll. 76-79.
[208] Cf. Bod., *Pol. Schauspiele* (1768), p. 319: here he acknowledges Shakespeare as the source for the dream.
[209] Bod., IV, 2, p. 67. Shakes., II, 2, ll. 87-90.
[210] Bod., IV, 3, p. 71. Shakes., II, 2, ll. 19-26.

quoted as typical of Bodmer's translations from Shakespeare:
"Aber feige Memmen sterben vor ihrem Tode; der Tapfere
schmeckt den Tod ein einziges Mal. Ha! es ist eitel Thorheit, daß
die Menschen ihn fürchten, sie sehen doch, daß er ein noth-
wendiges Ende ist, und kommen will, wenn er kommen will."[211]
Thus Bodmer was attracted by Shakespeare's use of the dream
motif; further dependence on the English dramatist is difficult to
document.

Our play is not without original features. Brutus appears in the
first scene in conversation with Portia, uncertain and timid about
undertaking an attempt on Caesar's life. This fear is based upon
two considerations, first, a natural reluctance to harm the man
who had saved his life and showered favors and benefits upon
him; and secondly, the probability that the death of the dictator
will not remove the roots of his dictatorship, unless at the same
time it inspires the people with a spirit of order and republicanism.[212] Portia seeks to dispel his fears in both respects. Quite unhistorical and unconvincing is the scene in which Caesar attempts
to gain Brutus' consent for the assumption of the royal diadem. In
this discussion Brutus appears as Caesar's equal and makes un-
guarded, even bitter, retorts. Thus when the despot accuses Brutus
of harboring a prejudice against him and gives this as the reason
for not approving the assumption of the diadem, Brutus replies:
"But the excellent republic that you have destroyed has shaken
me in my innermost viscera, and how am I to presume to despise
the rule, but love the ruler?"[213] Bodmer's conception of Caesar's
character is a mixture of benevolent despotism and haughty disdain of popular opinion. He compares the people under his unlimited power to sheep and hares in all except their refusal to
grant him the title of king.[214] Still he desires to use this power
with indulgence and justice in order to make them feel that their
burdens are lighter than those which were imposed upon them

[211] Bod., IV, 3, p. 72. Shakes., II, 2, ll. 32-37.
[212] Bod., I, 1, p. 9.
[213] Bod., II, 2, p. 34: "Aber die vortreffliche Republick, die du umgekehrt hast, hat
meine Eingeweide erschüttert, und wie soll ich es angreifen, die Beherrschung zu
verabscheuen, und den Beherrscher zu lieben?"
[214] Bod., II, 1, pp. 22 f.

under the republic.[215] Bodmer puts into Caesar's mouth an interesting defense of his actions as being consistent with the practice of Roman conquest and domination:

Never did they [the Romans] make an honest peace settlement; their treaties were only advances intended to carry everything along with them if the opportunity was favorable. The title of their confederates implied subjection. . . . They attacked not only the power, but even the person of kings. After they had first accustomed nations to obey them as free peoples, they commanded them as subjects and swallowed them up in the republic. I have followed the same fundamental rules of politics and no others.[216]

The inference which Bodmer would draw here is that as the republic fell, so Caesar must fall, since he is pursuing the same policy. Cinna, the poet, appears at the end of the play, but does not die as Plutarch reports. Instead, in inflated speeches, he lauds the murder as a worthy sacrifice for the sake of Rome's order and freedom, and exalts the virtues of Brutus to the Romans in such bombastic style that at last the object of this extravagant eulogy commands him to be silent.[217]

Marcus Brutus is concerned mainly with drawing a picture of the despot Julius Caesar and is chronologically Bodmer's first attack on that historical figure. His selfish ambition, his arrogance and conceit, the arbitrary use of his unlimited power are for Bodmer the sins of tyranny and despotism. The spirit of his attack on Caesar's character is more intense than that of Plutarch. The influence of Shakespeare is not apparent on the political side of the theme, but is limited mainly to the exploitation of the dream motif. The essentially political nature of Bodmer's experience goes back to antiquity, and although Shakespeare may have inspired

[215] Bod., II, 2, pp. 28 f.

[216] Bod., II, 2, p. 31: "Niemals machten sie [die Römer] einen aufrichtigen Frieden; ihre Verträge waren nur Aufzüge, in der Absicht mit guter Gelegenheit alles mitzunehmen. Der Titel ihrer Bundsgenossen führte Knechtschaft mit sich. . . . Sie griffen die Könige nicht nur in ihrer Macht, sondern in ihren Personen an. Nachdem sie erst alle Nationen gewöhnet hatten, als freye Leute zu gehorsamen, geboten sie ihnen als Unterthanen, und verschlungen sie in der Republick. Denselben Grundregeln der Politick, und keinen andern hab ich gefolget."

[217] I have been unable to locate the source of Cinna's speeches in Vergil's *Georgics* referred to by Bodmer.

him to treat the material, he has no importance for Bodmer's notion of the political society of Rome.

TIMOLEON VON KORINTH

Timoleon was written in 1764[218] and was published in 1768,[219] with the following quotation on the title page:

> The fair Corinthian boast
> TIMOLEON, tempered happy, mild, and firm,
> Who wept the brother, while the tyrant bled.

Klotz spoke of the play as an attempt to combine the art of a juggler with that of an actor.[220] He took strong exception to the part played by Ceres in the action, and objected to the language as inappropriate to a tragedy. Then he quoted at length from Bodmer's text to show the burlesque nature of the play, as he termed it.

The plot is briefly as follows. Aeschylus, returning to Corinth after a long exile in Egypt, is incensed by the dictatorship which Timophanes wields over the city. Satyrus tells him of Timophanes' rise to power through bribery and unlawful political scheming. This hatred of a dictatorial state is shared also by Timoleon, brother of Timophanes. The latter is now planning to execute Satyrus on grounds of treasonable conduct and Timoleon is resolved to die with him. In an interview between Satyrus and Timophanes, the despot is very suspicious of Aeschylus, whom he regards as a spy, and this suspicion increases when Aeschylus refuses to accept the king's magnificent hospitality. This causes a strain in the relations of the two brothers, Timoleon and Timophanes. In the third act Ceres appears to Timoleon in the guise of Satyrus and declares that the salvation of the city lies in ridding it of his brother. Convinced by Aeschylus and Satyrus that the vengeance of the Furies will not fall upon him in consequence of such a deed, Timoleon plans and carries out the murder of Timophanes.

Bodmer found this material in the *Timoleon* of Nepos and in that of Plutarch. The latter reports that Timoleon was greatly

---

[218] Baechtold, *Tagebuch*, p. 199.
[219] *Pol. Schauspiele*, 1768, pp. 223-69.
[220] *Deutsche Bibliothek*, II (1768), 219-22.

distressed and tried to turn his brother from his ambitious and tyrannical ways, that in this violent scene Timophanes lost control of himself and was murdered by Aeschylus and Satyrus, while Timoleon stood somewhat apart without participating in the deed.[221] In this Plutarch follows Nepos' account closely.[222]

The picture of Timophanes as a tyrant and the degradation into which the city of Corinth has fallen represent Bodmer's attack on government by a dictator. The lack of such virtues as thrift, morality, and good taste in cultivating the simple joys of life has brought the city to such a low state of resistance that it was not difficult for Timophanes to assume complete control. He is described by Aeschylus as "an empty head without genius or talents."[223] Timophanes defends the despotism of his rule as the height of human achievement, because it gives him privileges almost as unrestricted as those accorded the gods. The state is for him a restriction of all for the advantage of one individual, and in this point of view his mother supports him. Timoleon objects to such a state, because it is not founded in the nature of man: "How tractable that nation must be which can transform itself into the person of a single man! I cannot conceive that this disposition is rooted in human nature."[224] He will recognize Timophanes' benevolent attitude toward the people only when palaces shall have been destroyed, and in their place institutions set up, "where our fathers administered justice in the name of the people."[225] When Timoleon attempts to reform his brother, his plea is based upon a like plea in Plutarch.[226] But he must come to the conclusion that no amount of persuasion can accomplish this reform and that hardened tyranny can be eradicated only by violence.

In accordance with his conception of the political drama as a means of spreading the doctrine of republicanism in opposition to a dictatorship, Bodmer built his play about Timoleon as "a hater

[221] Plutarch *Timoleon* IV. 5.

[222] Nepos *Timoleon* I. 4.

[223] Bodmer, *Timoleon*, I, 1, p. 226.

[224] Bod., II, 2, p. 247: "Das mag mir eine gelenkige Nation seyn, die sich selbst in die Person eines einzigen Mannes verwandeln kann! Ich kann nicht begreifen, daß diese Gemüthsfassung in der Natur des Menschen gegründet sey."

[225] Bod., II, 2, p. 249.

[226] Plut. *Timol*. IV. 3.

of tyrants and of base men."[227] He tried to exclude the element
of brotherly hatred as a possible motive for the deed. For this
reason he introduced a scene in which the goddess Ceres appears
to Timoleon and urges him to murder Timophanes, because it is
so inscribed "on the tablets of fate."[228] Timoleon is at first hesi-
tant, and only when Ceres proves her divinity by means of a
"cornstalk" growing in her hand and exhaling "an ambrosial fragrance," and further assures him that the Furies will not pursue
him, does he accept his divine appointment as the savior of the
state. This *deus ex machina* was introduced by Bodmer in order
to give more unity to the action and to give a more convincing
motivation for the murder. This is clear from a letter to Schinz in
which Bodmer wrote that he wished to place Timoleon's hatred of
tyranny above his fraternal attachment to his brother and that
the command of Ceres was supposed to relieve Timoleon of any
scruples of conscience: "I did not want to attribute to Timoleon
any feelings for his brother which would have weakened his aver-
sion to tyrants. . . . Moreover, the judgment and command of the
goddess had to deprive him of all scruples."[229] A further motivation for killing the despot is found in his threat to execute Aeschylus, Satyrus, and Timoleon. It is at this point that the murder
becomes inevitable. Aeschylus throws the tyrant to the ground,
Satyrus covers him with a coat, and Timoleon stabs him.[230] The
action takes place in the palace of Timophanes.

[227] *Ibid*. III. 2.
[228] Bod., III, 3, p. 258.
[229] Bodmer to Schinz, Feb. 17, 1768, MS ZBZ.: "Ich hatte dem Timoleon keine
Empfindungen für den Bruder beylegen wollen, welche den Abscheu vor den Tyran-
nen geschwächt hätten. Und ich glaubte, er muß desto weniger Zärtlichkeit für
ihn haben, weil er mehr für Korinth haben müsse. Zu dem mußte das Urtheil und
der Befehl der Göttinn ihm alle Scrupel benehmen."
[230] In Plutarch (IV. 5) Timoleon weeps while Aeschylus and Satyrus kill Timophanes. Bodmer may originally have followed the ancient biographer, for he writes:
"Im Timoleon wäre vermutlich Ihrer Critik vorgebogen gewesen, wenn ich gedichtet
hätte: Aeschylus hätte dem Timophanes ein Bein unterschlagen, Timoleon ihm den
Rock über den Kopf geworfen, und Satyrus ihn erwürgt. Satyrus als ein Priester ist
sonst ein Schlächter, und zu dem Opferer der Tyrannei schon bequem." Bodmer to
Schinz, Feb. 17, 1768, MS ZBZ. The ending mentioned in this letter is the one
which was finally incorporated into the printed version. Aeschylus addresses Satyrus
as the worthy priest of divine Ceres. Bod., I, 1, p. 226.

PELOPIDAS

Bodmer wrote *Pelopidas* in 1767[231] and published it in the following year.[232] In a letter to Schinz he said that the subject of the play was the same as that of Weisse's *Die Befreyung von Theben,* the characters of which he described as "majors in the imperial army."[233] He had already published an attack on Weisse's drama and was especially incensed because the latter's conception of the Theban rebels was not conceived in the spirit of Plutarch's biography of Pelopidas.[234]

So Bodmer set about writing a piece which would be a worthy account of the democratically minded men who rescued Thebes from the control of the oligarchs in December, 379 B.C. His play opens at the palace of Charon in Thebes, where the latter and the nobleman Epaminondas are awaiting the arrival of political exiles from Athens. A carefully laid plan to kill the tyrant Archias and assume control of the city has been drawn up. Pelopidas and Melon have stolen into Thebes and arrive at Charon's palace. Another Theban patriot Hipposthenides reports the arrival of other conspirators at his home. The city is celebrating the festival of Ceres, and Charon has arranged for the polemarch Archias and his friends to enjoy the company of the most beautiful Colchian women to be had. As the conspirators are perfecting their plans, Charon is summoned by messenger to appear before Archias. As a pledge of his loyalty he leaves his son in the custody of the plotters. He returns soon with the comforting news that they are as yet undiscovered, although Archias has learned that some of the banished fugitives are in the city. The scene now changes to a room in the palace of Philidas, where Archias' banquet is in progress. A messenger brings the despot a tablet from Athens. It contains a disclosure of the plot, but Archias, in his intoxicated condition, puts it aside unread. The conspirators appear disguised as the promised women, throw off their garments, and attack the

---

[231] Baechtold, *Tagebuch,* p. 201.
[232] *Pol. Schauspiele,* 1768, pp. 271-318.
[233] Bodmer to Schinz, Jan. 25, 1768, MS ZBZ.
[234] Bod., *Neue theatral. Werke,* pp. 313-32. Meissner treats this as a satire. *Op. cit.,* pp. 77 ff.

revellers. Archias is killed and a report arrives that Leontidas has also been killed. The play closes with the prospect of the unification of the people of Thebes.

In most of these events Bodmer has followed Plutarch.[235] In selecting the material he limits his play to the murders and events immediately preceding them. The entrance of the fugitives into Thebes, as reported by Pelopidas, is copied from Plutarch's description. Twelve of their number steal through the gates of the city dressed in the short coats of hunters and pretend to be game beaters. Others clothed as peasants pass through the city unobserved because a blizzard has cleared the streets of citizens.[236] Other details are introduced from the Greek biography, such as the abortive attempt of Hipposthenides to postpone the revolt by sending a message to this effect to Melon and Pelopidas.[237] To emphasize the loyalty of Hipposthenides to the conspiracy, Bodmer represents him as harboring in his home two of the plotters and later as being wounded in the fray.[238] The murder of Leontidas is also reported and not included in the main action.[239] In the climax Bodmer introduces his own version, when Charon's son Callicrates stabs Archias; Plutarch is not clear as to the slayer of the polemarch. The part played by the boy is interesting. He appears during Charon's absence at the palace of Archias and, echoing his father's sentiments, is fired with a desire to take part in the plot. He pleads with his mother Arete: "Ist ein Leben ohne Staat und populare Rechte besser? Und kann man leben, wenn die Edelsten, von Thebens Göttern angewehet sie zu erretten, in der Erde liegen, verweset, fühllos, kalt und dunkel, lichtloser, eckelhafter Staub?"[240] Callicrates is permitted to join the conspirators after his father's return. He comes to the banquet in women's clothing and kills Archias at a given signal. Two years later in a letter to Schinz Bodmer took occasion to compliment himself on this device of disguise as introducing an element of action into

[235] Plut. *Pelopidas,* VIII-XI.
[236] Bodmer, *Pelopidas,* I, 2, pp. 278 f. Plut. *Pelopidas* VIII. 2, IX. 1.
[237] Bod., I, 3, p. 282. Plut., VIII. 3 f.
[238] Bod., I, 3, p. 281; III, 6, p. 314. Plutarch does not mention this.
[239] Bod., III, 6. Plut., XI. 3 ff.
[240] Bod., II, 4, p. 298.

the play.[241] Bodmer introduces the boy's mother into the play under the name of Arete, but after a few solicitous, maternal remarks concerning the hazards of the undertaking and the safety of her son, Charon bids her withdraw to the women's apartments.[242] The messenger who brings the disclosure of the plot in the unread tablet comes from Ceres' priest in Athens rather than from the hierophant Archias, as Plutarch reports. Bodmer wanted to avoid confusing two persons bearing the name Archias, the one in Thebes and the other in Athens, and substituted the name of his favorite goddess Ceres.[243] The disagreement with Weisse's interpretation of Epaminondas' character as a "major in the imperial army" led Bodmer to present him as a passive figure in the revolt. He does not forget to include Plutarch's description of Epaminondas as a recluse who is devoted to the muses and voluntarily leads a life of poverty.[244] He appears at Charon's house among the conspirators, approving of their action and supporting it with advice and experience, but he disappears from the scene before the murders take place. His character is best described by Pelopidas as a determined soul who governs his actions by a well-ordered reason and who is conscious of his own virtue. Bodmer follows Plutarch in this conception of Epaminondas but not in allowing him to appear before the murder of Archias. The last scene of the play opens up the prospect of unifying the people of Thebes and liberating Cadmaea from Lacedaemonian domination. It is with this program that Melon points to the future: "If Athens helps us, then let us say that the first step has been taken in this night to break the bonds that Sparta has for so long forged about all the states of Greece, chains so strong that no one believed it any longer possible to break or remove them."[245]

[241] Bodmer to Schinz, Aug. 1, 1770, MS ZBZ.: "Es ist kaum eines von meinen politischen Schauspielen, welchem es an Action fehlt. . . . Sie erinnern sich . . . der Verkleidung im Pelopidas."

[242] Bod., II, 4.

[243] Ceres appears also in Bodmer's *Timoleon* and *Die Rettung in den Mauern von Holz.*

[244] Bod., I, 4, p. 284. Plut., III. 3, V. 3.

[245] Bod., III, 8, p. 317: "Wenn Athen zu uns steht, so wollen wir sagen, daß in dieser Nacht der Anfang gemacht ist die Ketten zu zerbrechen, welche Sparta so lange Zeit über alle griechischen Staaten geworfen hatte; so starke Ketten, daß man glaubte, es wäre nicht mehr möglich sie zu zerbrechen oder aufzulösen."

Pelopidas is another expression of Bodmer's hatred of despotism. Again his interest is in the characters that incorporate his ideals and determine the course of events. He has exalted the idealism of the youth Callicrates and minimized the part of Pelopidas in the assassinations in an attempt to offset the bravado of Weisse's character Epaminondas.

KARL VON BURGUND

In 1771 Bodmer published in an obscure periodical a short play entitled *Karl von Burgund.*[246] Its plot is based on the defeat of Charles the Bold by the Swiss in the battles of Grandson and Morat in 1476, but in form the play is an imitation of the *Persians* of Aeschylus. In the preface to the play the author acknowledges that its organization and thoughts are those of Aeschylus. The political aspect of the theme was suggested to Bodmer through an article on the *Persians* by Jean Lévesque de Burigny in the *Histoire de l'académie royale des inscriptions et belles lettres.*[247] Seuffert has given an analysis of the play in his reprint and has compared Bodmer's with that of Aeschylus.[248] The German version is composed mostly of long accounts which Count Imbercurt gives to Mary of Burgundy of Switzerland and the bravery of its people while these two are waiting for a report of Charles the Bold's campaign against Berne. Chaligni arrives with this report and relates at some length the defeat of the Burgundian forces at the hands of the Swiss. In the last act the ghost of Philip the Good appears to Mary, hears the sad news, and advises her to dissuade Charles the Bold from further combat with this enemy; as the play closes, the latter arrives to mourn his lost heroes and lament the defeat.

Bodmer has altered the contents to conform to his material. The Persian court is turned into the ducal palace in Brussels; Salamis becomes Berne. Xerxes becomes Charles the Bold, Atossa appears as Mary of Burgundy, and the ghost of Darius is represented by

---

[246] *Schweizer-Journal* (Bern: B. Ludwig Walthard, 1771), VI, 33-83: these signatures of the journal were rebound later in L. Meister, *Schweizer Allerlei*, 1787. Cf. also *Karl von Burgund*, hrsg. von B. Seuffert, "Deutsche Litteraturdenkmale des 18. Jahrhunderts," Nr. 9, Heilbronn: Henninger, 1883.

[247] Vol. XXVI, 1764. Cf. Seuffert, *op. cit.*, p. vi.

[248] Seuffert, *op. cit.*, pp. v-xii.

that of Philip the Good. The chorus of Aeschylus is replaced by the three counts, Imbercurt, Hugonet, and Ravenstein. Seuffert presents examples to show that Bodmer has changed the historical "costume." The outrage against Poseidon is replaced by the murder of Ludwig of Orleans and the ancient prayers assume a Christian tone. But the greatest similarity lies in the parallelism of the words and scenes, which Seuffert maintains, is close enough to warrant the statement that Bodmer's play is "less an imitation than a translation of the *Persians,* in fact the first one into German."[249]

In addition to the influence of Aeschylus the play assumes significance as an indirect praise of the virtue and bravery of the Swiss people. This is most apparent in certain parts of the descriptions of battle. Imbercurt ascribes the bravery of the Swiss to their independence, to their resourceful spirit, which is not under the domination of overlords or an autocratic senate, but is inspired by their freedom and democracy.[250] Chaligni refers to these same qualities in his praise of the invincibility of the Bernese citizenry.[251] It is the spirit of freedom that breeds the unshakable courage to which their leaders appeal on the eve of battle: "Sons of the Alps, hard as the stony cliffs which you inhabit! on to battle!"[252] Mary of Burgundy is astonished to learn that such bravery exists outside of her own country. By use of this historical material Bodmer has stressed the character of Swiss patriotism under the cloak of an ancient form. *Karl von Burgund* is thus a significant attempt to unite the spirit of antiquity with that of medieval Switzerland.

DESPOTS

JULIUS CÄSAR

Bodmer wrote his *Julius Cäsar* early in the year 1762[253] and published it in the following year.[254] His friends in Zurich, to

---

[249] Seuffert, *op. cit.,* p. viii.
[250] *Karl von Burgund,* I, 2, Seuffert, *op. cit.,* p. 10.
[251] *Ibid.,* II, 2, p. 14.
[252] *Ibid.,* II, 2, p. 16.
[253] Baechtold, *Tagebuch,* p. 197.
[254] *Julius Cäsar, ein Trauerspiel.* Leipzig: M. G. Weidmanns Erben und Reich, 1763.

whom he read the manuscript, detested the play, as Bodmer wrote
to Zellweger. The author was pleased to interpret this attitude as
an approval of his views against tyranny, rather than as a condemnation of the drama.[255] In July, 1762, Bodmer took the manuscript with him on a trip to Winterthur and Tös.[256] Then he sent it
to Johann Gottfried Gellius in Leipsic, who was to find a publisher for it. After some complicated negotiations, it appeared under the editorship of Gellius with a preface by him. In this he
sought to praise Bodmer's version at the expense of Shakespeare,
but in the end had to acknowledge the latter's work on the theme
as the better of the two.[257]

The play was received unfavorably and the attack on it was
led by Weisse, who reviewed it in Nicolai's *Bibliothek*.[258] He satir-
ized the work as "a frivolous caricature," pointed out by a series
of quotations its obvious lack of dramatic merit, and expressed his
sympathy for any actor who would have to play a part in it.[259]
He called Marc Antony "the meanest of sycophants and also Caesar's court jester."[260] He accused Bodmer of wilful falsification
of the material in assigning as the reason for the actions of Caesar
and Brutus "their joy in committing deeds of violence" rather
than the historical motive of "necessity."[261] He ridiculed the
cringing servility of Antony as like that of a common slave to his
sultan and he objected to Cicero's effeminacy and his womanish
tears.[262] Concerning this Bodmer remarked sarcastically to Schinz
that Cicero's tears were republican tears that were not worthy
of being shed in Brandenburg.[263] In this manner Weisse directed
his attack against all of the characters and refused, as unworthy

[255] Bodmer to Laurenz Zellweger, May 2, 1762, MS ZBZ.: "Ich habe meinen Cesar
etlichen von meinen Freunden gelesen. Sie haben ihn verabscheuet. Ich habe dieses
für ein gutes republicanishes Zeichen aufgenommen."
[256] Bodmer to Sulzer, July, 1762, Zehnder-Stadlin, *op. cit.*, p. 397.
[257] Cf. Baechtold, *Gesch. d. d. Lit. i. d. Schweiz*, p. 643. The Bodmer *Nachlaß* in
Zürich has four letters from Gellius to Bodmer.
[258] *Bibliothek der schönen Wissenschaften*, X (1763), 133-46: Weisse was editor
of the journal at this time.
[259] *Ibid.*, p. 136.
[260] *Idem.*
[261] *Ibid.*, p. 138.
[262] *Ibid.*, p. 139.
[263] Bodmer to Schinz, n.m. 19, 1764, MS ZBZ.: "Und die Thränen des Cicero sind
republikanische Thränen, die in Brandenburgen . . . nicht würdig sind zu weinen."

of the effort, to compare Bodmer's play with that of Shakespeare, although he had originally intended to do so. An unknown author, quite possibly Bodmer himself, promptly wrote an extended defence of the work in the *Züricher Anzeigen*.[264] Weisse was accused of showing a great "lack of thoroughness,"[265] and his objections were answered point for point. Caesar's deeds of violence were the natural result of his overweening ambition and quite in accord with the figure in history.[266] The criticism of Antony was refuted as unjust; his language did not "offend the dignity of the language which the tragedy demands."[267] Antony was a subordinate figure in the play, and there was no reason for making his character a sublime one. The review defended the conception of Caesar as a sultan and as embodying a higher kind of despotism than was implied in the words "crown and king."[268] As his parting shot the reviewer called upon Weisse to write a criticism without invective or prejudice and to support his statements with reasons, but this challenge went unheeded.

A modern version of Weisse's attitude is found in the treatment of the theme by Gundolf.[269] He describes the piece as an extreme caricature originating in a fanatic's interest in freedom, and calls it an historical pamphlet in dialogue. He points out the extravagance of ascribing to Caesar the ambition to found an empire in the Orient.[270] Gundolf's treatment consists of a brief, discursive summary of the plot, interspersed with remarks emphasizing the exaggeration in both language and ideas. In general it is an eminently just estimate, for *Cäsar* certainly does not rank very high as a piece of literature.

The play opens with a long scene in which Caesar describes to Antony his plan to build up a complete domination over the empire

---

[264] *Wöchentliche Anzeigen zum Vortheil der Liebhaber der Wissenschaften*, I (1764), 245-56.

[265] *Ibid.*, p. 246.

[266] *Ibid.*, p. 247.

[267] *Ibid.*, p. 249.

[268] *Ibid.*, p. 251.

[269] Fried. Gundelfinger, *Caesar in der deutschen Literatur*. "Palaestra," Nr. 33 (Berlin: Mayer & Müller, 1904), pp. 102-06.

[270] *Ibid.*, p. 105: "Bodmers Hauptquelle waren die Gerüchte des hauptstädtischen Pöbels über Caesars orientalische Herrscherpläne, die Sueton beiläufig verzeichnet." The passage in Suetonius is probably *Caesar* LXXXIX. 3.

by instilling into every Roman the fear of Caesar as a deity. His pride will not be satisfied until he has wiped out every supporter of the republic and every concept of freedom, even at the expense of much bloodshed. "My pride will not rest," he declares, "as long as the concept of freedom exists, as long as even one person is living who wants the republic. I will change the citizens of Rome until they shall no longer have any feeling for such things. . . . Fear shall consume every bit of boldness and shall leave no feeling for ambition."[271] Calpurnia pleads with Caesar to take greater precautions for his life. He plans to call the senate together on the morrow in order to test its loyalty by demanding the diadem and the scepter. Both Cicero and Brutus refuse to support him in this scheme. In the second act Brutus expresses strong sentiments against Caesar and makes plans to oppose the dictator, even at the cost of his own life: "One shall not say that I have always cringed. I will rise from the dust and at least die as a Roman."[272] Portia, his wife, does not wish to outlive him. Servilia, his mother, urges him to share power with Caesar, pointing out that he can help the republic more by living for it than by dying, because the ruler has no natural heir. With the arrival of Cassius, the plan to murder Caesar is developed. Only Brutus and Cassius are privy to it at this stage; Cicero's aid is not enlisted. The third act takes place on the next day. Caesar tries to allay Calpurnia's fears, which arise from certain evil portents seen by her in a dream. Caesar has had a dream too, in which the dead arose threateningly against him; but he was enshrouded by Venus in a cloud of ambrosial fragrance, which burst into flames and destroyed his enemies. He goes to the senate despite Calpurnia's fears, and soon thereafter Antony appears spattered with blood and reports the murder. At the end of the play Trebonius and Albin seek Antony, finally find him disguised in women's clothing, and carry him off

[271] Bod., *Jul. Cäs.*, I, 1, p. 15: "Mein Stolz ist nicht ruhig, so lange der Begriff von Freyheit noch ist, so lange noch einer lebt, der die Republik wünscht. Ich will die Römer verwandeln, bis baß sie keine Empfindung mehr für diese Sachen haben. . . . Die Furcht soll allen Muth verschlingen, und kein Gefühl von Ehrbegierde übrig lassen."

[272] Bod., II, 1, p. 38: "Man soll nicht sagen, daß ich immer gekrochen bin; ich will mich aus dem Staube aufrichten, ich will zum wenigsten als ein Römer sterben."

to prison. The first act is taken up with the futile attempt of Caesar to win Antony, Cicero, and Brutus to support his plan, the second with the development of the plot on the despot's life, and the third with its execution.

Bodmer makes no statement concerning his source for this play. We have seen that he knew Shakespeare's work on this theme. Gundolf favors the account of Caesar's life in Suetonius as the source for the German play and reduces the influence of Plutarch to a minimum.[273] The relation of Bodmer to Suetonius and Plutarch is a difficult one to establish completely. Some of the material is found in both ancient authors, such as the failure to find a heart in the sacrificial victim,[274] and Caesar's dream during the night before the murder; for this latter Bodmer probably took from Suetonius the comparison of Caesar with Jupiter and from Plutarch the cloud of fire on which his throne hovers.[275] Common to both sources is the well known warning against the Ides of March,[276] and the details of Caesar's assassination.[277] Some of Bodmer's material is found only in Suetonius, such as the refusal of Pontius Aquila to rise when the dictator passed in triumphal procession before the benches of the tribunes,[278] and the rumor that Caesar planned to withdraw from Rome and found an empire in the East.[279] The moralist Bodmer did not fail to introduce from Suetonius Caesar's license which permitted him to marry any woman in Rome.[280] Among the borrowings from Plutarch, as distinct from Suetonius, may be mentioned the honor which permitted Caesar to share the temple dedicated to Clemency,[281] and the convocation of the senate for the purpose of having the scepter conferred upon him.[282] The attitude of Brutus toward his ruler and the fact that Caesar had saved Brutus' life at Pharsalia occur in

[273] Gundelfinger, op. cit., p. 105.
[274] Bod., Cäsar, I, 2, p. 18. Suet. Julius LXXVII. Plut. Caesar LXIII. 2.
[275] Bod., III, 2, pp. 63 f. Suet., LXXXI. 3. Plut., LXIII. 2.
[276] Bod., III, 2, p. 65. Suet., LXXXI. 2. Plut., LXIII. 3.
[277] Bod., III, 6, p. 72. Suet., LXXXII. 1 ff. Plut., LXVI. 4 ff.
[278] Bod., I, 1, p. 15. Suet., LXXVIII. 2.
[279] Bod., I, 3, pp. 22 f. Suet., LXXIX. 3.
[280] Bod., II, 3, p. 48. Suet., LII. 3.
[281] Bod., I, 1, p. 13. Plut., LVII. 3.
[282] Bod., I, 3, p. 24. Plut., LXIV. 2.

the narrative of Plutarch.[283] From the same author comes the report that Brutus revealed the plot against the dictator's life to Portia after she had proved her loyalty and willingness to die by drawing blood from a self-inflicted wound.[284] That Cicero was not admitted to the confidence of the conspirators is mentioned twice by the ancient biographer.[285] Finally Bodmer introduces from Plutarch the attempt of Antony to hide after the deed, when he disguises himself in strange clothing.[286] The conclusion to be drawn from the above consideration of Bodmer and the ancient biographers is that he used more material from Plutarch than from Suetonius, although he did apparently consult both authors. The importance attached by Gundolf to Suetonius as the main source for the play applies to Bodmer's exploitation of Caesar's Asiatic ambitions rather than to the extent of the material borrowed. Gundolf has been influenced largely by the attitude of Weisse in his attack on Bodmer's interpretation of Caesar as a sultan.

In treating this material Bodmer has made several interpretations of his own. The first of these is his strong emphasis on Caesar's greed for the throne, for the title of sultan. The author intends to leave with the reader a picture of the force of tyranny working against the tradition of the republic. This force expresses itself in Caesar's purpose completely to subjugate the Roman citizenry and to break its spirit. He proposes to accomplish this by prohibiting freedom of speech,[287] and by eradicating every vestige of freedom and ambition,[288] in the belief that he has been appointed by the gods to the mastery of the earth. "Imagine," he says to Brutus, "that the gods have placed this great gift, the mastery of the earth, in Caesar's hands."[289] Secondly, Bodmer has three scenes in which Caesar attempts to win from Antony, Cicero, and Brutus, respectively, their approval and support of his

---

[283] Bod., I, 5, pp. 32 ff. Cf. Plut. *Brutus* V-VII.
[284] Bod., II, 2, pp. 40, 43. Plut. *Brutus* XIII. 2 ff.
[285] Bod., II, 5, p. 57. Plut. *Brut.* XII. 2. *Cicero* XLII. 1.
[286] Bod., III, 6, p. 71. Plut. *Caesar* LXVII. 2. *Brutus* XVIII. 3.
[287] Bod., I, 1, p. 13: "Der kühnste von ihnen darf nicht reden, wie er denkt."
[288] Bod., I, 1, p. 15.
[289] Bod., I, 5, p. 34: "Stelle dich vor, daß die Götter dieses große Geschenk, die Herrschaft der Erde, in Cäsars Hände übergeben haben."

plan to demand the diadem from the senate.[290] He is unsuccessful in each of these three attempts. Cicero's answer is typical: "Never shall you win from me the avowal that I have given Rome a king."[291] Thirdly, Bodmer has given Servilia, mother of Brutus, more attention than either Plutarch or Suetonius, both of whom, however, mention briefly Caesar's intimacy with her. She tries to win her son's support for Caesar's cause in the hope that he will one day succeed the ruler.[292] But she turns from Caesar when she is informed that he has assumed the right to take any woman in Rome as his wife, for this is a moral liberty she cannot condone.[293] In a later scene she attempts unsuccessfully to arouse Calpurnia against the despot.[294] Fourthly, Bodmer has introduced new elements into the dreams of Calpurnia and her husband. In both of these Caesar is sitting on a throne under a canopy decorated with pearls and jewels; in both the dead arise to attack Caesar. In Calpurnia's dream these dead appear as Roman generals: Pompey, Marcellus, Brutus, and Cassius.[295] In Caesar's dream he destroys his enemies by shaking fire down upon them.[296] These omens do not frighten him, as at first in Suetonius and Plutarch, from attending the senate meeting. In these four respects Bodmer has given his own peculiar emphasis to the material of his sources, but he has weakened the theme by excessive repetition, particularly in the scenes designed to win Antony, Cicero, and Brutus to Caesar's point of view.

Julius Cäsar differs from *Marcus Brutus* in its greater emphasis on Caesar's personal ambition and in approaching the material more directly from the standpoint of Caesar as a despot than from that of Brutus and Antony as patriots. This is seen most clearly in the first three scenes of the play, where the haughty arrogance of Caesar is brought out as a personal characteristic. In this play

[290] Bod., I, 1; I, 4; I, 5.
[291] Bod., I, 4, p. 31: "Nimmermehr sollst du das Bekenntnis von mir haben, daß ich Rom einen König gegeben hätte."
[292] Bod., II, 3, p. 48.
[293] Bod., II, 3, pp. 48 f.
[294] Bod., III, 4, pp. 67 f.
[295] Bod., III, 2, p. 62: neither Plutarch nor Suetonius mentions names here.
[296] Bod., III, 2, pp. 64 f.

Bodmer has also placed more stress on Caesar's immorality. As in *Brutus,* the conspirators figure conspicuously in the plot against the despot, but Bodmer has left out of *Julius Cäsar* Cinna's extravagant praise of the conspirators' bold and noble action. He has also shown more independence of Shakespeare than in *Brutus.* At the same time the theme of the two plays was so nearly the same that Bodmer could not avoid repeating parts of the material in this second treatment of Caesar's death. The political aspect of the theme is common to both and is the author's chief interest in his treatment.

TARQUINIUS SUPERBUS

Bodmer goes back to an earlier period in Roman history to treat the rape of Lucretia and the expulsion of the Tarquins in his *Tarquinius Superbus.* He wrote most of the play in May, 1764,[297] and characterized it as having more politics than poetry.[298] Schinz copied the manuscript, which then lay in Bodmer's desk for three years[299] and was finally published in 1768.[300] The long delay was due in part to the author's fear that it would be misinterpreted by the public, for early in 1765 he confessed to Schinz that the people of Zurich were afraid he was setting a bad example for his pupils.[301] Klotz criticized the play as a poor tragedy,[302] contenting himself with quoting several passages which he described as extravagant. He was incensed most of all by the bombastic speech of Lucretius over the body of his dead wife.

As the play opens, Sextus Tarquin, son of Tarquin the Proud, is in command of the Roman troops engaged in the siege of Ardea. He appears one morning unexpectedly at his father's palace in Rome. In explanation of his absence from camp he relates that on the preceding evening certain officers, being in their cups, had become excited over the merits of their respective wives and had repaired to Rome to settle the dispute. All conceded the prize for beauty and virtue to Lucretia. As Sextus takes leave of his father,

---

[297] Baechtold, *Tagebuch,* p. 199.
[298] Bodmer to Sulzer, May 26, 1764, MS ZBZ.
[299] Bodmer to Schinz, Mar. 26, 1767, MS ZBZ.
[300] *Pol. Schauspiele,* 1768, pp. 105-57.
[301] Bodmer to Schinz, Jan. 17, 1765, Zehnder-Stadlin, *op. cit.,* p. 462.
[302] *Deutsche Bibliothek,* II (1768), 216-18.

he meets Junius Brutus, who under pretence of being an idiot has long awaited a favorable opportunity to expel the Tarquin family. Brutus is silent but later tells his friend that his feigned idiocy has been discovered by Sextus. They agree that the next arbitrary act of the king shall be the signal to stir the people to revolt. Immediately after their decision the rape of Lucretia is reported. Their course of action is now clear. In the second act they bring the body of the dead woman into a meeting of the citizens. In long speeches Lucretius, Valerius, and Brutus recite Tarquin's shameful deeds of injustice and capricious tyranny, and attempt to excite the populace to overthrow him. The day is carried by the faction of Brutus in a scene where Lucretia's husband Collatinus swears oaths of vengeance over her body: "I will take vengeance for your virtue and your death on the evildoer and the house of his father . . . I will pursue them and every one of their family with fire and sword."[303] As Tarquin and his wife Tullia lament their predicament, Herennius comes to announce that the army, aroused by Sextus' dastardly deed, has abandoned him and declared its allegiance to the senate and rebels. The drama closes when Brutus brings the senate's decision that the Tarquins are to be banished.

Bodmer, who knew Livy's *History* well, made substantial borrowings from it for the play. The explanation offered by Sextus for his presence in Rome is a good paraphrase of the passage in Livy which describes the officers' discussion of the merits of their respective wives and the incident in Rome:

Wir schwatzeten von unsern Frauen; jeder pries die seine für die schönste, wir wurden hitzig. Collatinus sagte, man dürfte seine Lucretia nur sehen, um ihr den goldenen Apfel zu geben; wer daran zweifelte, könnte sich von seinen eigenen Augen belehren lassen. In dem Feuer des Wortstreites saßen wir zu Pferde, wir trafen sie am späten Abend an einer Stickrahme an, wo sie in ihrem häuslichen Gewand jedem das Bekenntnis abnöthigte, das wir ihrem Gemahl verweigert hatten.[304]

[303] Bodmer, *Tarquinius Superbus*, II, 3, pp. 138 f.: "Ich will deine Keuschheit und deinen Tod an dem Übelthäter und an dem Hause seines Vaters rächen . . . ich will sie und jeden Freund von ihnen mit Feuer und Schwerdt verfolgen."

[304] Bod., I, 1, p. 108. Livy *History* I. lvii. 6 ff.: "Forte potantibus his apud Sex. Tarquinium, ubi et Collatinus cenabat Tarquinius Egerii filius, incidit de uxoribus mentio; suam quisque laudare miris modis. Inde certamine accenso Collatinus negat

From the same author Bodmer has taken the prophecy motif; Brutus and Sextus were once returning from Delphi, where the oracle had promised the rule of Rome to that one of them who should kiss his mother first. As soon as they landed Brutus kissed the earth, the mother of all mortals.[305] The details of the violation of Lucretia correspond in both source and drama; these include the entrance of Sextus into the girl's chamber, his threat to kill her if she refuse to comply with his desire, as well as the second threat to kill her and lay by her side a naked slave, in order to give the impression that justice had overtaken her in the shameful act.[306] When Lucretius describes Lucretia's end, he uses Livy's vocabulary in a free translation: "Plötzlich zog sie einen Dolch aus dem Rocke hervor, und stach sich in ihre schwellende Brust."[307] As Collatinus grasps the fatal knife and kisses the blood on it, he swears a determined oath over his wife's body to avenge her on the Tarquin family; in Livy it is Brutus, not Collatinus, who makes this speech.[308] In all these passages Bodmer has followed Livy closely in longer extracts, but he has also used many less extended details from this source. Thus he recalls the murder of Servius Tullius and he has Tarquin disclose his policy of weakening the senate by reducing the number of its members.[309] Brutus mentions Livy's report of Tullia's crime when she ordered her carriage to be driven over the body of her dead father Tullius.[310] As the Latin historian, the Swiss author has Lucretia's body brought into the market place, and repeats from the same source the words of Lucretius reminding the people that they have not only sacrificed their lives in war, but are being made to build temples with their servile labor.[311] Much of the scene in which

---

verbis opus esse, paucis id quidem horis posse sciri, quantum ceteris praestet Lucretia sua. . . . Incaluerant vino; Age sane! omnes; citatis equis avolant Romam . . . sed nocte sera deditam lanae inter lucubrantes ancillas in medio aedium sedentem inveniunt. Muliebris certaminis laus penes Lucretiam fuit."

[305] Bod., I, 1, pp. 111 f. Livy, I. lvi. 10 ff.

[306] Bod., I, 4, p. 118. Livy, I. lviii. 2 ff.

[307] Bod., I, 4, p. 119. Livy, I. lviii. 11: "Cultrum, quem sub veste abditum habebat, eum in corde defigit."

[308] Bod., II, 3, pp. 138 f. Livy, I. lix. 1 ff.

[309] Bod., I, 1, p. 110. Livy, I. li. 9, xlix. 6.

[310] Bod., I, 4, p. 120. Livy, I. xlviii. 7, lix. 10.

[311] Bod., II, 1, pp. 127 f. Livy, I. lvi. 1, lix. 9.

Brutus and Valerius harangue the populace, enumerating Tarquin's misdeeds and acts of violence and exhorting the throng to expel the ruler, is based on Livy's report of Brutus' speech,[312] as is that in which Tarquin boasts of his conquest of the provinces of Suessa Pometia and Gabia and the heavy tribute which he has levied on them.[313] In the senate's decree of banishment, Bodmer has introduced the dispensation which allowed the Tarquins to take a carriage laden with their effects from Rome.[314]

Several interesting interpretations of the material have been made by Bodmer. Unhistorical is the scene (II, 2) just before the senate hands down its decision on the fate of the Tarquins. In it the elder Tarquin and Brutus face one another; the former disclaims all responsibility for his son's deeds and seeks to defend his own material achievements and his regency as god-given.[315] Brutus then accuses him of having destroyed the freedom of Roman citizens and forever discredited monarchy as a form of government: "You yourself, Tarquin, destroyed the confidence that we can enjoy freedom, security, and a fatherland under the rule of a monarch, when you made an arbitrary prince out of the king."[316] Bodmer is also original in introducing Herennius to play an active part in stirring up the soldiers "to fight for Rome, freedom, and the senate."[317] Entirely Bodmer's invention is the stinging attack which Herennius launches against powerless Tarquin, ending: "But now you stand there like a plucked stork, and it will be a long time before your feathers grow again."[318] Perhaps suggested by an earlier mention of Delphi is the prophecy in verse invoked by Brutus to express the moral of the play, as well as Bodmer's conception of ancient simplicity. In deeply felt words it praises the love of home and country above all other desires:

[312] Bod., II, 1, pp. 126 f. Livy, I. lix. 7 ff.
[313] Bod., II, 2, p. 133. Livy, I. liii. 2 ff.
[314] Bod., III, 4, p. 155. Livy, II. iv. 3.
[315] Bod., II, 2, p. 133.
[316] Bod., II, 2, p. 135: "Du selbst, Tarquin, hast das Vertrauen zerstört, daß wir Freyheit und Sicherheit und Vaterland unter der königlichen Regierung haben können, als du aus dem König einen eigenwilligen Prinzen gemachet hast."
[318] Bod., III, 2, p. 149.
[317] Bod., III, 2, p. 146.

Love of one's self, of one's household gods, the state, and one's country will be Rome's passion and will absorb all others. Each will identify his welfare with that of his class. Equality of possessions and laws which guard against wealth will give the city a morality that will preserve it in poverty. Thus will the dangers of victory and spoils be avoided. Generals will go from the plow to the battlefield and after victory will return to the peaceful pursuit of agriculture. Splendor will appear in morals not in treasures. Thus will victory follow victory, until the lowly state becomes the master of the earth.[319]

The overthrow of the Tarquin king and the setting up of a liberal government in Rome have given Bodmer an excellent opportunity to attack the failings of a monarchy and of despotism. The case against this type of rule is prosecuted with vigor and feeling by both Brutus and Lucretius in their enumerations of the excessive liberties of the royal family and their rejection of absolute power in the hands of one leader. In the words of Herennius Bodmer has stated the political axiom which is fundamental in the thought of all his political dramas: "Man is born free; freedom is his oldest right and springs from his very nature."

NERO

Nero was written in June, 1764,[320] but was not published until 1769.[321] During these five years it lay in Bodmer's desk. Ten years after the play appeared the author published in the Zurich *Literarische Denkmale* certain additions containing a scene in which the emperor's ashes are collected by Acte, his freedwoman. Introducing these additions, he gave the subject of the drama as "the despotic drunkenness with which he [Nero] despised the

---

[319] Bod., III, 4, pp. 154 f.:

> Liebe sein selbst, des Hausaltares, des Staats und des Landes
> Wird Roms Leidenschaft seyn, die alle die andern verschlinget;
> Jedermann wird sein Wol mit des Standes Wolstand vermischen,
> Gleichheit der Güter, Gesetze, die Rom vor Reichthum bewahren,
> Werden ihr Sitten geben, die sie in der Armuth behalten;
> So verhütet sich, daß ihr Sieg' und Beute nicht schaden.
> Feldherrn gehen vom Pflug ins Schlachtfeld, und nach dem Triumphe
> Wieder zum friedsamen Pflug; die Herrlichkeit wird in den Sitten,
> Nicht in den Schätzen seyn: so verbindet sie Siege mit Siegen,
> Und so wird der niedrige Staat zum Beherrscher der Erde.

[320] Baechtold, *Tagebuch,* p. 199.
[321] *Pol. Schauspiele,* II, 73-157.

Romans and the human race."[322] A single review, again by Klotz, appeared in 1769; it was restricted to a selection of events from the play, chosen with the purpose of ridiculing the theme and Bodmer's treatment.[323] Klotz' characterization of the work as a "puppet-show" is not fair, although the satirical attack on Bodmer's exaggeration of Nero's artistic talents is justifiable.

The play deals with the suicide of Nero in 68 A.D. The tyrant appears following a conversation between Silius Italicus and Flavius Sabinus, in which they lament the emperor's despotic actions and see salvation for Rome in the election of Galba as its ruler. Nero welcomes the report of Julius Vindex's revolution in Gaul as an opportunity to plunder that province and thus to replenish his depleted treasury. He does not realize the seriousness of this uprising, for he is firmly convinced that he is protected against downfall until his seventy-third year by the prophecy of an oracle. Nor does he attach any importance to the report of his freedman Phaon that the streets of Rome are being filled with libelous handbills. He is, however, incensed and determines to investigate. When his secretary Epaphroditus brings a tablet announcing the revolt of the legions in Spain, he loses his temper, but is calmed when presented with an ivory carving, on which is depicted a Roman soldier dragging a dead Gaulish soldier by the hair. Aroused by the revolutionary spirit abroad in the city, he plots revenge. He orders the conscription of more men and wealth, while his unsettled brain contemplates violence against the senators and the destruction of the city by fire. But with the arrival of the report that the guards have abandoned the palace, Nero decides to flee and orders the imperial fleet to be ready to sail. Temporary refuge is sought in Phaon's villa in Salaria, where the last act takes place. When he arrives, the despot protests in vain against the bare, unpretentious quarters and service and longs for his sumptuous palace, but finds some consolation in the love of Acte, a woman who has followed him into exile, and also in

[322] Bodmer to Schinz, July 30, 1777, MS ZBZ.: "Die Handlung im Nero ist die despotische Trunkenheit, wormit er die Römer und das menschliche Geschlecht verachtet." The additions: "Zusätze zu dem Drama Nero," *Literarische Denkmale* (Zürich: Orell, Geßner, Füßli und Comp., 1779), pp. 154-63.

[323] *Deutsche Bibliothek*, III (1769), 403-07.

his own singing and cither-playing. Phaon brings a report that the senate has accused Nero of high treason and has sentenced him to death by flogging. The tramp of horses bearing those in search of the emperor indicates that discovery is imminent, and finally Nero summons enough courage to stab himself. In the addition to the play, Acte collects his ashes and deposits them in their final resting place.

In treating the theme Bodmer has taken many of his facts and incidents from Suetonius' *Nero*. From this source come Nero's decision to fill his depleted treasury by a thorough pillage of Gaul, because it revolted,[324] as well as his order to punish Vindex by decree of the senate, mainly because he had criticized the emperor's ability as a poet and singer.[325] Bodmer has woven into Nero's speech the saying attributed to him by the Latin biographer: "A humble art affords us daily bread."[326] The despot's confidence in his mastery over the city while adverse events point to his downfall, is based on the oracle's report in Suetonius that Nero should have no concern for his power until he had reached his seventy-third year.[327] He is enraged at the grumbling of the people, especially as expressed in certain lampoons which were being circulated about him. He is compared to the matricides Orestes and Alcmeon, as in Suetonius, who quotes them in Greek:

Drey fluchwürdige Nahmen, Orest, Alkmäon und Nero!
Mörder der Frau, die sie an das Licht des Tages gebohren!

A second one runs: "Nero erwürgte die Braut, und die neue Braut war die Mutter!"[328] The effect of the carving in ivory, of a monument in the Latin, with the favorable interpretation which Nero attaches to it is a paraphrase of the report in Suetonius.[329] Bodmer has also portrayed the emperor's desire for revenge on the insubordinate Gauls after the manner of his source. He orders

[324] Bodmer, *Nero*, I, 2, p. 82. Suetonius *Nero* XL. 4.
[325] Bod., I, 2, p. 88. Suet., XLI. 1.
[326] Bod., I, 2, p. 90. Suet., XL. 2.
[327] Bod., I, 2, p. 91. Suet., XL. 3. Bodmer mistakes the age of the prophecy, giving it as sixty-three instead of seventy-three, but has used the correct number in *Brittannicus* (p. 27).
[328] Bod., I, 3, p. 92. Suet., XXXIX. 2.
[329] Bod., I, 4, p. 103. Suet., XLI. 2.

the conscription of men and money for the campaign and disregards the people's displeasure with such levies;[330] he commands that his women be taken along, with their hair trimmed in the fashion of men and equipped as soldiers.[331] Nor has the Swiss author neglected to mention the emperor's insane intention of poisoning the senators at a banquet, or setting fire to the city, and of releasing the wild beasts of the royal zoological garden in order to hinder any efforts to extinguish the fire.[332]

As in the Latin historian's account, so in the German drama, calamity soon befalls the ruler, and Bodmer follows his source here step by step. The semi-starved populace rises in indignation when it learns that a ship, reported as bringing grain from Alexandria, discharges at Ostia a cargo of sand for the wrestling floor in the palace.[333] After the revolt of the army, Nero summons the officers of the Praetorian guard and orders the fleet to be prepared for instant departure,[334] but as in the Latin account, the guards abandon their posts in the palace.[335] Both the emperor's first thought to drown himself in the Tiber[336] and his decision to accept Phaon's villa are found in Suetonius.[337] Bodmer's description of the Golden House in Rome, which Nero contrasts with the primitive quarters of Phaon's dwelling, is a good passage with which to illustrate Bodmer's use of Suetonius in paraphrase:

How these black walls, these tables, these knotty-wooded floors differ from those panelings, striped with inlaid designs of ebony and tortoise shells! How different this room is from those dining halls, where the ceilings of sumptuous art-work opened at my bidding to sprinkle down upon my table, now delicate flowers in all shapes and forms, now aromatic essences and gummy perfumes! There I had a house in which the spirit of one's body could live in style.[338]

[330] Bod., II, 1, p. 105. Suet., XLIV. 1 f.
[331] Bod., II, 2, pp. 113 f. Suet., XLIV. 1.
[332] Bod., II, 2, pp. 108 f. Suet., XLIII. 1.
[333] Bod., II, 3, pp. 115 f. Suet., XLV. 1.
[334] Bod., II, 4, p. 119. Suet., XLVII. 1.
[335] Bod., II, 4, p. 118. Suet., XLVII. 3.
[336] Bod., II, 6, p. 122. Suet., XLVII. 3.
[337] Bod., II, 6, p. 123. Suet., XLVIII. 1.
[338] Bod., III, 1, p. 126: "Wie ungleich sind diese schwarzen Wände, diese Tischbretter, diese knorrichte Fußboden jenen Vertäfelungen, die ganz mit eingelegter Arbeit von Ebenholz und Schildkröten durchstreift waren; jenen Speisesälen, wo

Nero's end corresponds in both versions; he is declared a traitor to his country and is condemned to die by being stripped and flogged with his neck in a fork.[339] All hope of rescue is lost when, his horse rearing, his covered face is exposed to recognition.[340] As the tramp of his captor's horse is heard, he stabs himself,[341] after urging his companions not to allow his head to be severed from the trunk of his body.[342] In these borrowings from Suetonius, Bodmer has used the material noted above in close paraphrases of the Latin.

Bodmer wished to give a clear picture of the despotic excesses of Nero and has pointed all his material to this end. He has exaggerated the emperor's egotistical confidence in his artistic talents. The frequent occasions on which Nero takes up his cither and sings verses, when he should be considering the weighty facts of a national crisis, are used to make this appear as the real cause of his overthrow. When the news of the revolt in Gaul arrives, Nero thinks it unimportant, but he is sorely offended by Vindex' criticism of his voice. Even in flight he consoles himself with his verse, boasting: "My head is a repository where the muses have gathered their sweetest treasure."[343] Coupled with this vain egotism is also his cruelty, which is strongly emphasized. Contrary to the statement of Suetonius, Bodmer's Nero orders the punishment of the authors of the libelous sheets which have been posted about Rome. When the people demur at the conscription of men and money, he seeks revenge: "The human race must feel my anger."[344] Bodmer's judgment of Nero is best summed

die Decke von palladischer Kunst auf meine Winke sich öffnete, bald Frühlingsblumen von allen Gestalten und Fragen, bald balsamische Essenzen und Gummi auf meine Tafel herabzugießen! Dort hatt' ich ein Haus, in welchem ein Geist, der im Körper lebt, noch ohne Schande wohnen könnte." Suet., XXXI. 2: "In ceteris partibus cuncta auro lita, distincta gemmis unionumque conchis erant; cenationes laqueatae tabulis eburneis versatilibus, ut flores, fistulatis, ut unguenta desuper spargerentur. . . . Eius modi domum cum absolutam dedicaret, hactenus comprobavit, ut se diceret quasi hominem tandem habitare coepisse."

[339] Bod., III, 3, p. 141; 4, p. 151. Suet., XLIX. 2.

[340] Bod., III, 3, p. 142. Suet., XLVIII. 2.

[341] Bod., III, 4, p. 156. Suet., XLIX. 3.

[342] Bod., III, 4, p. 153. Suct., XLIX. 4.

[343] Bod., III, 1, p. 137: "Mein Haupt ist ein Magazin, wo die Musen ihre süßesten Schäze gesammelt haben."

[344] Bod., II, 2, p. 108: "Das Geschlecht der Menschen muß meinen Zorn fühlen."

up in the words of the officer on finding the dead emperor: "His cruelty and his wantonness have done away with him."[345] With this conclusion the author sets the seal of moral condemnation on the despot.

The figure of the freedwoman Claudia Acte, introduced as a solace to Nero during his last hours at Salaria, has a certain basis in history, but is developed quite independently. She is presented as the only woman who loved Nero for himself and her affection is in some measure a substitute for his loss of power and wealth. Bodmer developed this motive further in the addition to the play. Here Acte repeats her love for Nero and collects the ashes of the man "who forgot in my arms that he was the master of the world."[346] In history she appears as the person who was responsible for the final breach between Nero and his mother Agrippina. Inasmuch as Bodmer has not concerned himself with the complications of Nero's family, Acte's part in the play seems to have little connection with the rest of the plot, and merely introduces a sentimental note into the grim tragedy of the tyrant's end.

SUMMARY

In reviewing Bodmer's treatment of political themes it becomes clear that he followed his sources closely, as usual, and selected from them two types of characters, both of which illustrate the inner experience he derived from his study of ancient historians. The supporters of democracy and republicanism constitute the first type, and the elevation of these patriotic spirits to a place of distinction as directors of the destiny of history represents Bodmer's own political ideals. The treatment which he gives to each of these figures justifies Bodmer's thesis regarding such men as Cicero, Paetus, Caius Gracchus, Timoleon, and Pelopidas, namely, that from the deeds and ideals in each specific case a general truth is to be derived. It is a political truth and may be phrased in general terms: Freedom of political thought and self determination of political organization is inherent in the nature

[345] Bod., III, 5, p. 157: "Seine Grausamkeit, seine Leichtfertigkeit haben ihn fortgeschaffet."

[346] Zusätze zu dem Drama Nero, loc. cit., p. 163: "der in meinen Armen vergaß, daß er Herr des Erdkreises war."

and existence of all men, and the democratic organism, the republic, resulting from this attitude must be defended at all costs, even at the expense of life itself. Ancient history had vitality and interest for Bodmer in so far as the organization of society conformed with his political creed. In *Cicero* the emphasis has fallen lightly upon him as a champion of political freedom, but more directly upon him as a thinker. *Thrasea Pätus* is to be regarded as one of the best plays from which to study the expression of Bodmer's political ideal, while *Caius Gracchus* is equally important as the best statement of the doctrine of popular rights and the need of the people for proper guidance in the establishment and preservation of their rights. The weakest of all the plays as a political drama is *Brutus und Kassius Tod*. A possible explanation for this may be that it was written in 1781, twenty years after Bodmer's first political drama, *Marcus Brutus*, at a time when death was approaching and political thoughts probably no longer stirred the author as they had in 1761. Cicero, Paetus, and Gracchus are more passive figures than Brutus, Timoleon, and Pelopidas. This difference is reflected most directly in the plots of the latter group against despotism and their bold execution of the tyrants. The dramas dealing with Brutus, Timoleon, and Pelopidas are no less idealistic in their aims than those in which Cicero, Paetus, and Gracchus appear as central figures, but they are more energetic and forceful in their action. If the former are dynamic figures, then the latter are static, but the underlying ideology is the same.

In these works Bodmer has been successful in recapturing the spirit of his sources within the limits of the material selected, but he has a tendency to repeat and this detracts somewhat from the interest of some of the plays. For instance, the assassination of Julius Caesar is treated in two plays, and although Bodmer attempts consciously to give a different emphasis in each of these, he is unable to avoid the repetition of certain parts of the material. This is also true of the repetition of similar phrases used by characters to attack despotism or to defend democracy.

The next type of character used by Bodmer complements that which has just been described. It includes the despots, who are attacked as the usurpers of democratic rights and powers. From his treatment of such figures as Caesar, Nero, and Tarquin, Bodmer preaches against despots in general, and he has not endowed any one of these with any laudable virtues whatever. The conquests and military ability of Caesar are forgotten in the effort to convey to the reader the evil nature of his ambition; the services of Tarquin in improving the civic beauty of Rome and in enlarging the boundaries of the country are minimized in the effort to show the defects of the monarchical system. Such an interpretation of the facts of history indicates how intensely Bodmer felt the source of ancient history as a means of discrediting the Eighteenth Century conception of government by an individual or a small group of vested interests. Of the three plays, *Julius Cäsar, Nero,* and *Tarquinius Superbus,* the first ranks highest as a convincing attack on this type of ruler, not because this play has any more aesthetic merit than the others, but because Caesar was for Bodmer the arch-despot of antiquity, and the attack is therefore more vehement and prosecuted with greater sincerity of purpose than is the case with either Nero or Tarquin. These three plays represent the negative side of Bodmer's interest in antiquity.

VI

POEMS

Although Bodmer had made translations from ancient authors
as early as 1752, it is the decade from 1770 to 1780 that stands
out as a period devoted to this interest. In these years he completed and published his translation of Homer (1778), and brought
out also a rendering of Apollonius' *Argonauts* (1779). In addition he made a number of shorter translations which were not
published until after his death.[1] This interest is further reflected
in several poems in hexameters, in which Bodmer undertakes to
retell more or less in his own words certain legends from antiquity.
These poems have no such tendentious purpose as most of the
dramas, and the themes attracted Bodmer mostly because of
their literary merit. Chronologically, the composition of five of
the seven poems treated here falls in the years 1771 and 1773,
when Bodmer was engaged in his translation of Homer, and this
work undoubtedly led him to select the hexameter as the meter
best suited to his purpose. Our aim in introducing this material
is to show briefly the nature of the subject-matter and where
Bodmer found it, rather than to make a critical study of his style
and meter.

In 1767 Bodmer published *Monima* in uneven hexameters.[2]
It deals with Plutarch's report of the marriage of Mithridates,
King of Pontus (†63 B.C.), to the Milesian beauty Monimé and
with her death as a result of his command, when he fled before
victorious Lucullus at Cabira.[3] The poem is built up of several
descriptions: the beauty of Monimé, the courtship of the king,
the years of his wife's unhappy marriage, the rout of Mithridates'
forces by Lucullus, and the death of Monimé. The first and third
of these descriptive pictures are more original than the others,
which are narrative and follow Plutarch closely. Bodmer differs

---

[1] Cf. the appendix for a complete list of Bodmer's translations from ancient
authors.
[2] J. J. Bodmer, *Calliope* (Zürich: Orell, Geßner und Comp., 1767), II, 381-86.
[3] Plut. *Lucullus* XVIII. 2 ff.

from his source only in his conception of Monimé as a "sacrifice to devout obedience," for she agrees to become queen only because her ambitious father commands her to do so. Her heroic death stands out as the element in the theme that attracted Bodmer most.

In 1777 Bodmer brought out three more poems: *Evadne, Kreusa,* and *Telemach und Nausikaa.*[4] Concerning them he wrote Gotter: "They have been printed for friends only and are to be regarded as manuscripts."[5]

Evadne was written in 1773.[6] The author had no illusions about its success, for he told Schinz that the Germans were too unlike the Greeks to appreciate it.[7] Early in November, 1776, he reported to the same correspondent that it was in the hands of the compositor.[8] He pointed to the *Suppliants* of Euripides as his source, but we shall see that this drama did not supply all of the material.[9] *Evadne* is a narrative poem in hexameters and tells the story of the suicide of the heroine because she wished to be united in death with her husband Capaneus, one of the seven chiefs who fought against Thebes. The first half of the poem describes the fighting before the city and is based largely on the *Phoenician Maidens* of Euripides, from which Bodmer has copied quite faithfully the description of the bravery of Parthenopaeus in battle.[10] Likewise the account of Polyneices' attack on the Fountain Gate is modelled on the Greek,[11] and the description of the attack by Arcas, his cry for brands with which to fire the city, and his end when his

[4] *Evadne; und, Kreusa. Zwey griechische Gedichte.* Zürich: Bürgklische Drukerey, 1777. In the appendix, with special pagination, appears *Telemach.* The latter was printed without place or date and is also called *Nausikaa;* it was written in 1771. Baechtold, *Tagebuch,* p. 202. At the end of 1776 Bodmer sent it to Schinz. Bodmer to Schinz, Dec. 27, 1776, MS ZBZ.

[5] Bodmer to Gotter, May, 1777, G. K. Jenny, *Miltons Verlornes Paradies in der deutschen Literatur des 18. Jahrhunderts* (St. Gallen: Zollikofer, 1890), p. 96.

[6] Baechtold, *Tagebuch,* p. 203.

[7] Bodmer to Schinz, Feb. 18, 1773, MS ZBZ.: "Evadne ist so griechisch und die Deutschen sind so ungriechisch . . . daß sie all für unsere Zeiten, Sitten und unsern Geschmack unpassend und fremd wird verworfen werden."

[8] Bodmer to Schinz, Nov. 5, 1776, MS ZBZ.

[9] Bodmer to J. G. Schulthess, March 14, 1776, MS ZBZ.: "Die Geschichte der Evadne, des Ion . . . und bey nahe alles, den Plan ausgenommen, liegen in Euripides IKETIΔEΣ und sein Sohn Ion ist der Kreusa Sohn von Apollo."

[10] Bodmer, *Evadne,* p. 6. Euripides *Phoenician Maidens* 1104 ff.

[11] Bod., p. 7. Eurip., 1123 ff.

head is crushed under the impact of Periclymenus' shield are paraphrased closely from this source.[12] Bodmer translates freely the passage in Euripides which describes the death of Capaneus;[13] he scales the wall, enraged and defying Zeus, but just as he reaches the top of the rampart, the bolt hurled by Zeus strikes him and his flaming body is thrown earthward. In other details of the battle Bodmer has recast the original into German freely, as for instance in the interpretation of Zeus' fire-bolt as an omen of defeat of the Argives,[14] and the single combat between the two brothers Eteocles and Polyneices.[15]

The last half of the poem is modelled on the *Suppliants* of Euripides. It tells of the campaign of Theseus undertaken against Thebes to recover the bodies of the slain chiefs and ends with the death of Evadne. The appearance of the women, led by King Adrastus, at the temple of Ceres is described as in the original.[16] Evadne enters the scene when the recovered bodies are about to be burned on a huge funeral pyre; in the German the passage describing her appearance is handled quite freely.[17] This is also true of her lamentation over her husband's body and her desire to be united with him in death. A typical illustration of Bodmer's adaptation of the original is presented in the following description of Evadne's appearance:

> Der Brand, wo der Leib lag,
> Welcher von Jovis Feuer versengt war, lehnt' an den Fuß sich
> Eines Felsen, der über ihm thürmt'. Auf dem Gipfel des Felsen,
> Über den Rand hervorgebeugt, wie ein Vogel zum fliegen,
> Stand ein fürstliches Weib.[18]

[12] Bod., p. 8. Eurip., 1153 ff.
[13] Bod., p. 8. Eurip., 1172 ff.
[14] Bod., p. 9. Eurip., 1187 ff.
[15] Bod., pp. 9 f. Eurip., 1223 ff., 1377 ff.
[16] Bod., p. 12. Euripides *Suppliants* 95 ff.
[17] Bod., p. 17. Eurip., 980 ff., 1045 ff.
[18] Bod., p. 17. Eurip., 984 ff., 1045 ff.:

> Evadne the princess renowned!
> On yon cliff why is she found
> Whose crags above this fane tower?
>   .   .   .
>
> Here am I on the rock.
> Even as a bird, my father, hang I poised
> In misery o'er the pyre of Capaneus.

(The translation is that of A. S. Way in the "Loeb Classical Library.")

Thus Bodmer's version varies from close adherence to Euripides
to freer treatment at times by the use of loose paraphrases of the
original.

Kreusa, also in hexameters, was written in February, 1773.[19]
It was also dependent on Euripides, as Bodmer wrote Sulzer,[20]
being the story of *Ion.* Ion has been abandoned by his mother
and brought up in the god's temple at Delphi. Years later, as the
barren wife of Xuthus, Creusa journeys to the temple. Here Ion's
identity is established, after the mother barely escapes death at
his hands. Bodmer follows his source, paraphrasing, translating
freely, and summarizing. Thus in the description of the temple
he has taken over directly from Euripides the picture of the
stricken dragon Enceladus and the mention of Castaly's fountain,[21]
while the passage in which Ion first addresses his mother and her
reply are paraphrases.[22] The story of Creusa's life, as developed
in the dialogue and narrated by Bodmer, differs in no essential
details in the two versions.[23] A good passage to illustrate Bodmer's borrowings is that where Creusa proves to Ion by means of
three articles that she is his mother: a piece of weaving by her,
a figure of a serpent with golden jaws, and an olive wreath:

Ein unvollendetes Kleid, in der Mitte die Gorgon gestiket,
Um der Aegide Rand die lokigten Schlangen gewunden.

.   .   .

Dann Antiken, geschmiedete Schlangen, die Schnäbel von Golde.

.   .   .

Endlich ein Kranz von dem Zweige des Baumes, den Pallas erschaffen,
Welcher, noch nicht verwelkt, die grünen Blätter noch hatte.[24]

[19] Baechtold, *Tagebuch,* p. 203.
[20] Bodmer to Sulzer, Nov. 9, 1774, MS ZBZ.
[21] Bodmer, *Kreusa,* p. 20. Euripides *Ion* 209 f., 144 ff.
[22] Bod., p. 20. Eurip., 237 ff.
[23] Bod., p. 21. Eurip., 260 ff.
[24] Bod., p. 35. Eurip., 1417 ff.:

> See there the web I wove in girlhood's days.
>
> .   .   .
>
> No perfect work; 'twas but a prentice hand.
>
> .   .   .
>
> A Gorgon in the mid-threads of a shawl.
>
> .   .   .
>
> 'Tis fringed with serpents—with the Aegis-fringe.
>
> .   .   .

Telemach is a fairly short poem based on the sixth book of the *Odyssey*. On the day following the departure of Odysseus from the land of the Phaeacians, Nausicaa is wandering along the shore, lost in reverie on his beauty and the memory of his visit. Telemachus appears suddenly and explains that he is in search of his father. He describes the arrogant behavior of the suitors toward Penelope. Nausicaa relates in some detail the visit of Odysseus to her shores, after which Telemachus resumes his journey. The poem is a loosely constructed narrative in which Bodmer has followed Homer in general outline. Telemachus and Nausicaa never meet in Homer, and Bodmer has introduced in the poem a modification for which he has no authority, nor does he seek to explain the reason for this freedom.

In 1778 Bodmer published two more poems on Greek themes, *Makaria des Euripides* and *Sigowin*.[25] The first of these is fairly short and was written hurriedly in two days in the year preceding its publication.[26] It is in hexameters and tells the story of Euripides' *Children of Hercules*. Under the leadership of Iolaus, they take refuge from Eurystheus, King of Argos, at the altar of Zeus in Marathon. They are defended by Demophon, and to insure victory, Macaria is sacrificed to Ceres in accordance with the demand of the oracle. The relation of the poem to its source is even closer than is the case with those previously discussed.[27] The refusal of Demophon to deliver the children to Eurystheus is a paraphrase from the Greek play,[28] but the speech of Macaria, as she enters the scene, is a free translation which condenses the demand of the oracle as spoken by Iolaus.[29] How Bodmer handled

---

Serpents, an old device, with golden jaws—

. . .

A wreath of olive set I on thee then:
Athena brought it first unto our rock.
If this be there, it hath not lost its green,
But blooms yet.

[25] J. J. Bodmer, *Drey epische Gedichte. Makaria. Sigowin. und Adelbert*. Zürich: Orell, Geßner, Füßli und Comp., 1778.

[26] Baechtold, *Tagebuch*, p. 206.

[27] Cf. Olga Franke, *Euripides bei den deutschen Dramatikern des achtzehnten Jahrhunderts*. "Das Erbe der Alten," 2. Reihe, Nr. 16 (Leipzig: Dieterich'sche Verlagsbuchhandlung, 1929), p. 160.

[28] Bodmer, *Makaria*, p. 8. Euripides *Children of Hercules* 464 ff.

[29] Bod., p. 9. Eurip., 474 ff.

this material may be illustrated by a few lines from the heroic speech of Macaria in which she offers herself as a sacrifice to placate the goddess:

> Ich zeug', ich betheure,
> Daß ich um meiner Brüder, um mein selbst willen ersterbe!
> Ohne Verlangen zu leben, ist mir in meine Gedanken
> Aufgestiegen, des schönen, des würdigen Todes zu sterben.[30]

A similar adherence to the original marks the farewell admonitions of the heroine before the sacrifice.[31] The long report of the battle, given by a servant in Euripides, is paraphrased with especial emphasis on Hyllus' offer to settle the issue by single combat, which is refused by Eurystheus, the rejuvenation of Iolaus in answer to his prayer to Zeus, and Iolaus' capture of Eurystheus.[32] In these and other details Bodmer has rendered the play of the Greek dramatist into a narrative poem which may be described as a very free translation or a fairly close paraphrase.

Sigowin. Nach Homers Μνηστηροφονία is a long poem in hexameters[33] and goes back in composition to July, 1771, when Bodmer wrote to Schinz that he wanted a copyist for his manuscript. He hoped to achieve in it the same moral aim, as he said, which Homer had in mind in writing the *Odyssey*.[34] Baechtold has given the contents of the poem and has pointed out that Bodmer has followed step by step Homer's story of the slaughter of the suitors.[35] The truth of this statement is evident from even a casual comparison, but Bodmer has substituted German names for the Greek figures throughout. The description in the German of the demoralized situation brought about by the licentious suitors at

---

[30] Bod., p. 11. Eurip., 531 ff.:

> Yea, I pledge me now
> For these my brothers' sake, and mine, to die.
> For treasure-trove most fair, by loving not
> Life, have I found,—with glory to quit life.

[31] Bod., p. 12. Eurip., 574 ff.

[32] Bod., pp. 13 f. Eurip., 800 ff.

[33] *Drey ep. Gedichte,* pp. 16-49.

[34] Bodmer to Schinz, Aug. 22, 1771, MS ZBZ.: "Warum fragen Sie mich nicht, was für einen moralischen Nutzen ich mit diesem Gedichte vorhabe? Wenn ich Ihnen antwortete, daß er der Nutzen wäre, den Homer mit der Odyssee vorgehabt hat, so würden Sie vielleicht einwenden, daß wir diesen nicht mehr nöthig haben." Cf. also Bodmer to Schinz, Nov. 5, 1776, MS ZBZ.: "Sigowin hat so viel von Homer, daß er die Verurtheilung der Odyssee ist, wenn er verurtheilt wird."

[35] Baechtold, *Gesch. d. d. Lit. i. d. Schweiz,* pp. 622 f.

Fredegunde's palace is modelled largely on the report which Odysseus receives from Eumaeus.[36] Sigowin's disclosure of his identity to his son Manfred follows that of Odysseus to Telemachus,[37] and Sigowin's plan for vengeance on the suitors is a paraphrase of that of Odysseus.[38] Bodmer has summarized Homer's description of the treatment which Odysseus, in the disguise of a beggar, receives during the banquet,[39] as well as that of Fredegunde's visit to the banquet hall and her words to her son Manfred, which correspond to those spoken at the appearance of Penelope among the wooers.[40] In telling of the revelry of the suitors and the taunts which are hurled at Sigowin, the Swiss author follows the Greek epic poet more freely, as is best illustrated in the insulting speech of Eberwin's sister:

> Ich vermuthe,
> Eine Bräms' hat den alten Mann in die Nase gestochen,
> Welcher so unverschämt zu der Tafel der Herren sich zudrängt,
> Und uns itzt Lehren giebt, die ihn ein Mucker gelehrt hat;
> Oder er hat die Schmähsucht im vollen Becher getrunken.
> Packe dich in dein Loch, das Nest des Bettelgesindes,
> Dort verdünste den Wein, der dich so grob und so frech macht.[41]

The actual slaughter of the suitors by Sigowin goes back directly to Bodmer's source.[42] Only the minstrel Münegüre and the cupbearer Steinmar, in Homer the minstrel Terpes and the herald Medon, are spared because Manfred intercedes for them.[43] Interesting is the German medieval setting which Bodmer has given to the Homeric story. The names are not translations but are selected apparently for their suggestion of knighthood and romance. Thus Odysseus becomes Sigowin of Thurheim, Eumaeus

---

[36] Bodmer, *Sigowin*, p. 20. Homer *Odyssey* XVI. 68-128.
[37] Bod., pp. 21 f. Homer, XVI. 186-200.
[38] Bod., p. 23. Homer, XVI. 267-83.
[39] Bod., pp. 25 ff. Homer, XVII. 327-430.
[40] Bod., pp. 28 f. Homer, XVIII. 206-25.
[41] Bod., p. 31. Homer, XVIII. 327 ff.: Wretched stranger, thou art but a crack-brained fellow, unwilling to go to a smithy to sleep, or to a common lodge, but pratest here continually, unabashed in the company of many lords, and hast no fear at heart. Surely wine has mastered thy wits, or else thy mind is ever thus, that thou dost babble idly. (The translation is that of A. T. Murray in the "Loeb Classical Library.")
[42] Bod., pp. 43-45. Homer, XXII. 1-88.
[43] Bod., pp. 46 f. Homer, XXII. 344-74.

is turned into Lütold, Penelope into Fredegunde, and Telemachus receives the name of Manfred, while the goatherd Melanthius becomes Eberwin. Antinous is Wolfbrand of Balme and Leiodes corresponds to Hugo of Liebefels. The baptizing of ancient personnel with German names is accompanied by a shift of scene to the full Middle Ages. Sigowin is represented as returning from a pilgrimage to the Holy Land. In line with this Bodmer made his most important change in the narrative by substituting for the trial of the bow in Homer a shooting contest. The target is a dove fastened to the end of a pole. No one of the suitors hits it until the last one, Wolfbrand of Balme, severs the bird's bond with his shot. It then flies into the air and is immediately attacked by a bird of prey, which Manfred kills with a clever shot. The dove alights on the shoulder of Sigowin. Wolfbrand claims the hand of Fredegunde as his prize; this is contested by Manfred, and thus the immediate cause for the slaughter of the suitors is given.

A curious mixture of Greek and Hebrew legend is Bodmer's poem in hexameters *Menelaus bey David*, which was written in May, 1781,[44] and published in the following year.[45] In it Menelaus, driven by storms, appears at David's camp. He relates the story of his family and his experiences, and hears in return the story of Israel and its religion. He aids David in a successful expedition against raiders who have carried off David's women. The Greek warrior receives a goblet studded with precious stones and presents David with a pearl necklace. The virtues of Israel's god give Menelaus cause for some doubt about the superiority of the Greek gods. Finally, after a great farewell ceremony, he sails for Argos.[46] The poem demonstrates again Bodmer's lack of epic gifts, but is interesting as a rare attempt in German literature to bring together figures from antiquity and the Old Testament. One aspect of the narrative is striking for originality of treatment: Menelaus' faltering in his faith in the Greek gods. He is plunged into doubt when he hears a priest extol the superiority of Jehovah, and thinks

[44] Baechtold, *Tagebuch*, p. 212.

[45] In the appendix to Bodmer's *Der Levit von Ephraim* (Zürich: Orell Geßner, Füßli und Comp., 1782), pp. 35-56.

[46] Cf. Baechtold, *Gesch. d. d. Lit. i. d. Schweiz*, pp. 623 f.

that David's victory over the marauders is due largely to the god's help. In comparison with the grandeur of the Hebrew conception, the gods of Greece seem to be a lawless crew indeed:

Wie kann ich glauben den Unsinn,
Habe Latona, des Iovis vermählte, gebohren, und kann ich
Tantalus Mahlzeit glauben, der seinen Sohn in der Schüssel
Aufgetragen, zur Speise den Göttern? Ich kann es nicht denken,
Daß solch Böses sich mit der göttlichen Güte vertrage.[47]

After this statement, however, no further mention is made of Menelaus' lack of faith in his Greek gods. If Bodmer hoped to recapture the Homeric tone in this poem, his effort was certainly far from successful.

With the exception of *Telemach* and *Menelaus*, these poems document further Bodmer's interest in the heroic element of ancient literature; and the selection of women to exemplify his heroism, as in *Monima, Evadne, Kreusa,* and *Makaria*, is in line with his emphasis on their importance, as we have observed in the case of the dramas. The poems have little connection with the author's selection and treatment of history and legend in the dramatic form, except, perhaps, Sigowin, whose revenge on the suitors Bodmer regarded in the ethical light of a triumph of the good over the bad. *Telemach, Sigowin,* and *Menelaus* grew out of the author's rendering of Homer, and the first two of these may be regarded, along with the drama *Patroclus,* as preparation for the larger work of translating the great epic into German. In form the hexameter is common to all the poems and its use is under the influence of Homer.

[47] *Menelaus,* p. 53.

VII

CONCLUSION: BODMER'S INTERPRETATION OF THE ANCIENT WORLD

In his use of ancient material Bodmer makes no distinction in the treatment of legend as distinguished from history. He adopts without discrimination the legendary material which had been treated by Sophocles in *Oedipus* and the more historical material of Herodotus in *Die Rettung in den Mauern von Holz*. Without concerning himself about the accuracy of his source, he does not hesitate to write his *Ulysses* in imitation of the Italian play by Lazzarini, apparently without studying the legend as treated by ancient authors. On the other hand, he takes over and translates long passages from such a reputable historian as Livy in *Cato*. Between the legend and mythology of the poets on the one side and the annals and historical accounts on the other we find Bodmer's favorite source in the historical biography of Plutarch. The material in nine of the plays we have examined is taken in great measure from that author. In general, Bodmer took his material where he found it without any attempt to test its historical or literary historical accuracy.

Bodmer's power of invention is limited. This has become apparent in our study of his relation to his sources. His attitude toward ancient material is, in the main, that of a student of history who reads his texts, taking notes on those passages which interest him. For our author the selection falls upon the ethical and political side of antiquity, and this interest goes back to his youth. His prose style was influenced by this procedure. One may characterize it as learned, indeed pedantic, or at least so teeming with historical and mythological citations and allusions as to produce this impression. Often the classroom looms in the background, and repetition for the sake of emphasis is a common device. Histrionism, as we have seen, was not part of Bodmer's life or dramatic aims; its lack is reflected in the use of long, extended passages which could never captivate an audience. His language can make a claim to quaintness, but never to stylistic distinction. It is sometimes casual, often drab; and although it is seldom lacking in the seriousness of purpose that gives it emphasis, it never produces the tensity required of good drama.

One of the first general observations which strikes the reader of these plays is that their action is anecdotal, their style narrative and descriptive rather than dramatic or dynamic. Most of the plays are built around an incident, and the material which is used to bring out the main event is lacking in any convincing motivation. In *Timoleon* the event is the murder of Timophanes; but except for the appearance of Ceres to Timoleon, the whole play is a series of passages describing the attitude of the characters rather than a sequence of interrelated happenings. In *Pelopidas* the death of Archias is the main incident, and the scene for this is set almost at the beginning of the piece. When Charon is summoned to Archias' palace and the former's son enters into the action, the only effect thus produced is to provide an opportunity for the reiteration of the conspirators' pledge to do away with the tyrant. So in *Die Tegeaten* the action centers around the combat of the brothers, which Bodmer has borrowed as an anecdote from Plutarch, without any attempt to lead up to this by preparatory tension. Indeed, there is little trace of dramatic tension, *Spannung,* in any of his plays. In *Die Rettung in den Mauern von Holz* the anecdotal quality of the action is embodied in the fulfillment of a prophecy. In *Cicero* the author chooses the incident of the orator's death, without attempting to construct a dramatic sequence of events, while in *Cato* even the main anecdote, the repeal of the Oppian Law, is not introduced as part of the action, but merely forms the background for the spirited oratory of Cato, Valerius, and the women. In *Octavius Cäsar* even the anecdotal quality of the action is lost in the portrayal of the wrath of Augustus at the insulting accusations of his profligate daughter and granddaughter. In *Nero* the situation that forces the emperor to withdraw from Rome is fully developed before the play opens, and most of the text is devoted to a narration of his illogical reactions to the events. The theme in *Thrasea Pätus* is the description of his trial in the senate and there is no other action in the play. In *Brutus und Kassius Tod* there are two incidents: the appearance of Caesar's ghost to Brutus and the battle at Philippi, both of which are reported as anecdotes. In *Aristomenes* there are also two anecdotes: the plan to capture Sparta and the treachery of Aristocrates, but the first of these is not developed. *Patroclus* and *Julius Cäsar* have a more consecutive course of action and are less anecdotal; and this is also true of *Tarquinius Superbus*. To say that Bodmer's plays have an anecdotal quality means that he does not use a plot involving dramatic action, and this is quite in accord with his disagreement with Aristotle's emphasis upon action in the drama.

The characters are for Bodmer more important than the action. In presenting these he never undertakes to show a development within a given play, but seeks to portray and describe them as heroic figures who are either to be praised or condemned. The insistence upon the importance of the character runs through all Bodmer's writings, the critical as well as the dramatic. His technique in treating figures from antiquity is to select some aspect of a character and to illustrate this by means of biographical data. Thus Timoleon is characterized as a hater of tyrants and of base men, and this attitude governs his actions. This is likewise true of Pelopidas and his relations to the oligarch Archias. In *Die Tegeaten* Critolaus is portrayed as devoted to the welfare of the state, and Euphorion appears as the symbol of Athenian weakness in *Die Rettung in den Mauern von Holz*. Aristomenes and Patroclus are endowed with a spirit of bravery and loyalty. In every appearance of Caesar, Bodmer emphasizes his ambition for power, while Brutus appears as the defender of freedom and democracy. Cicero represents the caution of a contemplative man, who through his resignation and his belief in immortality looks to an after-life of freedom of thought and political beliefs. Cato is stamped as the harsh moralist who objects to luxury as a sign of decadence, while his opponent Lucius Valerius stands for equality in the sharing of Rome's wealth. Tarquin appears as the usurper of the people's rights; Junius Brutus is the champion of these rights. Augustus' character is portrayed as that of a libertine; Nero is pictured as a crazed poet, whose illusions of grandeur and genius cause him to neglect the demands of his office, while in *Brittannicus* he is hounded by fear and uncertainty. Paetus is a political martyr who is resigned to his fate at Nero's hands and Caius Gracchus is characterized by his faith in the people and their rights. With almost the first appearance of each of these characters his particular stamp is evident and all of his utterances and actions follow as expressions of this dominant trait. In this respect Bodmer exemplifies the attitude which he had set forth in his *Critische Betrachtungen,* where he stresses the value of character portrayal and considers Plutarch one of the outstanding masters in this treatment of historical figures. Bodmer's exploitation of character in his dramas was, as we have seen, a part of his program. Through this type of portrayal of heroic figures and their virtues or defects Bodmer sought to uplift the political morality and patriotic loyalty of his country. The result of his effort must have been insignificant; his plays were not widely read in his day, were never performed, and the adverse criticism of the reviewers did not help to spread their popularity.

The theme which appears most frequently in these dramas is the doctrine of democracy. For Bodmer the positive side of this political theme appears in the glorification of the figures of antiquity who stood for a republican form of government. In general such figures appear in the plays as plotters for the overthrow of dictatorship and tyranny. This is true of *Timoleon, Pelopidas, Julius Cäsar, Marcus Brutus, Tarquinius Superbus, Thrasea Pätus,* and *Cajus Gracchus.* The leaders of the rebellion in each conform to a type. Common to them all is the arraignment of tyranny, the thesis that a despotic state represents a betrayal of the people's freedom and is an autocratic usurpation of power founded upon intimidation and bolstered up by armed force. The conspirators are practical men, and the author does not allow them to delve deeply into the theoretical aspects of political organization. Their attitude is based on a common assumption, which is best expressed by Herennius: "Man is born free; freedom springs from his nature and it is his oldest right." In preaching democracy and freedom in the dramas on ancient themes Bodmer follows the same approach to historical material that he used in treating material from Swiss national history. In his manuscript drama *Die Schweizer über dir, Zürich* (1757) he symbolizes in the death of the patriotic burgomaster of Zurich, Stüssi, the high worth of freedom and the just claim of each part of the confederacy to its own rights, while his opponent Reding is the supporter of special privilege and of the suppression of equal rights. In his manuscript play *Rudolf Brun* (1758) Bodmer seeks to glorify another Swiss champion of the people's rights. Brun leads the people against the obstinate councilors, who are finally driven out of the city of Zurich, an historical event of 1336. In his version of the Tell story in *Die gerechte Zusammenschwörung*, which was written in 1761, Bodmer sets up an historical figure as the ideal supporter of people's rights.

The negative side of Bodmer's political picture is to be found in his attack on the autocratic figures of history. The tyrant Timophanes in *Timoleon* symbolizes the degradation of Corinth under a despot's rule, as Archias in *Pelopidas* represents a dissolute oligarchical government. Caesar is for Bodmer the worst tyrant and oppressor of democracy in antiquity and is introduced into several plays, where the author emphasizes persistently his greed for power. In *Nero* we have the picture of a tyrant who, half crazed by illusions of artistic genius, has lost all sympathy with the people under him and by his oppressive rule has destroyed the foundation and basis of a thriving political organism, namely a contented and willing populace. In *Gracchus* it is the senate as a class that bears the brunt of Bodmer's attack.

Rationalist that he was, Bodmer interpreted the aim of literature as didactic, and this applies also to his treatment of historical themes. As early as 1741 in the *Critische Betrachtungen* he had said that history, in describing ultimate truth, must also teach some useful lesson.[1] In addition to political democracy his dramas seek to deal with the moral aspect of antiquity. His thesis may be stated as follows: anti-democratic leaders in ancient political society exemplify in their moral character the degradation of manners and morals in their states. Or, expressed in other words, a decline in fundamental moral virtues and an excess of material

---

[1] P. 126: "Die Historie, die es [das Wahre] beschreibet, wie es ist, hat dabey den Endzweck, zu unterrichten, und zu nützen."

luxury make possible the rise of dictatorships and absolute despots. The Eighteenth Century should learn a lesson from antiquity. In speaking of the Epicurean attitude toward life as a contributory factor in Rome's decline, Bodmer wrote to Schinz: "A more potent cause was the enormous treasure of Greece and Athens. It brought about a hardening of conscience and contempt, not only for the gods, but also for honesty, loyalty, and faith."[2] It is impossible to understand Bodmer's treatment of history, especially Roman history, without taking into consideration his hatred of luxury as breeding political corruption. This attitude explains and conditions his selection of ancient themes. *Cato* is Bodmer's best attack on luxury, but *Octavius Cäsar* is also a condemnation of ancient society on moral grounds. In *Tarquinius Superbus* the rape of Lucretia by Sextus is treated as the immediate cause of the expulsion of the royal family. So, too, the moral degradation of Nero in the play of that name, and the capricious selfishness in *Thrasea Pätus* are presented as symptoms of the decadence that the author saw in despotism. This is less true of the Greek themes, although in *Pelopidas* Bodmer has used the riotous revelry of Archias as the background for the murder of the oligarchs. In *Aristomenes* he has chosen to make the bribery and treachery of Aristocrates the cause of Aristomenes' resignation to defeat. In so far as Bodmer's plays are an attack on the luxury of antiquity and its accompanying national effeteness on the negative side, and a glorification of simple virtues, social liberty, and political democracy on the positive side, just so far may Bodmer be considered a disciple of Rousseau, whose influence on his view of life cannot be denied.[3]

In addition to the characteristics of Bodmer's dramatic style discussed above, his plays show a remarkable fondness for dreams and prophecies. His admission of the world of spirits into poetry, especially in connection with Milton's use of angels and devils, is well known; for him these spirits belonged within the realm of the probable, and he admitted the use of such figures from what

---

[2] Bodmer to Schinz, Dec. 7, 1777, MS ZBZ.: "Eine mächtigere Ursache [des Sittenverfalls] waren die ungeheuren Schätze von Griechenland und Athen. Aber sie verursachten Verhärtung des Gewissens, Verachtung nicht nur der Götter, sondern der Redlichkeit, der Treue, des Glaubens."

[3] Cf. Betz, *op. cit.*, pp. 204 ff.

he termed the "invisible world" without respect to their contradiction of natural phenomena.[4] Both for this reason and as an attempt to recapture the spirit of ancient literature, Bodmer's use of oracles is not unnatural; the number of instances is nevertheless striking. Orestes in *Electra* is commissioned by an oracle to kill his mother. In *Ulysses* the sacrifice of Theodotus is ordered from Delphi, and Samgar, the priest, reports another prophecy to the effect that Ulysses would murder his own son and be guilty of incest with his own daughter. In *Oedipus* Laius comes in an apparition to his son, accusing him of the murder of his father. The goddess Ceres in *Timoleon* appears in order to persuade him to kill his brother Timophanes. The action in *Die Tegeaten* proceeds directly from the oracle's order to settle the issue by single combat; so also *Die Rettung in den Mauern von Holz* is built around a prophecy concerning the safety of Athens. Bodmer has used in *Julius Cäsar* omens of a sacrifice and warnings in two dreams, while a prophecy from Delphi foreshadows the victory of Junius Brutus over Tarquin in *Tarquinius Superbus*. It may be pointed out that Bodmer borrowed the dream motif for *Marcus Brutus* from Shakespeare in 1761, before Wieland began to publish his translations from the English. Due to the character of the mythological sources, the use of such prophecies is more frequent and more natural in the treatment of Greek themes than Roman themes.

In the main, while Bodmer has selected themes and motives that agreed with his own view of the world, he has not, as a rule, tampered with the *Weltanschauung* of the ancient world as reflected by its poets and historians. However, a few exceptions may be noted. In two of the earliest plays he introduces a rationalistic, if not a Christian, element into ancient ideology. In *Ulysses* Samgar approaches the revelations of ancient oracles with the skeptical mind of a rationalist. In the end he supports a belief in a god of forgiveness who is closer to the Christian deity than to a heathen god, and the words of an invisible angel comfort Ulysses. The prophet Teiresias in *Oedipus* revolts against the power of the ancient priests because it is based on obscurantism and orders Oedipus to obey his own reason rather than the priests. The reason to

[4] Cf. *Crit. Betrachtungen*, p. 591.

which Bodmer refers here is not the power of logic but a humanizing force that draws its vitality from man's soul. In the poem *Menelaus bey David*, as we have seen, Bodmer made a formal and unconvincing attempt to bring together the religious ideas of the Greeks and of the Old Testament. A similar attempt is recorded in *Brittannicus*, but the juxtaposition of these two religious attitudes is neither a serious effort nor is it far-reaching in its effect. It represents rather a liberalizing and humanizing of the material. This is also found in the increased attention paid by Bodmer to the women in his plays. In this emphasis he has given the material a new interpretation, especially in the themes from Roman history.

One cannot speak of a development in Bodmer as a writer of dramas. Our plays were written between the years 1759 and 1782; of the twenty-one plays considered in our study, four were written as early as 1759, two in 1762, and seven during the year 1764. It is obvious that one can hardly show any real development under conditions of such rapid composition. Those written in the years between 1761 and 1764 are all political in nature and reflect Bodmer's activity as the leading spirit of the "Historische-politische Gesellschaft zu Schumachern," where the type of theme treated in these political plays constituted a great part of the weekly discussions, which were pedagogical in purpose. There is then a logical relation between the political plays of Bodmer and his personal activity during this period, even if there is no development in Bodmer as a dramatist.

Finally, a question which arises in connection with the present study is that of Bodmer's relation to Winckelmann. Unfortunately there is little material to document an intimate contact between the two men. Baechtold does not bring Winckelmann into his account of Bodmer's life and works.[5] De Reynold states only that from the standpoint of aesthetic doctrine Winckelmann is a disciple of Bodmer.[6] At any rate the latter knew Winckelmann's *Geschichte*

[5] *Gesch. d. d. Lit. i. d. Schweiz:* this is still the most complete and authoritative treatment of Bodmer's life and works as a whole.

[6] *Op. cit.*, p. 641: he mentions only that both Eighteenth Century writers considered painting, poetry, and music as having the same purpose and method and that they differed only in the medium of expression.

der Kunst des Alterthums and borrowed from it in his *Octavius Cäsar*. In a letter to Schinz in 1765 Bodmer mentions quite incidentally Winckelmann's *Abhandlung von der Fähigkeit der Empfindung des Schönen in der Kunst* (1763).[7] In the summer of 1778 the Swiss patriarch read the *Monumenti antichi inediti spiegati ed illustrati* (1767) and was surprised, as he wrote Schinz, to learn that such critics as Scaliger had entertained false notions about the customs and clothing of the ancients, and that he himself had erred with them in translating Homer.[8] He admired in Winckelmann's work the drawings from Homer's epic and remarked that they would make excellent illustrations for his own translation. In another very interesting letter Bodmer erects a monument to the famous historian of ancient art on the occasion of reading Winckelmann's published letters to his friends in Switzerland.[9] He praises the revealing tone of these letters and expresses regret that he had not come personally into contact with their author. "I must deplore the fact," he says, "that no one has spoken to me of Winckelmann with the enthusiasm which his letters have produced in me. Had I been shown some of these letters, I would have become enthusiastic about him."[10] It is unfortunate for the development of Bodmer that the relations of these two men were not more intimate.

[7] Bodmer to Schinz, Nov. 28, 1763, MS ZBZ.

[8] Bodmer to Schinz, Aug. 26, 1778, MS ZBZ.

[9] Bodmer to Schinz, July 20, 1778, MS ZBZ. The reference is to Joh. Casp. Füßli, *Winckelmanns Briefe an seine Freunde in der Schweiz.* Zürich: Orell, Geßner, Füßli und Comp., 1778. There is no record of any correspondence between Bodmer and Winckelmann.

[10] Bodmer to Schinz, July 20, 1778, MS ZBZ.: "Ich muß klagen, daß man nicht mit der Wärme zu mir von Winckelmann gesprochen hat, in welche seine Briefe mich gesetzet haben; hätte man mir einige dieser Briefe gezeiget, ich wäre für ihn enthusiasmirt worden."

APPENDIX

1752 *Die geraubte Europa, von Moscus. Dieselbe von Nonnus.* n.d.
(cf. Baechtold, *Tagebuch,* p. 191.) That of Moscus reprinted
in Bodmer's *Calliope* (Zürich: Orell, Geßner und Comp., 1767),
II, 20-27. That of Nonnus in *Ibid.,* II, 28-32.

1753 *Die geraubte Helena, von Coluthus.* Zürich: Conrad Orell und
Comp., 1753. Reprinted in *Calliope,* II, 1-19.

1755 Passages from the *Odyssey:*
"Ulyssens Wiederkunft bei seinem Vater; aus der 24. Odyssee."
Odyssey XXIV. 204-412. J. J. Bodmer, *Fragmente in, der erzäh-
lenden Dichtart* (Zürich: Conrad Orell und Comp., 1755), pp. 1-
8.
"Telemachs Besuch bei Nestorn; aus der 3. Odyssee." *Ody.* III.
1-134. Bodmer, *Fragmente,* pp. 9-14.
"Telemach bei Menelaus; aus der 4. Odyssee." *Ody.* IV. 1-350.
Bodmer, *Fragmente,* pp. 15-27.
"Ulyssens Abschied von der Calypso; aus der 5. Odyssee." *Ody.*
V. 1-281. Bodmer, *Fragmente,* pp. 28-38.

1760 *Vierter Gesang; und Sechster Gesang der Ilias.* In Hexametern
übersetzt. Zürich: Conrad Orell und Comp., 1760.

1767 "Die ersten Gesänge der Ilias." Bodmer, *Calliope,* II, 157-306.
First six cantos.

1771 Horace *Odes* III. xi. J. J. Bodmer, *Der neue Adam* (Bern, 1771),
pp. 20-23.
Horace *Odes* II. i. Bodmer, *Der neue Adam,* pp. 24-27.

1778 *Homers Werke.* Aus dem Griechischen übersetzt von dem Dichter
der Noachide. Zürich: Orell, Geßner, Füßli und Comp., 1778.
2 vols.

1779 *Die Argonauten des Apollonius.* Zürich: Orell, Geßner, Füßli
und Comp., 1779.
"Juvenals fünfzehnte Satyre." J. J. Bodmer, *Literarische Denkmale* (Zürich: Orell, Geßner, Füßli, und Comp., 1779), pp. 87-
92.
"Der Aeneis erster Gesang." Bodmer, *Lit. Denkmale,* pp. 128-51.

1783 "Fragment aus dem V. Buch der Aeneis v. 604 folg. Der Brand
der Schiffe." *Bodmers Apollinarien,* hrsg. von Gotthold Friedrich
Stäudlin (Tübingen: Johann Georg Cotta, 1783), pp. 53-60.
Aeneid V. 604-84.
"Des Orpheus Höllenfahrt." *Bodmers Apollinarien,* pp. 76-81.
Vergil *Georgics* IV. 464-527.

"Verzeichnis der Schiffe im 2ten Gesang der Ilias." *Bodmers Apollinarien,* pp. 106-28. *Iliad* II. 527-759, 816-877.

"Dido in der Hölle." *Bodmers Apollinarien,* pp. 155-69. *Aeneid* IV. 1-172.

"Meleager." *Bodmers Apollinarien,* pp. 170-93. Ovid *Metam.* VIII. 271-546.

"Die Hochzeitfeier des Peleus." *Bodmers Apollinarien,* pp. 223-52. Catullus *Peleus and Thetis.*

"Der Tartarus." *Bodmers Apollinarien,* pp. 253-72. *Aeneid* VI. 426-665.

"Philemon und Baucis." *Bodmers Apollinarien,* pp. 273-81. Ovid *Metam.* VIII. 624-724.

"Medea." *Bodmers Apollinarien,* pp. 314-26. Ovid *Metam.* VII. 1-158.

BIBLIOGRAPHY

I. BODMER'S WORKS

(Only those treated in the text are listed.)

Aristomenes von Messenien. Bodmer, *Politische Schauspiele,* III, 187-256.

Atreus und Thyest. Bodmer, *Neue theatralische Werke,* pp. 137-311.

Brief-Wechsel von der Natur des poetischen Geschmackes. Zürich: Conrad Orell und Comp., 1736.

Brutus und Kassius Tod. Basel: Carl August Serini, 1782.

Cajus Gracchus, ein politisches Schauspiel. Zürich: David Bürgklj, 1773.

Cato, der Ältere, oder der Aufstand der römischen Frauen. Bodmer, *Neue theatralische Werke,* pp. 81-134.

Critische Abhandlung von dem Wunderbaren in der Poesie und dessen Verbindung mit dem Wahrscheinlichen. Zürich: Conrad Orell und Comp., 1740.

Critische Betrachtungen über die poetischen Gemählde der Dichter. Zürich: Conrad Orell und Comp., 1741.

Der Tod des Brittannicus. Ein Trauerspiel. MS ZBZ., 1764.

Die Discourse der Mahlern. Zürich: Joseph Lindinner, Bodmerische Druckerey, 1721-23. (with Breitinger) (Second edition: *Der Mahler der Sitten.* Zürich: Conrad Orell und Comp., 1746.)

Die Rettung in den Mauern von Holz. Bodmer, *Politische Schauspiele,* III, 113-86.

Die Schweizer über dir, Zürich (Stüssi). MS ZBZ., 1757.

Die Tegeaten. Bodmer, *Politische Schauspiele,* III, 8-110.

Drey neue Trauerspiele. Zürich: Heidegger und Compagnie, 1761.

Electra, oder die gerechte Übelthat. Ein Trauerspiel. Zürich: Conrad Orell und Comp., 1760.

Evadne; und, Kreusa. Zwey griechische Gedichte. Zürich: Bürgklische Druckerey, 1777. In the appendix: *Telemach und Nausikaa.* (special pagination)

Friederich von Tokenburg. Bodmer, *Drey neue Trauerspiele,* pp. 95-204.

Helvetische Bibliothek, bestehend in historischen, politischen und critischen Beyträgen zu den Geschichten des Schweitzerlands. Zürich: Conrad Orell und Comp., 1735-41. 6 Stücke.

Julius Cäsar, ein Trauerspiel. Leipzig: M. G. Weidmanns Erben und Reich, 1763.

Karl von Burgund, ein Trauerspiel. Schweizer-Journal, 6. Stück (1771), pp. 33 ff. Reprinted: *Karl von Burgund* von J. J. Bodmer, hrsg. von Bernard Seuffert. "Deutsche Litteraturdenkmale des 18. Jahrhunderts," Nr. 9. Heilbronn: Gebr. Henninger, 1883.

Kreusa. Bodmer, *Evadne; und, Kreusa* (Zürich: Bürgklische Druckerey, 1777), pp. 19-36.

Makaria, des Euripides. Bodmer, *Drey epische Gedichte* (Zürich: Orell, Geßner, Füßli und Comp., 1778), pp. 3-14.

Marcus Brutus. Ein politisches Trauerspiel. Bodmer, *Politische Schauspiele* (1768), pp. 1-103.

Marcus Tullius Cicero. Ein Trauerspiel. Zürich: Orell, Geßner und Comp., 1764.

Menelaus bey David. Bodmer, *Der Levit von Ephraim* (Zürich: Orell, Geßner, Füßli und Comp., 1782), appendix, pp. 35-56.

Monima. Bodmer, *Calliope* (Zürich: Orell, Geßner and Comp., 1767), II, 381-86.

Nero, ein politisches Drama. Bodmer, *Politische Schauspiele*, III, 73-157.

Neue theatralische Werke. Lindau: Jakob Otto, 1768.

Octavius Cäsar, ein Drama. Bodmer, *Politische Schauspiele*, II, 2-72.

Oedipus, ein Trauerspiel. Bodmer, *Drey neue Trauerspiele*, pp. 205-320.

Patroclus. Ein Trauerspiel. Augsburg: Johann Jakob Mauracher, 1778.

Pelopidas; ein politisches Trauerspiel. Bodmer, *Politische Schauspiele* (1768), pp. 271-318.

Politische Schauspiele. Zürich: Orell, Geßner und Comp., 1768.

Politische Schauspiele. Zweytes Bändgen. Aus den Zeiten der Cäsare. Lindau und Chur: typographische Gesellschaft, 1769.

Politische Schauspiele. Drittes Bändgen. Von griechischem Innhalt. Lindau und Chur: typographische Gesellschaft, 1769.

Polytimet. Ein Trauerspiel. Zürich: Conrad Orell und Comp., 1760.

Rudolf Brun. MS ZBZ., 1758.

Sigowin. Bodmer, *Drey epische Gedichte*, pp. 16-49.

Tarquinius Superbus; ein politisches Trauerspiel. Bodmer, *Politische Schauspiele* (1768), pp. 105-57.

Telemach und Nausikaa. Bodmer, *Evadne; und, Kreusa*, appendix (special pagination, pp. 1-16).

Thrasea Pätus. Ein Trauerspiel. Bodmer, *Politische Schauspiele*, II, 158-237.

Timoleon von Korinth; ein politisches Trauerspiel. Bodmer, *Politische Schauspiele* (1768), pp. 223-69.

Ulysses, Telemachs Sohn. Ein Trauerspiel. Zürich: Geßner, 1760.

Von dem Einfluß und Gebrauche der Einbildungs-Krafft. Frankfurt und Leipzig, 1727. (with Breitinger)

2. SERIALS

Bibliothek der schönen Wissenschaften und der freyen Künste. Leipzig: Dyck, 1757-65.

Deutsche Bibliothek der schönen Wissenschaften, hrsg. vom Herrn Geheimdenrath Klotz. Halle: Gebauer, 1767-71.

Freymüthige Nachrichten von neuen Büchern, und andern zur Gelehrtheit gehörigen Sachen. Zürich: Heidegger und Compagnie, 1744-63.

Nouveau journal helvétique; ou, Annales littéraires et politiques de l'Europe et principalement de la Suisse. Neuchâtel: Société typographique, 1769-1782. (Title varies)

Schweizer-Journal. Bern: B. Ludwig Walthard, 1771.

Wöchentliche Anzeigen zum Vortheil der Liebhaber der Wissenschaften und Künste. Zürich: Heidegger, 1764-66.

3. WORKS RELATING TO BODMER

Baechtold, Jakob. "Bodmer's Tagebuch (1752 bis 1782)," *Turicensia. Beiträge zur zürcherischen Geschichte,* pp. 190-216. Zürich: S. Höhr, 1891.

———— *Geschichte der deutschen Literatur in der Schweiz.* Anastatic reprint of 1892 edition. Frauenfeld: J. Huber & Co., 1919.

———— *Kleine Schriften,* hrsg. von Theodor Vetter. Frauenfeld: J. Huber & Co., 1889.

———— "Von und über Bodmer," *Archiv für Litteraturgeschichte,* VI (1877), 86-91.

Betz, Louis P. "J. J. Bodmer und die französische Litteratur," *Johann Jakob Bodmer. Denkschrift,* pp. 163-239.

Bodemann, Eduard. *Johann Georg Zimmermann. Sein Leben und bisher ungedruckte Briefe an denselben von Bodmer, Breitinger.* Hannover: Hahn'sche Buchhandlung, 1878.

Bodmer, Hans und Hermann. "J. J. Bodmer. Sein Leben und seine Werke," *Johann Jakob Bodmer. Denkschrift,* pp. 1-48.

Johann Jakob Bodmer. Denkschrift zum CC. Geburtstag, hrsg. von der Stiftung von Schnyder von Wartensee. Zürich: Alb. Müller, 1900.

Braitmaier, Friedrich. *Geschichte der poetischen Theorie und Kritik von den Diskursen der Maler bis auf Lessing.* 2 Theile. Frauenfeld: J. Hubers Verlag, 1888-89.

Brandl, Alois. *Barthold Heinrich Brockes. Nebst darauf bezüglichen Briefen von J. U. König an J. J. Bodmer.* Innsbruck: Wagner, 1878.

Danzel, Theodor W. *Gottsched und seine Zeit. Auszüge aus seinem Briefwechsel.* 2d ed. Leipzig: Dyk'sche Buchhandlung, 1855.

Donati, L. "J. J. Bodmer und die italienische Litteratur," *Johann Jakob Bodmer. Denkschrift,* pp. 241-312.

Finsler, Georg. *Homer in der Neuzeit von Dante bis Goethe.* Berlin und Leipzig: B. G. Teubner, 1912.

Franke, Olga. *Euripides bei den deutschen Dramatikern des achtzehnten*

Jahrhunderts. "Das Erbe der Alten," 2. Reihe, Nr. 16. Leipzig: Dieterich'sche Verlagsbuchhandlung, 1929.

Füssli, Joh. Heinrich. "Bodmer," *Schweitzersches Museum,* I (July-Sept., 1783), 1-37, 97-148, 193-222; II (Oct., Dec., 1783), 289-328, 481-523; III (Feb., 1784), 673-724; IV (April, 1784), 865-915.

Gardthausen, V. *Augustus und seine Zeit.* 2 Bde. Leipzig: B. G. Teubner, 1891.

Gundelfinger, Friedrich. *Caesar in der deutschen Literatur.* "Palaestra," Nr. 33. Berlin: Mayer & Müller, 1904.

Jenny, Gustav Karl. *Miltons Verlornes Paradies in der deutschen Literatur des 18. Jahrhunderts.* St. Gallen: Zollikofer, 1890.

Klopstocks Werke. 12. Bde. Leipzig: Georg Joachim Göschen, 1798-1817.

Körte, Wilhelm. *Briefe der Schweizer Bodmer, Sulzer, Geßner.* Zürich: Heinrich Geßner, 1804.

Largiardèr, Anton. "Die Ahnentafel Johann Jakob Bodmers. Ein Beitrag zur zürcherischen Personengeschichte," *Schweizer Archiv für Heraldik,* XLII (1928), 145-59.

Lazzarini, Domenico di Morro. *Ulisse il Giovane, tragedia.* Padua, 1720.

Löen, A. von. "Eine Reliquie von Johann Jakob Bodmer," *Blätter f. Lit. Unterhaltung,* I (1856), 32-35.

Meissner, Erich. *Bodmer als Parodist.* Naumburg a. S.: H. Sieling, 1904.

Meister, Leonhard. *Über Bodmern. Nebst Fragmenten aus seinen Briefen.* Zürich: Orell, Geßner, Füßli und Comp., 1783.

Morgenstern, Hofrath v. "Briefe deutscher Dichter und Gelehrter aus den Jahren 1740 bis 1771," *Morgenblatt für gebildete Stände,* IV (Aug. 3, 1810), 737-38.

Mörikofer, Johann Caspar. *Die schweizerische Literatur des achtzehnten Jahrhunderts.* Leipzig: S. Hirzel, 1861.

Raccolta di tragedie scritte nel secolo XVIII. 2 vols. Milano: Società Tipogr. de' classici italiani, 1825.

Reynold, Gonzague de. *Bodmer et l'école suisse.* Lausanne: Georges Bridel & Cie, 1912.

Schmitter, Jakob. *J. J. Bodmers Übersetzungen von J. Miltons Verlorenem Paradies 1732. 1742. 1754. 1759. 1769 sprachlich verglichen.* Zürich: Gebr. Leeman & Co., 1913.

Servaes, Franz. *Die Poetik Gottscheds und der Schweizer.* "Quellen und Forschungen," Nr. 60. Strassburg: Karl J. Trübner, 1887.

Stäudlin, Gotthold Fried. *Briefe berühmter und edler Deutschen an Bodmer.* Stuttgart: Gebrüder Mäntler, 1794.

Sulzer, Johann Georg. *Allgemeine Theorie der schönen Künste.* 2d ed. 4 Theile. Leipzig: M. G. Weidemanns Erben & Reich, 1786-87.

Tobler, Gustav. *J. J. Bodmer als Geschichtschreiber.* "Neujahrsblatt

herausgegeben von der Stadtbibliothek in Zürich auf das Jahr 1891."
Zürich: Orell Füßli & Co., 1891.

———— "Bodmers politische Schauspiele," *Johann Jakob Bodmer.*
Denkschrift, pp. 115-62.

Vetter, Theodor. "Bibliographie der Schriften J. J. Bodmers und der von
ihm besorgten Ausgaben," *Johann Jakob Bodmer. Denkschrift*, pp.
387-403.

———— "Bodmer's persönliche Anekdoten," *Zürcher Taschenbuch,*
XV (1892), 91-131.

———— "J. J. Bodmer und die englische Litteratur," *Johann Jakob*
Bodmer. Denkschrift, pp. 313-86.

Wieland, C. M. *Ausgewählte Briefe von C. M. Wieland an verschiedene*
Freunde in den Jahren 1751-1810 geschrieben, hrsg. von H. Geßner.
4 Bde. Zürich: Geßnersche Buchhandlung, 1815-16.

Wolff, Eugen. "Briefwechsel Gottscheds mit Bodmer und Breitinger,"
Zeitschrift f. deut. Unterricht, XI (6. Heft, 1897), 353-81.

Zehnder-Stadlin, Josephine. *Pestalozzi. Idee und Macht der menschlichen*
Entwicklung. Gotha: Thienemann, 1875.

INDEX

VITA

Anthony Scenna was born on July 29, 1906, in Revere, Massachusetts. After attending the public schools of Melrose, Massachusetts, he entered Amherst College in the fall of 1923 and received the degree of Bachelor of Arts from that institution in June, 1927. The next two years, 1927-1929, he spent at Columbia University as a student in the Department of Germanic Languages and received the degree of Master of Arts in German in February, 1929. During the next academic year he continued his studies in Germanics as a German-American Exchange student at the University of Frankfort-on-the-Main, Germany. While at Columbia University he taught German in its Extension Division. During the year 1930-1931 he held an instructorship in German at the University of Buffalo, Buffalo, New York. In September, 1931, he was appointed instructor in German at Amherst College and has held that position continuously since that time.

COLUMBIA UNIVERSITY GERMANIC STUDIES

EDITED BY ROBERT HERNDON FIFE

NEW SERIES

NUMBER SIX

LITERARY CRITICISM IN THE WORK OF
LUDWIG ACHIM VON ARNIM

LITERARY CRITICISM
AND ROMANTIC THEORY
IN THE WORK OF
ACHIM VON ARNIM

BY HERBERT P. LIEDKE

COLLEGE OF THE CITY OF NEW YORK

AMS PRESS, INC.
NEW YORK
1966

To

K. B. L. and F. K.

PREFACE

The completion of this study is due largely to Professor Robert Herndon Fife, at whose suggestion I started the work and for whose invaluable guidance and constant encouragement I wish to express my sincerest gratitude. I am indebted for kind advice and continued interest to Professor Edwin C. Roedder of the College of the City of New York, to Director Dr. Ernst Beutler, and to Dr. Franz Götting of the Goethe Museum in Frankfort for the permission to avail myself of hitherto unpublished material. I also wish to express my gratitude for pertinent information given by the von Arnim family, by Dr. Otto Mallon, and Mr. Ernst Henrici. From the Columbia University Library, the Goethe Museum in Frankfort, the Goethe-Schiller Archiv in Weimar, the Universitätsbibliothek in Heidelberg, and the administration of the Preussische Staatsbibliothek in Berlin I have received many courtesies which I wish to acknowledge.

ABBREVIATIONS

Arnim-Bettina	Reinhold Steig, *Achim von Arnim und die ihm nahe standen*, Bd. II. *Achim von Arnim und Bettina Brentano*. Stuttgart, 1913.
Arnim-Brentano	Reinhold Steig, *Achim von Arnim und die ihm nahe standen*, Bd. I. *Achim von Arnim und Clemens Brentano*. Stuttgart, 1894.
Arnim-Grimm	Reinhold Steig, *Achim von Arnim und die ihm nahe standen*, Bd. III. *Achim von Arnim und Jacob und Wilhelm Grimm*. Berlin, 1904.
Bettina-Goethe	Reinhold Steig, *Bettinas Briefwechsel mit Goethe*. Berlin, 1922.
DNL, CXLVI, I.	*Deutsche National-Literatur*. Bd. CXLVI. *Arnim, Klemens und Bettina Brentano, J. Görres*. Teil I. Hrsg. v. Max Koch, Stuttgart.
HeidelbJbb.	*Heidelbergische Jahrbücher der Literatur*.
NHeidelbJbb.	*Neue Heidelberger Jahrbücher*.
Werke	*Ludwig Achim's v. Arnim sämtliche Werke*. Neue Ausgabe. Berlin, 1857.

ABBREVIATIONS

Arnim-Bettina	Reinhold Steig, *Achim von Arnim und die ihm nahe standen*, Bd. II. *Achim von Arnim und Bettina Brentano.* Stuttgart, 1913.
Arnim-Brentano	Reinhold Steig, *Achim von Arnim und die ihm nahe standen*, Bd. I. *Achim von Arnim und Clemens Brentano.* Stuttgart, 1894.
Arnim-Grimm	Reinhold Steig, *Achim von Arnim und die ihm nahe standen*, Bd. III. *Achim von Arnim und Jacob und Wilhelm Grimm.* Berlin, 1904.
Bettina-Goethe	Reinhold Steig, *Bettinas Briefwechsel mit Goethe.* Berlin, 1922.
DNL, CXLVI, I.	*Deutsche National-Literatur.* Bd. CXLVI. *Arnim, Klemens und Bettina Brentano, J. Görres.* Teil I. Hrsg. v. Max Koch, Stuttgart.
HeidelbJbb.	*Heidelbergische Jahrbücher der Literatur.*
NHeidelbJbb.	*Neue Heidelberger Jahrbücher.*
Werke	*Ludwig Achim's v. Arnim sämtliche Werke.* Neue Ausgabe. Berlin, 1857.

INTRODUCTION

In this study an attempt has been made to explore Arnim's activities and attitude as a literary critic, a field that has heretofore been almost completely neglected. The material for such an investigation is not easily accessible. None can be found in the three editions of Arnim's *Sämtliche Werke,* published by his widow with the help of Wilhelm Grimm between 1839 and 1857. These editions lack all of Arnim's reviews, essays, anecdotes, and short stories, as well as his correspondence. Only minor attempts have been made to collect and to reprint Arnim's extensive journalistic writings, which originally appeared in about forty different periodicals.[1] The wealth and quality of the material on which this study is based has become known only recently through the publication in 1925 of Otto Mallon's scholarly *Arnim-Bibliographie,* which furnishes an excellent reference work in the field. Furthermore, the auction of Arnim-Brentano manuscripts and posthumous works from the family archives in Wiepersdorf in 1929-30 brought to light additional and important material.

For the present work all of the published writings of Arnim have been examined. In addition a certain number of unpublished essays and fragments, found chiefly in the Goethe Museum in Frankfort, have been read. A further important expression of Arnim's critical views is that which is found in his correspondence. The letters to Clemens Brentano, to Joseph Görres, and especially to Jacob and Wilhelm Grimm contain much that is necessary for an understanding of his views on literature, particularly for his ideas concerning popular poetry. These are in the main accessible in the volumes of Reinhold Steig (*Achim von Arnim und die ihm nahe standen*), which have contributed much to Chapters IV and V of this investigation. Some unpublished letters from Arnim and

[1] Ludwig Geiger, "A. v. Arnim's Beiträge zum Literatur-Blatt", *Zeitschrift für vergl. Literaturgeschichte,* XII; Ludwig Geiger, *L. A. v. Arnim, Unbekannte Aufsätze und Gedichte,* Berlin, 1892 (cited below as *Unbekannte Aufsätze*), contains selected reprints of Arnim's contributions to *Der Gesellschafter;* Otto Mallon, "A. v. Arnims Beiträge zum literarischen Conversationsblatt", *Preussische Jahrbücher,* 1931.

others, in part also in the Frankfort Goethe Museum, have been used, as will appear in the following pages.

The scope of such a study as this cannot, however, be limited to a discussion of the reviews, essays, pronouncements, notes, and letters, or the other purely critical material that flowed so easily from Arnim's pen. By his very nature he was obliged to stamp whatever he wrote with the quality and force of his own personality. All of his writings, published and unpublished, are the expression of a *Weltanschauung* that struggled for utterance. All that he put before the public was a challenge to the literary and social world of his time. Obviously, his critical position and his contribution to literary criticism cannot be understood unless we widen the boundary of our investigation to include aspects of personality and characteristic productions in other fields than the critical. The explanation and the excuse for such an extension of our discussion are to be found in Arnim's nature and in the totalitarian character of the romantic spirit.

The conceptions which form the basis of Arnim's critical work are to be sought in the spiritual legacy which the younger romantic generation received from that immediately preceding it, and also in the unique personality of young Arnim. Our investigation begins, therefore, with these aspects. The first chapter tries to survey and define the critical approach to literature which Arnim found in his predecessors, chiefly in Herder, and the form and interpretation which he gave to the idea of "spirit" (*Geist*) in its historical and popular expressions. The second chapter traces the background of family tradition and character development that throws light on the peculiar soul structure of Arnim. With the third chapter we enter, then, on an examination of his critical activities. The history of these may be divided roughly into four periods. The first includes his student days at Halle, beginning in 1799, and at Göttingen, and the years of his "grand tour." Here again the boundaries of our study must be widened to include his interest in the natural sciences. This was his first field of scholarly activity and an understanding of his attitude toward it throws light on his approach to literature. It has also been felt necessary to trace the relation of Arnim to the scientific and pseudo-scientific literature of the time with some care for the reason that this side of his work has heretofore received rather insufficient treatment. Coincident with the development of this critical interest in the natural sciences, came the beginning of a critical interest in literature, evidenced as early as 1803 in his contributions to Friedrich Schlegel's *Europa* and confirmed in the spring of 1804 by his confession to Clemens that he would like to make journalism his life career.

The maturing of his work as a literary critic follows, from 1808 to 1810. This is treated in our fourth chapter, which deals with his writings for the *Heidelbergische Jahrbücher* and the *Einsiedler-Zeitung,* and includes the important discussions of critical questions which he carried on with members of the group of Heidelberg romanticists. The third period of his critical activity falls, then, in Berlin, beginning in 1810, and embraces the nationalistic propaganda that preceded the War of Liberation, the period of his association with Heinrich von Kleist's *Berliner Abendblätter* (1810-1811) and with the *Preussische Correspondent* (1813-1814). The fourth and last period, which is characterized by a wider range of critical interest, covers the years from 1814, when he withdrew from public affairs to live on his estate at Wiepersdorf, to his death in 1831. In these years his more important critical work appeared in Gubitz' *Gesellschafter* and Brockhaus' *Blätter für literarische Unterhaltung.*

This periodization furnishes, in the main, a framework for the organization of the results of our investigation. However, a strictly chronological treatment of the material was found to be impracticable. Arnim's interest in natural sciences overlapped his development as literary critic; indeed, it will be noted below that it experienced a revival in 1810 and reappeared here and there in the later decades of his life. Equally important with any chronological arrangement for a complete view of his critical work is an investigation of his relationship to literary groups. To his attitude toward older romantic contemporaries and toward Goethe special chapters have been devoted. Particularly his relation to the Weimar master has been treated extensively. Its importance for an understanding of his ideas concerning literature will be obvious.

Nowhere, not even in the interchanges with Brentano, do the literary aspirations and views of Arnim stand out more clearly than in his contacts with Goethe.

It will be apparent from the foregoing that the present work has been obliged to go somewhat further than its title indicates. Any investigation of Arnim's literary criticism must soon overstep the commonly recognized boundaries both of literature and of criticism. The reasons for this lie in the character of the man and his epoch. Arnim regarded the works that came into his hand as subject matter for the expression of ideas that were not bounded by considerations of literary history or convention, genre or style. In such matters as these, in the field of aesthetic discrimination, he was certainly inferior to Brentano and possibly to Görres. Nevertheless, it cannot be denied that Arnim had a feeling for works of literature and a talent for discussing them. Journalistic essays and studies, notes of the most varied content flowed even more readily from his pen than from that of any other member of the Heidelberg group, even including Görres. He brought to his critical work a spirit that was peculiar to himself. This appears even in essays on insignificant topics. It can best be described as a spirit of consecration. He felt himself called to a mission: to change the spiritual attitude of his people. As will appear below, he wrote only on those books that interested him positively or negatively, and the spiritual and patriotic ground-tone of his critical purpose can be noted everywhere. It is this that gives to his literary criticism a certain consistent seriousness and an essential dignity.

I
THE ROMANTIC APPROACH TO LITERARY CRITICISM

The object of early Romanticism was to arouse the literary world and to create new idealistic standards. It opposed the utilitarian rationalism of men like Nicolai and turned against the philistine spirit of Kotzebue and Iffland. It turned at first with enthusiasm to the classical harmony and perfection idealized by Goethe, but speedily passed on to new fields of speculation and literary and artistic interest. The generation of early romanticists had experienced during the most impressionable years of youth the emergence of new ideas in natural science, and the new development of idealistic philosophy, and it was now to carry its theorizing to unlimited extremes. In the political field the last decade of the Eighteenth Century was comparatively quiet in Germany, and the petty bourgeois mind was little affected by the revolutionary ideas which held sway on the other side of the Rhine. Political and politico-social questions, such as Rousseau's interpretation of the relation between the individual and society, did not interest the great men of letters, or at most, only as a stimulus for aesthetic and ethical theorizing. National sentiment, as the Nineteenth Century understood it, did not enter into their range of ideas. In this "peaceful" atmosphere the early romanticists spun their thoughts regarding the individual and the universe. Fichte carried this system of idealistic philosophy to a dazzling height. Novalis surpassed him with his "magical idealism," and in literature Friedrich Schlegel created the concept of "progressive universal poetry."

Ten years later men of letters were facing an entirely different situation. The French Revolution had failed to bring about the "Golden Age," men were looking more realistically into prevalent concepts, such as "innate goodness of man," *"liberté, egalité et fraternité."* Napoleon had appeared on the political horizon, and Germany had begun to realize the danger of the French imperialistic policy. Not German territory alone, German "Kultur" also was to be defended against a foreign invasion.

Particularly the younger generation of Romanticists, the group of young poets and scholars which embraced Arnim, Brentano, Görres, and their friends from Cassel, the Grimm brothers, were among the first to awaken to this danger, while older, well-known leaders in literature, like Goethe and Voss, realized more slowly the changed situation. Following the path opened by Herder, the Heidelberg group began to emphasize actively the cultural tradition of Germany and the hidden treasures in her art and literature. It was their feeling that if the German people could be led back to this wealth, the present would be enriched, and art and literature would receive an impetus hitherto undreamed of. They cherished the belief that the senility of the age had almost killed the delicate flower of true creative art, and that it had to be revived through a reawakening of the spirit of the people. On the one hand, unassimilated forms of expression from abroad had smothered native endeavors; on the other, a narrow-minded philistinism and a love of bombastic display still held the attention of the public as they had since the Thirty Years' War. To the mind of the young men of Heidelberg the nation was waiting for a reappearance of creative genius such as it once possessed in the Nibelungenlied, in the Minnesang, and in Hans Sachs. It is understandable that this absorbing quest for *Volkspoesie* was sometimes exaggerated and pursued with a disregard of the aesthetic standards erected by the preceding generation. Thus Arnim, with the unbounded spirit of youth, wrote that in folklore he liked that which was most free and liberal and did not even mind the burlesque.[1]

Very early in the new century, therefore, the cultural consciousness and historical-philosophical thinking of Romanticism in Germany had struck out in two directions. The earlier of these expounded the cult of the individual, of the ego, as a supreme, incomparable entity in its relation to society (*Allgemeinheit*). The second, more concretely historical in attitude, was absorbed in a wealth of historical material, and was endeavoring to formulate a literary-historical philosophy in the train of Herder. Single phenomena like nature, man, history, and society were viewed as the

[1] Arnim-Brentano, p. 169: "Mir gefällt auch das Freieste, auch das Burleskeste."

expression of a dynamic world organism moved by spirit. Spirituality became the sole basis for the interpretation of all life.

Romantic historical thinking built upon a not entirely unprepared soil. The transition from the principle of reason to that of spirit, the tendency to emphasize the rôle of history in the concept of the universe had been long under way. In the preceding century Johann Jakob Winkelmann and Justus Möser approached the historical organism in a manner that was intuitive and emotional.[2] Hamann's philosophy opened the way for the disintegration of German rationalism. Sensitivity and emotion took the place of reason; art was no longer a literal and rational reflection of nature, but rather of the artist's soul and feelings. "It is the spirit that creates life; the letter is flesh, and your dictionaries are rubbish!"[3] The spiritual element was emphasized especially in the evolution of history.[4] Herder, and later Schelling, gave a new impetus to the recognition of the metaphysical basis of existence and to the spirit as a force in life. The former in his treatise "Vom Geist des Christentums" found the *spirit* to be the essence of religious consciousness, and in his philosophical essays on mankind he regarded the *spirit* as the universal basis of all human endeavors. The peculiarity or essence of every phenomenon Herder designated as "spirit," "genius," or "character."[5] For the philosophers of the Enlightenment these concepts had individualistic, structural meanings, while Herder applied them to collectivistic ideas. The Heidelberg Romanticists and the romantic historical school employed the term *spirit* to explain an historical reality. They assumed an autonomous rule by the spirit of the people (*Volksgeist*).[6]

In accordance with these ideas, art must necessarily become the

[2] Wilhelm Dilthey, *Das 18. Jahrhundert und die geschichtliche Welt;* also Josef Heimann, *Möser und Herder* (Diss. München 1924), p. 372.

[3] *Hamanns Schriften,* hrsg. von Friedrich Roth, Berlin, 1823, IV, 146.

[4] *Ibid.,* p. 50: "Jede Geschichte trägt das Ebenbild des Menschen, einen Leib, der Erde und Asche und nichtig ist, den sinnlichen Buchstaben, aber auch eine Seele, den Hauch Gottes."

[5] Herder thus speaks of "Geist der Sprache, Geist der Poesie, Geist der Erdichtung, Geist der Literatur."

[6] The concept of "Volksgeist" may be traced to the philosophers of the French Revolution, especially Montesquieu. Herder used the following terms: "Volksgeist", "Nationalgeist", "Zeitgeist"; cf. Herders *Werke,* hrsg. von Suphan, III, 30; XVII, 80; XX, 117; also Rothacker, *Einleitung in die Geisteswissenschaft,* 1930.

expression of the creative spirit of a people, not an individualistic expression. Thus Herder spoke of the *Volksgeist* as the creator of the folk-song as well as of all other poetry.[7] Many of the Heidelberg romanticists were disciples and friends of Schelling and Savigny, who had enlarged and built upon Herder's ideas. The idealistic-historic *Weltanschauung* which they held looked upon the spirit as the ultimate force behind all matter. Schelling's theory of the unconscious evolution of the absolute spirit was the climax of Herder's ideas. In Savigny's philosophy of history and the state and in Hegel's system one finds a further elaboration of the idea *Volksgeist.*

One looks in vain for frequent references to Herder in the writings of Arnim, Görres, Brentano, or the Grimm brothers. For this circle, however, his concepts and phraseology had become accepted facts and presuppositions of general usage. "Did I write the same once before?"[8] asks Jacob Grimm naïvely, referring to Herder's "Zerstreute Blätter." Arnim also must be regarded as one of the chief sponsors of the theory of the spirit. Throughout his writings the word "Geist," meaning genius or spirit, occurs frequently in many contexts and combinations, such as *Volksgeist, Zeitgeist, aufgeregter Geist,* etc.[9]

In addition to "spirit" (*Geist*) one must note also the frequent occurrence of *Genius* and *Genie* in the works of the romanticists. These words had already an interesting history in Germany.[10] As foreign words, *Genius* and *Genie* became in German Eighteenth Century usage identical with *Geist,* just as in English "genius" became synonymous with "wit" and "spirit," and in French with

---

[7] Cf. Herder's summons to collect folksongs in 1767, also in 1773 his "Briefwechsel über Ossian und die Lieder alter Völker."

[8] *Briefwechsel zwischen Jacob und Wilhelm Grimm aus der Jugendzeit,* 1881, p. 43.

[9] No check-up on the frequency of the word *Geist* or *Genius* is possible, because an index is lacking, but in Oehlke's Bettina edition it ranks first in frequency. In Bettina's "Königsbuch" one finds an elaboration of Arnim's concept *Geist,* i.e., *Volksgeist.*

[10] Cf. Rudolf Hildebrand's discussion of *Geist* in Grimms' *Deutsches Wörterbuch* Bd. I. Teil II, Spalte 2623-2741. Also Herman Wolf, *Versuch einer Geschichte des Geniebegriffs in der Ästhetik des XVIII. Jahrhunderts,* Bd. I, Heidelberg 1923; also Hellmuth Sudheimer, *Der Geniebegriff des jungen Goethe,* "Germanische Studien," Heft 167, Berlin, 1935; Julius Ernst, *Der Geniebegriff der Stürmer und Dränger und der Frühromantiker,* Zürich, 1906.

"esprit."[11] With the advent of a flourishing German literature *Genius* was so extensively misused that Immanuel Kant once suggested—though in vain—*eigentümlicher Geist* as a good German substitute. Nevertheless the word continued to be in great vogue, and various philosophical movements interpreted it each in accord with its peculiar *Weltanschauung*.[12] To the *Kraftgenies* of Storm and Stress genius was divine. Its creations were intuitive visions. Herder used the word *Genius* as identical with "being original and inventive." However, Herman Wolf in his "Die Genielehre des jungen Herder" admits that any clear-cut definition of the nature of genius is hardly found in young Herder's works.[13]

In the important essay "Von Volksliedern" Arnim wondered respecting the proper meaning of the term *Genius* and suggested the study of all the different contexts:

The habit of playing with words in our times has put art and genius at opposite poles; in poor imitations one speaks of much art and little genius, although many works are without genius. . . . If genius is the creative force, then art is the mode of appearance of this creation.[14]

He distinguished between *Genius* and *Genialität*, however. A great poet possesses *Genius;* the dry sophisticated scholar who just manages to show off and glitter and fails to create anything of lasting spiritual value is possessed of *Genialität*. In Arnim's *Wintergarten* the woman of genius is his mouthpiece: "Stop speaking of *Genialität*," she cries, "this empty expression which is meaningless in our time."[15] In one of his letters he remarks: "What the mob calls *Genialität*, I call devil. I appreciate all originality, but I am a solid rock against that so-called originality which wants to rule the world as if it were law."[16] The originality which he does appreciate, Arnim generally designates as "spirit" (*Geist*) or "genius," following the customary terminology. He is as ready as his predecessors to use the word in combinations and compounds. In general he prefers the German word *Geist* to the foreign *Genius*

[11] Benedetto Croce, *Estetica*, 4th edition 1912, pp. 189-190, translated into English by Douglas Ainslie, London 1922.

[12] B. Rosenthal, *Der Geniebegriff des Aufklärungszeitalters*, Berlin, 1932.

[13] Herman Wolf, "Die Genielehre des jungen Herder", *Vierteljahresschrift für Literaturwissenschaft und Geistesgeschichte*, Bd. III, 1925 H. 3, pp. 401-430; especially page 406.

[14] DNL, CXLVI, I, 57-8.   [15] Werke, V, 77.   [16] Arnim-Bettina, p. 203.

and *Genie,* yet is inclined to use the terms without distinction in meaning.

Like Herder, Arnim regarded the creative spirit as the fundamental basis of all art. "Art without genius," he says, "is comparable to a point without dimensions;" and again, "art is only the visible appearance of the genius."[17] He supports Goethe's profound observation that the nature of poetry is the truthful expression of the aroused spirit (*Divan,* p. 378).[18] In July, 1805, in the essay on the folksong, referred to above, when speaking of the interdependence of the future, past, and present,[19] Arnim emphasizes the eternal continuity of the rule of the spirit: "The world is spirit and does not need us,"[20] he writes to Wilhelm Grimm. Arnim's "Lehrgedicht an die Jugend" is an exhortation to pay heed to the good spirits.[21] In his poem "Träume" he identifies "words" as human spirits, to be esteemed and cultivated, because spirits are holy.[22] In Arnim's opinion the manifestations of the spirit are quiet, unobtrusive, and unnoticeable, and are revealed in their full importance only later by history. Man is but a tool of the spirit, predestined to fulfill his fate, to follow unknowingly the spirits, and thus to become, like Frederick the Great, a *tool* of the *Volksgeist.*[23]

A summons to exaltation of the spirit, a sincere plea for the spiritualization of his age, he voiced most emphatically in the introductory chapter to the *Kronenwächter.* One may justly call this chapter "a hymn to the spirit."[24] Here Arnim declares that

---

[17] Werke, XIII, 453; cf. also DNL, CXLVI, I, 57-8, Arnim's essay "Von Volksliedern."

[18] Ludwig Achim von Arnim. *Unbekannte Aufsätze und Gedichte.* Hrsg. von Ludwig Geiger, cited below as *Unbekannte Aufsätze,* p. 53.

[19] Cf. DNL, CXLVI, I, 78.

[20] Arnim-Grimm, p. 12.

[21] Werke, XXI, 68.

[22] *Ibid.,* V, p. 92;

> "Was die Worte nur sind?
> Es sind die Geister der Menschen,
> Und ich achte das Wort,
> Weil mir heilig der Geist."

[23] *Monatliche Beiträge zur Geschichte dramatischer Kunst und Literatur,* hrsg. von K. v. Holtei, Berlin, 1812, II, 1-42; cf. Arnim's "Sammlung zur Theatergeschichte": "Er (Frederick the Great) aber mußte hier, wie in so vielen Fällen tun und erfüllen, wozu er bestimmt war, ohne diese seine Bestimmung zu kennen."

[24] Werke, XV, 3-9.

in the writings of former centuries we have documents which cannot be made our own without effort: "Genius loves its finite creations as a symbol of eternity which we can attain neither through our earthly activities nor by reasoning." The evaluation of these documents differs according to the trend and interests of different periods. There is no absolute standard for the productions of genius in its spiritual realm: "Who honors the boundary lines he drew? Who recognizes the originality of his ideas? . . . There exists no law to protect works of the spirit against sacrilege." The spiritual holds within itself the ultimate secret of the universe, more precious in its wisdom than anything voiced in history. Contemporaries may not grasp the significance of its workings, but true history ("Geschichte in höchster Wahrheit") will transmit visions of them. It is only poetry which has an insight into this secret of the universe. Poetry is the knowledge of this secret, born of spirit and truth, communicated from the past to the present.

With Arnim the word "spirit" (*Geist*) was a concept of mood and feeling (*Stimmungsbegriff*). Thus it appears in *Volksgeist*, the "soul of the people." Herder had said of the *soul of the people:* "What a mysterious and peculiar phenomenon the soul and character of a people are, unexplainable and indestructible, as old as nature, as old as the country."[25] Arnim uses the expression *Volksgeist* as early as 1805 in his essay "Von Volksliedern," likewise such words as *Zeitgeist, Gemeingeist, Volkstätigkeit.* In one place he contradicts the philosophers who make it their task to oppose sentimentalism, defined by Arnim as the imitation and exploration of emotion. He hoped that the living *Volksgeist* would terminate their activities. The country lacks *Volkstätigkeit.* Only when the poet has become the *"spiritus familiaris"* (*Gemeingeist*) in the community of the world, will it be possible to live in true poetic enjoyment.[26]

The most interesting discussion and definition of the *Volksgeist* is found in Arnim's *Wintergarten,* where he compares this force to a slumbering giant, who must be awakened by the people themselves. The *Volksgeist* is of divine origin and becomes potent

[25] Herder's Werke, hrsg. von Suphan, XX, 181.
[26] DNL, CXLVI, I, 50.

through divine grace. Then "he will stand, free, a strong, pious hero, looking up above to where the hopeful days of the new earth glow in a thousand colors."[27]

The belief of Arnim in the awakened giant (potent *Volksgeist*) looking forward to hopeful days must be compared to Novalis' and Hölderlin's ideas of the Golden Age. While their version was more romantically abstract, Arnim introduced political and national ideas. In this connection he tried to formulate in an idealistic manner his conception of the real mission of the nobility, a question much discussed in his day. This appears in the poems "Der Götter Adel" and "Adel."

> Nicht die Geister zu vertreiben
> Stand des Volkes Geist einst auf,
> Nein, daß jedem freier Lauf,
> Jedem Haus ein Geist soll bleiben,
> Nein, daß adlich all' auf Erden,
> Muß der Adel Märtrer werden.[28]

> Die neuen Zeiten
> Sie nennen Adel
> Was ohne Tadel
> Die Geister leiten.
> Der Schein, die Plage
> Versinkt am Tage.[29]

Allusion to this role of the nobility may be found in others of his poems and in the *Gräfin Dolores*. In this work Graf Karl is the protagonist of Arnim's vision. Karl is morally superior to the Gräfin. He strives for one lofty ideal, namely, to lead the people to a higher moral plane. Arnim's preoccupation with ideas for the spiritual rejuvenation of the nation was shown repeatedly during the War of Liberation, 1813-14. To Clemens he wrote in August, 1814: "My soul is bound for hours by the enchantment of ponder-

---

[27] Werke, V, 251.

[28] *Ibid.*, XXI, 172; "Lieder aus einem ungeschriebenem Roman," also the interesting version of this stanza in the poem entitled "Still bewahr' es in Gedanken":
> Nicht die Geister zu vertreiben,
> Steht des Volkes Geist jetzt auf,
> Nein, daß jedem freier Lauf,
> Jedem Haus ein Geist soll bleiben:
> Nein, daß adlich all'auf Erden,
> Muß der Adel Bürger werden.   (Werke, XXI, pp. 232-3)

[29] *Ibid.*, XXI, 177.

ing over the tower of Babel; how all may be united which I consider of profound value in the Germans."[30] After the war, however, a more pessimistic note is struck in his letters to Görres: "We expected fine times for Germany and worked hard, thinking she would unite the world like a wonderful many-sided mirror."[31]

Unlike Herder, Arnim and his circle used the concept *Zeitgeist* to denote something undesirable and even despicable. They saw it manifest itself in Germany in arrogant intellectualism, rooted, in their opinion, in the cult of reason of the French Revolution. The *Zeitgeist* also appeared to them in the philistinism of the petty German bourgeoisie. Arnim charged that the *Zeitgeist* "belittles everything magnificent" and that empty arrogance and boasting prevails among the educated classes.[32] A result of the *Zeitgeist* appears in the miserable productions in literature betraying a lack of talent and of imagination, such as occasional poems without a real underlying experience or cause.[33] He pitied contemporary Germany for "silencing beauty, forgetting excellence, and desecrating sincerity."[34] Two contemporary works dealing with the *Zeitgeist* did not remain unnoticed by Arnim. They are Ernst Moritz Arndt's *Geist der Zeit* (1805) and Madame de Staël's posthumous work, *Considérations sur les principaux événements de la révolution française,* (1818). He disagreed with both writers, particularly with Arndt's pessimism about his own day and about the future of Germany. To be sure, the author's fruitless efforts, Arnim admits, may well have brought him to the verge of despair, but in spite of this he has not lost faith in the greatness of his fatherland. Arndt's denunciation of Prussia he considered most unjust,[35] as he wrote to Clemens in July, 1806.

Madame de Staël's book was discussed at length in a review in Gubitz' *Gesellschafter* in 1818.[36] While acknowledging the

---

[30] Arnim-Brentano p. 338.

[31] Joseph von Görres, *Gesammelte Briefe,* hrsg. von Marie von Görres; letter of January 23, 1816; cf. *Werke,* VIII, 481-4.

[32] Cf. Arnim-Brentano, pp. 262, 280, 338; Arnim-Bettina, p. 333; Herder's "Was ist der Geist der Zeit," Werke, XVII, 77-81.

[33] Arnim-Brentano, p. 238.

[34] *Ibid.,* p. 238.

[35] *Ibid.,* p. 184.

[36] *Der Gesellschafter oder Blätter für Geist und Herz,* hrsg. von F. W. Gubitz, Berlin; cited below as *Ges.* 1818; Arnim's "Frau von Staël und Herr von Haller", pp. 734-738. Republished in *Unbekannte Aufsätze,* pp. 38-43.

excellence of her portrayal of the spirit of the French Revolution, particularly its noble and heroic element, Arnim criticizes and pities her for her failure to understand the true origin of a state and for her hostility to feudalism. It is evident that Arnim shared here Karl von Haller's point of view as set forth in his *Restauration der Staatswissenschaft*. According to Haller, the state owes its origin and existence to the feudal system and to private ownership of land. Feudal forms tie the spirit of the present with that of the past and future. The spiritual element in the origin of a state Haller sees in family life, while possession of land constitutes the material element; the state is an historic organism in which the spiritual dominates the material. However, Arnim shared only Haller's historical, not his political views. He rejected Haller's theory, which derived all civic rights from land ownership and endowed the church with considerable political control, as just as impractical as Rousseau's *contrat social*. Haller's conception of the state as the creation of the spirit of a people in its historical development was accepted by Arnim and by other members of the German nobility united under his leadership in the *Christlich-deutsche Tischgesellschaft*.[37] These were men who had lost much through Napoleon's ascendancy and his invasion of Germany. However, they wanted to solve the German question by a progressive movement and not by un-German or reactionary methods based on outworn traditions, such as became the program of Metternich and of the Prussian government during the ascendancy of Hardenberg.

Arnim endeavored not to be submerged by the *Zeitgeist*, to avoid infection by the poisonous trend of the time, and to preserve his own individuality. He wanted, as he says, to blow away the noxious spirit like "the smoke of a strange pipe."[38] In his efforts to escape from the *Zeitgeist*, however, he went to such extremes of eccentricity that Wilhelm von Humboldt in 1809 would not recommend him for service in the government. Humboldt felt

[37] In an essay "Ein Wort über die jetzige Gesetzmacherei", Leopold von Gerlach, another member of the *Tischgesellschaft*, compares the predominating spirit of the time to that of the French Revolution, "which abolished with one stroke many honorable institutions without consideration of historic events, yet history is the greatest teacher of the human race and dreadful prophet of the fate of nations."

[38] Arnim-Brentano, p. 159; Arnim's letter to Clemens, January 25, 1806.

sorry he could not do something for the *"Wunderhorn* man." It
was out of the question, as he said, "because this man who quarrels
rudely with Voss and Jacobi, wears an impossible fur cap, and
has similarly impossible whiskers, is in ill-repute."[39] The loss of
many promising and valuable contemporaries Arnim attributed
to the deadening effects of, or the strenuous struggle against, the
Zeitgeist. One of the victims was his friend August Winkelmann,
taken away in the prime of life: "The times killed him," Arnim
wrote to Brentano.[40] Eight years later, the great Fichte succumbed
to the *Zeitgeist*, in Arnim's opinion. This he affirms in the poem
which concludes his eulogy of Fichte in *Der Preussische Correspondent*:

> Auch Dich hat uns die Pest der Zeit entrissen,
> Dich mutigsten Bestreiter schlechter Zeit,
> Du hattest Dich als Opfer ihr geweiht,
> Als Du ihr strafend riefest ins Gewissen.
> Bekämpft die Zeit in EUCH mit heiligem Willen!
> So riefest Du.—Den Bogen spannt im Stillen
> Die tück'sche Zeit—auch Du mußt ihr erliegen.[41]

This new attitude toward the world and life as an expression
of the spirit necessitated a new direction in art and literature.
This meant a new criticism, which had its roots likewise in Herder's spiritual and historical approach to literature. Productive
criticism in Germany had found its first champion in Lessing.
However, Lessing's methodical, standardized, and regulated procedure had been rejected by Hamann and Herder, for genius
hates classification and comparison.[42] Both objected to limitation
in literature and to comparison as a critical method. Instead of
using classical antiquity as a standard for modern poetry, the
method in vogue among the critics of the Enlightenment, they
advocated another approach, namely, to regard each poet as a
product of his age, his people and his environment. Bearing this in
mind, the reader should try to penetrate, understand, and appre-

[39] Wilhelm von Humboldt to Caroline, February 28, 1809; *Wilhelm und Caroline
von Humboldt in ihren Briefen 1808-1810*, hrsg. von Anna von Sydow, 1909,
pp. 101-2.
[40] August Winkelmann died in February, 1806.
[41] Quoted by R. Steig, Arnim-Brentano, p. 324.
[42] Herder's *Werke*, hrsg. von B. Suphan, XIII, 138.

ciate the work of art. In this manner intuitive criticism, often assuming the form of characterization, was pitted against analytical criticism. Herder advanced and deepened interpretative criticism (*Auslegergeist*),[43] which has also been called "apocalyptic criticism."[44] He distinguished between objective and subjective, or "higher" and "lower" criticism. Only genius is capable of objective criticism of high standing. Herder went one step farther in his innovations, so important for future generations, and emphasized the national and historical elements as factors to be considered in criticism: "To pass judgment without taking into account time, country, and language," he declares, "is stupid"....[45] "Sound criticism the world over demands that one enter into the spirit of the author, his public, his nationality, and last but not least, into the spirit of his creation, in order to appreciate fully a piece of literature."[46]

These views entered into conflict with the destructive, narrow-minded criticism which had dominated during most of the Eighteenth Century, and gradually won their way. This was due in large measure to the wide range of Herder's influence, which extended to Goethe and the romanticists. During the last decade of the century a progressive criticism in art, with the slogans: understanding, interpretation, intuition, and characterization, had supplanted the former subjective method. The romanticists had taken cognizance of Herder's views on aesthetics. They emphasized even more than he the inter-relationship between literature and history. All phenomena were to be explained in their dependency on time and civilization. According to Friedrich Schlegel, criticism was to be the link between the solitude of the literary world on its lofty heights of idealism and active, realistic, national life.[47]

Even as a youth Arnim was well acquainted with the aesthetic currents of his age, and with most of the leading advocates of these ideas. He could not but accept the principles of Herder's

[43] *Ibid.*, I, 41.
[44] Cf. Sigmund von Lempicki, *Geschichte der deutschen Literaturwissenschaft*, 1920, p. 369.
[45] Herder's *Werke*, III, 232.
[46] *Ibid.*, VI, 234.
[47] HeidelbJbb., 1808. I, Abt. 5, p. 379.

criticism as broadened by Goethe, Tieck, Schelling, and the Schlegel brothers. The great mission of literary criticism in his day as he saw and interpreted it was to acquaint the reader with the "remote and forgotten in literature."[48] The task of the critic was thus to be educational and constructive. Furthermore, he wanted to curb unnecessary so-called learned discussion. Criticism was not the primary thing; it was only a necessary tool to purify the spirit.[49] Art, he declared, should never be subjugated by criticism, as it unfortunately was in his day. These views were bound, sooner or later, to come into conflict with another attitude that developed simultaneously out of the romantic movement, the scientific approach to the past. A method of criticism like Arnim's, which endeavors to acquaint the reader with the "remote and unknown," will often overstep the boundary line of literary historical research. As Lempicki says, "Jacob Grimm's opposition to Brentano and Arnim reveals the line of demarcation between the literary criticism historically oriented and scientific research in literature."[50]

Arnim's essay "Von Volksliedern"[51] must be regarded as the first document in the development of his critical style. It takes the form of a characterization and description of the history of civilization, written in an entertaining and stimulating manner. Here he presents, not only his observations of different countries, districts, and ages, but also a cultural program which was to form the basis for his later activities. This is centered around the creation of a new spiritual life of the people. He believed that culture had degenerated during the preceding centuries because, since the ending of the Middle Ages, one had looked askance at the simple enjoyment of life. Unhealthy materialism, gluttony, fear of death were substituted. Only an awakening of the people to an active communal life could lead humanity back to a higher

[48] Arnim's letter to Goethe, April 1, 1808 in *Schriften der Goethe-Gesellschaft,* Weimar, XIV, 126; cited below as *Schriften der Goethe-Ges.*

[49] *Briefe an L. Tieck,* hrsg. von Karl von Holtei, I, 12; Arnim's letter to Tieck, December 3, 1807.

[50] Sigmund von Lempicki, "Über literarische Kritik und die Probleme ihrer Erforschung," *Euphorion,* XXV, 501-517.

[51] This essay had been partly published as early as 1805 in the *Berliner Musikalische Zeitung,* and appeared in completed form in 1806 as appendix to the first volume of *Des Knaben Wunderhorn.*

plane of living, prepare the ground for a new poetry of the people (*Volkspoesie*) and usher in a new era of understanding and reconciliation. *Volkspoesie* will inspire people to a noble and deep understanding of each other and put an end to disputes such as those about Christian and heathen, Hellenic, and Romantic.[52] In further development of this idea he proceeds to expose and attack what he regards as harmful elements in the art and literature of the nation, dwelling especially on pseudo-originality, *Genialität*, as mentioned above, and on the wretched state of contemporary criticism. This kind of critical gossip, he says, is not of German origin, but has become the fashion. In the eyes of the people these pedantic critics do nothing but spin sophisms and throw dirt at everything for the sole purpose of gathering questionable laurels for themselves.[53]

This then was Arnim's entry into the field of literary criticism and this was the spirit and the program which marked his work throughout life.

[52] Cf. DNL, CXLVI, I, 70.
[53] *Ibid.*, p. 76, footnote.

II

THE BACKGROUND OF FAMILY TRADITION AND CHARACTER DEVELOPMENT

If we glance through a list of the poets and other writers in Germany at the beginning of the Nineteenth Century, we discover many aristocratic patronymics. Most of the bearers of these betray their noble origin in their writings. There is none for whose work family tradition and background were more important than for Ludwig Achim von Arnim's; none whose literary conceptions were more strongly moulded by such forces. It is surprising that such a small amount of biographical data should have come down to us from a man of such a prominent family and of such poetic importance.[1] Max Koch declares, "there is scarcely a modern German poet about whose early years we have so little information as about those of Arnim."[2] We have, however, a good deal of information about his forefathers, their way of living, and their personalities.[3] From these sources we may venture some deductions as to the part played by heritage and milieu in the formation of Arnim's attitude toward life and art.

In analyzing Arnim's background, three elements are very striking. These are, first, the connection of the Arnim family with its native district, the Mark Brandenburg, and with the Prussian ruling house during many centuries; second, the intelligent, objective outlook on life characteristic of the family; and third, the artistic inclinations of Achim von Arnim's father and his maternal grandfather. Ludwig Achim von Arnim was first of all "a genuine squire of the *Mark*."[4] The tradition of the family, which had for seven hundred years lived on the soil of Brandenburg, was powerful within him. He felt himself to be a link in the chain of his ancestors and a part of the great historical events in which they

[1] Both Max Koch and Reinhold Steig deplore this fact.
[2] Cf. DNL, CXLVI, I, p. V; Arnim-Brentano, p. 10.
[3] Otto Devrient, *Das Geschlecht von Arnim*, Vol. I, Leipzig, 1914; Arnim-Crieven, *Beiträge zur Geschichte des Arnimschen Geschlechts*. 1. Teil, Berlin, 1883.
[4] Josef Nadler, *Die Berliner Romantik,* p. 154.

had played a rôle, as well as of national customs and life that had surrounded them. Love for his native land was born in him. The wide expanse of the North German plains and the rugged folk who dwelt there were dear to his heart. In contrast to his great master Goethe and his best friend Clemens Brentano, he was not of urban stock. In rural life he found always invigorating strength and peace of mind.

Thus the attachment to homeland and to family and local tradition held him with unbreakable bonds. He regarded it as one of his chief tasks to cultivate the past, which had for him "a peculiar austerity and sanctity."[5] Yet he did not want to live for the past alone. To him it was merely the source for a better understanding of the present and future, a fixed point from which to spin threads of the historical web further on to his German people and his fatherland. His master, Goethe, was almost entirely independent of local or national limitations. He was not merely the great poet of his native town or of Weimer, but a great world genius and an internationally minded artist. To Arnim, on the other hand, poetry, fatherland, and nation were one. He does not say, "I want to build a castle dedicated to art on German soil"; his goal is more restricted: he wants to build this structure on the sturdy soil of the *Mark*.[6] This love and admiration for his Prussian fatherland and his own people may always be found as the underlying note of his critical approach. Even when he steps into the "beautiful, simple, free Greek temple," he is in his thoughts still in the oak forests of Eastern Germany.[7]

However, in Arnim there was not merely the heritage of an old Prussian, land-owning family. In him there was also a strong artistic element which made him one of the most ardent of the romanticists. Furthermore, he revealed himself as an outstanding student and scholar, with a broad horizon, taking an interest in almost all fields of intellectual endeavor. The scholarly bent was especially strong in his youth, and it is noticeable again at the end of his career: "He is too diligent, too prone to versatility; he shows a thirst for knowledge and a wide reading in all fields."

---

[5] Arnim-Brentano, p. 270.
[6] *Ibid.*, p. 67.   [7] *Ibid.*, p. 35.

Thus a school report describes him.[8] This universality of intellectual interest permeated all his writings, especially his essays and reviews. Arnim feels himself compelled to bring his accumulated wealth of knowledge into relation with his own ideas; and it reappears sometimes clothed in fantastic garb, in his artistic creations.[9]

As a young student in Halle, Arnim's first interest was in the founding of a scientific club, and immediately thereafter, he prepared a series of articles for Gilbert's *Annalen der Physik*. These articles show a more objective attitude of mind than would be expected of the author of his fantastic poetic creations. He bases his discussions on Kant, Volta, and Priestley and opposes the pseudo-scientific notions so common at this period. The impression which we get of Arnim in his later period is similar to this early one. Interest in the factual and practical is a strongly marked characteristic and persisted throughout life. In the depressing years after 1806 he is the typical North German Junker, worrying incessantly about his financial and administrative obligations and always struggling to make ends meet. His interest in these days was of necessity concentrated much more on political and economic than on artistic problems. In his later years he saw the political sluggishness of his fatherland reappear, as well as the dull trends in literature against which he had fought so vigorously for over a decade. A certain resignation took possession of him. He came to realize more and more that he had lost in the struggle for the great cause to which he had dedicated his life, and he wearied of preaching his literary and political gospel to deaf ears.

This practical side of Arnim was in strong contrast to his romanticism.[10] Both combined in a dual personality, and he endeavored

[8] Ibid., pp. 7-8.

[9] Reinhold Steig in "L. A. v. Arnim als Tagesschriftsteller", *Nationalzeitung*, 427 (Berlin 1892), makes the following comment: "Dieser Trieb nach praktischer Betätigung dessen was er geistig empfand, führte ihn früh dazu an der Tagesschriftstellerei Teil zu nehmen."

[10] This contrast is best pictured by young Adolf Friedrich von Schack, who met Arnim in 1829: "Ich dachte, alle seine Reden müßten außergewöhnlich und von denen der gewöhnlichen Sterblichen verschieden sein. Aber bald fand ich mich sehr enttäuscht, da Alles, was er sagte, so einfach und schlicht wie möglich war . . . zu meinem großen Verdruß sprach er meistens von Landwirtschaft, welcher er sich mit großem Eifer widmete, und hie und da von Politik. Über Literatur hingegen floß auch nicht die kleinste Äußerung von seinen Lippen. Ich selbst wagte

all his life to reconcile the one with the other. As a child he was, he declares, highly romantic: "When I was a child, I thought as a child and believed in everything I thought. At that time, I was sure that I saw many marvellous things both in heaven and on earth."[11] But the romantic urge in him was checked through many years by various influences: after the early death of his parents, the strict, prosaic upbringing in the house of his grandmother, the Baroness von Labes, and the rationalism prevailing in the school system to which he was subjected. He mentions "the early artificial measures of the Roman school poets who were the torment of my youth."[12] Nevertheless an enthusiasm for poetry and romance was too essential a part of his character to be smothered by a rationalistic education. Indeed, an artistic strain lay in the family. His father was *directeur des spectacles* at the Berlin court from 1776 to 1778, and on terms of close friendship with the musician and composer, Johann Friedrich Reichardt. To his maternal grandfather Arnim ascribes "a soul of a very peculiar sort, an odd mixture of broad, liberal experiences and of the narrow attitude of his day, a distinctive personality with a great deal of eccentricity."[13] This description might apply almost as well to Arnim's own personality.

The only contact Arnim had with art and journalism in his youthful years in Berlin was at the home of Reichardt.[14] A close

nicht von diesem Thema anzufangen, und so habe ich denn von dem Urheber der 'Isabella von Aegypten' und so vieler phantastischen Erfindungen keinen anderen Eindruck erhalten, als von manchen sonstigen Landedelleuten, deren geistiger Horizont sich nicht weit über ihre Roggen- und Weizenfelder hinaus erstreckt . . . Der literarische und persönliche Charakter müssen bei Arnim in auffallender Weise im Widerspruch gestanden haben. Denn mein Vater, der nach damaliger Studentensitte mit ihm das nämliche Zimmer bewohnt hatte, versicherte mir wiederholt, er sei schon in seiner Jugend, wie immer nachher, ein praktischer, keineswegs überspannter Mensch gewesen. . . ." Adolf Friedrich Graf von Schack, *Ein halbes Jahrhundert. Erinnerungen und Aufzeichnungen* (Stuttgart, 1889), I, 14-16.

[11] Werke, I, p. XVII; Anrede an meine Zuhörer, im Herbst, 1811.

[12] *Ibid.*, p. XIX, cf. also in Arnim's essay "Von Volksliedern" (DNL, CXLVI, I, 62, footnote), "Wenn ich es verkehrt nenne, wie die Alten in vielen Schulen betrieben, so ist es meine Erfahrung. An allen Orten des Altdeutschen war nichts, des Lateins zuviel, des Griechischen zu wenig. Verkehrt nenne ich der Annäherung-Schulen nationale Geschichte, das Eigenste des Volks, den Alten nachzubilden, da doch diese nur wegen dieser erschöpfenden Nationalität vortrefflich sind."

[13] Arnim-Brentano, p. 1.

[14] Reichardt published the periodical *Deutschland*, beginning 1796, and the *Berlinische Musikalische Zeitung* from 1805.

friendship united him with this family all his life. It was Reichardt
who first called Arnim's attention to Herder and to many collections of folksongs, and some of Arnim's critical writings were
published in Reichardt's *Musikalische Zeitung*.[15] However, it was
men like Tieck, Schelling, and especially Clemens Brentano who
first aroused Arnim's artistic temper. Once awakened it soon
mounted to fantastic heights. When he met Arnim at Göttingen in
May, 1801, Brentano had just passed through three years of intimate association with the Jena romantic group. Years of rare
friendship were to follow on this first meeting. During this time
Arnim's literary critical ideas were subjected and conformed to
Brentano's. When this bond of friendship gradually loosened, however, it seems that Arnim's somewhat cooler nature gained the
upper hand. Brentano's share in shaping Arnim's critical point
of view should not be overestimated. He had had, it is true, a
longer literary experience. They had a common interest in folklore and a similar attitude toward their contemporaries. However,
before Arnim came to Göttingen he had gone through a thorough
training in the scientific and philosophical thinking of his age.
Here Brentano was never able to follow him, nor into the realm
of nationalistic enthusiasm, which is such a vital element in Arnim's criticism. Their opinions differed also with regard to Goethe
and on religious matters.

At the end of July, 1801, Arnim left Brentano and Göttingen
and went on his "grand tour." This was his first experience of travelling into greater Germany, away from his immediate Prussian
surroundings. From early childhood, love of the Mark Brandenburg and his *engere Heimat* was strong in him; now for the first
time he experienced the color and variety of the many different
German states and their varying landscape. Still, different as they
were, a similar culture united them; and he found the same folksongs and legends in Prussia and on the Rhine, in Switzerland and
in Austria. He was much impressed by Munich and Vienna, both
larger and more distinctly cultural centers than Berlin at this
time. Here he found the old German traditions united with a new
artistic life. He regretted much that cultural unity was divided

[15] Cf. Otto Mallon, *Arnim Bibliographie*, pp. 10, 23; cited below as "Mallon."

by political boundary lines, and expressed the hope that North and South Germany might be united in the future. The solitude of the Swiss mountains inspired his fantastic plan for the conservation, revival, and world-wide dispersion of German lyrical poetry. He was not enthusiastic about France, sharing the attitude of most of his German contemporaries, who disapproved of French culture and especially of Paris, the cosmopolitan center, with its artificial modes of life. He criticized French art in an article, "Erzählungen von Schauspielen," published at this time in Friedrich Schlegel's *Europa*.[16] It was his conviction that French forms of art were unsuitable for Germany and would lead only to pretense and bombast. In Paris longing for home seized him: "Oh, my hallowed fatherland, here among strangers I still feel the breath of thy inspiration!"[17]

His "grand tour" also took him to England, in the summer of 1803. Here also he could not feel at home, in spite of many beautiful scenic impressions and his admiration for the English people. He shared the great enthusiasm of his time for Shakespeare. While in London he found that tragedy was still presented in great perfection and still enjoyed great popularity.[18] Above all, he was interested in Walter Scott's Scottish ballads and romances.[19]

In the fall of 1804 Arnim returned from his tour. Though still a young man, he had already seen and experienced much, and had associated with many distinguished people. He had also won his spurs as an author, having published his first novel, *Hollins Liebeleben* in 1802, and in 1804, *Ariels Offenbarungen*. By this time he had also had his first experience as a literary critic. Following his many contributions as a student of natural science to Gilbert's *Annalen der Physik* after 1799, Arnim had now found recognition as a critic of literature from no less an authority than Friedrich Schlegel. His "Erzählungen von Schauspielen," had been published, as we have seen, in Schlegel's *Europa*. The three years which he had spent abroad were not without results in the shaping of his character. We might have expected him to return home

[16] *Europa*, hrsg. von Friedrich Schlegel, 1803, pp. 140-192.
[17] Arnim-Brentano, p. 68.
[18] *Ibid.*, p. 95.
[19] *Ibid.*, p. 95.

equipped with cosmopolitan ideas. On the contrary, his stay abroad had made him more German than before. His interest in folklore had increased through his correspondence with Clemens Brentano and the attainment of a deeper insight into the writings of Walter Scott, Percy, and Macpherson.

Arnim came back to Germany with a fixed resolve to do for his fatherland in the field of folklore that which had already been accomplished for England and Scotland. He went about this task with dauntless optimism, supreme confidence in himself and in a better future for Germany, and with a complete faith in divine providence. This confidence in the future of the fatherland remains characteristic of him throughout his whole life; it is expressed in all his writings on cultural and political questions concerning Germany. In the program for his planned weekly *Der Preusse, ein Volksblatt,* announced in 1806 Arnim says with characteristic optimism:

We shall call this paper *Der Deutsche* as soon as Germany has recovered from the long illness which destroys all individual and collective strength which we had gathered and cultivated silently and joyfully.[20]

The quality of his optimism is expressed in the lines of Goethe, which Arnim quotes in his introduction to *Wunder über Wunder:*

Liegt dir Gestern klar und offen,
Wirkst du heute kräftig frei;
Kannst auch auf ein Morgen hoffen,
Das nicht minder glücklich sei.[21]

Even in the depressing years after 1806, when Ernst Moritz Arndt struck a very pessimistic note in the first volume of his *Geist der Zeit,* and when a well-known publicist, Archenholtz,[22] expressed the fear that the German language would die out, Arnim still believed in the future greatness of Germany, a result, however, which could come only through the cultivation of the treasures to be found in folk-art and folk-literature. It is this faith that gave the impulse for the rise of the historical school in language and

[20] *Ibid.,* p. 191; Mallon, pp. 22, 23.
[21] Werke, XIX, 266; *Landhausleben, Wunder über Wunder, indisches Mährchen, Mittwochs-Erzählung des Direktors der Theaterschule.*
[22] Johann Wilhelm von Archenholtz, 1743-1812, published in Hamburg from 1792-1812 the periodical *Minerva, ein Journal historischen und politischen Inhalts.*

literature and for publications such as the *Wunderhorn* and the *Zeitung für Einsiedler*.

In Arnim this optimism goes hand in hand with an absolute faith in God. He was a convinced Protestant and believed confidently in "a heart of eternal love that throbs through the entire world." God, he felt, would not permit His own destruction, for the love of God is the will of the world. If mankind has to suffer, it is because mankind has failed in recognizing the divine will.[23] Beginning with early childhood, Arnim had a very strict religious education, both in his grandmother's home and during his school and student days at Berlin and Halle. From these years dates his admiration for Luther. His romantic nature was later to draw him in a mystical direction similar to that of Jung-Stilling and young Zacharias Werner.

Such, broadly, was Arnim's background when he started out on his critical activities. In Heidelberg he hoped that the *Zeitung für Einsiedler* would become his "Opera omnia," and he took a very active part in the beginning of the *Heidelbergische Jahrbücher*. Nevertheless, the former, his own periodical, survived less than half a year, and he soon had to withdraw as collaborator from the *Heidelbergische Jahrbücher* in the face of a rising antagonism towards him on the part of members of the university circle. In Berlin, his critical activities, his association with the *Abendblätter* and with the *Preussische Correspondent*, were all short-lived. These failures show conclusively that he was not popular as a critic and journalist.

To understand the reason for this failure it is necessary to analyze some additional features of his personality. Arnim was throughout life the simple, forthright *Junker*. He was not really born to become an acute and subtle critic. Nature seems to have intended him rather to be an officer in the king's army. The inner conflict between the desire for the free life of the soldier and the urge to take part in the tedious struggle for the spiritual rejuvenation of his country came particularly to the fore during Napoleon's rule in Prussia. At that time he deplored that his weapon had to

[23] Werke, XX, 278; Arnim's favorite maxim was, "Gott ist die Liebe, und wer in der Liebe lebt, lebt in Gott." Cf. Arnim-Bettina p. 362.

be the pen instead of the sword. During this conflict with himself he writes to Bettina:

Again the same old regret takes hold of me that tormented me in Königsberg, the feeling that perhaps I have taken the wrong course. Instead of letters, I ought to have taken the sword. Now it is too late, habit with its millions of invisible threads has bound me so firmly that I can never free myself entirely from it.[24]

These profound contradictions within his personality made it difficult for him to achieve the inner harmony and balance so necessary for the exercise of the critic's office. There were also other reasons. Arnim lived and wrote only in and for his own idealistic world. He never wrote merely for pecuniary reward.[25] Often he clung to his opinions in an obstinate and uncompromising manner. Theories, schools, or literary groups had little meaning for him. "He kept away from all literary cliques," says Reinhold Steig,

His concern was ever with the matter itself, never with disputes about it. In judging the work of others, he fixed his attention first of all on what had actually been accomplished, in order to be able the more easily to overlook any weakness. Not a single one of his reviews or observations contains anything to wound the feelings. He had too rich and noble a soul for that.[26]

[24] Arnim-Bettina, p. 268; March 10, 1809; cf. also *Ariel,* autobiographical sketch of the *Siebente Winterabend:* "Ich stamme aus rühmlichem und reichem Geschlechte; meine erste Neigung würde mich zum Soldaten gemacht haben, doch das läppische Wesen, das durch lange Friedenszeit in diesen Stand gekommen, machte ihn mir verächtlich; ich wählte das Buch statt des Schwertes. Was mich ergreift, dem ergebe ich mich ganz, meine ganze Lebensweise entwickelte sich darnach, meinen Büchern, dieser lieben Gesellschaft aus alter Zeit zu leben, alle Wissenschaften und Künste suchte ich mir nach möglicher Kraft anzueignen. Bald genügte es mir nicht, dies allein in mir zu treiben, ich fühlte einen Drang andre damit zu ergreifen und zu durchdringen, ich knüpfte reisend mit Unzähligen an, wir hofften auf eine schöne Zeit für Deutschland, und arbeiteten fleißig, es sollte wie ein wunderbarer allseitiger Spiegel die Welt vereinigen. Schnell über und fort, wie eine wilde Taube im Sturm, der Krieg brach ein, zerschlug den Spiegel; wohl recht sagt Sophokles, er raubt die Guten nur. Ich hätte gern mitgefochten aber ich konnte das Schwert nicht führen; tausend Gewohnheiten hielten mich gefangen, die eben darum sich hielten, weil sie nicht leer, sondern in würdigen Zwecken erworben, doch fühle ich, wenn ich auch meinen Sinn und meine Bemühung achten mußte, daß ich etwas Verkehrtes getrieben, was in der verderblichen Zeit nicht paßte, ich trauerte tief und hoffte dann wieder abwechselnd mit aller Torheit." Werke, V, 110-14.

[25] Arnim-Bettina, p. 308: "Die Schriftstellerei für Geld ist einmal mir verhaßt . . . von anderer Gnade zu leben wäre mein Tod."

[26] "Achim von Arnim als Tagesschriftsteller," *Nationalzeitung,* Nr. 427, Berlin, 1892.

This nobility of mind was not entirely advantageous to his career as a critic. Often his friends in Heidelberg complained that he was too lenient in the quarrel with Voss and the *Jenaer Literaturzeitung*. Wilhelm Budde, while a young student in Heidelberg, gives us in his diary a sketch of Arnim in those days, as "a man of noble and self-contained nature. His intelligent face wears an expression of youthful, good-natured irony."[27] Arnim himself recognized this trait, and declared that his worst fault was too great softness of character.[28]

In addition to these characteristics, it must also be emphasized that Arnim lacked completely a sense of order and form. He neither co-ordinated nor systematized the facts, ideas, and outer form of his writings. He wrote as the spirit moved him. He would often incorporate into his writings symbolical comparisons and far-fetched ideas. He liked to interpolate anecdotes and sententious remarks. His basic trait of character, his hatred for any kind of system, fostered this manner of writing. Brentano bemoaned the great confusion in Arnim's papers. He wanted to live near him in order to help him organize his ideas and his work.[29] In his criticisms Arnim almost never discusses form, style, or other external characteristics; only the spirit and the thought of a work attract him. He prefers to deal with writers and ideas close to his heart and of his own way of thinking. He sympathizes with poets "whose only purpose is to express their ideas," and he contrasts them with those who value ideas only when clothed in perfect form.[30] This one-sided and undisciplined approach to literature sometimes impaired his perception of literary values and hampered his objective judgment. In this respect he was unlike Brentano, who possessed excellent critical faculties.[31] In Arnim's writings one searches in vain for analytical discussions, but one finds abundant expressions of feeling and many hasty, subjective conclusions. His entire critical production is an *Erlebniskritik* based on *Tendenz*

[27] H. Wilhelm Budde, 1786-1858, studied in Heidelberg for two semesters, beginning Easter, 1807. *Heidelberger Tagebuch*, p. 267, 1807-8.

[28] Arnim-Bettina, p. 269.

[29] Arnim-Brentano, p. 105.

[30] HeidelbJbb., Abtlg. I, 153, 1810; Arnim's review of *Friedrich Schlege's Gedichte*, Berlin, 1809.

[31] Cf. Arnim-Brentano, p. 354 (Anm. 188).

and thus constitutes a continuation of the method of approach of Hamann and Herder, who looked upon such topics as nature, spirit, mankind, the nation in literature subjectively, uniting them monadically into a great harmony of the *All*.

It was for the realization of this great harmony in literature and art that Arnim struggled. For him it was exemplified in the creations of the Middle Ages and the old German past generally. He desired also that this harmony might enter into his personal life. He tried to put an end to the conflict between life and art inherent in almost all of the younger Romanticists. He wished to attain to the lofty height of a romantic monism and to the full unity of spirit and nature found in Goethe.

His *Lebensgefühl* is definitely in this direction and is therefore positivistic and joyfully optimistic.[32] He wished to overcome obstacles and conflicts in a grand manner, to let his literary creations spring from the wealth of his overflowing soul and the richness of life itself. It was his aim to grasp the "sublime life":

> Es trägt nur freie Kraft durchs hohe Leben
> Vertrauend soll sich jeder ihr ergeben.[33]

The same thought when applied to literature is expressed in a passage in the *Zeitung für Einsiedler:* "The blind conflict between the Romanticists and the so-called Classicists is coming to an end: what remains is life itself."[34] At the same time he strove to retain a popular appeal, the ability to be understood by all social classes, something that he always admired in other writers. What he valued and sought to attain was, as he expresses it, the ability to give distinction to ordinary things in such a way as to make what is sublime appear as nothing unusual or out of the ordinary.[35]

[32] Even though Arnim appeared as a happy, carefree human being, there was a deep seriousness hidden in his nature. But he preferred to express himself often in a jesting manner. When critical, he inclines to good-natured irony of an entirely different character from Tieck's romantic irony. Thus, in announcing the *Zeitung für Einsiedler,* Arnim admonished the reading public: "Nehmt alles ernsthafter, als wir es Euch sagen, und Ihr werdet den Sinn fassen." *Arnim's Tröst Einsamkeit. Hrsg. von Fridrich Pfaff* (Frieburg i.B. und Tübingen 1883), p. 4, cited below as *Tröst Einsamkeit.* Similarly he confided to Bettina that behind the comic mask of his journal a more serious face was concealed. Arnim-Bettina, p. 91.

[33] Werke, I, p. XXI; "Anrede an meine Zuhörer."

[34] *Tröst Einsamkeit,* p. 71, Anmerkung.

[35] Arnim-Bettina, p. 239.

A prerequisite for the attainment of this *hohe Leben* was the spiritual rejuvenation of his fatherland, for life in his age was too prosaic to inspire a poet: "In our time one cannot be a poet, one can only do something for poetry," Clemens wrote him.[36] To the Count in his *Gräfin Dolores* Arnim assigned one purpose in life: service to his fellow-countrymen.[37]

However, it was not given to Arnim to reach these lofty heights of spirit and nature, of desire and accomplishment in life. Comparatively early in his life he had to realize that his hopes and capacity did not balance. Shortly before his marriage to Bettina he cautioned her not to look for too much that was good in him: "I know better than anyone how much I have wanted to do and how little I have accomplished".[38] His *Spiegelmensch*, against which he struggled in vain all his life long, is a Wilhelm Meister type. In a discussion of *Wilhelm Meister* in his later years he gives unconsciously a fine bit of self-analysis which emphasizes the conflicting elements in his own soul:

> Wilhelm's goodheartedness and weakness, his great aspirations and his pliant nature, his desire for development and his continual talk about it, and the constant interruption of this development by capriciousness, his isolation from the world and then his attachment to it, his doubts of himself, although he is always falling back on himself,—all this makes him a faithful though intellectualized image of gifted young men in a period which ended with the Revolution. He makes only a pretense of contact with the life of the middle classes; public life arouses his disgust and suspicion. He is only persistent in the effort for his own development and he sticks to that like a bird to a lime twig . . . he is endowed with all the admirable powers of his time and is subject to all the evil temptations, with no force to urge toward a goal selected by his own genius.[39]

Like Wilhelm Meister, Arnim lacked the determination and driving force of the genius who is able to master the contrasts in himself and those of his age.[40]

[36] Arnim-Brentano, p. 106.

[37] Werke, XVIII, p. 455.

[38] Arnim-Brentano, p. 401; letter of July 29, 1810.

[39] Werke, XIX, 267/8; Arnim-Brentano, p. 54: "Lies einmal im Wilhelm Meister . . .das dritte Capitel des fünften Teils, Wilhelms Brief an Werner, und Du hast was Savigny und Winkelmann über mich urteilen. . . "

[40] Arnim-Brentano, p. 54; Klinger's *Weltmann und Dichter* likewise reminded Arnim of the two realms which he could not reconcile.

But although Arnim never could attain to the greatness and wisdom of Goethe, he was spared the fate of many of his contemporaries who, like Brentano, for instance, became the fragile toys of their romantic whims. The whirlwind of romantic sentiment, the wild intoxication of spirit never entirely gained the upper hand in Arnim, because his Mark Brandenburg tradition kept his feet on the ground. Hence in his critical writings one encounters a novel accent which distinguishes him from contemporary thought and throws light on the transition to, first, a national and later, a realistic outlook on life.

In conclusion, one may say that like his other works, his critical writings are the outgrowth of a vague, groping idealism. His philosophy and his art did not appeal to his contemporaries, and Arnim died lonely and misunderstood. Nor was he appreciated by the next generation, with the exception of a chosen few. Among these was Heinrich Heine, who praised Arnim's writings very highly in his *Romantische Schule*,[41] and paved the way for his subsequent fame. There are many interesting comments on Arnim's personality by those who knew him,[42] but none of these describes the conglomerate which formed the basis for his critical work more strikingly or more aptly than that by Wilhelm Grimm his most faithful and understanding friend:

He was a man of decision, but of mild temper; to even the most insignificant person he would give sunshine and warmth. Thoroughly nonpartisan in character, he maintained a noble attitude of detachment amid the dissensions of the time. He was not a poet of despair revelling in the agony caused by the dissonances of his own soul. He rose superior to turmoil and prejudice. With hope for the future he brought the most extraordinary and astounding things without hesitation into close companionship with those of general acceptance, the simplest songs that appeal to every human heart with those mysterious ones whose meaning he alone might fathom. He seemed like one who could suddenly leave a party and surrender himself to his own thoughts in the depths of a forest.[43]

[41] *Heines Sämtliche Werke*, Insel Ausgabe, VII, 128-136.

[42] Goethe to Reichardt, October 10, 1810; Wilhelm von Humboldt to Caroline, *Briefe*, III, 101-2; Immermann, *Jahrbücher für wissenschaftliche Kritik*, pp. 760-6, 1827; K. A. Varnhagen von Ense, *Tagebücher* X, 414, 14-16.

[43] Introduction to *Arnims Sämtliche Werke*, I, VIII.

III
FROM SCIENCE TO LITERATURE

Arnim was relatively late in discovering the field of literature. Not until his twenty-first year, in 1802, did he begin to look at poetry as "the focus of life and affairs."[1] As a student of eighteen, however, he had found the path to critical journalism in the field of science. In May, 1798, he matriculated at the University of Halle as a student of law but felt himself attracted by the field of natural science. On July 15 of the same year he presided at the organization of the "Freunde freier Untersuchungen,"[2] a student society devoted to the cultivation of research. The results of his studies were embodied in the following year in a book, *Versuch einer Theorie der elektrischen Erscheinungen,*[3] and in sixteen contributions to Gilbert's *Annalen der Physik.*[4] It was the age of revolutionary discoveries in the field of science. The startling problems of electricity and magnetism occupied the leading minds; but metaphysics and mysticism were also strongly in vogue. The relationship between experiment and deductive reasoning in the approach to nature was by no means clear. Scientific and poetic activities had their origin in the same soil. In Middle Germany the universities particularly engaged in scientific speculation were Jena, Halle, Göttingen, and Würzburg. These centers were becoming widely known through the activities of men like Fichte, Schelling, Ritter, and Novalis.

While Arnim was a student at Halle, a strictly scientific attitude toward nature was prevalent there. The dominating figure in scientific circles was Ludwig Wilhelm Gilbert (1769-1824), who had been professor of mathematics and physics at Halle since 1795. He was Arnim's teacher and was chief editor of the *Annalen der Physik,* founded by Albert Carl Gren. This journal was much

[1] Arnim-Brentano, p. 38.
[2] *Ibid.,* p. 8.
[3] Mallon, p. 1.
[4] *Ibid.,* pp. 1-3; also Ernst Darmstaedter, "Achim von Arnim und die Naturwissenschaft"; *Euphorion,* 1931, pp. 454-76.

concerned with polemics against the pseudo-scientific mysticism fashionable in those days. This attitude is emphasized in the concluding paragraphs of Editor Gilbert's preface to the first volume of the *Annalen* (1799):

> Nothing in my opinion is more incompatible with true science than the passion for novelties and the snatching at sensational news, instead of being satisfied with thorough studies and research. I am concerned only about the promotion and propagation of true science and disdain this passion for sensational pseudo-scientific novelties.[5]

Influenced by the point of view of his teacher, Arnim in his first published work warns against an unscientific, unsystematic spirit:

> I would not advise the acceptance of any mere semblance of knowledge in the field of natural science where there is an illegible passage in the book of nature, nor would I, like the freebooter in Homer, be satisfied to show my tracks in reverse, leaving the reader in uncertainty as to what path had led me to the goal.[6]

This objective attitude was strikingly in contrast with that of Arnim's mystical Romantic contemporaries. One of these, Christian Brentano, some years later accuses him of a too materialistic approach to physics. "Men on earth," he writes Arnim, "have to seek refuge with God and his religion, not with mechanism or philosophy or whatever it may be."[7]

The *Versuch einer Theorie der elektrischen Erscheinungen,* from which the quotation in the foregoing paragraph is taken, is based on Kant's dynamic conception of nature. Arnim rejects all mechanistic materialism and adopts as a working hypothesis the principle of a formative force (*gestaltende Kraft*).[8] His briefer contributions to the *Annalen* are partly translations and announcements drawn from French scientific publications, and partly reports on the author's own researches, or critical reviews of other

---

[5] *Annalen der Physik,* hrsg. von Ludwig Wilhelm Gilbert. Vol. I, Vorwort, Halle, 1799.

[6] "Ich würde raten, in der Naturlehre weder den Schein des Wissens anzunehmen, wo im Buche der Natur eine unleserliche Stelle ist, noch, wie jener Homerische Freibeuter, die Fußtapfen umgekehrt zu zeigen, und die Leser bei dem erreichten Ziele über den zurückgelegten Weg in Ungewißheit lassen." *Versuch einer Theorie der elektrischen Erscheinungen,* p. 3, also DNL, CXLVI, 11.

[7] Christian Brentano's letter to Arnim (unpublished), July 23, 1805, quoted partly in K. E. Henrici, *Auktions-Katalog* 149, p. 31.

[8] Moritz Carriere, *Achim von Arnim,* p. 13.

publications. These and Arnim's later articles on scientific subjects are clear and objective, and are therefore quite in contrast with the writings of certain contemporary students of the natural sciences, like the famous Jena physicist, J. W. Ritter, whose works make a very mystical and confusing impression. A glance at Arnim's topics reveals that he did not choose pseudo-scientific subjects.[9] The significance of his scientific contributions has recently been confirmed in a paper by Ernst Darmstaedter.[10]

Important and interesting in this connection is a closer study of Arnim's relationship to the two men who played such an important rôle in formulating the philosophic conception of this romantic period, Johann Wilhelm Ritter (1776-1810) and Friedrich Wilhelm Schelling. The names of Ritter and Arnim have been mentioned together very often.[11] August Winkelmann, who was in close contact with Ritter in Jena, wrote in the preface to his *Einleitung in die dynamische Physiologie,* published in 1803, a dedication to "his friends," Ritter and Arnim.[12] If Bettina may be relied on, Clemens Brentano in a letter of May, 1801, referred to Arnim as Ritter's great rival in the field of physics.[13] Such references to Arnim's relation to Ritter are especially noteworthy if one recalls the leading position young Ritter held among his romantic contemporaries in that field. The brilliant career of the self-

[9] Mallon, pp. 1-5.

[10] Ernst Darmstaedter, "Achim von Arnim und die Naturwissenschaft," *Euphorion,* XXXII (1931), 454-476. Unlike Schönemann, who maintains that Arnim was ill prepared to discuss philosophically the results and problems of scientific research (L. A. von *Arnims geistige Entwicklung an seinem Drama "Halle und Jerusalem" erläutert*), Darmstaedter comes to the conclusion that young Arnim displayed a rare independence in scientific thinking (p. 47).

[11] The only article I have found on Arnim's relations with Ritter, that of Paul Hoffmann, "Achim von Arnim über J. W. Ritter" (*Archiv f. Gesch. d. Mathematik, Naturwiss. u. Technik*, X, 357), is misleading. Apparently Hoffmann overlooked completely two publications containing valuable information: R. Steig, "Zeugnisse zur Pflege der deutschen Literatur in den Heidelbergischen Jahrbüchern" (NHeidelbJbb., 1902), and Alfred Kloss, *Die Heidelbergischen Jahrbücher der Litteratur,* 1918. From Hoffmann one gets the impression that Arnim reviewed Ritter's book in dutiful compliance with the editor's wishes, while as a matter of fact, the review was Arnim's choice. Furthermore Arnim's attitude toward Ritter was essentially different from Hoffmann's view of it. He quite misinterprets Arnim's statement, "den Ritter habe ich mit Lust und Liebe und ganz in allgemeiner menschlicher Beziehung geschrieben," NHeidelbJbb. (1902), p. 247; quoted from Arnim's letter to August Böckh, March 12, 1810.

[12] Arnim-Brentano, p. 9.

[13] *Frühlingskranz,* p. 246; letter to Bettina, May, 1801.

educated young peasant was the result of strenuous and intensive effort; indeed, overwork, accompanied by a dissolute life, was responsible for his untimely death. Arnim was familiar with Ritter's queer habits of living and working, and describes them vividly in a letter to Clemens Brentano:

> Intensive work for a few days; hunger, then sleep, drink, and gluttony for the next days; love making, despair, artificial stimulation, interspersed with insult and truth, absurd and futile literary endeavors.[14]

Arnim and Ritter were interested in similar questions, chiefly galvanism and magnetism, and they influenced each other mutually, as is apparent in their writings. Arnim wrote two reviews of Ritter's early scientific papers, his *Beweis, daß ein beständiger Galvanismus den Lebensprozeß im Tierreiche begleite* (Weimar, 1798) and his *Beiträge zur Kenntnis des Galvanismus* (Bd. I, Jena, 1802).[15] Ritter, likewise, noticed Arnim's scientific contributions published in the *Annalen der Physik* in 1800[16] and discussed them in his *Beiträge* (II, 17). Here he contended that some of Arnim's hypotheses had become antiquated. Arnim was offended by this criticism and in a letter to Gilbert, October 29, 1801, maintained his views with youthful stubbornness.[17] Furthermore, in his "Versuche und Bemerkungen über den Galvanismus der Voltaischen Batterie," a series of letters addressed to the editor of the *Annalen der Physik,* Ritter criticized severely Arnim's paper "Bemerkungen über Voltas Säule," published in the *Annalen* in 1801,[18] and expressed his surprise that Arnim, otherwise so well acquainted with the laws of electricity, should overestimate the importance of wet bodies.[19]

While Ritter was a great rival of young Arnim, Schelling, the

---

[14] *Arnim-Brentano*, p. 187. Here Arnim compares Winkelmann's life with that of Ritter: "Er (Winkelmann) ist an einem Typhus gestorben, den seine Art von wilder Praxis gefährlicher gemacht hatte. Er hat sich auch eigentlich nicht durch Liederlichkeit geschwächt—denn das soll mehr Redensart gewesen sein—sondern durch sein altes, Ritter nachgebildetes ungewöhnliches Leben: langes Arbeiten für einige Tage, Hungern, dann Schlafen, Trinken, Fressen für den folgenden, Verliebttun, Verzweifeln, eine künstliche Empfindungsmanege. . . ."

[15] These two reviews appeared in the *Annalen der chemischen Literatur,* hrsg. von Friedrich Wolff, I, 197-399, Berlin, 1803. Cf. Mallon, Nr. 20.

[16] Mallon, No. 4.

[17] *Annalen der Physik*, IX, 494-496.

[18] Mallon, No. 10.

[19] *Annalen der Physik*, IX, 212-262, esp. 238, 239.

greatest nature philosopher of his generation, was a stimulus to him, and was probably responsible for his abandoning science and entering the field of literature. Arnim and Schelling never met. Intermediaries between the two were the Reichardt family, who during Arnim's student years resided at Giebichenstein Castle at Halle. Here many of the prominent figures of the day were accustomed to meet. Later on, in 1808, Bettina, while visiting in Munich, seems to have started a short-lived correspondence between Arnim and Schelling, of which only one letter, from Arnim to Schelling, is available.[20] Arnim had an intimate knowledge of Schelling's writings. In his *Versuch einer Theorie der elektrischen Erscheinungen* he discussed them critically, and Schelling took favorable notice of young Arnim's scientific articles in his *Zeitschrift für spekulative Physik*, 1801-1802.[21]

The common ground of interest in these earlier exchanges was the phenomenon of electricity. In the *Versuch* Arnim felt obliged to inform his readers that he had not found any novel point of view in his study of Schelling.[22] This youthful approach of Arnim to the problem of electrical manifestation is purely scientific (in the modern sense), taking as its basis only the actual physical data and paying no heed to the universal character of the thought of Schelling, who endeavored to find the "all" behind single phenomena of nature. Only when he began a study of Schelling's *Weltseele* and *Ideen zu einer Philosophie der Natur* did Arnim begin to realize the importance of relating spiritual life and art to science.

The *Ideen zu einer Philosophie der Natur*, published in 1797, and the study *Von der Weltseele, eine Hypothese der höheren Physik zur Erklärung des allgemeinen Organismus*, published a year later (in the spring of 1798), were two brilliant works on natural philosophy. They gave, indeed, an entirely new, transcendental outlook on the world. In the *Ideen* Schelling expounded the thesis that scientific achievements are of secondary importance and can not explain the wonders of the world. It is rather the task

---

[20] Partly published by K. Henrici, *Auktions-Katalog* 149, p. 15; not mentioned in Arnim Bibliography.

[21] Jena, 1800, Vol. I, 142-8, 1801, Vol. II, 152-3.

[22] *Versuch einer Theorie*, p. 120.

of philosophy, the instrument of the spirit, to interpret scientific facts.[23] Chemistry furnishes only information on the elements, physics only such as concerns formulas (*Silben*), mathematics only details with respect to nature, while philosophy alone is able to synthesize and expound the data. In *Von der Weltseele* Schelling departed still further from logical, scientific thinking and empirical procedure and delved deeper into metaphysics and mysticism. He declared that behind the antagonism of forces and the yawning dualism of nature, in the last analysis a single natural principle manifests itself, namely the "World Soul," as the ancient Greeks called it without being able to define it more adequately.[24] From both these works, the *Ideen* and the *Weltseele*, extensive quotations are found in Arnim's *Versuch* of 1799. Four years later, in the essay "Erzählungen von Schauspielen," published in Friedrich Schlegel's *Europa*,[25] we find Arnim making use of expressions and ideas drawn from Schelling, such as "World Soul," and the "inner essence of all nature."

Of the greatest influence on Arnim's conception of art was a third work of Schelling, his *System des transzendentalen Idealismus* (1800). This was the book which forced Goethe to declare that he would have to depart from the traditional method of science.[26] In the sixth chapter of his *System* Schelling declares that art is the pattern of science and that science must associate itself with art;[27] for art, which can spring from genius alone, is "the sole and eternal revelation."[28] These ideas must have stirred Arnim deeply, as one can readily see in the "Lebensplan," which he submitted to Clemens in a confidential letter of July 9, 1802.[29] In other letters which he wrote in the following years on his

[23] *Schellings Werke*, hrsg. von K. A. Schelling, Abt. I, Bd. II, 6: "Aus der Innerlichkeit des Geistes soll die Natur gedeutet werden."

[24] *Ibid.*, p. 562.

[25] *Europa*, II, 163, 173; Frankfurt, 1803. Here Arnim says: "Die Weltseele scheint noch wie ein unerzogenes Mädchen in ihren Bildungen aus Erdschollen zu spielen, sie hängt immer einen gewaltigen Geist und ein gewaltiges Schicksal einem schwachen Körper zum Schabernack an."

[26] In April, 1800, Goethe wrote to Schelling: "Ich glaube in dieser Vorstellungsart sehr viele Vorteile für denjenigen zu entdecken, dessen Neigung es ist, die Kunst auszuüben und die Natur zu betrachten."

[27] *System*, pp. 460, 468, 469.

[28] *System*, pp. 460, 468, 469.   [29] Arnim-Brentano, pp. 38-9.

grand tour, particularly those written during the time when he felt most strongly the conflict between the call to a scientific career and to an artistic one, Arnim echoes Schelling's statement that even science has to serve art.[30] In the letter to Clemens just referred to he had declared that "everything that occurs in the world is on account of poetry."[31] Similarly, Schelling's emphasis on the sacredness of art inspires Arnim's appeal to the poet not to show pride, but the greatest virtue.

Very early in Arnim's letters we note an inclination to approach literature through nature. His attitude was similar to Goethe's: "to practice art and observe nature." In 1802 he proclaims that a mighty spirit of poetry breathes throughout all nature, revealing itself at one time as history, at another as a phenomenon of nature. The poet need only catch a few faint echoes of this spirit in order to see clearly into the profoundest depths of the emotions.[32] Schelling maintained that perfection (*das Vollendete*) can be reached only by genius.[33] With a truly romantic egotism Arnim feels that he is a genius according to Schelling's definition, and in the somewhat turgid language characteristic of Schelling, he declares that he recognizes in himself the "pole," e.g., the focal center of all languages, "without which nature must of necessity fade into indefiniteness."[34]

Arnim was attracted to Schelling because of the latter's very broad definition of poetry and art. In his "transcendental idealism" Schelling considered poetry and art as the main-spring of life. Arnim felt that genuine greatness and glory were attained only by creative artists, such as Goethe, Tieck, and his friend Brentano when he gave to the world his *Godwi*. He held it to be his immediate task to bring new life to humanity through poetry: "Art must take a hand in the transformation of the world," he declared many years later in the *Kronenwächter*.[35] This was to be the

---

[30] *System*, p. 468.

[31] Arnim-Brentano, p. 38.

[32] *Ibid.*, p. 35. Schelling expressed this idea as follows, "Nature and history are the two poles proper which combine to a new third unity, namely art."

[33] Schelling interprets poetry (*Poesie*) as "the realistic element by means of which the infinite is moulded into the finite." *Werke*, I, V, 479, 468. Cf. also Heinrich Knittermeyer, *Schelling und die romantische Schule*, p. 345.

[34] Arnim-Brentano, p. 32.

[35] *Kronenwächter*, II, 387.

poetizing of reality for which Novalis, Hölderlin, and Tieck had struggled; yet Arnim set for it more immediate goals. As early as December 1803, he came to believe that he could thus render a service to mankind which would never be possible in the natural sciences. In retrospect he now views his work in physics as useless. He does not want to write for bookworms: "My mind stood open like a chalice to the light of poetry."[36]

Appreciating this philosophy of Arnim in the light of Schelling's "transcendental idealism," one can understand now fully his "plan of life," (*Lebensplan*). The framework of this romantic universalism contained, however, definite goals which Arnim pursued seriously in succeeding years. National boundaries were not to put a limitation on these goals. In the first place, a *Sprach- und Singschule* was to be founded, where a standard modern German language was to be created which would soon be accepted by all people in Germany and later also by all nations of the world. This would bring about at once a closer association and more intimate unity among Germans of all tribes. All the agitation and quarreling of their princes would cease, for Germans would not fight against their brethren. Even the foreigners, no longer supported by selfish individual German princes, would ally themselves with united Germany. Thus Arnim hoped that Germany would become the "lightning rod of the world."[37] It is evident that these ideas of Arnim's can be traced ultimately to Schelling's romantic monism.

Romantic monism presupposed thinking and planning on a grand scale with the final purpose of integrating the individual with the universe. Thus Friedrich Schlegel advocated a world revolution; Novalis, a universal church; and Arnim, a Golden Age, to be realized by the "poetizing" of the world. Direct references to romantic monism cannot be found in Arnim's writings, as he generally seems to abhor philosophical discussions. He hardly mentions Spinoza and Leibnitz. However, he was well acquainted with the works of Hamann and Herder, whose philosophy, emphasizing feeling and nature, he adopted. With Herder he recognized the bond between the individual and the universe

---

[36] Arnim's letter to Clemens Brentano, Christmas, 1803, Arnim-Brentano, p. 104.
[37] *Ibid.,* p. 39.

which led finally to the concept of the "folk-soul." Arnim, like Herder before him, listened intently to the expressions of the "soul of the people," and he believed that he saw it reflected in the history of mankind throughout the ages. Leibnitz' monad, e.g., the original force (*Urkraft*), became for both of them the national force (*Volkskraft*), manifesting itself in the national spirit (*Volksgeist*).[38] These ideas not only stimulated literature and art, but also led Arnim's contemporaries to productive research in universal history and comparative linguistics. With the men engaged in these studies Arnim kept in close touch.

Monistic thinking can be traced throughout Arnim's life. It is found especially in his literary theories. The idea of the totality of expression and of literature as an organism, an organic unit, he expounded in great detail in his correspondence with Jacob Grimm on the problem of "nature-poetry" and "art-poetry." "You will understand," he writes to Jacob on April 5, 1811, "that I deny the assumption that poetry, history, and life in general are to be set off in contrast with each other," a practice, he goes on to say, for which contemporary philosophy has a predilection.[39] To contrast nature and art appeared ridiculous; he wanted rather to derive the whole universe, including art, from nature. He regarded Goethe as the living example for this thesis:

It is not possible to trace in Goethe the boundary between art and nature. Often the intuitive character of his personality takes him by surprise; the expression of this is then called art.[40]

As appears from the foregoing, Arnim's transition from science to art seems to have been rather sudden. In reality he remained for many years in close contact with science. Nevertheless, as soon as he becomes interested in art, he begins with youthful arrogance to ridicule science and theoretical thinking. He now has the "courage" to describe an idealistic philosophy of life. He now believes he has overcome the "fear and laziness" of the days when he saw the only salvation in science.[41] Satirizing the too

[38] Compare paragraph on *Volksgeist, Zeitgeist* in Chapter I.

[39] Arnim-Grimm, p. 110.

[40] *Ibid.*, p. 109.

[41] Arnim-Brentano, p. 52. Arnim's youthful, somewhat dry, scholarly inclinations can be partly explained as an after-effect of his Berlin school days. He wrote to Goethe from Berlin, February, 1806, "Es steht hier noch wie eine Mauer, die trübe

abstract theories in Fichte's and Schelling's philosophy, he writes
to Clemens in November, 1802:

You probably know the subject of the quarrel between Fichte und
Schelling. The former says: the ego = the universe; the latter, the
universe = the ego. Mathematically speaking, both equations amount to
the same. But Schelling, proud of his ego and productivity, emphasizes
that he bases his ideas on productivity; Fichte, on reflection.[42]

Clemens, answering this letter from Düsseldorf, Christmas, 1802,
notes that Schelling's lectures have lately become rather un-
popular because of his obscure barbarism.[43] Arnim turned away
from the natural science of those days chiefly because he detested
its scholastic disputes and the resultant theoretic confusion. He
felt that working in this field was too remote from life and reality.
He hoped to find the true well of life in art and poetry.[44] There
was still another reason for his desertion of the sciences. He
declares that "success came too slowly in this field." He recognized that he had not enough original ideas. At Christmas, 1803,
he wrote to Clemens: "I did not discover anything in physics
which was not published at the same time by Ritter, Schelling,
or others; indeed, many papers I have torn to pieces because
the others were ahead of me."[45]

However, as noted above, Arnim's scientific interests and
activities did not terminate suddenly and forever. When the concentrated efforts ceased which the publication of the *Wunderhorn*
had required, and he again settled down to a quieter life, we notice
a revival of his scientific activities. The very year which witnessed

---

gepreßte Luft einer zwangvollen Kinderstube, aus der ich mich in verzweifelnder
Langeweile in allerlei Gelehrsamkkeit stürzte, die nachher in wärmerer Sonne bis
auf wenige Neigen rein verdampfte." *Schriften der Goethe-Ges.*, XIV, 83.

[42] Arnim-Brentano, p. 53.

[43] *Ibid.*, p. 59.

[44] What Friedrich von Raumer, at eighty years of age, recorded in his memoirs
about Arnim's transition from science to literature can hardly be taken seriously.
He and Arnim had been schoolmates at the Joachimsthaler Gymnasium and also
studied together at Halle und Göttingen. Raumer tells us that while in Halle,
Arnim pursued preferably the study of science (physics); when in Göttingen, he
turned to belles lettres because his lady love there complained that his studies in
physics and chemistry polluted the atmosphere with unpleasant odors. Therefore
he discarded these studies, bought himself new clothes and fine perfumes and
wrote *Hollins Liebeleben*. Friedrich von Raumer, *Lebenserinnerungen und Briefwechsel* (Leipzig, 1861), pp. 29, 43.

[45] Arnim-Brentano, p. 104.

the appearance of the *Wunderhorn,* 1806, saw also Arnim's venture into a second "science" period with the publication of a short article in the *Annalen der Physik.*[46] In 1807 he wrote another brief article for the same periodical,[47] and the three following years bring his best criticism and interpretations of natural philosophy. In 1808 two important books on natural philosophy appeared, *Ansichten von der Nachtseite der Naturwissenschaften* by the Dresden philosopher, Gotthilf Heinrich von Schubert, and *Theorie der Geisterkunde, in einer Natur-, Vernunft- und Bibelmäßigen Beantwortung der Frage: Was von Ahnungen, Gesichten und Geistererscheinungen geglaubt und nicht geglaubt werden müsse,* by Heinrich Jung-Stilling. Both books stirred Arnim's imagination. That of Schubert, he recommended highly. With regard to Jung-Stilling's, he wrote to Clemens, October 22, 1809, "What a magnificent, ponderous, and at the same time very human book it was, like a Greek mythology."[48] Without being invited, Arnim wrote at once a review of this "magnificent" work for the *Heidelbergische Jahrbücher.* In 1808 also Arnim met in Heidelberg Zacharias Werner who introduced him to his mystical *Naturlehre* and *System der Liebe.* The next year, while living in Berlin with Pistor, who was then engaged in making instruments for physics laboratories,[49] Arnim fell a victim to the political restlessness of those years and to discouragement over his own none-too-successful literary endeavors and resolved to go back to science as an academic profession. First, he thought of taking his doctor's degree at Heidelberg, but when the Berlin University was founded he hoped for a career at this institution.[50] However, this plan did not materialize. In 1810 appeared the last important publication of the unhappy physicist J. W. Ritter, *Fragmente aus dem Nachlasse eines jungen Physikers,* which Arnim immediately reviewed for the *Heidelbergische Jahrbücher.*[51]

These are but the general data of Arnim's second "science" period. It is marked by an entirely different attitude towards

[46] *Annalen,* XXII, p. 331, essay on "Steinregen".
[47] *Ibid.,* XXVI, pp. 479-80; "Eine Berichtigung, die Haarröhrchen betreffend."
[48] Arnim-Brentano, p. 261.
[49] *Ibid.,* p. 280.
[50] Cf. NHeidelbJbb., XI, 227, Anm. 2; 221, 231 235, 253.
[51] HeidelbJbb., Abt. I, Bd. II (1810), pp. 116-125.

science than that of a decade earlier when, under the spell of his teacher Ludwig Gilbert, he was working for the promotion of "true" science. Now he approached science under the influence of natural philosophy, and as a mystical romanticist, adopted an all-embracing monistic view of the universe. This *höhere Weltor-ganisation,* the unity behind all matter, was to be searched for intuitively, as Schelling's "World Soul" had taught him. This changed attitude appears in his review of Jung-Stilling's *Theorie der Geisterkunde:*

In our opinion, modern German physics cannot deny the existence of the spiritual world and is forced to adopt the idea of animal magnetism and a higher organization of the world, because physics notices and recognizes that from lower organisms, described by purely physical laws, higher beings evolve. The mechanistic view in physics is destroyed with Kant.[52]

Arnim's reviews of Ritter's *Fragmente* and Jung-Stilling's *Theorie der Geisterkunde* are extremely interesting as documents of a Romanticist's spiritual and scientific attitude towards the world and his own period, and they deserve to be discussed here at greater length. While both reviews were intended for the *Heidelbergische Jahrbücher,* only one, that of Ritter's *Fragmente,* was accepted for the philosophical section of this periodical.[53] August Böckh, representing the anti-Romantic clique of editors, rejected as too fantastic the review of Jung-Stilling's book, but it was finally published in F. W. Gubitz' *Gesellschafter* in 1817.[54] Here, indeed, the editor passed it on to the printer rather unwillingly.

Ritter had died in poverty in 1810, deserted by most of his former admirers. Arnim had throughout his life an appreciation and an understanding of Ritter's tragic personality. This sentiment is frankly expressed in his review of Ritter's *Fragmente*[55] and in his brief note on Ritter's death.[56] In the latter Arnim

---

[52] *Unbekannte Aufsätze,* pp. 22-23.

[53] August Böckh's letter to Arnim, April 2, 1810; cf. NHeidelbJbb., 1902, pp. 250-3.

[54] *Ges.,* 1817. pp. 385-6, 389-91, 394-5.

[55] HeidelbJbb., Abt. I, Bd. II, pp. 116-125; Arnim was especially interested in books of a biographical nature and preferred to review them: "Auf Biographien, besonders auf Selbstbiographien, bin ich auf steter Jagd." Arnim-Bettina, p. 374.

[56] This note was held up by the censor and never published during Arnim's life

objected to the false stories about Ritter and the unfair criticism directed against his intellectual associate:

During his life he found little encouragement and recognition among us, such as would have promoted his efforts and assured us of the fame of possessing such a man. His achievements were recognized abroad, where an effort was made to free him from oppressive poverty when it was too late. To a foreign country he bequeathed all of his writings, of which he had published only a small part in his remarkable *Fragmente eines jungen Physikers.*

More light on this human angle of Arnim's interest in Ritter is given by his review of Ritter's *Fragmente*. Although the review considers mainly Ritter's personality, it also touches upon his scholarly endowment. Here Arnim looks at him as a conservative man would, and in a tactful but critical tone deplores the direction that Ritter's life had taken, yet he praises his great talents.[57] Contemporaries were attracted, he declares, by Ritter's talents, but repelled from any sympathy with his scientific efforts by his disputatious nature. A friendly relationship with him was not possible on account of his biting, satirical attitude. He had all the self-confidence and air of superiority of a self-educated person. At Jena he showed that he could practice economy and maintain himself on a modest scale by his writings, and he understood how to exploit the fame that came to him. He drew around him those who were inclined to loose living and incapable of understanding him, as well as certain people of culture who in Jena at that time gave themselves over to a kind of frivolous life and whom Ritter formed to his taste. It was not without justification that Ritter complained of the type of culture he encountered in the educated circle at Jena. The flashy, superficial impressions of art which he received there stirred up the wish to do something extraordinary and to make himself conspicuous. This led to the premature

time, because he accused the government of negligence. It appeared first in "Gesammelte kleine Bemerkungen zu Dichtern und Schriftstellern des 18. und 19. Jahrhunderts" by R. Steig, *Euphorion*, Ergänzungsheft, XV (1923), 70-1.

[57] Arnim and Brentano must have tried to become more intimate with Ritter. In the spring of 1802 Brentano was for a short time in frequent correspondence with Ritter. Cf. Brentano's letter to Arnim, May, 1802; Arnim-Brentano, p. 34; Brentano's letter to Arnim, September, 1802; *ibid.*, p. 45: "Ritter, der mir viel schreibt . . . " later, in a disappointed vein: "Ritter hat mir keine Zeile mehr geschrieben. . . ."

announcement of discoveries, which in some cases were not realized, a behavior which was quite contrary to his nature. The alternation of dissipation and extreme want cut short fruitful efforts on Ritter's part and drove him to over-exertion. This was the cause of much slipshod work. It broke down his health and prevented proper scientific observations. At times he could do nothing at all; at times, supported by stimulants, he would write half a volume in a few nights. This, as Arnim sagely remarks, caused a different type of exhaustion from that which followed on the natural, prodigious exertions of a Luther or a Newton. In Ritter's *Fragmente* Arnim notes a religious attitude that lacks respect for the body which was made in God's image; and he accuses Ritter of making useless experiments to the damage of his own body, such as exposing his eyes to the sun. For his part, Arnim is convinced that experiments harmful to the investigator's life, by which young scientists of his day sought to prove their courage, have never led to important results.[58]

The beginning of Arnim's review ostensibly showed Ritter's attitude, but actually Arnim's attitude toward science in relation to the problems of the nation and the universe. The hopes and aspirations of the romanticists reflect here the restlessness of political life during these years. Like Ritter, Arnim questioned whether now (1810) it was still necessary to urge German youth to closer unity and collaboration in science, since political events had welded the nation and hence also the different branches and schools in science into one united front. German science was just as youthful and strong as the German nation, and was already showing signs of even greater vigor in comparison with science in other countries. Arnim alluded here to France, and he expressed the belief that with the birth of a new political world over there, Germany was proceeding to a new unification of knowledge and science which would fuse the peculiar and separate elements of all disciplines and the efforts of single scholars into a unified whole. Encouraged by the apostle (here Arnim referred to Ritter), the German nation has put all prophesies and all faith into science and art. Every German feels the urge to learn and to invent. Politics is only a hateful distraction, for a secret voice seems to

[58] Arnim's review of Ritter's *Fragmente*, p. 120, cf. note 51, above.

whisper that while the affairs of politics and the world are now
the task of other nations, it is the German's destiny to show his
love for the fatherland in devotion to science and art. From such
whole-hearted devotion patriotic and political devotion will spring
when called for.[59]

Finally Arnim discusses Ritter's religious beliefs and comes to
the conclusion that they were the outgrowth of his conception of
natural philosophy. Both Ritter and Arnim were deeply religious:
"Uns bleibt Glaube, Liebe, Hoffnung . . . aber die Liebe ist die
größte unter ihnen," Ritter quotes in his fragments. Arnim found
that Ritter's autobiography was written in this spirit:

> We feel that his religion is not the product of inheritance and educa-
> tion, but rather the outgrowth of his innermost conviction and deep feel-
> ing, as in many contemporaries, who pondered much and forgot religion
> only to become deeply religious again when speculating on God and
> religion.[60]

In this connection he evaluated Ritter's contributions to science
and natural philosophy. The conclusion is brief but enthusiastic:

> Part Ten, on animal magnetism, is perhaps the finest thing that has so
> far been written on the subject and serves well to characterize the soul
> of the author, whose beautiful words in this connection are not based
> on novel experiences, but on well-known phenomena. The reader should
> compare him here with Gotthilf Heinrich von Schubert's book *Über die
> Ansichten von der Nachtseite der Natur*. How he loves to organize the
> universe and bring it closer to us, with how much sagacity he uses phi-
> losophy without losing himself in it! . . . Never before has the new
> organic physics been proclaimed so brilliantly.[61]

To this extent then, Arnim defended Ritter's life and work in
public. However, in his confidential letters to Bettina he strikes
a more critical note. Speaking of the *Fragmente* in a letter of
September 29, 1809, when he had just heard of the book, but had
not yet read it, he voices the opinion that it must be highly entertaining and scandalous, provided it is a truthful account.[62] Later,
in a letter of February 26, 1810, he regrets that Ritter's life fell
short of the hopes and expectations of others; nevertheless, he
thinks that one could say many good things about the book if a

[59] *Ibid.*, pp. 116-18.
[61] *Ibid.*, pp. 123-4.
[60] *Ibid.*, p. 123.
[62] Arnim-Bettina, p. 335.

group of Ritter's intimate friends could be gotten together.[63] However, romantic natural philosophy did not reach its mystical climax in the *Fragmente*.

The intermingling of science, philosophy, and religious mysticism is still more characteristic of Jung-Stilling's *Theorie der Geisterkunde*. Here the mystical author not only records his personal observations on magnetism, but correlates them with spiritualism and the conjuration of spirits. All is based on feeling and belief, not on experimental proofs. His view of nature and science was completely transcendental. He meditated on the supernatural, on presentiments and visions in a deeply mystical, religious way. This was particularly congenial with Arnim's thinking and feeling, for he found in Jung-Stilling's writings as well as in his philosophy of life a confirmation of his own attitude toward science, art, and life. Jung-Stilling's *Theorie der Geisterkunde* and *Heimweh* revealed "the author's matured faith in the world beyond, which is reflected in this visible universe,"[64] and the author is, in Arnim's opinion, the "honorable champion of a living faith" who with quiet confidence brings about a closer unity of kindred spirits. With this personal high esteem for the man and author it is comprehensible when Arnim in his capacity as reviewer either omits or shows kindly tolerance for many weak points in Jung-Stilling's *Theorie der Geisterkunde,* on which the enlightened critics of the *Jenaer Allgemeine Literatur-Zeitung* concentrated their attacks.[65] Arnim, with his scientific background, cannot help mentioning that many of the author's theories are antiquated; that hypotheses which should explain add only to the confusion of the difficult subject; that the manner in which the author employs concepts of time and space is questionable; that his emphatic opposition to mechanistic philosophy is uncalled-for and just as unnecessary as his discussion of the Copernican system. Yet, as Arnim goes on to show, all these are only minor issues within the brilliant major theory expounded by Jung-Stilling: "The wrestling human soul grows strong with the aid of miracles" (*Des*

[63] *Ibid.,* p. 384; compare also Bettina's remarks on Ritter, Arnim-Bettina, p. 373.

[64] *Unbekannte Aufsätze,* p. 18.

[65] Cf. *Jenaer Allgemeine Literatur-Zeitung,* 1808, pp. 809, 817.

Menschen Geist ringt sich am Wunderbaren stark). Thus deep insight and great wisdom make the *Theorie der Geisterkunde* the book of books among all that have been written about spirits and spiritualism. Arnim calls attention to the human ability for presentiment and vision which Jung-Stilling has demonstrated in the ordinary walks of life. Without this gift not even the humblest true verse is made, and it reveals itself in science and poetry in its best, purest, and holiest aspects. However, we can grasp the miraculous ether which pervades everything and surrounds us only if our faculties are sufficient. Dante possessed such spiritual greatness and thus became a believing, visionary poet, uniting the theological system of his age with his own world and with the knowledge of his time through the medium of art.

The review is the last milestone on Arnim's long, exploratory path through the field of science. It shows clearly the transformation which he had undergone. He had started with a materialistic approach and had finally come to realize how helpless and hopeless human reasoning is when it tries to lift the veil of the Beyond. Not reasoning power, but the soul and spiritual insight have the ultimate word in science. However, a spiritual approach is impossible without faith, the belief in a higher organization of the universe. Like Jung-Stilling, Arnim rejected all secrecy, hypocrisy, and coercion in matters of faith, as well as the "brutality which regards any faith as weakness and illness."

Man is in need of the grace of God and must receive it humbly. . . . All our knowledge does not yet enable us to impart to a blind man the powers of his missing fifth sense by means of the other four senses he possesses, how much less can reason ferret out what is needed and meant for the heart. No eye has seen nor ear heard that which comes into the heart and is its future.[66]

This was Arnim's final answer respecting the problems confronting him in science: he saw only one way out, faith and trust in a higher being. It is no mere coincidence that at the time when he reviewed Ritter's *Fragmente* and Jung-Stilling's *Theorie der Geisterkunde* he was working on his own *Halle und Jerusalem*. He used this fantastic play as the vehicle to give artistic expression to his visions and his mystical religious philosophy of life. Was

[66] *Unbekannte Aufsätze*, p. 18.

Halle und Jerusalem intended to be the *Divine Comedy* of the Nineteenth Century?

Arnim's desertion of science was often deplored by his intimate friends. Josef von Görres expresses this feeling in his brilliant eulogy of Arnim, written in 1831 for the *Literaturblatt zum Morgenblatt* (Nr. 27-30):

> I often told him how much I regretted that he had abandoned this field, for I have always been under the impression that exclusive occupation with poetry has a disadvantageous and weakening effect; however, he never seemed to show any inclination to return to this neglected interest.[67]

Tieck voiced his regret still more forcefully, saying it was a pity Arnim had, to his own disadvantage, deserted a promising career in physics for literature, since he lacked poetic talent. He claimed that Arnim had stolen everything worth while from Schiller and himself.[68]

While still in the first flush of enthusiasm for natural science young Arnim came into contact with some of the leading figures in German literature. Soon production in this field came to take the place of his interest in scientific research. His early work and his critical attitude toward literature bear definite signs of the influence of three well-known men of letters of his time: Goethe, Tieck, and Brentano. The youthful Arnim had personal contact with all three of them, and they were to play an important rôle in his future, as is apparent in his "plan of life." Even as a young student Arnim became Tieck's faithful disciple in the matter of folk poetry. They differed only as to the proper methods of propagating the poetry of the people. While Tieck tried to interest the educated classes in "folkbooks" (*Volksbücher*), Arnim suggested taking the reverse path by appealing to the masses, for he believed that educated people, captivated by the refined form and conventional ideas of French poetry, would never appreciate fully the charm of popular poetry. He shared with his generation the admiration for Goethe, and considered it one of his tasks to make Goethe popular with the masses. In fact, it was his ultimate goal

---

[67] Cf. Josef Görres, *Ausgewählte Werke und Briefe*, hrsg. von Wilhelm Schellberg, 1911, I, 433.

[68] Reinhold Steig, *Brentano und die Gebrüder Grimm*, pp. 34, 63.

that Goethe's works should become as beloved as the old chap-books. The close ties of friendship which existed between Arnim and Brentano are well known. They were cemented through their joint editing of *Des Knaben Wunderhorn*. It must be emphasized, however, that the *Wunderhorn* represents only the realization of a small fraction of their early idealistic plans for the revival of popular poetry.

Of the three poets, Goethe, Tieck, and Brentano, Tieck was Arnim's earliest acquaintance. They met in the Reichardt house in Halle as early as July, 1799, and Arnim then accompanied Tieck on a trip to Leipsic.[69] Two years later the first long stop-over of his "grand tour" was in Dresden, where he saw Tieck daily for three weeks. It is not possible to give instances of Tieck's early influence on him. But Arnim must have appreciated highly the association with the author of the *Volksmärchen für die Deut-schen*, for he wrote to Clemens Brentano from Dresden on November 7, 1801, that it was a joy to him to be with Tieck, and that in his company he could always shake off the dust from his wings and return happily and courageously to the innermost springs of his soul.[70] At that time Tieck had already written his *William Lovell* (1795-6), his *Volksmärchen* (1797), the *Sternbald* (1798), and *Genoveva* (1799).

Arnim always kept himself well informed about the progress of Tieck's writings. He expressed his admiration for the elder poet in his letters to Clemens and in his own first literary attempts. He praised Tieck's "splendid poems," particularly the *Romanzen* in the *Muselalmanach 1802*.[71] In *Lovell* he saw a wealth of poetic innovations, a heavenly seed on the old, dry field of Richardson's influence.[72] Among Tieck's *Volksmärchen* Arnim must have liked best *Die schöne Magelone*, for Maria in Arnim's first novel, *Hollins Liebeleben*, is obviously elated when Hollin questions her about Tieck's story and passes the book over to him "with an indescribably joyous glance."[73] The epistolary form of Arnim's first novel reminds one of Tieck's *Lovell*, where we also find a

[69] Arnim-Brentano, p. 8.   [70] Arnim-Brentano, pp. 25-6.

[71] *Ibid.*, pp. 26, 51; Arnim's letter of December, 1801.

[72] *Ibid.*, p. 41; Arnim's letter of summer, 1802.

[73] *Hollins Liebeleben*, hrsg. von J. Minor, p. 45.

correspondence which is carried on between several persons.

Both Brentano and Arnim had great hopes that Tieck might play an important rôle in German literature, especially in the drama. Brentano tried in vain to secure for him a position as theatrical manager at Frankfort, and Arnim wished that Tieck might move to Marburg, "in order to lecture there on the very timely subject of literature." "Literature," he adds, "has been used long enough merely as an introduction of materia medica."[74] The continuous travels of the next years loosened Arnim's relationship to Tieck. Furthermore, the latter did not encourage the two rambling idealists, Arnim and Brentano, in their poetic enthusiasm, as they had probably expected.[75] Still, for several years to come, Arnim looked up to him as the superb, shining German minstrel,[76] and Brentano lost no time in informing Tieck of his friend's high esteem, associating himself with it unreservedly. In January, 1802, he writes to the object of their enthusiasm:

> Arnim, whom you know and surely love, writes me his first letter from Regensburg, telling how delighted he is to know you and your work. I am certain that perhaps Arnim is the only German who reads your books as you would wish them to be read. If there are any who want to do or sacrifice something for you, they are Arnim and myself; he for the cheerfulness of your muse, I for its melancholy.[77]

With Goethe young Arnim was not so intimate as with Tieck.[78] He approached Goethe as a young apprentice, filled with deep reverence for the master, not like the older Romanticists, with a set program representing a literary school. In youthful enthusiasm he built a shrine for Goethe in his soul, and he felt himself called upon to bring Goethe's message to the whole world. Because of his scientific training, it is not surprising that he was at first

[74] Arnim-Brentano, p. 28.　　　　[75] *Ibid.*, pp. 43, 53; Holtei, III, 337.
[76] *Ibid.*, p. 23.
[77] Brentano's letter to Tieck, January 11, 1802.
[78] The relationship between Arnim and Goethe has never been sufficiently treated. Herman Grimm and Reinhold Steig intended to devote one of the volumes of *A. v. Arnim und die ihm nahe standen* to Arnim's relationship with Goethe as a man and poet. To a limited extent this subject is touched upon in the second volume *Arnim und Bettina*. More material is in the letters of the Weimar Goethe-Ausgabe, Vol. XIV; *Schriften der Goethe Ges.; Jahrb. Freies deutsches Hochstift; Bettinas Briefwechsel mit Goethe*, hrsg. von R. Steig; and Felix Scholz, *Clemens Brentano und Goethe*, Leipzig, 1927. Cf. Ch. VI, below, where the critical attitude of Arnim to Goethe is treated in detail.

interested in Goethe as a naturalist. As a young student he wrote long essays on Goethe's *Farbenlehre*.[79] Again in later life his interest in this side of Goethe's genius was renewed. He valued it more than Goethe's literary work, which he criticized as pretentious and full of dogmatic expressions.[80] When Goethe visited Göttingen in 1801, Arnim, together with other students, arranged a welcome for him, and he then received an invitation from Goethe to visit him.[81] Soon afterwards he set out on his "grand tour," which prevented closer personal contact with Goethe at this time, although Goethe's spirit and Goethe's works accompanied him on this trip. The landscape and places he saw reminded him of Goethe's former journeys or the descriptions of scenery in Goethe's works. While travelling along the Rhine, he began to understand and appreciate fully the beauty of Goethe's *Hermann und Dorothea*.[82] Riding through the Italian campagna, he and his brother sang Goethe's famous "Kennst Du das Land, wo die Citronen blüh'n," set to music by Reichardt.[83] During his trip Arnim also read and studied Goethe's *Wilhelm Meister,* the apprenticeship novel which proved to be so important for the problems of his own life.[84] He also read Goethe's most recently published works, the comedy *Was wir bringen* and the tragedy *Die natürliche Tochter.* The latter had on him, in his own words, "a very pure and tragic effect."[85]

Arnim's first literary attempt, *Hollins Liebeleben,* shows plainly traces of Goethe's influence, for his novel might be classified as a miniature *Werther,* put into new and peculiar garments. Arnim was aware of this poetic dependency and acknowledged freely in a letter to Clemens that this form of imitation was wrong and unworthy and might suppress the best of his own creative genius: "The demonical Werther and my misdirected admiration of Goethe's forms seduced me then to omit the best of *Hollin*," he declared, November 8, 1802, "in *Ariel* I shall create unhampered."[86]

[79] Cf. K. E. Henrici, *Auktions-Katalog, Nr. 149*, 1929, No. 5, p. 2.
[80] Bettina-Goethe, p. 238.
[81] Goethe's *Tagebücher,* June 8 and 21, 1801.
[82] Arnim-Brentano, p. 35.
[83] *Ibid.,* p. 42.   [84] *Ibid.,* p. 54.   [85] *Ibid.,* p. 71.
[86] *Ibid.,* pp. 51, 52; and Kummermann's remarks in *Halle und Jerusalem,* p. 251,

It must be emphasized at this point that the Heidelberg Romanticists would never have come into such sympathetic contact with Goethe during the years immediately following if Goethe had not abandoned, around 1800, his classical approach to literature in favor of popular poetry and returned to a more genuinely German lyric style. Goethe's poems published in the *Taschenbuch auf das Jahr 1804,* which were modeled after the style of folksongs, now became the pattern for the romanticists. It was this Goethe whom Arnim approached after returning to Germany, in the hope of benefit to his fatherland and to his own poetic efforts.

This enthusiasm for Goethe and Tieck Arnim shared with Brentano,[87] whom he met in the summer of 1801 in Göttingen. The two students soon became intimate friends. Bretano read his *Godwi* to Arnim, who had come to Göttingen to continue his studies in natural sciences, though his interest in literature was now gaining more and more the upper hand. The first plans for *Hollins Liebeleben* can be traced back to these student days in Göttingen. The end of the summer semester parted the two friends, and Arnim started on his "grand tour." During the next three years they met only once, when Arnim spent a week with Brentano's family in Frankfort, and then took a trip down the Rhine in Clemens' company, the journey so admirably described in Bettina's *Frühlingskranz.* The long and frequent letters exchanged between the two friends during the next two years reveal,

---

ought to be interpreted as Arnim's own opinions, not those of Brentano. Schönemann took them to be solely Brentano's (cf. p. 110): "Hieran erkenne ich mein eigenes jugendliches Treiben und Fühlen—ich habe auch so übertriebne Zeit gehabt, wo ich mit Werther liebetrunken schwärmte, nun bin ich weiter kommen. Es scheint mir nun un-Werther, die Liebe zu der Sünde, zu dem Altertume, die Verstocktheit gegen christliche Gesinnung, ein ewiges Verklären aller Nichtigkeit; so fühle ich, daß eine Kunst in unserer Zeit unmöglich sei; ich ließ mein Studium der Dichter und wendete mich hin zur göttlichen Natur, die ewig allein lebt. So weit bin ich gekommen."

[87] Arnim's criticism of Brentano's writings are found in letters to Brentano, Bettina, and others. It was a very understanding, friendly, yet frank criticism. In January, 1809, Arnim wanted to review all of Brentano's writings in the *Heidelbergische Jahrbücher,* but the editor Böckh preferred only a review of Brentano's latest book *Der Goldfaden.* Arnim complied, sending this review to Zimmer, but it was never printed. Instead an announcement by Wilhelm Grimm appeared (cf. NHeidelbJbb., 1902, pp. 199, 204). A brief review of Brentano's *Victoria und ihre Geschwister* by Arnim appeared in the *Gesellschafter* of the year 1817. Cf. reprint in *Unbekannte Aufsätze,* p. 82.

as one might expect, their thoughts and ideas on current literary problems and discuss also their own poetic creations. In these we find Arnim's views of the works of Brentano which appeared during this period, the second part of *Godwi* (1801), *Die lustigen Musikanten* (1802), and *Ponce de Leon* (1803).

Any discussion of Arnim's first criticism of Brentano's writings must take into consideration their intimate friendship and Arnim's youthful literary dependency on Brentano. In spite of this, frankness and honesty prevail to an astonishing degree. Arnim had himself participated in the second part of *Godwi*, and had written the "Rede auf dem Schützenfest zu G. vom Freunde A. gehalten," which, however, was not finally incorporated into the novel. Arnim did not regret the omission, writing Clemens that the book had become too serious for it.[88] Almost an entire year elapsed before he returned to a discussion of *Godwi*. In the meantime Brentano assumed the rôle of a severe critic of Arnim's productions. He felt obliged to judge Arnim's verse as superficial and slovenly[89] and explained his own fundamental principles as a literary critic: "I criticize only in order to do for myself what I request from others, namely to become just and severe toward myself."[90] Arnim, in youthful self-confidence, turned a deaf ear to criticism, declaring that "a thinking poet is a fool."[91] Soon, however, Brentano's frank strictures invited similar remarks from Arnim, who took up again the subject of *Godwi*. While praising highly Brentano's portrayal of "a young poet in the making," he nevertheless criticized details of the plot. It seemed to him that it was not well to have the young poet die. While he was in a fainting spell among the grief-stricken people, a happy piece of news should have come to bring about his recovery. It is all right for Diderot to have "Religieuse" turn out in the end to be nothing but a joke, an imaginary character, but to declare that of a serious and fascinating work, as Brentano does at the end of *Godwi*, is to destroy the effect intentionally, for the young poet in *Godwi* and Godwi himself have aroused the reader's interest more than the one who writes about them.[92] Arnim regretted that

[88] Arnim-Brentano, p. 25.   [89] *Ibid.*, p. 50, with reference to *Hollin.*
[90] *Idem.*   [91] *Ibid.*, p. 52.   [92] *Ibid.*, p. 53.

Brentano had not carried through the plan outlined in his preface to the second part of *Godwi,* instead of having one of the chief characters, the young poet, fail and die right at the beginning of his career. He recalled in this connection the principle set forth in *Wilhelm Meister* to the effect that the reader is more vitally interested in a hero who strives for and reaches a high goal than in one who fails.[93]

Arnim also criticized Brentano's *Die lustigen Musikanten* because of the vagueness of its plot and the inadequate treatment of the wealth of material. The scenes are too brief and too few and could have stood more elaboration and detail. Just as in the case of *Godwi,* Arnim was impressed by the seriousness of this *Singspiel.* He writes to Brentano; "They are not merry; on the other hand, it is one of the most thoroughly touching pieces that I know."[94] For *Ponce de Leon* on the contrary, Arnim had nothing but praise and admiration. Here he saw again in Brentano the great talented artist in whose footsteps he would have liked to follow. At that time he wrote to the author that he wished he could write something comparable to this perfect comedy, so full of suspense from beginning to end, and like a balloon finally disappearing in the bright sunlight.[95] He thought that Brentano had observed excellently the fundamentals of comedy-writing; and in this connection defined the nature of comedy: "It is to fuse with us completely; not to have the effect of medicine, like tragedies and farces, but to nourish us like food and drink, and cause us to grow, love, and become active."[96]

These lines were written on September 20, 1804. In December of the same year, Brentano, longing to see again his "song-brother," arrived in Berlin. A new era now began for both. The first plans for the *Wunderhorn* were made in those Berlin days. A year later, this work, which was to assure them of immortality in literary history, was given to the world.

[93] *Ibid.,* p. 54 (cf. Brentano's own interpretation, p. 58).
[94] *Ibid.,* p. 93.   [95] *Ibid.,* p. 113.   [96] *Ibid.,* p. 112.

IV

THE CRITIC AND THE HEIDELBERG CIRCLE

The great collection of folksongs, so important as a fountain of inspiration to the lyrical poetry of Germany in the following century, does not belong to our discussion. Suffice it to say that the year in Heidelberg which brought the first volume of the *Wunderhorn* into being was a golden period in the life of both young men. For Arnim it shines the more brilliantly because it was followed by the distressing events of 1806 and 1807, the military collapse of Prussia which swept him into the remote Northeast and finally awakened him fully to national consciousness. The maturing of this sentiment in its effect on his critical work will be examined in a later chapter. For the moment he was still under the ban of the *Wunderhorn;* and as soon as the way was clear for his return to the South, he set forth again for the university town on the Neckar.

When he rejoined the Heidelberg circle in January, 1808, it was his intention to take again an active part in reviving and propagating old German literature and art. He looked forward to a period of fruitful endeavor, as carefree and happy as that in the spring of 1805, when in a short time the first volume of the *Wunderhorn* was given to the world. But those joyful days were not to return. The experience of the war of 1806-7 had changed much in Germany. General uneasiness prevailed about the future of German culture. August Wilhelm Schlegel wrote at the time that the need of the hour was a direct, wide-awake, energetic and above all, patriotic poetry, not poetry of a dreamy sort.[1] Arnim himself had grown more mature and serious-minded. His views on art and life had taken on more definite shape, and were colored to a greater degree by patriotic feeling. This tendency found its chief expression in the efforts he made to perpetuate old German literature. His name had now penetrated literary circles and his opinions were respected by friends and enemies alike.

[1] Schlegel's letter to Fouqué, March 1806; Böcking, VIII, 144.

Heidelberg and its cultural life had also experienced a change. The university, recently restored to its former prominence, had attracted many friends, but also not a few enemies of the "Wunderhornists." To the former belonged Görres and the Grimm brothers. Görres had arrived in Heidelberg in the fall of 1806. He was soon well-known as an inspiring lecturer and much admired for his versatile knowledge. Brentano and he became close friends and Arnim soon completed the trio. Brentano had already gained the interest and support of the Grimm brothers for the Heidelberg movement. In 1807 he wrote to Arnim that the Grimms were his "beloved, Old-German, intimate friends, . . . they know far more of everything than Tieck . . . you will grow very fond of these fine people, who are quietly at work preparing to publish later on a history of German poetry."[2] The future enemies of the Wunderhorn pair also had become well established in Heidelberg. Foremost among them were Johann Heinrich Voss, who had accepted a chair at the University of Heidelberg as early as 1805, and his son, Heinrich Voss, who was appointed professor there in February 1807.

In addition to working on the continuation of the *Wunderhorn*, Arnim hoped to devote himself largely to his much cherished journalistic pursuits, which he regarded as a very useful task for German cultural life and as a means of expression for his own ideas. As early as 1802 he bemoaned the fact that a people with as much reverence and love of art as the Germans were served by literary periodicals of extremely poor standing,[3] and in 1804 he regarded a journalistic career to reform this lamentable situation as his supreme calling.[4] Many years later, Görres, recalling the days in Heidelberg when they started out on their literary mission, characterized the situation as follows:

The journals and newspapers, superficial, trivial, and uninspired beyond belief, compete in their base attitude. . . . The past, as it lived on through its poetic manifestations, seemed to Arnim, and with right, the most potent force to revive in some manner the stagnant present. And

[2] Arnim-Grimm, p. 4.
[3] Arnim-Brentano, p. 68: "Kein Volk habe so viel schlechte kritische Blätter wie das deutsche, und doch herrsche bei ihm stets die Ehrfurcht vor der Kunst."
[4] Arnim-Brentano, p. 106.

the poetry of the people just as it had never failed in its duty to earlier centuries, seemed also to offer its services here in order to bring the people into its own.[5]

Arnim hoped to obtain the co-operation of Brentano and the Grimm brothers, with whom these journalistic plans had been discussed in Cassel in November, 1807.[6] When the war of 1806-7 ended, he thought that the time had now come to start a new literary periodical to serve their purposes. In 1808 this ardent wish for a "periodical of the old style" (*Zeitung alter Art*)[7] was fulfilled when the *Zeitung für Einsiedler* appeared. Both Arnim and Brentano set forth on various occasions[8] the principles, the general make-up, and the aims which were to guide the editors. The *Zeitung für Einsiedler* was to take the form of an imaginary literary paper of the Middle Ages; it should become an attractive collection of an artistic character, making accessible to the public valuable contributions to art and literature from the past. Contemporary art and intellectualism were to be strictly excluded. In that manner Arnim hoped to create a periodical that should tower far above the superficial, wordy publications of his time. He realized that with these ideals he had thrown down the glove to the philistine public, but he hoped that the youth of his country would rally to his support. One question still to be solved was, how to make the new periodical palatable to the reading public. A keen sense of humor, comical announcements, a play on the curiosity of the public were to aid here. The paper should, in Arnim's words, become a "storehouse of merriment" (*eine Fundgrube von Lustigkeit*)[9], but the editors should not lose sight of the chief purpose of the paper, which was after all a very serious one, namely, to educate people in art and to bring them to an understanding of true cultural values. As Arnim wrote to Bettina, behind a comical mask for attracting people a serious face was

[5] Görres in a memorial sketch after Arnim's death; Menzel's Literaturblatt, 1831, No. 27-30, pp. 104-117.

[6] Brentano's letters to Zimmer, Nov. 1807.

[7] Arnim-Brentano, p. 238.

[8] *Ibid.*, "Ankündigung der allgemeinsten Zeitung. Zeitung für Einsiedler," Heidelb-Jbb., 1808, pp. 33-4 (Int. Bl. 4); also pp. 75-7 (Int. Bl. 9); Brentano's letter to Zimmer, November, 1807.

[9] Arnim-Bettina, p. 90.

to be hidden.[10] Likewise, in "advertising" the new paper he requested his readers to take serious account of everything it contained, even if it was presented in a frivolous manner. Only then would they grasp the true meaning.[11]

Similarly the editors emphasized that they intended to depart from the customary type of literary criticism. In the first place, they considered criticism very often superfluous. A work of art or literature can speak for itself, is self-explanatory, and should not need commentaries. Keeping this premise in mind, we can understand that Arnim's purpose, to "acquaint the reader with the remote and forgotten," was the next logical step in this "new" criticism.[12] In a letter to Tieck, Arnim admitted that criticism was not superfluous in connection with literary fragments or writings which might be difficult to understand because of a change in language or other peculiarities. He was also willing to let criticism of contemporary writings stand if it was in a spicy, humorous vein.[13]

Arnim's attitude toward criticism is expressed at various places in his *Zeitung für Einsiedler*. The introductory poem "Der freie Dichtergarten" contains several stanzas entitled "Kritik." The youthful poet's lyric effusion is here compared to the nightingale, bursting forth into song, in its rapture undisturbed by the cuckoo's call. The cuckoo, i. e., the critic, is questioned by children. Even the hawk—tricky criticism—is disarmed by the fresh beauty of the song and cannot harm the carefree nightingale:

> Fort kann der Falk sie tragen,
> Doch sieh den Falk
> Er hört ihr zu betroffen,
> Der lose Schalk,
> Und hält den Schnabel offen.[14]

In the "Rundgesang gegen Unterdrücker des Werdenden in der Literatur," the future poets are to flee away from the dark present

[10] *Ibid.*, p. 90.

[11] *Tröst Einsamkeit*, 4. Compare also Arnim's letter to Tieck: "So leicht meine Zeitung aussieht, ich wünsche viel Ernsthaftes damit und fühle mich rein von leerer Sonderbarkeit und parteiischer Begrenztheit." March 31, 1808, Holtei, I, 14.

[12] Arnim's letter to Goethe, April 1, 1808, *Schriften der Goethe-Ges.*, XIV, 126.

[13] Arnim's letter to Tieck, March 31, 1808; Holtei, I, 14.

[14] *Tröst Einsamkeit*, p. 22.

to the divine old songs and faith of the past, like a lark ascending the skies:

> Alter Glanz ist nun verflogen,
> Gestern ist ein leeres Wort,
> Scham hat unsre Wang' umzogen,
> Doch der neue Tag scheint dort.
> Unerschöpflich ist die Jugend,
> Jeder Tag ein Schöpfungstag,
> Wer mit froher reiner Tugend
> Fördert was sein Volk vermag.[15]

In the "Geschichte des Herrn Sonett" Arnim carries out his principle that criticism should be put into pleasing, humorous garments. Various contemporary literary quarrels are touched upon here, but his satire is chiefly pointed towards the older Voss, who reminds him of the philistine Wagner, and he introduces into his poems lines from the Wagner scene in Goethe's *Faust* with telling effect. The spirit of Faust admonishes the noisy fool (Voss?) for his pompous wordiness:

> Es trägt Verstand und rechter Sinn
> Mit wenig Kunst sich selber vor;
> Und wenns euch Ernst ist was zu sagen,
> Ists nötig Worten nachzujagen?
> Ja eure Reden, die so blendend sind,
> In denen ihr der Menschheit Schnitzel kräuselt,
> Sind unerquicklich wie der Nebelwind.[16]

Thus far we have seen that for Arnim the chief purpose of criticism was to open to his readers the literature of the past. Criticism in its ordinary sense he considered superfluous, or desirable only if it clarified the meaning of an otherwise obscure piece of literature. Furthermore, criticism, particularly criticism of contemporaries, should be put into a pleasing, humorous frame. He also suggests that criticism should not be poisoned by cheap publicity, that it should rather, like a true educative force, be brought into play as within an intimate circle, or even more confidentially, just as between two persons, the critic acting as the encouraging teacher. As a fine example of such positive criticism

[15] *Ibid.*, p. 314.
[16] *Tröst Einsamkeit*, p. 383; *Faust*, Part I, lines 197-203.

he published in the *Zeitung für Einsiedler* selections from letters of Schiller to a young poetess ("Auszüge aus Briefen Schillers an eine junge Dichterin").[17] In these letters, Schiller, with fine psychological insight, first called attention to the young writer's talent, whenever it revealed itself, thus encouraging her. He criticized only by making suggestions for minor changes, whenever she might feel herself in the right mood for it. This discussion illustrates the kind of literary criticism which Arnim put into practice in the *Zeitung für Einsiedler*. The periodical was therefore of necessity different from any other of its time. Virtually all its pages are pregnant with implied criticism of literary tendencies of the period. The periodical is thus a monument to literary criticism as Arnim conceived it.

The *Zeitung für Einsiedler* was published only for a period of five months, Goethe's good wishes to the editors notwithstanding. Apparently it did not appeal even to the chosen group of readers on whose interest Arnim had counted. For this failure, a bitter experience for Arnim, he blamed solely the reading public, to whom he addressed a sort of valedictory after publication of the *Zeitung* had ceased.[18] Taking off the "Einsiedler's" mask, he now declares very frankly his disappointment with the body of German readers. He has lost all confidence in it and intends in the near future to write of the origin and decay of the reading public. Apparently, he declares, the masses cannot appreciate real literature unaided; they must always have an authority for their guidance, they are incapable of enjoying anything genuine and feel only the urge of the times to pass judgment and criticise destructively. Thus they have remained blind to the purpose of his journal, which did not publish daily news and historical events. It had sought rather to reveal the dignity of the common national culture, to bring about a return "to a more remote, forgotten art of word and picture, to undertake a search for the national element and that which has been forgotten in every kind of popular enjoyment, in folklore, for all that which once affected our Germany so deeply, . . . but above all, [it sought] the awakening and

[17] *Tröst Einsamkeit,* pp. 196-9.
[18] *Tröst Einsamkeit,* "An das geehrte Publikum," p. 6.

revitalizing of the naive poetic and religious spirit of which our times are still capable."[19]

The failure of his periodical was a very bitter experience for Arnim. However, he was only twenty-seven years old, and still a novice in the literary field. Many possibilities were open to him, and his most important writings were yet to appear. Even in Heidelberg, he felt that he need not abandon his journalistic activities. Now he could throw all his efforts into the much better-managed *Heidelbergische Jahrbücher*. This prospect mitigated the disappointment over his experience with the *Zeitung für Einsiedler;* and he resolved to avail himself of this excellent opportunity, hoping that his Heidelberger collaborators and friends would do the same. Thus they would be able to make the *Jahrbücher* a mouthpiece for their literary ideas. His numerous reviews in this periodical during the years 1809 and 1810 show how fully these expectations were realized.

The young Heidelberg romanticists began their collaboration with the *Heidelbergische Jahrbücher* under the most favorable circumstances. They were in sympathy with the spirit of the periodical, and Friederich Creuzer, in charge of its philosophic-historical devision, approved and encouraged their endeavors. Creuzer, a classical philologist, shared in general Arnim's historical outlook, and the two were strongly attached to each other. They first met in March, 1808. Creuzer made a very scholarly and pleasant impression on Arnim, who characterized him as a very spirited man, possessing a soul susceptible to impressions.[20]

The spirit and ideas expressed in the announcement of the *Jahrbücher* and in Creuzer's first essay[21] were much like those of Arnim's *Zeitung für Einsiedler,* which had come into the world almost simultaneously. It was Creuzer's idea that a new national and productive spirit should prevail in the publication, a spirit not found in contemporary periodicals. The critical attitude to be adopted was laid down in the "eighteen rules" of the announcement, which contain the following declarations: "The age warns

[19] HeidelbJbb., 1808 (int. Bl. 8), pp. 75-7; "Anzeige des Inhalts des April und Maiheftes der Einsiedlerzeitung."
[20] Arnim-Bettina, p. 105.
[21] HeidelbJbb. 1808, I, Abt. 5, pp. 3-24: "Philologie und Mythologie, in ihrem Stufengang und gegenseitigen Verhalten."

of the degradation of literary criticism for the sake of profit and literary partisanship and dictatorship. Scholarly genius prohibits such a debasement."[22] Reviews were to set forth whether an author's writings contained anything worth while; anything novel, genuine, and creative, and therefore adapted for the enrichment of knowledge. The reviewer should not squander undue praise; his judgment should be fearless and firm.

While Arnim devoted himself to the investigation of German history and ancient culture in their relation to art, Creuzer envisaged this relationship as a problem of classical philology:

How have the philologists administered the religious inheritance of the peoples entrusted to them? Have they appreciated its worth, and through its virtues sought to increase the worth of their own knowledge? Particularly, have they established it on a documentary basis and transmitted it to mankind, to whom it belongs, in its original and pure state?[23]

Creuzer also wanted to "acquaint the public with the remote and forgotten," voicing the trend of the historical school, and sharing in particular the point of view of the Grimm brothers, who were his highly esteemed collaborators on the *Jahrbücher*. It is not surprising, therefore, that Creuzer entrusted his young Heidelberg friends, Görres and Arnim, whose ideas were so much akin to his own, with reviews of outstanding works that were making a sensation and stimulating scholarly quarrels. Curiously enough, the third of the trio, Brentano, never wrote for the *Jahrbücher*, ignoring repeated invitations to do so.[24]

In 1808, because he was still very much occupied with his own periodical, Arnim contributed to the *Jahrbücher* mainly a few notices.[25] These referred to his *Zeitung für Einsiedler* and the *Wunderhorn,* and to the "Alte Bühne," which he planned at this time but never brought into being. His only extensive review was of F. H. Jacobi's *Über gelehrte Gesellschaften*. Here Arnim takes Rottmanner's criticism of Jacobi's work as his starting

[22] NHeidelbJbb., XI (1902), 182-4; R. Steig, "Zeugnisse zur Pflege deutscher Literatur in den *Heidelbergischen Jahrbüchern.*"

[23] HeidelbJbb., I, Abt. 5, 1808, p. 4.

[24] NHeidelbJbb., XI (1902), 207; Creuzer's letter to Jacob Grimm, April 10, 1809.

[25] A more detailed discussion of Arnim's contributions to the *Heidelbergische Jahrbücher* appears below; cf. pp. 42 ff., 89 ff., 92 ff., 100 ff., 123.

point.[26] In writing this article Arnim welcomes the opportunity to speak for a united Germany in opposition to the narrow, local patriotism of Jacobi.[27] In his work, Jacobi, a North German philosopher then resident in Munich, had ridiculed Bavaria's low state of civilization and had found fault with the institutions of the Middle Ages, such as feudalism and the religious hierarchy. Patriotic students at Landshut, among them Rottmanner, criticized strongly these ideas. Arnim supported the students, applauded their patriotism, and reproached Jacobi for his narrow outlook. Jacobi, as president of the Munich Academy, Arnim pointed out, seemed to be interested only in general humanistic principles and a program of enlightenment.

In 1809 and 1810 Arnim contributed more important reviews, chiefly on topics assigned by Creuzer. However, his first article, the criticism of Jacobi, had stirred the indignation of Voss and others, and they contrived that in the future Arnim's contributions were to appear anonymously.[28] They could not oust him altogether because of Creuzer's intervention. In the summer of 1808 the "Einsiedler" group had reached the zenith of its literary career in Heidelberg. Thereafter they had to give way to the elder Voss and his circle, whose maturity, literary prestige, and academic influence finally brought victory in this literary quarrel. Görres left Heidelberg at the end of the summer semester,[29] Brentano almost at the same time,[30] and Arnim went back to Berlin in November.

Arnim, who still contributed frequently to the *Jahrbücher* during the two years following, remained in close contact and correspondence with Creuzer. His letters reveal his attachment to Heidelberg and to Creuzer, and his vital interest in the maintenance of the original program of the *Jahrbücher*. However, only three months after his departure from Heidelberg, he had come

---

[26] HeidelbJbb., I (1808), pp. 362-372; Arnim reviewed the following three publications: F. H. Jacobi, *Über gelehrte Gesellschaften,* München 1807; Rottmanner, "Kritik der Abhandlung F. H. Jacobis über gelehrte Gesellschaften," Landshut; Aman, "Nachschrift über Etwas, was Fr. Heinrich Jacobi gesagt hat," 1808.

[27] In this connection the *Zeitung für Einsiedler* published an abstract of Jean Paul's *Friedenspredigt* and Viller's *Überblick der Universitäten.*

[28] NHeidelbJbb., XI (1902), 194; Creuzer's letter to Arnim, December 18, 1808.

[29] *Schriften der Goethe-Ges.,* XIV, 132.

[30] Arnim-Brentano, pp. 254-5.

to realize that his efforts were in vain, and in sadness he wrote to Creuzer:

I was not mistaken in my premonition that you would be the only one in Heidelberg to continue to think of me. Not a word has come from Zimmer, and perhaps you also are leaving soon. . . . Then Voss will rule Heidelberg. I am sorry, for I am still much attached to the faithful mountain and the airy castle.[31]

In April 1809, to Arnim's deep regret, the management of the philosophic-historical division of the *Jahrbücher* passed into the hands of Böckh and Wilken, Creuzer having accepted a call to the university of Leyden. Arnim felt keenly that Heidelberg was now deserted by all his friends and mourned the severance of all ties. He was afraid that the *Jahrbücher* might soon become nothing more than an expensive edition of the *Göttinger Anzeigen,* unless the new editors showed discretion and determination.[32] Everyone in favor of the romantic trend in the *Jahrbücher* suspected the new management. "I feel sorry for the *Jahrbücher,*" Arnim wrote to Creuzer, "because of the hopes others and I cherished, to see preserved in them freedom and impartiality of judgment."[33] In a letter to Görres, Creuzer complained: "It is going to be something very fine when these three people[34] undertake to arbitrate on theology, philosophy, literature, and art."[35]

These suspicions were indeed justified. The entry of the new editorial board signified a departure from the "Einsiedler" group. This became still more marked when Wilken's influence assumed greater proportions and Böckh gradually withdrew. In 1810 Wilken's and Thibaut's proposal to exclude Arnim was defeated by Böckh.[36] Nevertheless, the result was that for more than a year Arnim was not invited to contribute reviews. It is not surprising, therefore, that the young Heidelbergers were very indignant and expressed their disgust in strong language. They were justified in their attitude, for, indeed, literature and art fared badly in the hands of the new editors, and Arnim could well complain that important works like Goethe's *Wahlverwandtschaften* and

---

[31] NHeidelbJbb., XI (1902), 198-9; Arnim's letter to Creuzer, Jan. 25, 1809.
[32] NHeidelbJbb., XI (1902), 208; Arnim's letter to Cruezer, April 22, 1809.
[33] *Ibid.*   [34] Wilken, Böckh, and Thibaut.
[35] *Görres-Briefe,* hrsg. von M. Görres und Fr. Binder, 1858-74, II, 161-2.
[36] NHeidelbJbb., XI (1900), 146; Görres' letter to Arnim.

the writings of Jean Paul were not even mentioned in the *Jahrbücher*. Nevertheless, the standard of the *Jahrbücher* was still higher than that of other contemporary periodicals.

Arnim's connection with the *Jahrbücher* was re-established in November, 1811, when he visited Heidelberg on a trip to Strassburg and Frankfort. He was asked again to collaborate, and contributed two minor reviews in 1812 and 1813.[37]

In the meantime his literary pursuits and possibilities had gravitated from Heidelberg to Berlin. The depressing years of 1807-8, when social and intellectual life in Berlin stagnated, were followed by a period of forceful and brilliant activities. At Christmas, 1809, the royal couple again took up residence in their capital. The newly founded university had enticed several old acquaintances of Arnim's to come to Berlin, among them Savigny. Other important persons, like Heinrich von Kleist, Fichte, and Adam Müller, were now also there. They all found themselves united in the "Patrioten- und Kriegspartei" and in the "Christlich-deutsche Tischgesellschaft," where Arnim presided. Their united efforts were bent toward one goal: a spiritual and cultural renaissance of Germany and liberation from Napoleon's yoke.

However, the day of national uprising, so longed for by Arnim, was not to dawn for several years. The intermediate period, which witnessed the final break-up of the Heidelberg circle and the preparation for the resurgence of Prussia, provided ample leisure and the necessary stimulus for the execution of ideas and plans of long standing. Hand in hand with this went a greater clarification of the literary theories of the younger Romanticists. All the writings of this intermediate period, whether Arnim's or Brentano's, the Grimm brothers' or Görres', must be interpreted as the outgrowth or continuation of the literary movement that started with the *Wunderhorn* and the *Einsiedlerzeitung*. The five young men kept in close touch with each other during those years. After September, 1809 Brentano resided in Berlin in the same lodgings with Arnim, almost without interruption for two years.[38] Wilhelm

[37] Arnim-Brentano, p. 292. The two reviews were of *Gottfried August Bürgers Ehestandsgeschichte*, HeidelbJbb., 1812, Abt. 2, pp. 1199-1200, and Bornemann's *Plattdeutsche Gedichte, ibid.*, Abt. I, pp. 305-9.

[38] Arnim-Brentano, p. 286

Grimm came at this time for a visit. Without doubt the reunion of the trio meant a revival of discussions of their literary and philological plans. The question of a fourth volume of the *Wunderhorn* was debated. Von der Hagen joined in the discussion of the *Nibelungenlied*. An active search began for old books. After Wilhelm Grimm had left Berlin the exchange of ideas was continued in a correspondence of great literary interest.

A brief examination of the writings and plays which were planned for the near future by these five members of the former Heidelberg circle is instructive. It was indeed a time of great literary activity. Arnim had compiled from old sources the stories of his *Wintergarten*, published in 1809. His novel *Armut, Reichtum, Schuld und Busse der Gräfin Dolores* followed in 1810. The same year he completed the drama *Halle und Jerusalem*. In 1811 four short stories were published, and in 1813 the first volume of the *Schaubühne*. Brentano was working on the *Romanzen vom Rosenkranz*, on a collection of fairy tales, and on *Die Gründung Prags*. He was constantly on the look-out for rare old books, so that Arnim gave him the nickname "sleuthhound for godly books" (*Gottesbücherspürhund*).[39] He contemplated a philological study on the folksong, and Wilhelm Grimm wanted to entrust him with the writing of a modern version of the *Nibelungenlied*.[40] Now it was that the Grimm brothers joined the ranks of nationally known writers with the publication of Jacob's *Über den altdeutschen Meistergesang* and Wilhelm's *Altdänische Heldenlieder, Balladen und Märchen*. Between 1812 and 1815 they brought out the *Kinder- und Hausmärchen*, and three years later, 1816-1818, their *Deutsche Sagen* appeared. Görres' activities and interests were more akin to those of the Grimm brothers than to those of any other member of the Heidelberg circle during these years. No

[39] Arnim-Bettina, p. 342.

[40] Arnim agreed with Wilhelm Grimm that the *Nibelungenlied* either had to receive a new version which would enable it to drive its own roots from new sap, or that it should be handed down from generation to generation in its dry, unrelieved antiquity. In a letter to Tieck, December 3, 1807, Arnim voiced his regret that Tieck's version of the *Nibelungen* had not yet been published, for "I do not like Hagen's, with its baroque dialect, its boresome annotations, and the omission of all other tales which you had so cleverly interwoven." Karl von Holtei, *Briefe an L. Tieck*, I, 10-13. Cf. also the report on the discussion of the *Nibelungenlied* in Hagen's presence at Arnim's home on Nov. 12, 1809; Arnim-Grimm, pp. 26, 29.

wonder that Görres carried on a very active correspondence with the Grimms. In Görres' *Die teutschen Volksbücher* and *Mythen-geschichte der asiatischen Welt* the Heidelberg circle found much stimulating material for discussion.

This long list of novel and serious writings from the pens of the Heidelberg circle—all having folklore as their subject matter and all appearing within a decade—invited eager interest and much discussion among the reading public, and most of all, among the members of the romantic circle itself. There was dire need of profound discussion, for it must not be overlooked that these young men and their subject matter had risen to sudden promi-nence. Popular poetry (*Volksdichtung*) as a genre, its origin and characteristics, its value and purpose for literature, philology, and history, and especially as a national treasure, all this had to be clarified. Such questions as the following provoked discussion: Should a folksong be handed down to posterity in its original form, or was it permissible to subject it to alterations, additions, or subtractions, retaining the ancient spirit? Should the *Nibelungen-lied* or the *Edda* be published in their original form, merely with a commentary, or should they, for a better understanding, be modernized or only be translated into modern High German? This again entailed a discussion of the rank and rights of the modern poet in comparison to those of the poet of the people (*Volks-dichter*), and finally the very fundamental question of distinction between "popular" or "natural poetry" and "art poetry" (*Volks-oder Naturdichtung und Kunstdichtung*).

Already while collaborating on the *Wunderhorn* Arnim and Brentano had taken different points of view with regard to render-ing the folksong. In 1805 Brentano objected that Arnim had introduced changes into some folksongs. Later, in 1808, after publishing the third volume of the *Wunderhorn,* Arnim tried to justify his stand in a letter to Clemens. Arnim is for new creations which preserve the old form and old spirit, yet adapt themselves to modern taste and understanding, so that they have a universal appeal to the public.[41] In support he cites Macpherson's *Ossian* and Goethe, who had stated that he liked the most extreme combinations of the ancient and the modern, "for only in these

---

[41] Arnim-Brentano, pp. 225, 229.

has the vitality of antiquity stood the test."[42] Arnim also called attention to the uncertainties as to what and how much single poets had contributed to the *Iliad,* and referred to the use of ancient sources by Shakespeare, Plato, and Schelling.[43] He believed that a poem can be put into a different context without changing its content or characteristics, as a painter can change his grouping by means of different light effects.[44]

Arnim and Brentano cherished the hope that collections similar to the *Wunderhorn* would soon be started by their friends, and that the same program for reviving interest in folklore, by a simple editing rather than by learned discussion, would guide them. Görres had published *Die teutschen Volksbücher* in 1807, much to Arnim's chagrin, for it was a book about chapbooks rather than a new chapbook. He expressed his vexation to Brentano and Tieck in two similar letters, characterizing the book as superfluous, superficial, aesthetically wordy; superfluous, because it was not evident for whom the literary portion had been written; superficial because while treating one collection, it generalized about all of them, betraying, "with one word, the whole modern arrogance born out of a lack of talent and imagination." "It would have been better if he had followed our plan and reprinted fully and whole-heartedly from the best sources for the people, giving his own opinion only in a condensed form."[45] Arnim had the same criticism for Büsching and Hagen's collection of folksongs, which he found permeated with a "faulty critical spirit, holding life in its clutches like death, usurping beauty as well as ugliness with the same fervor."[46]

The literary-theoretical controversy was opened on a broad basis in the correspondence between Arnim and the Grimm brothers, conditioned by the fundamentally different outlook of the two parties. This became even more pronounced in the following years. The Grimms had a scientific approach to art, literature, and history, while in Arnim the poetic element dominated. Thus Arnim wanted to interpret to his contemporaries the past in an

[42] *Ibid.,* pp. 234-6. Like Goethe, Görres was a keen sponsor of new creations and combinations in old folksongs.
[43] *Ibid.*   [44] *Ibid.*
[45] Arnim-Brentano, p. 221; Arnim's letter to Tieck, Dec. 3, 1807. Cf. Karl von Holtei, *Briefe an L. Tieck,* I, 12.   [46] Arnim-Brentano, p. 220.

attractive poetic manner, while the Grimms, as philologians, had a scholarly, objective attitude.

The immediate cause of the debate was Jacob Grimm's essay, "Gedanken: wie sich die Sagen zur Poesie und Geschichte verhalten," published in Arnim's *Zeitung für Einsiedler*.[47] Here Jacob maintained that there is a clear-cut distinction between the "poetry of nature" and the "poetry of art," more specifically, epic poetry versus dramatic poetry, poetry of the uneducated versus poetry of the intelligentsia. "The former," Grimm contended, "is transmitted without any effort, like a sound carried from afar, so faithful, pure, and innocent are the heroic deeds and legends recorded, constituting a common sacred treasure." But the "poetry of art" expresses only individual feeling, opinion, and experience. "Just as these two forms of poetry are of fundamental, intrinsic difference, they are also of necessity separated by time and can never appear simultaneously."[48]

In a commentary, added to this essay of Jacob Grimm, Arnim demands historical proof, for in his opinion both types of poetry are current at present. In a letter to Jacob he elaborated this idea, adding that he could demonstrate both types even in the worst poetry, and a third element which disturbed and obliterated the distinction between *Natur- und Kunstpoesie*.[49] It is obvious that Arnim could not share Grimm's point of view, for it would have meant that not a single one of Arnim's own creations could anywhere near reach the standard nor compare in intrinsic value with what was in Grimm's opinion the superior "poetry of nature." Not even Goethe's works could qualify under this definition. Furthermore, Arnim as a philosopher and scientist had learned that art and nature, reflection and intuition, experience and revelation, fact and faith, must exist simultaneously and in all periods of the history of mankind. In his student days at Halle and Göttingen these questions had been much discussed. Schelling also had occupied himself with "national poetry," "popular poetry," "poetry of nature" in contrast with the "Poetry of Art."[50]

[47] *Zeitung für Einsiedler,* pp. 199-204.
[48] *Ibid.,* p. 200.   [49] Arnim-Grimm, p. 14.
[50] Arnim and the Heidelberger used Herder's "National-," "Volks-," and "Naturpoesie" interchangeably, preferring "Naturpoesie" as the all-inclusive term. A

With the publication of Arnim's *Gräfin Dolores* and *Halle und Jerusalem* in 1810 the divergent opinion of the Grimms' became still more apparent. Wilhelm did not quite share his brother's severe criticism of Arnim's recent literary creations, but both had now learned to esteem and honor to a still higher degree all national poetry, sagas and legends, because they were convinced that only in this type of literature artistic perfection was attained. "National poetry (*Nationaldichtung*) is written by God himself; no patching and mending is apparent as in human productions."[51] Hence they considered it their duty to protest emphatically against any alterations in the sagas. Jacob's chief objection to *Gräfin Dolores* and *Halle und Jerusalem* was that Arnim had offended against these principles. He had made superficial and pretentious use of historic material in *Halle und Jerusalem*. His novel was untrue, and its plot incredible.[52]

This conclusion grew also out of the knowledge of the Grimms' that Arnim had little interest in historical facts, and hence did not study carefully historical documents. The culprit made no attempt to clear himself of this charge, but admitted that he read the "Nibelungen" for the sake of poetry and not to collect data about its origin or its author.[53] His interest in the Minnedichtung and the Meistergesang, on which Jacob was working at that time, followed the same lines. Here he judged also from the poetic point of view, admiring the art of word-play in the Minnedichtung, criticizing the boresome and often clumsy composition of the Meistergesang. He disagreed with Jacob's thesis that Minne-

---

definition, as far as possible according to Herder's usage, may not be amiss. "Naturpoesie" are the saga and epic; the emphasis lies on the aesthetic and beautiful, and it is characterized by innocence and unconsciousness, pure objectivity, and infinite contemplation of its subject matter (cf. *Herders Werke*, hrsg. von Suphan, I, 399; VI, 27). "Volkspoesie" is the saga; the emphasis lies on the psychological and emotional; it is characterized by a penetration and a recording of the event, disregarding often place and time, and it lives on even if the nation in question has changed its boundary lines and affiliations (IV, 10, 12, 35, 45). "Nationalpoesie" emphasizes the national historical event, preferably the heroic. It takes account of place and time and obviously is recorded for, and adapted to, a definite audience (IV, 34). Cf. also Ernst Lichtenstein, "Die Idee der Naturpoesie bei den Brüdern Grimm und ihr Verhältnis zu Herder," *Dt. Vierteljahresschr. f. Lit. Wiss. u. Geistesgesch.*, VI (1928), 513-47; also Elisabeth Blochmann, "Die deutsche Volksdichtungsbewegung in Sturm und Drang und Romantik", *ibid.*, I (1923), 419-52.

[51] Arnim-Grimm, p. 89.   [52] *Ibid.*, pp. 72, 99.   [53] *Ibid.*, p. 76.

dichtung was predominantly "natural poetry" (*Naturpoesie*), while Meistergesang was "art poetry" (*Kunstpoesie*). In this controversy it was his belief that:

neither the one nor the other form of poetry can exist by itself unalloyed. Both always coexist in the creations of an individual, even though one or the other may predominate for a time. If in Minne poetry the impulse of nature, in the Mastersong a consciousness of art predominates, then it would be indeed interesting to note the occurrence and the details for the sake of history.[54]

Almost simultaneously with Jacob's *Über deutschen Meistergesang* Görres published his *Die Mythengeschichte der asiatischen Welt,* in those days a book of far-reaching importance for the formulation of literary-historical conceptions. Naturally the Grimm brothers rejoiced at the advent of such a book, for it confirmed their belief that there is *unity* in the fundamental mystical thoughts of all people, and that all myth has come into this world by divine revelation. The spirit of poetry, the divine, is the same in all peoples; the myth is the first sound uttered by this divine spirit when it begins to break the fetters of nature, and this first sound is poetry. Thus all myth was originally poetry, and all poetry was originally mythical.

Arnim discussed Jacob Grimm's and Görres' books in the same letter, addressed to the former. Again he emphasizes that the natural impulse (*Naturtrieb*) and art-consciousness (*Kunstbewußtsein*) coexist, a fact which, he declares, has been overlooked by Görres.[55] Jacob Grimm had gone so far as to attribute not only the origin of religion, of myth, poetry, and language to divine revelation, but also all forms of language and poetry, such as alliteration and rhyme. He believed that he could prove his contention by the fact that identical myths and poems are found in all languages. This could be possible only by transmission from a single source, namely, divine revelation, otherwise the same poems would have been invented and imagined by different individuals in different languages. In other words, Jacob gave no credit to the individual poet, something which Arnim considers a grievous injustice to the greatest individuals of all times.[56] In this connection Arnim points out that his own enthusiasm for

[54] Arnim-Grimm, p. 109.   [55] Arnim-Grimm, p. 109.   [56] *Ibid.*, p. 109.

popular poetry (*Naturpoesie*) is based upon the fact that it is good poetry which has stood the test of time, and not because it is, as Grimm seems to believe, poetry of a different nature and art than the one practised at present. This does not mean that Arnim denied outright the divine origin and successive development of myths. He agreed with Görres that all myth was derived from India and from there brought to other countries; nevertheless he criticized Görres' book as one-sided because it emphasizes too much this one aspect, popular poetry (*Naturpoesie*).[57]

The exchange of ideas between Arnim and Jacob Grimm had thus led to still more detailed and complicated distinctions. Unsurmountable obstacles now existed in the way of a common agreement as to *Natur- und Kunstpoesie*.

Wilhelm Grimm tried to mediate in this controversy between his brother and Arnim. He himself leaned more towards Arnim's point of view. With regard to Görres' *Die Mythengeschichte der asiatischen Welt*, Wilhelm rejected Jacob's single source of all myth: the divine revelation, and postulated a double one: the inner source, the *one* spirit of which all human beings partake;[58] and the external source, transmission of poetry by means of communication between nations. Wilhelm then summarized his conception of *Natur- und Kunstpoesie*, agreeing with Arnim that in "natural and national poetry" the element of reason, conscious artistic reflection, is present, citing the *Nibelungenlied* and Homer, which his brother Jacob classified as "natural poetry." On the other hand, Wilhelm saw in Goethe's "Fischer" and "König in Thule" folksongs, equaling the best in the *Wunderhorn* collection.[59]

Before starting on his extensive trip with Bettina to her native city of Frankfort, in August, 1811, Arnim desired to clarify his position in this dispute about *Natur- und Kunstpoesie*. From his final letters his ideas may be summarized as follows: Poetry is nourished by eternal springs, flowing at all times, even in those when no verses are made, and perhaps more purely in them. "At the moment, however, when inspiration creates an outer form and

---

[57] *Ibid.*, pp. 109, 125.
[58] Corresponding to Jacob's "divine revelation," the *only* source of *Naturpoesie*.
[59] Arnim-Grimm, p. 124.

tries to communicate its inner joy, it becomes a vehicle of observation, and is no longer entirely true to the unconscious spring by which it is nourished."[60] Therefore *absolute* natural poetry (*Naturpoesie*) does not exist; there exists only a difference of greater or less degree in the development of both, "natural" and "art poetry" (*Natur- und Kunstpoesie*).[61]

Arnim admitted that there is a difference between the ancient poets of the people (*Volksdichter*) and those of modern times. Nevertheless, it is not a question of talent and inspiration, but rather of environment. In former ages a people lived more simply and primitively; there was none of the complexity of the modern world in the national life; hence thought and social life were more uniform. Anyone with poetic inspiration could embrace the whole, and therefore was a poet of the people, and the creations of several popular poets (*Volksdichter*) could easily form a poetic unit. However, in modern times individual talent is restricted to a narrower field. But whoever understands and embraces three elements: the history, life, and love of a people, will have a universal appeal even today.[62] Thus Arnim ranks the modern poets with these of antiquity, and rejects Jacob's glorification of the latter, the *Volksdichter*. By reason of his national, philosophical outlook Arnim could not very well agree with Jacob Grimm. Unless he was to despair of the possibility of a spiritual renaissance in his fatherland, he had to have faith that the glorious past was not a closed chapter, never to be reopened, but that a continuous spiritual stream was flowing and effective still today.

Jacob Grimm had approached the problem historically. Popular poetry (*Volkspoesie*) was a thing of the past and could not be repeated. Herder, Goethe, A. W. Schlegel had an aesthetic approach. They regarded *Volkspoesie* as the expression of a noble but primitive civilization. Arnim, whose attitude was somewhat comparable to that of Tieck or Fouqué, believed with ardent expectation that the present complex civilization could yet be permeated with the noble spirit of *Volkspoesie* of past ages, and that this would replace the scholarly poetry of the intelligentsia. All poetical endeavors should be directed towards the attainment of this lofty aim. Not only in Germany, but also abroad Arnim

[60] Arnim-Grimm, p. 142.   [61] *Ibid.*, p. 134.   [62] Arnim-Grimm, pp. 134-5.

observed that the golden days of the poetry of the people had withered and that a poetry of the intelligentsia was predominating. The fate of *Volkspoesie* in France he pictured as follows: As late as the Fifteenth Century *Volkspoesie* still existed in France; thereafter it was confined to Paris and finally to the so-called noble society of Paris. When this society ceased to exist, *Volkspoesie* also vanished and now exists only in historical documents.[63] In another place he wrote:

In this turmoil of novel things, in this supposed rapid establishment of paradise on earth, also in France all folksongs were extinguished even before the Revolution. Perhaps the disappearance of folksongs hastened the coming of this state of social turmoil. Even now the French are poorly endowed with them—what could bind them to that treasure, which ought to be of lasting value to them as a people? In England, too, the singing bards and minstrel songs have become rare; in Italy the national folksong gives place to the opera, to please people of little depth; even in Spain folksongs are said to be lost and nothing important has been substituted.[64]

The poetry of the intelligentsia has also a universal appeal: not to the people, the masses, but rather to the higher social classes of all nations. It rises above the horizon of the common people. The language used in this literature is merely something accidental. The poet of the intelligentsia, enamored of strange material and novel forms of expression, cannot but produce works that are foreign to his people.[65]

The interest and research in folklore by the Heidelberg circle naturally included also the fairy tale. However, while it did not take long to bring about a revival of interest in the folksong and saga and the collection and study of these forms, interest in the fairy tale remained dormant for a while. Nevertheless, the Grimm brothers had been busily gathering material since 1808, and began the publication of the *Kinder- und Hausmärchen* by the end of 1812. On the other hand, Brentano's *Märchen* appeared very slowly and sporadically, some not until after his death.[66] Never-

[63] From Arnim's unpublished note-book.
[64] DNL, CXLVI, I, p. 51; Arnim's essay "Von Volksliedern."
[65] *Unbekannte Aufsätze*, p. 79.
[66] Cf. DNL, CXLVI, I, p. CXLVIII-CLI, also H. Hamann in *Die literarischen Vorlagen der Kinder- und Hausmärchen und ihre Bearbeitung durch die Brüder Grimm ("Palaestra," XLVII)*.

theless, Brentano with the publication of the fragment *Die Rose* in 1800 had been the first worker in this field among the Heidelberg Romanticists. Five years later Arnim's summons to start collecting sagas and fairy tales, instead of only folksongs, was the first signal for renewed effort in this direction.[67] The same year Brentano wrote Arnim that he was adapting Italian fairy tales for German children,[68] and that he wanted to publish a collection at Zimmer's press in Heidelberg in 1809.[69] During his stay in Berlin from 1809 till 1811, encouraged by Savigny and Schinkel, and later on his estate at Bukowan in Czechoslovakia, Clemens continued his work on fairy tales.[70] However, before they actually appeared, they were discussed and criticized in the circle of friends, who were already acquainted with Clemens Brentano's tales or had heard of them. One was especially anxious to compare them with Grimm's *Kinder- und Hausmärchen*.

We have ample proof that Arnim took great interest in the collection of fairy tales by the Grimms.[71] Here difference of opinion and old disputes made their appearance again. Are fairy tales "natural poetry" (*Naturpoesie*), or must they be assigned to the field of "art poetry" (*Kunstpoesie*)? Is it permissible for modern poets to make alterations? To what extent is it possible to regard the fairy tale as the expression of a pure and noble naiveté? In Arnim's opinion fairy tales are not fixed, but in constant flux. The purpose of the fairy tale is to occupy the child's mind and to stimulate the imaginative talent.[72] Children when they relate fairy tales are apt to omit incidents or add new ones. Here again Jacob Grimm had a different point of view. He insisted that fairy tales have been told with truth and honesty, so that they must be regarded as *Naturpoesie*, admitting, however, that a mathematical truth is impossible, even in the "truest, sincerest tale."[73] The purpose of the fairy tale is not to stimulate the child's imagination

[67] Arnim-Brentano, p. 151; "Aufruf von Dezember 17, 1805."

[68] *Ibid.*, p. 156.

[69] Brentano's letter to Zimmer, Dec. 12, 1809.

[70] Arnim's letter to Jean Paul, Jan. 1, 1811.

[71] Arnim-Grimm, pp. 213-273; e.g., *Die Kinder- und Hausmärchen*.

[72] *Ibid.*, p. 223.

[73] Cf. also Arnim's and Jacob Grimm's different views on translations. Jacob would publish the *Edda* only in the original version, with a detailed commentary. Arnim suggested a translation of the *Edda*, not a simple, literal one, but a more

to new inventions and self-occupation. Children do not invent, though they may forget beautiful incidents. Variations found in fairy tales are comparable to the dialects of a language.[74]

Arnim's "Anmerkungen zum Märchenbuch"[75] is a critical analysis of the Grimms' *Kinder- und Hausmärchen*. In the first place Arnim did not wish that children should themselves read the fairy tales, but held that adults should select from them for telling children. He would have liked to see this advice printed on the front page ("Für Ältere zum Wiedererzählen nach eigener Auswahl"). He made this suggestion for the simple reason that the different styles in fairy tales of this collection make them difficult for children to understand. A fairy tale in which one child kills another is entirely unsuitable for children. He wanted the *Geschichte vom Fischer und syner Fru* omitted from the collection, because especially this tale is not suitable for children. *Machandelbom* he considered also a little too cruel for a children's collection, and the story of *Frau Füchsin* perhaps unmoral and at least dubious.

Arnim's suggestions did not at first meet with Wilhelm's and Jacob's approval. While Wilhelm was ready to omit *Frau Füchsin*, Jacob refused, for he maintained that to the pure in heart everything is pure, and that they will not read another meaning into the story. For the same reason both brothers scorned Arnim's suggestion that the title page indicate that adults were to read the book and then select for children. There cannot be, and perhaps ought not to be, any book for children which they can fully grasp. If ideas and words are sometimes over their heads, so much the better, for they will sink in and bear fruit in later time. "This," Jacob declared, "was comparable to reading to children from the Bible, where they also might not understand the meaning of 'God' or 'devil'." Yet it is good for them to hear these passages, as the Grimm brothers knew from their own childhood experiences.[76]

It must be noted, however, that in later editions of the *Kinder-*

---

poetic rendering than the original (*poetische Erhöhung*). "Religious sincerity", he said, "lies at the bottom of all literal translations, but playful enjoyment alters old pieces of poetry." Cf. Arnim-Grimm. pp. 131, 137, 143.

[74] Arnim-Grimm, p. 255.
[75] *Ibid.*, p. 262.
[76] Arnim-Grimm, pp. 266-7.

und Hausmärchen all of Arnim's suggestions found due consideration.

While the Grimm brothers were publishing their Märchen, Brentano was also busy with the fairy tale, and his work was included in this discussion. A definite judgment of Brentano's fairy tales was not yet possible because of incomplete knowledge, due to fragmentary publication. Very apparent and much discussed, however, was the different approach of Brentano, his leaning to the poetic side. Arnim and his family had spent the summer with Brentano in Teplitz, where Brentano had given them an intimate acquaintance with his work. Arnim was thus in a position to give detailed reports to the Grimms. The fairy tales were "decorated with several new additions,"[77] as Arnim wrote to the brothers, adding, however, that Brentano's chief interest at the moment was in the drama, namely in his dramatic poem *Aloys und Imelde,* and in the mythical legends about the founding of Prague. In spite of the great hopes Brentano cherished for his drama *Libussa (Die Gründung Prags),* which centered around the founding of Prague, Arnim wrote less optimistically to the Grimm brothers: "*Libussa,* excelling in language and details, lacks unity of action and character, as may happen so easily with mythical stories. There are beautiful single passages, interesting situations, so that I regret extremely that he did not carry out his original plan to write an opera."[78]

In November, 1814, Brentano announced to Arnim that his *Libussa* was finished, completely rhymed and revised four times.[79] Even for the author Arnim had little encouragement, criticizing especially the superabundance of poetical words and untimely declamation.[80] He voiced a similar criticism in his later correspondence with Wilhelm Grimm, being unable to understand how such beautiful tragic material could be spoiled. Brentano was, he declared, in dire need that somebody should devise a plot for him.[81] The reaction of the Grimm brothers was characteristic. Wilhelm, polite and understanding, pointed out that excessive revising and polishing deprived Brentano's works of all vivacity and natural charm. Jacob referred again to the fallacy of adapt-

[77] *Ibid.,* p. 211.   [78] *Ibid.,* pp. 210-11.   [79] Arnim-Brentano, p. 306.
[80] *Ibid.,* p. 306.   [81] Arnim-Grimm, p. 320.

ing and rearranging myths and fairy tales. He reproached Clemens and all modern poets for their attempts to imitate *Naturpoesie;* a veritable weakness, he contended, probably never to be recognized by Clemens in his erroneous desire to create something better.[82]

Arnim felt hurt by Jacob's vigorous criticism, not only of Brentano, but of modern poets. He felt that with equal right he could criticize the tiresome and often mechanical old poets. He took great pains to explain to Jacob the poetic elements in Brentano's poetry, especially in his fairy tales. "These are *new* fairy tales, which his innermost soul urged him to write. One can criticize only Brentano's vain coquetry which prompted him to display his skill in words."[83] Arnim saw the fundamental difference between the Grimm brothers' fairy tale collection and that of Brentano in the fact that the latter did not meet the immediate needs of children but rather had to be adapted for them by adults. It was a collection that would stimulate the imagination of adults, who could fashion it into a constant source of fascinating enjoyment for children.[84]

Some years later, in the *Gesellschafter* of 1818, Arnim reviewed F. V. V. Schmidt's free translation of Italian fairy tales, which had been published in 1817 under the title *Die Märchen des Straparola.* To suit the taste of the German reading public Schmidt had omitted many questionable jokes and episodes from the original, a procedure which, as Arnim informs us, was justified and by no means cast any reflection on Italian morality. It was rather a difference in taste, which has to be considered in transmitting the literature from one nation to another. Like the Grimm brothers, Schmidt had equipped his translation with valuable notes.[85]

The fertile discussion with the Grimms, an attempt to clarify questions so vital to the Heidelberg romanticists, was interrupted by the war of 1813-14. The struggle, with its far-reaching consequences, and the new political constellation in Europe brought new issues, particularly to Arnim, Görres, and Brentano. During

[82] Arnim-Grimm, pp. 219-20.
[83] *Ibid.*, p. 223. Cf. the inconsistency of Arnim's opinion, *ibid.*, p. 263.
[84] *Ibid.*, p. 223.
[85] *Ges.*, 1818, p. 44; F. V. V. Schmidt, *Die Märchen des Straparola.*

the war years the friends did not meet and their meagre correspondence was concerned chiefly with political events. Then in September, 1814, after having been absent from Berlin for more than three years, Brentano returned to the Prussian capital. It seemed as if the stimulating influences and friendships he found in Berlin would bring the dawn of a new era of activity for him. Berlin society had attempted to revive and to cultivate again literary interests. Soon friendly bonds united Brentano with E. Th. A. Hoffmann, who had made Berlin his permanent residence in September, 1814, and with Karl Friedrich Schinkel, the great architect. Had Clemens also found the stimulation and assistance of his friend Arnim as in former years, he might have regained the inner peace of mind and the joy necessary for new and creative work. But as early as the spring of 1814 Arnim left Berlin again and for reasons of economy, settled on his family estate, Wiepersdorf, then almost a day's ride from Berlin. Furthermore, the shift in his literary interests and his constant financial worries prevented a renewal of the old ties of close association. For these reasons the two friends did not return to the brotherly intimacy of literary effort of former days.

Only one field attracted their mutual interest during the remaining years of Brentano's residence at the Prussian capital, from the autumn of 1814 to the autumn of 1818: the Berlin stage. Both wished now to realize their long-cherished plan of winning the stage for romantic plays. Earlier, both had attempted to gain entrance to the theater for their dramatic productions: Brentano unsuccessfully in Vienna, and Arnim, together with Kleist, in Berlin in 1810, also in vain. Now both, Arnim in the capacity of stage producer and Brentano as playwright, were eager to bring before the public their impressions of the stage of the day and their views of the necessary stage reforms. These ideas were set forth in a satirical and belligerent manner in the "Briefe über das neue Theater." These were fictitious letters which began to appear in the *Wünschelrute*,[86] in 1818. They were soon discontinued, for

---

[86] The *Wünschelrute,* hrsg. von H. Straube und J. P. von Hornthal, was a short-lived publication which was supposed to be the mouthpiece of the so-called "Poetische Schustergilde in Göttingen" (from January until June 1818). The "Briefe über das neue Theater" were published from March 19 to April 27, 1818.

the reason that Arnim's contemporaries were at a loss to understand the mixture of satire and seriousness which marked their style. From Arnim's letter to the publisher which accompanied the manuscript it is apparent that it was the intention of Arnim and Brentano to write an evolutionary history of dramatic production, setting forth the obstacles that had beset its path and their ideas for its future development. Arnim was to write in the capacity of a modern stage producer. As the spokesman for the stage producers, he soon discovered that these unfortunates had much reason for lamentation.[87] The two friends never tried to revive their project as a co-operative enterprise, but Arnim returned to the subject[88] a decade later in the "Sammlungen zur Theatergeschichte."

In this connection it is of interest to examine Arnim's attitude towards the later literary work of his close friend and colleague. Of all of his notes on Brentano's writings, only one deserves mention, an announcement of *Victoria und ihre Geschwister* in Gubitz's *Gesellschafter* of the year 1817.[89] Arnim classified it as a gay pageant, interspersed with serious commentaries, originally planned for the comic stage and now adapted for the reading public. He considered the commentaries, the Schoolmaster's serious remarks, especially valuable. These refer to the political situation of the time and contain a grave warning to the victorious nations not to be overjoyful and conceited.

The spheres of interest of the former friends now drew further and further apart. This separation reached a crisis when Brentano turned as a penitent to find refuge in the bosom of the Catholic Church, a step that was hastened by his unhappy love for the pious Luise Hensel. With the year 1817, news of the change in

[87] Arnim's letter to the publishers of the *Wünschelrute*, Prenzlau, February 23, 1918. Cf. *Literarische Mitteilungen, Festschrift zum zehnjähringen Bestehen der Litteraturarchiv-Gesellschaft* in Berlin (Berlin, 1901, Litteraturarchiv-Gesellschaft), pp. 76-8.

[88] "Sammlungen zur Theatergeschichte" in *Monatliche Beiträge zur Geschichte dramatischer Kunst und Literatur,* hrsg. von Karl von Holtei. II (1828), 1-42. Two other projects of the friends from an earlier time were a biographical collection by Bettina, Clemens, and Arnim, and a collection of war letters. Cf. Arnim-Bettina, pp. 333, 355.

[89] *Victoria und ihre Geschwister mit fliegenden Fahnen und brennender Lunte. Ein klingendes Spiel von Clemens Brentano,* Berlin, 1913. Ges. (Berlin 1817), p. 644.

Brentano began to be disturbing to the friends, for it seemed that his restless spirit was seeking refuge in Catholic mysticism. In recalling the happy days they had spent in Heidelberg, Arnim wrote to Jacob Grimm March 30, 1917:

A very pleasant time I had there, living with Clemens, and writing the first part of the *Wunderhorn*. His wife Mereau was still alive. At times he suffered from rheumatism or was in a bad humor, but he was more religious then than now, when he crosses himself, goes to confession, and acts like a converted sinner.[90]

In the fall of 1818 Brentano took a further step toward severing his relations with Arnim and to Berlin by his departure for Dülmen, where the "tired pilgrim" tried to find peace in the presence of the stigmatized nun, Anna Katherine Emmerich. When Arnim saw Clemens again during the latter's brief visit in Berlin in January 1819, Brentano impressed him as a Catholic fanatic. Nevertheless, he expressed to Görres his satisfaction that Clemens had at last found a path and an aim in life.[91]

In later years, in the correspondence between Arnim and the Grimm brothers, Brentano's life and work were still discussed occasionally. Arnim expressed enthusiasm for what he called Brentano's "beautiful fragment 'Der arme Heinrich,' " by which he probably meant "Der arme Johannes," and referred to *Aus der Chronika eines fahrenden Schülers*.[92] Finally, the year 1828 brought an end to the friendship. Arnim's letters to Wilhelm Grimm during the summer of that year, when Arnim was visiting Brentano in Frankfort, contain many interesting remarks. In these letters we hear a note of chagrin and disappointment that two of his best friends, Brentano and Görres, were now wasting their energies on behalf of the Catholic clergy. Political trends and confessional zeal had taken them into another camp. As South Germans, ardent Catholics, and Romanticists, they embraced whole-heartedly the ultramontane program, which Arnim, a stout Protestant and a North German, could not accept. Arnim blamed the *Zeitgeist* for their desertion. They were victims, he thought,

[90] Arnim-Grimm, p. 372.
[91] Arnim's letter to Görres, February 4, 1918.
[92] Arnim-Grimm, p. 369.

of the "bad times." In this sense he wrote to Wilhelm, February 29, 1828:

I can hardly tell you how desperate I am sometimes when I come to think how two men of such great talent as Clemens and Görres have been thrown off their path by this rubbish about faith, this malady of distorted views. I should not have objected, had they gone like hermits into the desert, or mounted the pulpit like Werner; but they are under some inhibition, full of complexes which they do not understand. In the last analysis, they have just gotten stuck in the mud of the time.[93]

While thus in the spring of 1828 Arnim only expresses regret at their going astray, half a year later, after visiting them in southern Germany, he condemns them more severely. His pan-German sentiments were deeply hurt. It was his conviction that such people were very dangerous to the nation because of their very inactivity and their negative attitude, and their contempt of the world.[94] Thus the beautiful friendship, born out of youthful idealism for the fatherland, had received its death blow at the hand of petty local politics and party spirit.

In later years Arnim paid little attention to Görres' literary-historical writings. He did review his *Altdeutsche Volk- und Meisterlieder* in the *Gesellschafter* in 1817. Here again he emphasizes the author's historical approach, the same method which had been employed by the Grimm brothers. Görres' work was an extensive collection of folksongs, containing valuable contributions similar to those in the *Wunderhorn,* together with a brilliant historical essay. Görres' interest centered on the historical aspect of poetry, whereas in the *Wunderhorn,* as Arnim points out, he himself had emphasized the artistic side of the folksong and interpreted its "soul" by means of selection and alterations in accord with the spirit of his own time.[95]

Among all his friends the Grimm brothers remained closest to him in later years. Arnim esteemed deeply their personal qualities, especially their kindness and modesty. However, the more they concentrated on literary-historical scholasticism, the less was Arnim able to follow them. This became apparent on the publication of the first volume of Jacob's *Deutsche Grammatik* in the

[93] Arnim-Grimm, p. 576.   [94] *Ibid.,* p. 582.
[95] *Unbekannte Aufsätze,* pp. 83-5.

spring of 1819. The poet Arnim had little interest in this book. He refers to it only humorously. On the whole, he seems to have considered the teaching of German grammar as superfluous, except in districts where dialects prevailed. In case it was to be taught, he advocated that a German grammar be added to a book on Latin grammar.[96] Again, in 1818, he reviews briefly the second part of the Grimms' *Deutsche Sagen,* published in that year.[97] Once more the old dispute as to how far legends *(Sagen)* were *Natur-* or *Kunstpoesie* is revived, and the critic believes that he has now the opportunity to define and clarify the point definitely. The most difficult problem is to determine what oral material successive generations have added to the nucleus of the original saga, which originated under simple conditions. Simplicity of life and culture distinguishes for Arnim the original element of a saga from the creations of the modern poetic spirit. Nevertheless, whatever is "good" in the poetry of all times has been written "out of inner necessity" by poets who "could think thus and not otherwise." This living treasure of poetry is eternal and will remain eternal.

Among the writings of the last years of his life, the essay on Jacob Grimm's *Deutsche Rechtsaltertümer*[98] is noteworthy as a formulation of Arnim's attitude toward an important creation of the German spirit through past ages. This work was very much to Arnim's taste, and was in his opinion entitled to a prominent place among the various collections of folklore. He had waited impatiently for the publication of the book, and on its appearance he hastened to express his appreciation and delight to Wilhelm Grimm:

This book I like best among all of his [Jacob's] writings because here he has created something highly important out of almost nothing, that is, he has collected something from sources hitherto unavailable, from manuscripts never used for such a purpose. You will understand, how pleased I am, for I have never liked the scholarly criticism of old poems, nor the grammatical discussions of language.[99]

It had been Arnim's intention to write an extended review of the

[96] Arnim-Grimm, p. 435.
[97] *Ges.,* p. 532; cf. *Unbekannte Aufsätze,* pp. 89-90.
[98] *Ges.,* pp. 156-8; cf. Arnim-Grimm, pp. 596-602.
[99] Arnim-Grimm, p. 581.

Deutsche Rechtsaltertümer, but he did not feel equal to the task, nor did he think that any contemporary scholar could qualify for writing critically on this monumental piece of work. As Arnim pointed out in his essay, Jacob's book did not deal merely with interesting linguistic forms, nor was it only a collection of ancient legal documents and customs, but rather something more organic and unified, revealing the ancient civilization, the free and noble system of old Germanic law. The "Weistümer" were not legal decisions dictated by reason, but rather a voice of the people in its own popular, poetic, rich, and sensuous language, which was at times phrased in the ancient alliterative form. Hence they were essentially, from the cultural point of view, on a par with the folksongs. As a champion of Germanic law, Arnim pointed out how easily these old laws had been accepted by the German people after they were reintroduced from French and English translations into German territory, e.g., into the kingdom of Westphalia in the "code Napoleon". He challenged two of Jacob Grimm's contentions. The first was the statement that in the province of Brandenburg, mostly inhabited by people of Slavic origin, no old Germanic laws were found. On the contrary, Arnim claimed to find many traces of these ancient laws in Brandenburg, and he concluded, therefore, that this province must have been inhabited by Germanic tribes before the advent of the Slavs. Secondly, he protested against Grimm's criticism of present-day conditions in his introduction. Here Grimm remarks that "the serfdom and slavery of the past were in many ways easier and more attractive than the oppressed existence of our peasants and factory workers."[100] As an aristocrat and landowner, Arnim must naturally have a different opinion on this issue; and he points out that since the overthrow of Napoleon land had been confiscated and allotted by the state for the purpose of creating an independent peasantry.[101] The extensive notes which conclude Arnim's essay on Grimm's work reveal his wide knowledge of folklore and legal subjects.

Less than a year after Arnim wrote this review he passed away. In his last letter to him Wilhelm Grimm urged Arnim to be more

[100] Jacob Grimm, *Deutsche Rechtsaltertümer* (1828), p. XII.
[101] Arnim-Grimm, p. 599.

active as a critic, a calling for which he was so well equipped and which was so well suited to his talents.[102] After his death Wilhelm Grimm published Arnim's collected works. By means of this edition and the deeply appreciative introduction that opened it, he set up a lasting monument to their friendship.

[102] *Ibid.,* p. 615.

V

OLDER ROMANTIC CONTEMPORARIES

The most significant literary acquaintances which Arnim made on his grand tour of 1801-4 were Friedrich Schlegel and his circle in Paris. When speaking critically of Friedrich Schlegel and August Wilhelm Schlegel Arnim preferred to make no important distinctions between the brothers, for he found their literary tastes and judgments to be similar, even though they differed widely in their writings. He would have preferred that they should have published their voluminous writings jointly, as they had done with the "Charakteristiken," instead of separately. In that manner, he thought, their work would have been of greater value for posterity.[1] Even though Arnim had not much in common with the Schlegels, as regards character and personality,—he thought them too arrogant and propagandistic,—he nevertheless esteemed them very highly as men of letters. In his writings he mentioned them often together with Goethe and Tieck.[2]

Prior to his meeting with Arnim, Brentano had known Friedrich Schlegel in Jena, and he told Arnim much about him. In their reserved attitude toward Schlegel, both Arnim and Brentano were influenced by Tieck. They wanted to prevent the cold current of Schlegel's criticism from chilling their own work. Arnim was always reminded of translations when thinking of Schlegel.[3] It was in agreement with Arnim's and Brentano's nature to choose the modest, quiet paths in art, following Tieck's example, instead of the "Programm-Romantik" of the Schlegel brothers, whose aggressive nature, "like an accursed trumpeting," disturbed the serenity of all artistic endeavor.[4] In his letters to Clemens from

[1] *August Wilhelm Schlegels poetische Werke*, reviewed by Arnim in the HeidelbJbb. (1811), pp. 1188 ff.
[2] Arnim-Brentano, pp. 247, 357.   [3] *Ibid.*, p. 58.
[4] *Ibid.*, p. 96; Clemens' letter to Arnim, August, 1803. In spite of this antagonism, Arnim's writings show traces of Schlegel's influence, e.g., in "Heymars Dichterschule," the use of paintings and stories in teaching. In *Halle und Jerusalem* Schönemann points out certain similarities to Schlegel's *Lucinde*. Cf. Schönemann, *op. cit.*, pp. 113-14, 145.

Switzerland during the summer of 1802, Arnim condemned Friedrich Schlegel's criticism of Jacobi's *Woldemar*,[5] and said that he intended to use the polemic activity of the Schlegels satirically as "one of the best episodes" in his *Ariel*.[6]

Arnim knew that he was going to live in the same boarding house with Friedrich Schlegel in Paris. Nevertheless, as he wrote to Clemens from Geneva on November 8, 1802, he had not the slightest intention of seeking Schlegel's association and friendship, much less of writing for his periodical *Europa*. With youthful zeal he wanted rather to challenge and to scold him, and to call him to his face a "Casso senza pensieri."[7] However, a few months later, in February, 1803, after he has met Schlegel, he changes his opinion very decidedly and writes to Brentano that Friedrich really would be a good fellow if financial adversities had not developed envy and affectation in his character. He finds him and his wife modest. Schlegel was at that time lecturing on the history of modern philosophy and literature in a manner which Arnim considered quite boring.[8] Most likely Arnim was also very much attracted by Schlegel's romantic-religious conception of art, which was opposed to the inadequate and hazy imitation of the ancients which was in vogue at this time.

Of all the members of the Paris circle, Arnim was perhaps the one whom Schlegel liked best. Apparently he appreciated very much his "Erzählungen von Schauspielen" written for the *Europa*, for he asked him for a similar article on the London stage.[9] In later years Schlegel also asked Arnim for contributions to his various periodicals and almanacs.[10] Arnim did not comply with these requests; on the other hand, Friedrich accepted readily Arnim's invitation and wrote for the *Einsiedlerzeitung* in spite of his hostile attitude toward the *Wunderhorn*.[11] Schlegel did not approve of the "Wunderhorn spirit"; to him it was an "unclean spirit," and he therefore held aloof from the rest of the "worthy

[5] Arnim-Brentano, p. 41. [6] *Ibid.*, p. 54. [7] *Ibid.*, p. 54.
[8] *Ibid.*, p. 67.
[9] Joseph Körner, *Briefe von und an Friedrich und Dorothea Schlegel*, 1926, p. 528.
[10] Especially to the *Poetisches Taschenbuch von 1806*. Schlegel also asked Arnim for a review of this almanach in the *Elegante Zeitung*, or in another equally suitable place. Cf. Arnim-Brentano, p. 163, and Schlegel's letter to Arnim, January 3, 1806.
[11] Josef Körner, *Schlegel-Briefe*, p. 505.

society in Heidelberg."[12] Nevertheless, he was polite enough not to attack Arnim in public.

In 1810 Arnim wrote a rather unfavorable review of *Friedrich Schlegels Gedichte*[13] for the *Heidelbergische Jahrbücher*. The review was characterized best by Schlegel himself in a letter to Friedrich Wilken, editor of the *Jahrbücher*: "Your periodical contained a well-meaning notice of my poem, by Arnim I think; only it had more in it about the *Athenaeum* than about my poems."[14] It is true that Arnim was apt to judge the writings of the Schlegel brothers only in the light of the *Athenaeum* and the literary-critical activities of the Jena group. In this review of Friedrich's poems he emphasized that a poet is not independent of his age and group, hence must be judged accordingly.[15] The attacks of the Schlegel brothers on current literary trends had met with Arnim's approval, and he gives expression to this in the review. He thought that valuable work had been accomplished by this drive against the tedious array of mediocre writers. What he objected to was, that the new trends were presented by the Schlegels in their characteristic bombastic manner.[16] In the review Arnim also expressed the opinion that the attacks of the Jena group would have reached their goal sooner had they been preceded by productive work; and he pointed to the example of Goethe, who had first shown the way to something better by his works, and then tried to bring about improvement by means of criticism. What the Schlegels expressed had been felt for a long time by all the better writers, who had kept silence only from a false reserve. In this connection Arnim referred to certain critical expressions in Heinse's correspondence:

For a long time the better class of writers had been disgusted with the useless shifting about of philosophical formulas and analysis, the mushy sentiment and syllable-counting, especially the ambitious manner of

[12] Schlegel to Boisseree in Heidelberg, February 16, 1811.
[13] HeidelbJbb., I (1810), pp. 145-153. The "Gedichte" were published (Julius Hitzig, Berlin, 1809) as the first volume of Schlegel's *Sämtliche Werke*. The volume contains the two longer works, *Alarkos* and *Roland*, in addition to such poems as "Andacht," "Der alte Pilger," "Spessart," "Frankenberg," "Windesrauschen," "Geistes Licht," "Eulenspiegels Rat."
[14] Josef Körner, *Schlegel-Briefe*, p. 131, March 13, 1811.
[15] HeidelbJbb., I (1810), p. 148.
[16] *Ibid.*, p. 147.

laying down narrow rules in judging works of art, a task which every one felt called on to undertake. It is easy enough now to give an opinion as to how the editors of the *Athenaeum* should have gone about their undertaking, but it was only at that moment that one could judge how much ridicule was necessary in order to blow up the old fortress of firmly established usage. Who could then stop to think of the few simple households that might see their activities endangered, I mean the few writers who were no longer finding a market and yet were writing only for the market.

He adds that it was remarkable that in those fateful days in Europe when the *Athenaeum* appeared in the only region which still enjoyed peace, the attention of every one could have been so riveted on literature. Thus it was that writers like those of the *Athenaeum* concentrated their zeal for reform almost entirely on literature, to the exclusion of every other form of life.[17] Arnim recognized clearly, however, the importance and far-reaching effects of the new conception of art originating in Jena, in contrast to many who felt that the efforts of the group had been useless: "What was then limited to that small town, belongs now to the whole world. Schlegel's ideas have become the subject of many university lectures, particularly those of his former enemies."[18]

Turning now to discuss Schlegel's poems, Arnim criticizes chiefly those of the youthful period. These he finds defective in meter, something which to him betrays a lack of practice. He also notes in them a detachment from reality, or at least, a reflection of the inner rather than the outer world:

The range of these poems shows in general rather a tendency to seize the vital aspects of what he has read, to develop ideas, than to present what has been a matter of genuine experience. I do not deny that many things were based on experience, but it was certainly experience in a different form. It is due to this, that when a factual experience quite permeates the inner realization, as in the case of people who wear glasses, there results no broad observation, but a strangely profound and penetrating look. It is not until later on the Rhine that we find more universal sympathy, a fellow-feeling, an interest in popular life in general.[19]

Finally Arnim discussed in detail the tragedy *Alarkos* and the epic *Roland*. Brentano had written to Arnim as early as Septem-

---

[17] *Ibid.*, p. 147.   [18] *Ibid.*, p. 148.   [19] *Ibid.*, p. 148.

ber, 1802, how much he disliked *Alarkos*, calling it the worst tragedy he knew, a tragedy, which because of its artificiality bordered
on the comic.[20] The chief fault Arnim finds is the neglect of fundamental stage principles: "One notices that the author's staging
and construction of the plot is faulty, and that he has not mastered
language, style, nor subject matter. Consequently he has not been
able to avoid many things that hinder a general understanding.
These may not cause difficulty in reading the work, but certainly
do on the stage."[21] He also finds fault with the *Roland*.[22] He considers Schlegel's version of this epic so inadequate and artificial
in comparison to the *Chanson de Roland* that it would probably
never attain the universal appeal of a folk-epic. Certainly, he
declares, the artificiality could have been avoided had the author
taken the *Nibelungenlied* as an example rather than seeking his
patterns in the Spanish romances. Since Schlegel has so often
praised the dignity of the Old Germans and their literature, he
should have put his theories into practice.[23] Finally he comes to
the general conclusion that the poems reveal Schlegel as a divided
personality. His reason and his ideas attracted him to Goethe's
perfected form of poetry, but his true nature was romantic, of that
enthusiastic originality which transcends all form, reminding one
of Jean Paul.[24]

Schlegel's reaction to Arnim's review consisted of a severe
criticism of Arnim's *Halle und Jerusalem* in a letter to Friedrich
Wilken, March 13, 1811. Here he declared that the work did not
even approach the standard that would make it worthy of being
treated in a review.[25]

The following years witnessed a gradual estrangement between
the two men. During the years of national revolt against Napoleon
Schlegel again approached Arnim, for he wanted to make contact
with men of Arnim's type who were seriously concerned with the
German language and learning. On February 17, 1813, he wrote
to Arnim, "recalling earlier friendship," asking for contributions
to the *Deutsches Museum*.[26] In view of this cordial approach, it is

[20] Arnim-Brentano, p. 45. [21] HeidelbJbb., I (1810), p. 151.
[22] *Roland. Ein Heldengedicht in Romanzen nach Turpins Chronik.*
[23] HeidelbJbb., I, p. 152. [24] *Ibid.*, p. 153.
[25] Josef Körner, *Schlegel-Briefe*, p. 131. [26] *Ibid.*, p. 179.

surprising to note that Friedrich wrote to Tieck only three months later: "I am very fond of Fouqué. To be sure, my enjoyment of him may possibly be much greater as a result of my disgust for Arnim and all the other freaks (*Fratzen*)."[27] Arnim did not answer Schlegel's request till six months later, in August, 1813, when Brentano was visiting Vienna, where Schlegel was then living. Through his friend Arnim sent an essay, a patriotic poem, and a copy of his *Schaubühne* for the *Deutsches Museum*. Schlegel could not use any of them since he was preparing to discontinue publication of the *Museum,* which came to an end the following year.[28] This was the last of their literary contacts.

Not so close, and less important, were Arnim's relations with August Wilhelm Schlegel. They met first in 1808 in Heidelberg, where Schlegel was in attendance on Mme. de Staël. Schlegel pictures Arnim in Heidelberg as follows: "a talented young man; however, not without an admixture of vanity and foolishness; nevertheless, one has to esteem his knowledge of old German books and his love for them."[29] Like his brother, August Wilhelm promised contributions to the *Zeitung für Einsiedler*. A brief correspondence ensued, in which Schlegel encouraged Arnim to begin researches in the history of the literature of the Sixteenth Century. Arnim rejected this suggestion because he did not consider the historical evaluation of literature so important as the revival and popular presentation of old Germanic literature and works of art: "One work of art is better than the whole history of literature. . . . Germany's chief passion now is skill in talk and chatter rather than action and achievement along any line."[30]

In the form of a review in the *Heidelbergische Jahrbücher* of the poetical works of A. W. Schlegel, Arnim published in 1811[31] an

[27] Holtei, III, 337; May 12, 1813.

[28] Arnim-Brentano, p. 317; Arnim-Grimm, p. 185. Arnim intended, in collaboration with Wilhelm Grimm, to write a review for the *Heidelbergische Jahrbücher* of Friedrich's *Deutsches Museum*, which would have turned out, most likely, not very complimentary for Schlegel. Cf. NHeidelbJbb., XI (1902), 132-3.

[29] Arnim-Bettina, p. 169; Schlegel's letter to Carl von Hardenberg, August 4, 1808.

[30] Arnim to Schlegel, September 26, 1808.

[31] HeidelbJbb., Abt. 4 (1811), pp. 1185-1195; Arnim's review of *August Wilhelm Schlegels poetische Werke. Erster und zweiter Teil.* Heidelberg bey Mohr und Zimmer. Wilhelm Grimm and Görres agreed completely with this review. Görres thought at first that Wilhelm Grimm and not Arnim was its author. Cf. NHeidelbJbb.

interesting character study of the author and an appreciation of his literary achievements. Apparently Arnim thought very highly of this review, for he wrote to Brentano that he believed that he had expressed some truths in it.[32] Here he greets August Wilhelm, who had been travelling around in Germany and abroad since 1805, as the "returning German Poet . . . who can live only in his home. Foreign lands produce many plans, but little fulfillment . . . the contact with his people and with his language will awaken within him all that foreign lands put to sleep when it was on the way to realization."[33]

Nevertheless, in spite of his long absence from Germany, August Wilhelm was for Arnim at this time the central figure in the controversies and literary battles that had been going on in Germany for the past decade. As in his review of Friedrich Schlegel's *Gedichte,* he saw the brothers' endeavors in literary criticism in a favorable light, and expressed again his conviction that such a house-cleaning process as had been accomplished by the Schlegels was a necessity for a healthy development of German literature:

The diseases, envy and arrogance, which brought about the political destruction of Germany; envy and debasement of every distinguished individual and of the German peoples in comparison with each other, and arrogance over against the grandeur of earlier history in order to magnify the present moment, these had shown themselves ever since the foundation of the *Allgemeine Deutsche Bibliothek,* especially in the critical journals of Germany. Perhaps Shakespeare and Calderon and Goethe would never have attained their universal recognition, perhaps our literature would have been hamstrung by criticism as French literature was after Racine, but for the fact that Schlegel united with the knowledge of the old forms of criticism that suited the masses, a feeling for all that had real greatness, and by giving clear expression to the contradiction of "to be" and "not to be," brought about a change in the weather and thereby cleared the atmosphere for genius.

Arnim recalled that Schlegel's reviews in the *Jenaer Literatur-zeitung* had stood up against many an enemy of poetry. It was

---

(1902), 149-150. Arnim's suggestion that Schlegel should publish a third volume of poetic translations was accepted by Schlegel, who made arrangements with the publisher Zimmer. His sudden departure for Russia, however, interfered with this plan.

[32] Arnim-Brentano, p. 300.

[33] HeidelbJbb., Abt. 4 (1811), pp. 1185-1187; Arnim's review of *A. W. Schlegels poetische Werke.*

especially his dispute with the *Jenaer* that toppled over the authority of the critical journals and brought it to pass that the present-day reading public was able to criticize the critics, and enjoy wit when it appeared, yet at the same time recognize the lasting and vital creations of the soul.[34]

This review is important for our purpose, as it gives evidence that Arnim was stimulated to his own journalistic activities by the procedure and methods introduced by the Schlegels. The critical analysis in Schlegel's *Europa,* of the different periodicals concerned with reviews,[35] Arnim regarded as a masterly achievement in literary criticism.[36] Yet Arnim wonders whether August Wilhelm Schlegel had not given too much time in the different periods of his life to the thankless task of criticizing the work of others, thus depriving himself and the world of his own creations and of more of the translations for which he had shown such marvellous talent: "Perhaps," Arnim continues, "his 'Tristan' would have been completed by now, perhaps also his 'Shakespeare' and 'Calderon,' and all the untruth and vain glory which he discovered and chastized in literature would have disappeared without effort before such magnificence."[37]

Arnim draws a parallel between the Silesian literary schools of the Seventeenth Century and the activities and interests of the Schlegel brothers. Both groups had cultivated an interest in the ancient and the Romance literatures and had adapted their forms to German literature. He praises A. W. Schlegel especially for restoring the sonnet and the elegy to their rightful place. Arnim must have welcomed the opportunity to raise his voice again for the sonnet as a poetic form.[38] He regretted, to be sure, that it, or for that matter, any literary form had been abused so much. In his elegies, Arnim declares, Schlegel had also attained perfection

[34] *Ibid.*, p. 1186.

[35] As Arnim said, "Es gibt wenig so Herrliches als die in der *Europa* von Schlegel (II. Bd., Seite 18) aufgestellte Charakteristik der meisten rezensierenden Institute, ja es ist vielleicht die erste Ermunterung zum Rezensieren für die geworden, welche es ernstlich mit Kunst und Wissenschaft meinten."

[36] HeidelbJbb., Abt. 4 (1811), p. 1187; Arnim's review of *Schlegels poetische Werke.*

[37] *Ibid.*, p. 1186.

[38] The so-called *Sonnettenkrieg* is reflected in the *Zeitung für Einsiedler* of 1808; cf. Fr. Pfaff's introduction to *Arnim's Tröst Einsamkeit,* 1883.

of form, except that in the elegy "Rom," which Schlegel considered as one of his best, the contents did not correspond to the excellence of its outer form, for, as Arnim puts it, it was a "historic abstract in verse."[39]

The classical drama *Ion,* which had been staged once under Goethe's direction in Weimar, is severely criticized, chiefly because Schlegel had failed here to put into practice his own theoretical principles of drama. In Arnim's opinion, no contemporary playwright can ever attain perfection merely by imitating or utilizing the subject-matter of the classics. Hence Schlegel's *Ion* as well as Goethe's *Iphigenie* were failures in Arnim's eyes. Schlegel had himself come out in favor of Euripides in contrast with Racine's *Phèdre* and his own attempts in the classical styles with their mingling of ancient and modern elements. He had also, the reviewer reminds him, called Goethe's *Iphigenie* a weak reflection of antiquity. His *Ion* is therefore exposed to much unfavorable criticism if we compare it with the best of all Euripides' dramas: "We have a strong feeling that Goethe's *Iphigenie* and Schlegel's *Ion* belong, as concerns details, to the most finished achievements of dramatic poetry, but as a whole they are not to be compared with the ancient stage."[40]

While Arnim could not see the possibility that any laurels could be earned by intermingling the modern with the antique, he was in favor of translating the ancient dramas. He was aware, however, of certain inherent difficulties: no literal, word-for-word translation was wanted, but rather a free rendering based on a deep insight into the dramatic effects to be produced, so that the richness and power of the ancient drama might be experienced fully by the modern audience.[41]

When Schlegel's *Tristan* appeared, it brought special joy to Arnim, champion of old German literature as he was; and he expressed the hope that Schlegel's future literary productions might be of this nature.[42]

Arnim, then, looked upon the Schlegel brothers as militant prophets of a new epoch in art. On the other hand, there is little

---

[39] HeidelbJbb., Abt. 4 (1811), pp. 1190-1191; Arnim's review of *Schlegels poetische Werke.*

[40] *Ibid.,* pp. 1191-2.   [41] *Ibid.,* p. 1193.   [42] *Ibid.,* p. 1194.

mention in his writings of Novalis, the third member of the triad which had been so active in formulating the program of the *Athenaeum,* who is often referred to as the high priest of early Romanticism. Only during the first years of his literary career do we find in Arnim's letters a few remarks about Novalis and his *Heinrich von Ofterdingen.* These make it quite apparent that he lacked any deeper understanding of this one of his contemporaries. To Arnim the high priest of the new spirit in literature and art was Hölderlin rather than Novalis, and he regretted deeply that neither of these poets saw the national arising and the new political era in Germany.

It is, indeed, easy to understand that the youthful Prussian Junker, filled with a zest for life, was not attracted to the dreamy nature of Novalis, whose spirit was occupied more with the Beyond than with the earthly present. They were opposite poles, in spite of the great power of romantic imagination which both possessed. Where Arnim is simple and bright as daylight, Novalis is as pensive and as supernatural as the powers of night. A critical comparison of the outstanding novel of each, *Die Kronenwächter* and *Heinrich von Ofterdingen,* would be interesting and illuminating. Briefly a few points may be indicated. Both novels are a glorification of the historic past, written in the vein of romantic imagination and romantic natural philosophy; but while Novalis chose as background the Middle Ages, with its mysticism and universalism, Arnim chose the restless years of the Renaissance. Novalis' hero is a dreamer searching for the mystic "blue flower," while Berthold in Arnim's *Kronenwächter* is destined to accomplish great national and practical tasks. Arnim's commentary on *Heinrich von Ofterdingen* was sketchy and rather insignificant. After praising Tieck's *Lovell* highly he turned to *Heinrich von Ofterdingen:*

In contrast, I must confess that I find Novalis' *Heinrich von Ofterdingen,* as a whole, thoroughly mediocre, although beautiful in many details. Is there any narrative episode in it as fine as one of a dozen in *Lovell?* The pedantic stupidity of the chatter of the peasantry through it all; most of all, the "Märchen," a bore if you can't spell it out, and insignificant if you do understand it! . . . The examination of the second volume of *Ofterdingen* left me in a queer frame of mind. I finished it with the conviction that literature cannot be written in such a manner in the future. It exhausts itself with the conception of the plan.[43]

At times in Arnim's writings, especially in *Halle und Jerusalem,* one finds what may be interpreted as a satire on Novalis. Now it is the "neo-poetic Christians" that are ridiculed, now "nature mysticism" or the exaggerated, distorted, philosophical descriptions.[44] It is regrettable that in later years, when he had acquired more mature judgment, Arnim attempted no general evaluation of Novalis and his work. Yet it should be noted that in 1828, when writing about Hölderlin and seeking a poet with whom he could compare Hölderlin's impressive characteristics, his thoughts turned to Novalis.[45] This, after all, must lead to the conclusion that in his later years he had a better understanding and appreciation of Novalis as a poet than in his Heidelberg period.

Arnim was the first critic who noticed the kinship between Hölderlin and Novalis. The common characteristics of their poetry are great sincerity, a depth of ideas, and a melancholy, restless element, which is of the greatest tragic effect. Both had only a small group of admirers at first, and it was much later that their genius was generally recognized. Hölderlin was one of the few poets whom Arnim accepted without any reservation. He liked to turn to him in the most serious hours of his life and remained deeply interested in his literary aesthetics until his death. When his first youthful enthusiasm had subsided, he was often critical of Goethe and Tieck, but never of Hölderlin. Caroline von Günderode certainly expressed the true sentiment of the Heidelberg group when she wrote that they rated Goethe and Hölderlin as the first great masters of Romanticism.[46] Arnim regarded Hölderlin as a great German idealist who was devoted to the mission of his art with a deep sincerity. With the greatest sorrow and sympathy he followed Hölderlin's tragic life. As he saw it, a lack of recognition by contemporaries was the common lot of Hölderlin and himself.

[43] Arnim-Brentano, pp. 41, 136: "Die Durchsicht des zweiten Bandes von *Ofterdingen* ist mir sonderbar bekommen; er hat mich fester überzeugt, daß so überhaupt keine Dichtung weiter entstehen kann, sondern daß sie da mit der Entwerfung des Planes aufgebraucht ist."

[44] Werke, XVI, *Halle und Jerusalem*, pp. 336, 308. Cf. Arnim-Grimm, p. 110.

[45] *Berliner Conversationsblatt;* "Ausflüge mit Hölderlin"; Nr. 33, 1828.

[46] G. Bianquis, *Caroline von Günderode* (Paris, 1910), p. 42.

The interest in Hölderlin finds its first expression in 1808 in the *Zeitung für Einsiedler,* which contained several specimens of Hölderlin's free verse.[47] In Arnim's "Briefe über das neue Theater" Hölderlin's *Hyperion* is given the same rating as the works of Shakespeare and Calderon.[48] How much *Hyperion* meant to Arnim personally, is apparent from a letter written in 1813, where he declares that beside his own work, *Hyperion* is the only poetic work that he still finds to his taste.[49] One can only regret that Arnim never carried out his intention of writing a book on literary aesthetics, which he had intended to base on *Hyperion.* About this plan he wrote to the Grimm brothers October 21, 1817: "Several years ago I intended to do a work on aesthetics, following Hölderlin's *Hyperion,* for by its very nature a system of literary aesthetics should depend on the elegy, and the most magnificent of all elegies would then be the occasion for it."[50] In the "Literary Notes" in the periodical *Der Gesellschafter* during the following year (1818) Arnim referred again to Hölderlin's art and tried to arouse interest in a collection of his works,[51] a task which he felt had been unduly neglected.[52]

On this occasion he also discussed the slow progress of poetic art during recent years. The essence and task of art is "to render a true picture of life, emphasizing moral values, i.e., to evoke an ethical enthusiasm."[53] One might take exception to this as a very limited definition of art, but Arnim mentioned that also Goethe, using the pastor in *Hermann und Dorothea* as his mouthpiece, emphasized the element of "ethical enthusiasm" (*sittliche Begeisterung*) in art.[54] Arnim did not give up hope that this "true" art would eventually come into its own and he consoled himself with Hölderlin's words, "O Seele! Seele! Schönheit der Welt! Du unzerstörbare, du entzündende mit deiner ewigen Jugend!"[55]

In a later publication "Ausflüge mit Hölderlin," written shortly

---

[47] *Zeitung für Einsiedler,* Nr. 10, May 4, 1808.

[48] *Wünschelrute* (Göttingen, 1818), Nr. 25-28.

[49] Arnim-Brentano, p. 316.   [50] Arnim-Grimm, p. 402.

[51] *Unbekannte Aufsätze,* p. 98.

[52] *Ibid.,* p. 98; in Arnim's own words: "Vollständig müßten sie gegeben werden, weil er nie ein leeres Wort geschrieben."

[53] *Ibid.,* p. 97: In Arnim's words, "Kunst ist ein treues Bild des Lebens, sie weiß die sittliche Begeisterung darzustellen, wie jede andere [Begeisterung]."

[54] *Ibid.,* p. 97.   [55] *Ibid.,* p. 97.

before his death,[56] Arnim paid the highest tribute to Hölderlin. Pigenot, one of the most discriminating critics of the great Swabian poet, refers to Arnim's "Ausflüge mit Hölderlin" as the best article on Hölderlin written in a long time.[57] Arnim's essay contains a forceful arraignment of the critical spirit in literature during the preceding decades and apparently includes ideas which he was going to elaborate in his proposed "Aesthetics." He expresses his delight that Hölderlin's name, that of "the greatest of all elegiac poets," has not appeared as yet in any aesthetics; hence it has not been misused, he adds ironically, in order "to praise his faults." How do critics become famous? asks Arnim: "By tearing to pieces the laurel wreaths of poets!" To avoid unjust criticism and misrepresentation by critics, he wished that the poets might rather give their own annotations or explanations; but he realized the difficulties, for a true artist creates unconsciously, follows the divine spark of his genius:

Authors, one might say, ought to call attention to their own views, to the real value of their efforts, but the modesty which prevents them from uncovering the roots of their work is so natural. They fear that these cannot find again the soil from which they sprang, the unconscious and the unknown. Yet especially in the case of Hölderlin we must regret that he attained to no explanation of this kind, still less to an autobiography, because his art is too serious to be confused by an effort of that kind; especially because his life for the world and for his own talents came to such an early end.[58]

Of Hölderlin's poems Arnim discusses here only those of the poet's later years, e.g., "Die Nacht," "Die Herbstfeier," and "Die Wanderung." He points out the novel and effective way in which Hölderlin utilized a simple vocabulary. Of Hölderlin's "Patmos-Hymne"[59] our critic gives a poor evaluation. He considers it Hölderlin's most peculiar poem, bearing marks that foreshadow his mental unbalancing. In conclusion he wonders how other poets would have treated the Patmos material. The only

[56] *Berliner Conversationsblatt*, "Ausflüge mit Hölderlin," Nr. 31-34 (1828).

[57] *Hölderlins Sämtliche Werke*, hrsg. von. Hellingrath, II, 545.

[58] *Berliner Conversationsblatt*, "Ausflüge mit Hölderlin," Nr. 33, 1828.

[59] The "Patmos-Hymne" was first published in 1808 in *Seckendorfs Musenalmanach*. "Ohne Kenntnis dieses Druckes, von A. v. Arnim im *Berliner Conversationsblatt*, vom 18 Februar 1828, in ganz entstellter Form veröffentlicht." Cf. Hölderlins *Werke*, hrsg. von N. von Hellingrath, IV, 353.

other competent one, he thought, would have been Novalis: "None other occurs to me who could have taken hold of this theme, except perhaps Lavater. However the sublime inspirations which he had were drowned in words. But neither Lavater, nor Klopstock nor any other contemporary of Hölderlin can be regarded as the spark of his flame."

Arnim himself valued this essay on Hölderlin highest among all of his articles and reviews,[60] and in this he certainly was justified. With increasing age and a better understanding of literary values he was becoming a critic with deep insight into the nature of the poet and his creations.

While Hölderlin was the greatest poetic genius among the early Romantiscists, the greatest dramatist of this group was Zacharias Werner. Today in literary history Werner appears chiefly as the inventor of the fate-tragedy; to his contemporaries he was the greatest dramatist after Schiller, indeed, some even set him above Schiller. Arnim met Werner first in Heidelberg in 1808.[61] In speaking of this meeting in a letter to Bettina he refers to him as a "theater-poet, who is an up-right but happy-go-lucky fellow."[62] In December of the same year Arnim and Werner met again, this time in Goethe's house.[63] What appealed most to Arnim in Werner's plays was the revelation of the dramatist's deep inner religious life, reminding Arnim of Jung-Stilling in its mysticism. However, Arnim refused to take seriously the so-called "love-system" which Werner expounded to him at length at their Heidelberg meeting. "All the time," he writes Bettina, "I vacillated between a terrible outburst of laughter and deep sadness, as he talked about himself again and assured me that he writes solely for the purpose of expounding his system."[64]

Werner's "love-system" was to be regarded as the key to an understanding of his dramas. Two years after their first meeting Arnim wrote for the *Heidelbergische Jahrbücher* a review of Werner's *Attila*.[65] Here he tries to do justice to this peculiar feature

[60] Böhmer's letter to Jacob Grimm, Oct. 23, 1839.
[61] Arnim-Bettina, p. 175.
[62] *Ibid.*, p. 176; Arnim's letter of July 12, 1808.
[63] Bettina-Goethe, p. 322.
[64] Arnim-Bettina, p. 176; Arnim's letter of July 12, 1808.
[65] HeidelbJbb., I, 1810, pp. 8-15, 145-153.

of the playwright's creation by calling attention to this hidden "system" running through all of his plays, like *Die Söhne des Tals, Das Kreuz an der Ostsee, Luther,* and *Attila.* The review is not limited to a discussion of this tragedy, but is much wider in scope, in fact it is a general appreciation of the romantic playwright, with many interesting comparisons to Schiller. According to Arnim, Werner's "love-system" is based on the belief that the transcendental world manifests itself to our senses and becomes comprehensible to the individual through the medium of love. It is love also which forms the ties in human institutions, in society and the state.[66] Arnim points out that Werner's "love-system" is rooted in the Biblical statement, "God is love, and whosoever lives in love, lives in God." This would explain the abundance of religious and ecclesiastical motives in all of Werner's plays, which he uses chiefly for the presentation of "an eternal community of goodness."[67]

As most of the titles suggest, Werner took the subject-matter of his plays from history. Arnim, who associated poetry and all forms of literary expression so closely with history, in this review of *Attila* dwells at length on the question of historical truth in literature. Whenever history forms the background of a work of literature, he demands a detailed, faithful picture of a single historical event. His ideas coincide here, as a whole, with those of Herder, who in his *Ideen zur Geschichte der Menschheit* discusses the literary treatment of history with great seriousness and understanding.[68] Literature, Arnim declares, has to be a faithful presentation of history, otherwise it is a false and arbitrary allegory.

From this historical angle Arnim goes on to discuss each of Werner's dramas. *Die Söhne des Tals* is in his opinion the most accomplished one of these, revealing greater historical truth than all of Werner's later plays. Here Werner never deviated from historical facts, he only added what history forgot to relate, or con-

---

[66] *Ibid.,* pp. 9-10: "Es drückt sich aus in einer gleichartigen, sinnlichen Einwirkung einer übersinnlichen Welt, die sich dem Einzelnen in der Liebe versinnlicht, Staaten und heilige Gesellschaften in Staaten zusammenhält."

[67] *Ibid.,* p. 12.

[68] *Ibid.,* p. 13: "Mit tiefem Ernst und mit möglichster Treue gegen die Geschichte hat Herder in seinen *Ideen zur Geschichte der Menschheit* dasselbe allgemein durchzuführen versucht, aber ohne ein enges Anschließen an das Einzelne, schließt sich das Herz nicht auf."

densed in accordance with the requirements of dramatic art, as Shakespeare did in his historical dramas. Arnim does not venture to pass judgment on *Das Kreuz an der Ostsee,* since only the first part had been published, but he has the more to say on Werner's *Luther* and on *Attila. Luther* is entirely unhistorical. Wherever Luther's own words are rendered by the author, they leave one with a strange impression. In Arnim's opinion this "allegorical" play, as he called it, might well serve as a prologue to a truly historical drama on Luther. After seeing it performed on the Berlin stage, he writes to Brentano: "There is no trace, with the exception of a few expressions and anecdotes, of what you and I would expect from a Luther drama. Otherwise it is a peculiar product characteristic of Werner's art, betraying his singular imitative sense."[69] *Attila* shows the same defect in its lack of fidelity to history, but this play appears more authentic, because historical reports on Attila are scanty. Arnim mentions three historical sources: the report by the historian Jordanes, the *Nibelungenlied,* and a chap book from Venice entitled *Attila, flagelum dei,* which is little known. All three sources give different accounts of Attila's death. Werner in his *Attila* follows none of these accounts, but gives his own version of the death of the great Hun, something which does not serve to improve artistically the historical picture. In comparing *Attila* with Schiller's *Jungfrau von Orleans,* Arnim points out that Schiller commits the same *faux pas.* But Schiller knows far better than Werner how to unite artistically single historical events which have been torn away from their context into a great symbolic picture, as e.g., in the *Braut von Messina.* With Werner such symbolism leads only to meagre, empty scenes. In *Attila* as well as in *Die Jungfrau von Orleans* prophecies and visions occur too frequently to be effective. Actors will find it impossible to perform such scenes with continued natural beauty and art. The prophecies and visions will impress the audience the same way as letter-writing in novels, when these epistles appear just at the crucial moment to conclude the story. Arnim thinks that *Attila* was the outgrowth of the author's own imagination, his personal life and experiences rather than the

[69] Arnim-Brentano, p. 182.

product of an inspiration by historical prototypes. The play was boldly constructed and well reasoned out, and improves as the action progresses.[70]

In concluding the *Attila* review, Arnim hints again, as he had done at other times, at the unsatisfactory stage of Iffland. It had overlooked this interesting drama, he declares, because actors and managers were too lazy, and each stage manager had his own favored playwrights. If the stage manager happens to be an actor himself, even the worst playwrights are favored, since usually they are lenient in permitting alterations and arbitrary interpretations.

About Werner's best known fate-tragedy *Der vierundzwanzigste Februar* Arnim wrote only briefly to Brentano on September 14, 1811, after seeing the performance on the Weimar stage. "It is a sort of centaur," he reports, "beautifully mystical but gruesome in the beginning. But the conclusion is an ordinary creature which ruins everything."[71]

During the same year, 1811, Werner turned from Protestantism to become an ardent Catholic priest. He documented his conversion in his *Die Weihe der Unkraft*, which Arnim reviewed briefly in 1814[72] in the *Preussische Correspondent*. Naturally Arnim, a convinced Protestant, felt obliged to denounce this "horrible confession."[73] He can no longer take Werner seriously, and he ridicules his religious belief. Once he had been wrapped up in his "system of love." This he had now supplanted by a "system of mastership, fraternity, and discipleship (*Jüngerschaft*)." Arnim thinks that Werner's new confession as set forth in this work is full of errors, and that the author is least of all justified in seeking to teach and convert others with a few generalized and sententious phrases, for he is the one who is misled and ill advised.[74] Thus, Arnim's relation to Zacharias Werner ended on a disharmonious note.

---

[70] HeidelbJbb., I (1810), 151-2.

[71] Arnim-Brentano, p. 288.

[72] *Der Preussische Correspondent*, Berlin, 1814, No. 11, pp. 3-4.

[73] *Ibid.*, p. 3.

[74] *Ibid.*, p. 4; "Die ungerechteste Unkraft in dem Büchlein scheint es zu sein, daß der Unberatenste Rat geben will, und daß dieser Unkräftige die Lumpereien seines eigenen Lebens mit Kaisern und Königen und einigen allgemeinen Sentenzen durchgeknetet ganz Deutschland auf die Haustafel setzen will."

Strange as it may seem, in view of his idealism and sincerity of character, it is nevertheless true that most of Arnim's friendships and literary connections came to an early end. Among his many acquaintances of the Heidelberg period, it was with Wilhelm Grimm alone that Arnim retained a friendly intimacy until his death. His idealistic but very stubborn personality was a barrier to the cultivation of lasting personal connections, and this was also true of his relation with the older romanticists. Even the great admiration of the youthful Arnim for Ludwig Tieck and his devotion to this author gave way in later years to a complete disregard of this most congenial member of the older romantic school. As early as October 23, 1812, he commented sourly on Tieck's *Phantasus* in a letter to Brentano. "Is not the introduction a bad example of how a man who once wrote so enjoyably can degenerate in his writings to a mere play with words?"[75] Throughout his life Arnim maintained his definite idealistic views, reminding one in this respect of Herder. As we shall see in the next chapter the firm belief in the righteousness of his *Weltanschauung* was also reflected in Arnim's contacts with Goethe.

[75] Arnim-Brentano, p. 306.

VI

CLASSICISM

The great contrast between the so-called popular German ideology and the ancient Greek philosophy of life and art became a tragic issue in Hölderlin's career. The same problem confronted also A. W. Schlegel and Friedrich Schlegel. Arnim never experienced this antithesis, for he never felt himself attracted to ancient patterns in literature. He did not even go so far as Tieck, who in his drama *Niobe* had chosen one theme from the world of antiquity. In general, Arnim's opinion and appreciation of classic antiquity and its rôle in German culture had its roots in the teachings of Herder and Tieck and was largely molded by these authors. The former had said, "We want to learn to appreciate them (the Greeks), without becoming Greeks ourselves";[1] and the latter had objected to viewing Greek art as the *only* art.[2] Both had emphasized that the Greeks were an organically unified people and as such had given noble expression to their national spirit and their native characteristics. It would, they felt, be altogether illogical to attempt to build up a German national culture solely on imitation of the Greeks. Instead of devoting a great deal of time and energy to research into antiquity and to spreading a knowledge of its thoughts and ideals, it would be more appropriate to direct these efforts into more productive channels, namely toward acquiring a familiarity with the history and culture of the fatherland.

In his autobiographical references in "Wunder über Wunder," written in 1826,[3] Arnim described himself as having been a romantic child living in an imaginary magic world. His school-days were spoiled by severe requirements of memorizing and scanning Horatian verse and studying the artificial meters of the then fashionable Roman school-poets, thus blurring all impulses to

[1] *Herders Werke,* hrsg. von Suphan, XIV, 105.
[2] Tieck, *Kritische Schriften,* II, 251.
[3] *Landhausleben,* Werke, I, pp. XVII-XXI. Also in "Von Volksliedern," cf. DNL. CXLVI, 1, 62.

natural expression. After such a training in childhood, he felt like
a "trained horse, clicking automatically the time of the meter."
He became a severe critic of the curriculum in the German schools.
There was too much Latin and too little teaching of German history and culture, or none at all. His early years at the university
were devoted to the study of natural science, and he lived at this
time under the influence of Schelling and Ritter. It was as a natural scientist that he found his way to literature and art. Unlike
the Schlegel brothers, Lessing and Goethe, he had never delved
into the world of Hellenic thought and beauty; never had he felt,
like Goethe, a deep longing for the serene clarity of Rome. His
soul longed rather for the severity and mysticism of the northern
landscape.

It was Arnim's opinion that language and art had a great natural
rhythm of their own, which must be felt by the soul and in which
one must live. Greek declamation may be imitated, but for a German it can never become his own through personal experience.
Arnim's brief youthful discussion "Über deutsches Silbenmaß
und griechische Deklamation" (1805) voiced this conviction.[4]
Here he states quite naïvely that he has written poetry without
knowing the least thing about rhyme and meter, and yet has never
failed to achieve good poetry! He declares that he attaches no
value to the teaching of prosody. Just as one is far from being
a philosopher if one has merely mastered logic, no matter how
completely, one cannot become a poet if one is merely an expert
in prosody. One must keep in mind that the syllables are only
constituent parts of the original language (*Ursprache*). Whosoever uses this *Ursprache* without artificialities is a poet.[5]

Manifestly Arnim was not the man to ponder on these problems. It was rather a matter of instinct and of feeling with him
when he rejected the suggestion that classic antiquity alone was

[4] *Berlinische Musikalische Zeitung,* 1805, No. 32. Although published in 1805, this
essay was conceived and written earlier, on his grand tour in Switzerland in 1802.
[5] *Ibid:* "Ich habe früher gereimt, als ich das mindeste vom Silbenmaß wußte
und fast nie gefehlt; was ich davon weiß, entdeckte ich wie eine neue Ansicht in
der Schweiz auf den einsamen Wanderungen; ich las nachher mancherlei, und es
schienen mir alle diese prosodischen Versuche wie die Logik, wenn man in ihr das
gesamte der Philosophie zu erkennen glaubt. Silben sind Worte der Ursprache . . .
schwierig wird sie nicht dem, der darin lebt, sondern dem, der sie lernt und lehrt."

true art and should therefore be studied and made to penetrate German civilization, so that it might give to the Germans an art based on the classics. His references to these questions and remarks concerning them are not definite or precise, but are rather garbed in symbolical phraseology, as in the essay, "A Humorous Hodge-Podge on the Imitation of the Saint," (1808)[6] or in his poem "Dreams."[7] In the former he introduces a young man, shabbily elegant in appearance, who seeks to enlighten the mystical, monkish fools (the Romanticists) on paganism. He declares: "I am a pagan of the ancient Greek race and want to look at everything plastically." The audience demands why, then, is he dressed like other people; as a true pagan he should appear staging a tragic exhibition on a wheelbarrow, and collecting money for it. The young elegant takes this seriously and offers to donate the proceeds for the building of a central pagan temple for Germany, with casts of the gods. To be sure of genuine models, he is ready to take a trip to Italy: "I must tread classic soil. I have consecrated myself entirely to the pagan world." Arnim voices then his disdain for the imitative attitude of the German classicists through the comment of a wise old man: "Can you not feel and form your gods from your innermost soul; must you still put them together from broken fragments? . . . Art is a basilisk that destroys itself when it sees its reflection in the mirror."[8]

Similarly in his short story "Metamorphosen der Gesellschaft," published in 1826, Arnim declares that one does not become a true artist by selling oneself to paganism. True art in its quest for beauty emanates spontaneously from the genius, revealing his personality and emotions. But true art also bears the stamp of the time and the nation. Greek art is great art because it fulfills completely these requirements, and did not imitate. The Germans in their eagerness to imitate will never discover the beautiful. At present Richardson and Sir Walter Scott are widely read and

[6] *Tröst Einsamkeit*, pp. 60, 98, 260, 317, 324, 338.

[7] In *Der Wintergarten:* Werke, V, 192-198. First published in 1809.

[8] *Tröst Einsamkeit*, p. 319. The "Elegant" says: "Haben wir nur erst die obern Götter in guten Gypsabgüssen beisammen, die untern wollen wir dann schon kriegen, ich will mich selbst der Reise nach Italian unterziehen, nach den Korkmodellen läßt sich doch schwer bauen, ich muß den klassischen Boden betreten, ich habe mich ganz dem Heidenthum gewidmet."

praised in England in spite of their defects and weaknesses, because they "described successfully some features of the English national character."[9]

The concluding chapter of the "Humorous Hodge-Podge," "Der entfesselte Prometheus," brings a discussion, again symbolical in character, between the "Herzbruder," a young poet, and the Schoolmaster, a stubborn classicist and an undiscriminating critic. The latter is finally converted and has to admit that his belief in classicism and the world of Greek models as patterns for poetic form is entirely wrong. Neither Prometheus nor Hercules is a messiah, according to Arnim, speaking through the Schoolmaster. The one is dissolved and "flows away like lava, the other flies away in smoke."[10] However, from their ashes new gods arise; and the Schoolmaster is filled with new hope, for now he recognizes and supports whole-heartedly the true German poet, namely the "Hermit" (*Einsiedler*). Of course, Arnim and his circle are the "Hermits" who now bring to life again the only true poetry, the poetry of the people (*Volkspoesie*). Other poets and critics, as the converted schoolmaster rightly interprets from the warning hieroglyph in the temple of Sais, may be compared to a flock of foolish birds which swallow the same piece of undigestible food, i.e., classicism. This hieroglyph, it should be noted, was pinned to the invitation to the festival of the *Einsiedler* as a warning to all the "foolish birds" to stay away.[11]

The only other significant formulation of Arnim's attitude towards classicism is found in his poem "Träume," written in 1811. The writings of Winkelmann "der ein Landsmann von mir, mich dem Lande entzog," as Arnim puts it, had enticed him to dream of ancient Greece. Arnim relates then how once, when war and death had robbed him of friends and happiness, he longed for Greece, with its abundance of marble from which the creative artist fashions his work. But Greece and all its marble hold nothing but

[9] Werke, XVIII, pp. 11-12. "Metamorphosen der Gesellschaft": "Mag Richardson die Wahrheit durch übermäßige Reflektion unwahrscheinlich machen, mag Scott die abenteuerlichsten Gewächse und Bewerke, Staatsaktionen und Hof-Carrikaturen in unwahrscheinlicher Verwicklung aufstellen, die wohl bekannten schottischen Gesichter, die großartige Geschichte der britischen Völker bringen alles zur Wahrheit der Furcht und Hoffnung, erwecken in uns dieselbe Teilnahme. . . ."

[10] *Tröst Einsamkeit*, p. 347; "Der entfesselte Prometheus."

[11] *Ibid.*, pp. 347-8 (August 30, 1808).

illusions, and he turns away to dig in the sand of his native Brandenburg:

> Ach und wie tief ich grabe im Sande von Brandenburgs Erde,
> Immer nur find' ich den Sand und er ist mir so lieb,
> Ja ich beiße mich ein in diesen viel lockeren Boden,
> Schaff ich kein Leben darin, so begrab ich mich selbst.[12]

The main theme of this poem is the contrast between the Greeks and the barbarians in the worship of their gods. Barbarians of Taurus, visiting the Greek market, do not admire the perfect statues of the gods on the market place, but are attracted and deeply stirred by primitive childish models. The Taurian sees clearly that the Greeks, like Narcissus, honor only their own image, not the mystical and unfathomable, which reveals itself only to the innocent and unsophisticated:

> Toren, Ihr wollet verehren
> Euer menschliches Sein, diesen vergänglichen Glanz,
>
> . . . .
>
> Nur was die Kinder gemacht, ist rein in Unschuld geworden,
> Ach ich ehr, als Gott, weil ich den Sinn nicht versteh.[13]

The discussion which follows between Phidias and the barbarian shows a widely different conception of the gods. The Greek emphasizes beauty, strength, and physical enjoyment, all of which the barbarian condemns, for strength itself entails only greater servitude to the gods. The Greek puts himself almost on an equal footing with the gods. Reason and clarity predominate in his art and religion. Phidias says:

> Du schändest Götter, verachtest Du Armer Dich selber.
> Willst Du die Stimme des Gott's, horche der eigenen Brust.
> Wisse, das Beste an Dir, es sind die Herkulischen Muskeln.
> Daß von dem Göttlichen Stamm Dir ein Zeichen auch blieb.[14]

The god of the barbarian, on the other hand, is an awe-inspiring divinity. His splendor is set off by a dusky background and mystical symbols and he demands servitude or death from his trembling worshipers.[15] In the end, Greek and barbarian speak different languages; one does not understand the other; just as at home (in Prussia) masters and servants do not understand each other, due

---

[12] Werke, V, 192-3.   [13] Ibid., p. 196.   [14] Ibid., p. 196.
[15] Ibid., p. 197. The barbarian god Radegast is described as follows:

to the faulty and imperfect system of education. The final note, as so often in Arnim's writings, is an optimistic one. He believed that he could interpret with prophetic insight the history of art. From his dreams he awakens to "nordic work"; a peasant enters and shows him "Victoria."[16]

As set forth in a previous chapter, Arnim takes a similar position in a review of *August Wilhelm Schlegels Poetische Werke,* written in 1811 for the *Heidelbergische Jahrbücher.*[17] To mix the modern with the antique is utterly wrong, he holds. It is unnatural for a German writer to utilize classical subject-matter and to imitate its form, language, and style. The result will never be a great art like that of the ancient originals. Thus Goethe's *Iphigenie* and Schlegel's *Ion* can never endure comparison with their ancient prototype. If, however, modern poets prefer antique subject-matter, then they should follow Shakespeare's example and interpret ancient times in the modern spirit. Furthermore, translations are valuable, in so far as they are not simply literal and incomprehensible, but serve to enhance the artistic value of the original version.

It may be emphasized here that Arnim never spoke of classicism and romanticism as opposite literary tendencies, nor did he at any time take sides against the classicists. As is quite clear in his review of A. W. Schlegel's works, he felt no animosity towards classical literature and art as such. He was concerned only that Greek and Roman cultural achievements be assigned to their proper place in the frame of German culture. He was quite categorical in his statement that one can learn much from the ancient Greeks in contrast to the Roman poets, which were studied to exhaustion in German schools.[18] Nevertheless, the Greek poets should not be imitated literally by German poets, and at no time should Greek principles of art enslave German culture. In a foot-

---

Gräßlich blickt er uns an in nächtlicher Lampen Erleuchtung,
Wenn wir geblendet am Tag treten in's heilige Haus,
Zeichen zaubrischer Art umziehen die blutigen Wände,
Golden scheint sein Gesicht, Purpur sein flatternd Gewand,
Wen er verlanget zur Speise, den töten die harrenden Priester,
Immer verlangt er den, der sich von Arbeit befreit.

[16] Werke, V, p. 197.   [17] HeidelbJbb. II (1811), 1185-95.
[18] Werke, I, p. XIX.

note in the *Zeitung für Einsiedler* he emphasized that he sub-
scribed to none of the so-called literary schools or movements of
his age. In 1808, then, he believed that both classicism and romanticism were coming to an end, and that the literature which
would survive would be a unit, with genuinely German characteristics of inner strength and vitality. His periodical was to serve
for the purging of romanticism and classicism and for a discussion
of their striking peculiarities.[19] In an unpublished entry in his
notebook he declares that the fact that so much attention was
paid to antiquity is to be interpreted as a sign that the Germans
felt the need of an ancient art. If one would revive primitive and
ancient German art rather than Greek and Roman antiquity, one
would have a basis for the discussion of later and contemporary
German art.[20] It is to be noted that when he thus acted as the
champion of a new, vital literature, Arnim believed himself in
complete agreement with Goethe, whose fundamental concepts
also stressed the importance of a full-blooded literature, and for
whom it was of minor consideration whether such a literature was
plastic or romantic. He found that in *Dichtung und Wahrheit*
Goethe had preserved a feeling for the harmony and unity of the
past and present.[21]

While Arnim emphasized little the difference between romanticism and classicism, he did stress heavily the difference between a
vital national literature and the current literature of rationalistic
tone, with its philistine interpretation of ancient Greece. In his
opinion, the latter tendency was exemplified supremely by Johann
Heinrich Voss, a rationalist and a pedantic admirer of Greece,
without feeling for, nor faith in, an original, vital German literature, such as was sponsored by Arnim and Brentano. Voss, they
declared, was a "petrified spirit" (*versteinerter Geist*),[22] whose
chilly breath killed whatever was original and perfect, youthful

---

[19] *Tröst Einsamkeit*, p. 71, footnote: "Der blinde Streit zwischen sogenannten
Romantikern und sogenannten Klassikern endet sich; was übrig bleibt, das lebt,
unsre Blätter werden sich mit beiden und für beide beschäftigen; man lernt das
Eigentümliche beider Stämme wie in einzelnen Individuen erkennen, achten, und
sich gegenseitig erläutern, und in seiner Entwicklung erkennen."
[20] From Arnim's unpublished notebook; cf. Carl Henrici, Katalog 149, p. 5.
[21] "Von Volksliedern", cf. DNL, CXLVI, 85.
[22] Arnim-Brentano, p. 247, Brentano's letter to Arnim, March 15, 1808.

and courageous in art. Their antagonism was well founded. Very
soon Arnim had to give way to Voss and abandon his literary
endeavors in Heidelberg.

For Arnim the contemporary problem of classicism in Germany
crystallized itself in and revolved around Goethe as the central
figure. Neither Arnim nor the other Romanticists comprehended
and appreciated the greatness of Schiller.

On his way home from Heidelberg in December 1805, Arnim
visited Goethe for the first time.[23] The attitude of the Weimar
master toward the various literary movements was rather indefinite. Just at that time he was neglecting his Greek classical interests and turning more toward the primitive poetry of nature
and the people. He fully appreciated therefore a romantic publication like the *Wunderhorn*. Arnim was full of admiration for him
as a poet of the people, the author of popular ballads like "Der
König in Thule"; and he overlooked the "Greek" and the "pagan"
in Goethe. In this spirit he had dedicated the *Wunderhorn* to him
with great enthusiasm. Goethe gave Arnim a most cordial reception, invited him to dinner at his house, and travelled with him to
Jena. He was much impressed both by the enthusiastic young poet
and the handsome, accomplished aristocrat, and in return for the
affection and admiration of the younger man, the master continued
for a few years to extend to him a fatherly interest. On his return
to Berlin Arnim received from him an album-sheet with the motto:
"Consiliis hominum pax non reperatur in orbe,"[24] a gift which
made a deep impression on Goethe's young admirer. One can find
the echo of these words repeatedly in Arnim's later works: peace is
not regained by human action but rather by a new spiritual attitude. Goethe's affection for Arnim was an exceptional one. Brentano wrote enviously: "You have hardly started on your poetic
calling when you meet the master, who stretches out a friendly,
consoling hand. Goethe has befriended you; no other youth has
ever been so fortunate."[25]

After returning to his native Brandenburg Arnim cultivated the

[23] Arnim stayed in Weimar from Dec. 15 till Dec. 18, 1805. Cf. Goethe's *Tagebuch*.
[24] In answer to Goethe Arnim began his letter by translating these words as follows: "Nicht durch Menschen wird der Frieden wiedergewonnen." *Schriften der
Goethe Ges.*, XIV, 97.
[25] Arnim-Brentano, p. 157.

acquaintance with Goethe in a lively correspondence. Three long letters of the year 1806 show his devotion.[26] Here he writes interestingly of social life and mutual acquaintances in Berlin, and tells of his own life and travels in Brandenburg. In the first of the letters he expresses his gratitude to Goethe for the favorable review of the *Wunderhorn*,[27] which makes him believe that the master will grant further support and approval if he, Arnim, continues his literary endeavors along the same lines. He hopes that in the future he can count on Goethe as an ally in the struggle against barren scholasticism and philistinism: "I feel," he writes, "that my undertaking is justified since it has met clear-cut approval and disapproval; since it has found support in your kindness, and malice and hatred from the *Freimütigen*."[28] In still more glowing words he speaks to Brentano of his trust in Goethe: "I admire his determination to champion always the right cause, and if he has thus recognized our literary endeavors as worth while, he will do everything for us, will assist us and take an interest in our future path."[29]

In his controversy with Brentano about their treatment of the folksongs he wrote to Clemens that Goethe preferred the intermingling of old and new elements, for only in this way does the vitality of the old songs become apparent.[30] Goethe answered Arnim's letters very cordially. He writes how much it pleases him to become acquainted with the great city of Berlin through Arnim's descriptions. Again he speaks of the pleasure of cultivating new friendships: "It is fine to become better acquainted. Your full letters, perhaps mysterious to others, always put me into the mood in which you are and convey an enjoyable picture of interesting surroundings. . . . Do please continue to think of us, to write, and to send me something occasionally."[31]

The war of 1806-7 between Prussia and France made it more difficult for Arnim to keep in contact with Goethe. As soon as Middle and Southern Germany were accessible again, he retraced

[26] *Schriften der Goethe Ges.*, XIV, 82 (Feb. 1806), 97 (May 1806), 117 (Sept. 1806).

[27] *Jenaer Allg. Literaturzeitung*, I (1806), Nr. 18-19.

[28] *Schriften der Goethe Ges.*, XIV, 94.

[29] Arnim-Brentano, p. 163.   [30] Arnim-Brentano, p. 235.

[31] *Vierteljahresschrift der Goethe-Ges.*, 1936, H. II, 137; also *Schriften der Goethe Ges.*, XIV, 95.

his steps to Weimar from Eastern Prussia, where as a Prussian nationalist he had been a refugee. From November 8 to 10 he and Brentano and Savigny were daily callers at the master's house.[32] After this brief sojourn Arnim went on to Heidelberg, where he hoped to resume his idealistic literary pursuits, counting on Goethe's support and definitely on his sponsorship for his *Zeitung für Einsiedler*. Already in his last letter of 1806 Arnim had informed Goethe of his intention to publish a "Tageblatt für das Volk,"[33] and in the same letter poured out his hopes and fears for his youthful literary endeavors. He complained that criticism and controversies tended to cripple youthful efforts, while the political situation was forcing young men into early maturity. The mob and the philistine make no distinction between the mature and the immature. They designate all youthful attempts and creations as mere vanity and tear them to pieces with mockery.[34]

The *Zeitung für Einsiedler* began to appear in April, 1808. On the first day Arnim wrote to Goethe: "Surveying as editor the periodical which I sent you, I feel how poor it is to be submitted to you. It may satisfy the masses, and in their interest, which lies nearest the hearts of us both, I take the liberty to ask you for contributions."[35] Arnim's veneration for Goethe found discreet expression at various places in the periodical itself. The literary content of the first two numbers consists solely of Arnim's poem "Der freie Dichtergarten". He closed the first number with the motto that Goethe had written in his album, "Consiliis hominum pax non reparatur in orbe," and opposite this quoted from the Bible, "And God spoke, 'Let there be light!' and there was light."[36] Did this not imply that to Arnim, Goethe had given hope and light for the future? Goethe indeed was his god! In the eighteenth number of May 31, in Arnim's "Lehrgedicht an die Jugend," the symbol of the sun stands for Goethe's name in the following significant passage:

> Fühle Trost in jungen Jahren
> An dem Gott in Menschenkleid,

[32] Arnim-Brentano, p. 226.   [33] *Schriften der Goethe Ges.*, XIV, 124.
[34] *Ibid.*, 123.   [35] *Ibid.*, p. 125.
[36] *Tröst Einsamkeit*, p. 20.

Manche sich durch Schrift bewahren,
Einer lebt in unserer Zeit:
Will er mild den Arm dir reichen
Drück ihn nicht wie andre Freund',
Glück das paart sich nur in Gleichen,
Gott ist mehr als Menschenfreund.
Und erscheint als Gott dir ⊙
Auf der Menscheit höherm Thron,
O so glaubt der Abendröte,
Werd' nicht rot vor ihm mein Sohn;
Rüstig dann mit tücht'gen Händen,
Wirst du frisch zum eignen Werk, ...[37]

Arnim's great expectations for his *Zeitung für Einsiedler* were never realized. Its failure may be attributed largely to the complete indifference of Goethe to Arnim's undertaking. The great master in Weimar did not comply with his requests nor further his ambitions, obviously because he did not wish to interfere in the struggle between the "Einsiedler group" and the conservative group, headed by the elder Voss. As early as April 1, 1808, in the letter to Goethe which announced the publication of the *Einsiedler-Zeitung,* Arnim mentioned the formation of these two antagonistic camps and added that Voss regarded the periodical as a mockery of his person and interests.[38] After the period of the *Xenien* Goethe was ever wary of literary polemics. Even though he had little sympathy for Voss, the situation in Heidelberg struck him as unpleasant, and he did not wish to take sides. Consequently Arnim pleaded in vain for contributions for his new periodical, and it was only through Bettina's mediation that Goethe sent through her in May, 1808, a few obliging, but not very encouraging phrases.[39] Not until November 14, 1808, did Arnim hear directly from him in answer to his long letter of September 29 preceding. Again Goethe had only polite remarks. He indicated that he disapproved of certain things which he would prefer to discuss personally with Arnim.[40] The *"Wunderliche Zeitung,"* as he called Arnim's undertaking, evidently did not catch his fancy

[37] *Ibid.*, p. 182.　　　　　[38] *Schriften der Goethe Ges.*, XIV, 126.
[39] Bettina-Goethe, pp. 66-7.
[40] *Vierteljahresschrift d. Goethe-Ges.* 1936, H. 2, pp. 139-40. This letter, only recently discovered and published, moderates somewhat the traditional idea of Goethe's indifference and aloofness.

as the *Wunderhorn* had done. Its content was too strange and was beyond his realm of interest. In view of this, Arnim's friendly reception in Goethe's house December 19 to 24, 1808, on his return from Heidelberg to Berlin, should not be overrated. Goethe's cordiality was not meant for the poet and editor of the *Zeitung für Einsiedler,* but rather for the attractive Prussian aristocrat and friend of the Goethe and Brentano families.[41]

The year 1809 finally brought the realization to Arnim that he had overestimated Goethe's interest in the old-German movement. Then another of his attempts to gain Goethe's support failed, when the latter left unanswered his entreaty to write a brief introduction to Wilhelm Grimm's translations of the old Danish heroic legends.[42] Arnim was very anxious for this introduction, which should reveal Goethe's attitude definitely, for as Arnim declared in a letter, "Goethe's ballads 'Thule,' 'Fischer' and 'Erlkönig' contain the gruesome elements of Nordic poetry, while, on the other hand, all his ambitions and tendencies lie in the gracefulness of Greek art and the enjoyment of a rounded life."[43] Later he formulates in a letter to Wilhelm Grimm a similar conception of the dual nature of Goethe's literary interests.[44] In the year follow-

[41] Arnim-Bettina, 249. Nothing has come down to posterity about this meeting or any literary or personal discussions which may have taken place between Goethe and Arnim except a passage in Arnim's letter to Bettina; "Den ersten Mittag empfing mich Goethe mit zwei Küssen, was ihn Gott segne mit zwei Küssen höherer Liebe; seine Lippen wie die Finger großer Musiker haben eine eigentümliche Rundung, Bildung und Beweglichkeit, so daß man schon darin sehen und fühlen kann, wie er die Sprache wunderbar erregen und verbinden kann. Über meine Zeitung (für Einsiedler) sagte er wiederholentlich soviel Schönes, ebenso die andern, was mir besonders herzstärkend war. Voß erkannte er ganz genau." "Die andern" refers to Zacharias Werner und Kügelgen, who were Goethe's guests at the time of Arnim's visit (Bettina-Goethe, pp. 94, 332). Similar descriptions based on the impression he had of Goethe, are found in Arnim's writings. Thus in *Halle und Jerusalem* (p. 178), when Arnim speaks of Germany's master whom he had seen in Läuchstadt: "Ganz befangen von dem ernsten Blick, dem festen Gang, dem freundlich schön Vollendeten der Lippen, an diesen Lippen ist der Meister aller Worte, aller Sprachen zu erkennen, so zierlich sind sie geschnitten, ein jeder Hauch von ihnen ist ein Flötenton, kein falscher Ton fliegt je von diesen Lippen in die Welt."

[42] *Schriften der Goethe Ges.,* XIV, 142. They are the *Altdänische Heldenlieder, Balladen und Märchen,* which were not published until 1811.

[43] Arnim-Bettina, p. 333.

[44] Arnim-Grimm, p. 41. "Daß Goethe nichts hinzugefügt, ist mir nicht allein wegen des Honorars, es ist mir der Sache selbst wegen unangenehm, er hätte bei der Gelegenheit sicher viel Treffliches über den Eindruck der nordischen Sagen, Götterlehren, so wie sie ihm erscheinen, gesagt; während er sich selbst nach seiner Bildung so ganz nach den Griechen gewendet, hat seine Natur ihn doch in mehreren

ing the collapse of the *Einsiedler-Zeitung*, it was only through
Bettina that Arnim remained in contact with the master. She
assured Goethe repeatedly in most affectionate words of Arnim's
undiminished devotion to him.[45]

In 1809, while Arnim and his friends in Berlin were delving
still more deeply into old Germanic literature and folklore, Goethe
published his modern, most timely novel, *Die Wahlverwandtschaften*. Strange as it may seem, Arnim read this modern psychological novel with great interest. Its stimulating effect can be
traced in his own novel on a similar theme, *Armut, Schuld und
Buße der Gräfin Dolores*. Wilhelm von Humboldt testifies to the
depth of Arnim's penetration into the ideas of Goethe's work. In
a letter to its author he says that he could discuss the *Wahlverwandtschaften* better with Arnim than with anyone else.[46] Arnim
wrote to Bettina that he had discussed *Die Wahlverwandtschaften*
and argued about it a great deal, because some people sought to
interpret the novel in favor of Napoleon. He adds that he wants to
write a review of it for the *Heidelbergische Jahrbücher*. He did not
write the review; but he gives an indirect criticism of the work
in his *Gräfin Dolores* and makes incidental remarks concerning it
in various letters.[47] From these it is apparent that he found the
novel too long, a fault which he ascribed to Riemer's influence;
but that he was deeply impressed by the truth and perfection of
the descriptive elements and the philosophy which it contained.
However, he admitted he could not visualize the characters, except
the architect.

One might conclude, basing the deduction also on the ideas

---

seiner schönsten Gedichte, im Erlkönig, im König von Thule, wieder in jene Gesinnung und Gemütsfarbe zurückgeführt."

[45] Bettina-Goethe, p. 121. "Er hat Dich lieb ohne Rücksicht/ ohne Aber, ohne
Außerdem, er hat Dich lieb mit ungeschwächter Liebe/ er darf keinen Sinn leiten/ sie
gehen alle von selbst zu Dir, so wie meine auch/ darum sind wir beide höchst einig
mit einander, und werden es ewig bleiben. Wenn ich wieder zu Dir komme/ so werde
ich Dir manches von ihm erzählen/ wie ungemein groß edel diese Neigung zu Dir
ist, die Du erschaffen hast in ihm, mit einer Kraft/ deren Du selbst nicht wissend
bist. Oft hat er mir den Willen geäußert, mit mir in Deiner Nähe zu sein, er selbst
weiß nicht/ daß er zwischen mir und Dir sowie ich zwischen Euch beiden keine
Ruhe hab."

[46] Humboldt's letter to Goethe; February 10, 1810. *Goethes Briefwechsel mit den
Gebrüdern von Humboldt*, hrsg. von F. Th. Bratranek (1876), p. 236.

[47] Arnim-Bettina, p. 383; *ibid.*, p. 350; Arnim-Grimm, p. 83, *Goethe Schr.* XIV,
144-155.

Arnim developed in *Gräfin Dolores,* that he did not approve of the moral issue involved in the *Wahlverwantschaften* since it was in conflict with his own strict principles respecting religion and marriage. Arnim did not have the ability to write psychological novels, to delve into the intricacies of emotion and the life of the soul. He wrote his novels to illustrate ethical principles, consciously rejecting the exhibition of the inner life; and he considered Goethe's *Wahlverwandtschaften* chiefly as an excellent picture of the life and problems of a certain class in contemporary society. "Let us thank God and His servant Goethe," he says in a contemporary letter to Bettina, "that again a chapter of this dying age is faithfully preserved for posterity."[48] He wrote to Goethe expressing his deep gratitude, a gratitude perhaps mingled with sadness because of the tragedy so clearly presented in the novel.[49] It was, as he knew, a tragedy personally experienced by many contemporaries.

In the letter to Bettina mentioned above, Arnim was more specific about the contemporary social problem involved.[50] Goethe had succeeded in an enviable manner, he thought, in portraying in the first volume the boredom of the leisure class, and had, with keen observation, selected its best possible representatives, namely types from the educated country gentry. Arnim was only too well acquainted with this group, and agreed heartily with Goethe's ideas. All of its members, he declares, suffer from a peculiar morbid melancholy. Because of caste tradition and education, they feel superior to the active, landowning class of farmers, and are segregated from them. Without definite aims in life, they cook away at their own domestic soup until nothing is left in the pot. Anything new that enters this circle and interrupts its state of mutual ennui is felt to be a disturbance. There are more divorces among them than among any other class.

Bettina, Arnim, and others sought in vain for any hint of national consciousness or any patriotic element whatever in

[48] Arnim-Bettina, p. 350, Arnim's letter to Bettina, November 5, 1809. *Gräfin Dolores,* Part II, p. 50.
[49] *Schriften der Goethe Ges.,* XIV, 114-5.
[50] Arnim-Bettina, p. 349.

Goethe's characters, motives which Arnim had introduced into his
Gräfin Dolores. This is another instance of the wide difference in
outlook between Goethe and Arnim. Divergence in national attitude and in ethical principles were to become more and more pronounced as time went by.

Goethe's coolness and unfriendly attitude toward Arnim and
Bettina has been often attributed to a quarrel between their wives,
in September, 1811. It had, however, an earlier and deeper cause
which has been overlooked, viz., a fundamental difference in
Weltanschauung. As early as 1808, when the *Zeitung für Einsiedler* appeared, Goethe had already lost interest in Arnim and in
what the latter believed to be his poetic mission. The great man
was not only annoyed by the quarrel between the Heidelberg
group and Voss, but disliked heartily the chief literary interests
of the former, which centered on the revival of old-German literature. In October, 1810, one year before the quarrel referred to,
he had denounced vehemently this literary movement with its
slogan, "back to the Middle Ages," as "the foolishness of the
present day."[51]

Arnim was well aware of Goethe's lack of interest. He also felt
keenly the injustice of Goethe's indifference to Kleist, whose
friend Arnim had become in Berlin in 1810. Regretfully he wrote
Bettina in 1809 that Goethe was lost to their cause, since "all his
tendencies and ambitions lie in the gracefulness of Greek art and
the enjoyment of a rounded life."[52] Yet Arnim could not have
given up all hope of winning over the Weimar master, for at the
time of his and Bettina's marriage, March, 1811, the young
couple looked forward eagerly to making a surprise visit to
Goethe's home on the later's birthday in the following August.
Arnim announced their coming to Riemer, Goethe's secretary,
expressing his hope for "good weather," meaning that Goethe
might be in a good mood. He hinted that he feared the conspiracies
of old Voss in Jena. As mentioned above, the visit of the young
couple was cut short by the quarrel between Christiane and Bettina. After that Goethe's aloofness became still more apparent.

[51] Goethe's letter to Reinhard, Oct. 7, 1810.
[52] Arnim-Bettina, p. 332.

Preceding this quarrel Bettina does not seem to have had a clear perception of the difference in character and philosophy of life between Goethe and Arnim. When Arnim began to doubt as to whether he ought to follow in Goethe's footsteps as a poet, she tried to persuade him to do so: "Goethe lures you as a sunbeam lures the blossoms."[53] Goethe and Arnim were the two men of genius who had attracted her and whom she had come to adore. In them her restlessly striving personality and womanly vanity sought an object upon which they might expend themselves. To Arnim she writes, on November 21, 1809: "God desires that both of you should share the cup of my love, for never before has Goethe bestowed upon me such an abundance of kindness. . . . Thus Goethe loves both of us; let us press close to him that we may become quite like his children."[54]

Through the mediation of Riemer Arnim tried to mend the breach in their friendship caused by the quarrel of the women, but in vain. A second attempt in January, 1812, was also fruitless.[55] How earnestly he tried to cover up the unpleasant situation is apparent from a letter to Grimm on September 22, 1811, immediately after the sudden departure of the Arnims from Weimar. The quarrel between Christiane and Bettina is not mentioned. Arnim refers to Goethe's wife simply by remarking that her manners and behavior separate Goethe from all decent people.[56] It soon became apparent, however, that Goethe was no longer the idol of his disciple. Arnim's conception of Goethe as an outspoken, obstinate individualist interested only in the world of ancient Greece, became more intensified after the fateful visit. Goethe acted, he felt, as though he had to withdraw from the present, its events and ideas, and flee to the "Greek world of perfection." Arnim now reflected that it was ridiculous that he had told Goethe of his new ideas for literature, and he recalled that Goethe had then remarked in whimsical fashion, "Well, those are good jokes, but they do not concern me."[57] He had told Arnim repeatedly that he shunned all direct contact with the

[53] Arnim-Bettina, p. 271.   [54] *Ibid.,* pp. 351-3.
[55] *Idem.,* Bettina-Goethe, pp. 222 and 228.
[56] Arnim-Grimm, pp. 146-7.   [57] *Ibid.*

present world and avoided current literary discussions. He had never thought it worth while to comment on Wilhelm Grimm's translations from old Danish epics, and he was indifferent when Arnim praised the "nordische Romanzenmanier," which Goethe had previously derided as confused.

Goethe's impersonal attitude toward the urgent patriotic problems of devastated Germany brought Arnim to despair. He found the Weimar poet as much confused regarding German history as Johannes Müller. He noted in the same letter to Grimm that Goethe in revising his poem on Schiller had omitted all passages referring to the fatherland.[58] In all this he judged that Goethe certainly acted wrongly, but it was not his duty to call his attention to it.

At the time of the quarrel between the Goethes and the Arnims the first two volumes of *Dichtung und Wahrheit* had just been published. Arnim, a great lover of biographies, was keenly interested in the book. He held that critics should, because of the very nature of their profession, be very fond of autobiographies, for they represent a form of self-criticism and give a survey of uncompleted works.[59] It was quite natural that Arnim should have looked forward to the appearance of the work, since he knew Goethe personally and through Bettina and Clemens Brentano he had become familiar with the environment and circumstances of his youth in Frankfort. In fact, he had once intended to write a biography of Goethe. After reading the first two parts he wrote his impressions to Brentano and Grimm, praising the author's reticence. Nevertheless, he admitted that he had found the book a bit quaint. While Goethe had formerly wanted to embrace the whole universe, now, on reading the story of his life, it seems as if he wanted to withdraw and explore his own soul.[60]

The year 1812 brought no improvement in the relationship be-

[58] Arnim-Grimm, p. 147; letter of September 22, 1811.

[59] *Literatur-Blatt*, Nr. 66, August 16, 1822, p. 261.

[60] Arnim-Brentano, p. 289; Arnim-Grimm, p. 146. Note the interesting criticism of *Dichtung und Wahrheit*, Part I, by Jacob Grimm, who is also quite enchanted by the beauty of the book and praises in particular the first and last third. The middle is too drawn out, as are epics and history. This, however, makes them profound and more valuable. Arnim-Grimm, pp. 152-3.

tween the Goethe and Arnim families. In August of that year they stayed at the Spa in Teplitz at the same time, but ignored each other. Goethe, writing to his wife, says: "Take no notice of the Arnims, and I am glad that I have gotten rid of these crazy people."[61] Arnim's esteem for Germany's greatest poet, however, is still apparent. He continues to send him copies of his writings during the succeeding years: in 1814, *Die Befreiung Wesels;* in 1817, *Die Kronenwächter,* which he submits, "in well-founded loyalty."[62] This dedication seems justified when one considers that the *Kronenwächter* is a novel of apprenticeship like *Wilhelm Meister* and that Arnim to some extent was a disciple of Goethe's narrative art. In the *Kronenwächter* and still more in his later short stories he followed Goethe's example in the effort to create "reality" artistically. As early as 1809 Arnim was conscious of this principle of founding artistic creations on reality. In reviewing various novels by Ernst Wagner[63] and comparing them with Goethe's *Wilhelm Meister,* he wrote: "All poetry rests upon coarse, square reality and without this human feature, it would be super-human, a light without form."

In the same review he called attention to the novel in general as a tool of poetic expression and as a unique literary means of national education. This, he thinks, had become particularly apparent with the publication of *Wilhelm Meister.* In the search for quick methods of education, legends and the Bible have been brushed aside in favor of practical arithmetic, writing, etc. The theater cannot offer a substitute for the older material, because it is interested merely in female stars and not in the production of good plays. Thus only the novel remains. But novels must be written like *Wilhelm Meister;* the interest of youth must be kept in mind. The manner of presentation is negligible, while action and power, as in history,[64] and the development of character are

[61] Bettina-Goethe, p. 230.

[62] *Schriften der Goethe Ges.,* XIV, 148, 152.

[63] HeidelbJbb. 1809, pp. 169, 179. Here Arnim reviewed the following by Wagner: *Willibalds Ansichten des Lebens, Die reisenden Maler, Reisen aus der Fremde in die Heimat.*

[64] HeidelbJbb., 1809, p. 170: "Wer käme darauf, in der Weltgeschichte sich durchaus etwas anders denken zu wollen, als es geschehen, und viel authentischer sind Romane."

to be emphasized. In Wagner's *Wilibalds Ansichten des Lebens* Arnim found evidence of an imitation of *Wilhelm Meister* in the description and development of the hero, the rich inner life and balance of power with which he is endowed. Certain incidents in Wagner's book, like the countess' visit in the garden, are almost identical with Philine's visit in *Wilhelm Meister*. But Wagner and other novelists still have to learn from Goethe in other respects: 1) to practice due restraint in descriptions of nature and of the effects of music; 2) to show moderation in dramatic effects; 3) not to neglect the secondary characters in favor of the hero; 4) to avoid excessive emotionalism. Concluding, Arnim raises the question whether Goethe's ending in *Wilhelm Meister*, with Jarno's plan to migrate to America, has the hidden significance that in devastated Germany poetry may not survive, but it may find new roots in other lands.

Another novel under the influence of *Wilhelm Meister*, yet opposing some of Goethe's ideas, was *Die Versuche und Hindernisse Karls*, which originated in the Berlin "Nordstern" circle in 1808, and was written jointly by Neumann, Varnhagen and Fouqué. Arnim's criticism of this novel will be discussed in a later chapter.[65] However, in reference to *Wilhelm Meister*, it needs to be considered briefly here. In defense of Goethe, Arnim stresses that the poetic element in *Wilhelm Meister* was not destroyed when the hero abandoned the theatrical career and turned to the practical side of life. The authors of *Die Versuche und Hindernisse Karls* had made this accusation. Arnim points out that one need not cease to be an artist or to be interested in art merely because he gives up his ambition to become a reformer of the stage. Wilhelm Meister had left stage reforms to some successor, for whom he had paved the way and who might be even more successful than he. He had, however, only turned from the theater to interest himself in other fields of art, painting and the plastic arts of the past and present. Arnim reads this interpretation into the novel from the description of the house, filled with art treasures, in which Wilhelm Meister was to reside after leaving the theatrical group, and from Goethe's continuation of the novel in the

[65] Chapter VII, p. 139.

Tübinger Taschenbuch. Goethe in this continuation has stated the truth of the actual relationship between medieval treasures of art and those of the present; according to Arnim Goethe has emphasized that this age has now realized that art treasures of ancient times must be collected, appreciated, and incorporated into the art of the present and no longer regarded solely with religious feelings.[66] That this interpretation of *Wilhelm Meister* was much more a reflection of Arnim's wishes and feelings than of Goethe's, became, of course, apparent in later years, when the other continuations of *Wilhelm Meister* were published. Then Arnim probably had less reason for rejoicing.

These are the two reviews (of Ernst Wagner's novels and the *Versuche und Hindernisse Karls,* by the Nordstern circle) in which Arnim applied comparisons to *Wilhelm Meister* in detail. They both date from a time when he still saw in Goethe the spiritual leader of the nation, and they preceded the quarrel between the Goethe and Arnim families in 1811. From a much later date comes an interesting literary study by Arnim, based on *Wilhelm Meister,* which he designated as "a Wilhelm Meister echo." He gave it the odd title "Wunder über Wunder, indische Mährchen," and published it in his collection *Landhausleben* (1826) as a "Wednesday story" by the dean of the theatrical school. "Wunder über Wunder" is not an echo of *Wilhelm Meisters Lehrjahre,* but of his *Wanderjahre,* as published in Goethe's first version in 1821.

In this story, which is prefaced by a prologue, Arnim creates a counterpart to Goethe's "Pedagogical Province" of the *Wanderjahre*. The prologue is of greater interest to the literary historian. This introduction was necessary, for one might otherwise have been tempted to interpret Arnim's pedagogical narrative as another of the many parodies written on Goethe's novel by his contemporaries. Arnim expresses most emphatically his disgust with these numerous commonplace, and not even humorous, parodies, which, he declares, have failed to grasp the true *Wilhelm Meister*. In order, then, to guard against a wrong interpretation of his own "echo of Wilhelm Meister," he finds it necessary to write

[66] HeidelbJbb. 1810, pp. 347-9; review of *Die Versuche und Hindernisse Karls.*

this prologue. Here he becomes superlative in praise of the *Wanderjahre,* the "bright star on the firmament," which none of the many imitations or "false Wilhelm Meisters" can even approach in splendor, for these are dull and empty and are written in an imitative style that has grasped few details of the masterly original. He compares the tremendous influence of Goethe to a mighty stream, of which his conscious or unconscious imitators are but tributaries. Some of them are misled by their own arrogance, e. g., those who write these commonplace parodies.[67] Goethe's mighty influence was evident not only in true or false imitations, it had also opened new paths in literature and art. Arnim admits his own great indebtedness to the master. The delightful account of the "Pedagogical Province" has stimulated him to write "Wunder über Wunder." Whoever has seen Goethe knows how creatively his influence affects those who approach him:

> I have observed how the very tone of his voice, his posture, and movements, yes, even his favorite expressions were unconsciously imitated by a visitor; and when I called on him, I had to discover to my surprise that I formed no exception. . . . He compels one to exactitude and to limitation in new forms without sacrificing freedom. Like no one else, he is receptive to impressions from the world and then casts them into more beautiful, more comprehensible and lasting forms. . . . In addition to Goethe's poems, one has to count the innumerable poems which he stimulated in others and which they call their own, but which really belong to no one.[68]

In the prologue Arnim also rejects the belief, so often read into the novel, that Goethe portrayed himself in the character of Wilhelm Meister; and he assures the reader from his own acquaintance with Goethe, that none of Wilhelm's outstanding traits correspond with Goethe's. Wilhelm is rather the author's spiritualized conception of a talented youth of the period ending with the French Revolution. Arnim characterizes Wilhelm as kind, but weak; as zealous, persuasive, whimsical, egotistical, but also altruistic; he has an inferiority complex, but also great self-confidence. Above all, he is possessed by an inner urge for knowledge and education, while the world and public life concern him little; in short, he is the ideal of his period, equipped with all the

---

[67] Werke, XIX, 263. [68] *Ibid.,* pp. 263-267.

talents and good traits it admired and experiencing all the current temptations and vicissitudes. Nevertheless, no genuine talent drives him in a particular direction. If a whole nation were composed of people like Wilhelm, civilization might blossom but would soon be ripe for decay.[69] Thus the prologue expresses, indeed, admiration and love for the author of *Wilhelm Meister,* as well as gratitude to him.

In the story or study proper ("Wunder über Wunder") Arnim relates chiefly impressions from his own school days and sets forth the ideas growing out of these experiences, employing Goethe's "Province" as his frame and Wilhelm Meister as his mouthpiece. He scourges the conceit of contemporary educators and their so-called "education," "this peculiar, fashionable puppet."[70] Nevertheless, he is convinced that in the long run the indestructible spirit of youth will withstand the onslaught of these pseudo-pedagogues. In conclusion he sets forth his own ideas on education, applying Hölderlin's words: "You will never grasp why your pedagogical practices are useless; in the meantime the stars above follow their eternal course as ever."[71] Here, as frequently in later years, he turned to Hölderlin's wisdom.

The plot describes briefly the efforts of a pedagogue to create a better world by novel, unnatural methods of education in a school of stereotyped rules and regulations,[72] efforts which naturally failed. Only when Wilhelm Meister arrives on the scene and the pedagogue adopts enthusiastically his ideas of art and the theater as means of education, can excellent results be obtained. The pedagogue now transforms his school into a travelling theatrical school, which visits small, unspoiled towns and thereby accomplishes a twofold task: training the children to be great actors for the future and educating the adults who attend the excellent performances of masterpieces of literature and thereby satisfy the need of their souls to see a picture of human life and its vicissitudes[73] presented in a dignified, noble manner, unlike the circus-like contemporary theater, which emphasizes only external

[69] *Ibid.,* pp. 267-8.   [70] *Ibid.,* p. 313.   [71] *Ibid.,* p. 313.
[72] *Ibid.,* p. 271. The new educational plan was called "Schule der Gesetzmäßigkeit."
[73] *Ibid.,* XIX, 311-12: "Befriedigen im edlen Sinne das Bedürfnis, ein Bild der Menschheit im großen Wirken und im Gedränge aller Art geistiger Kräfte zu sehen."

effects. In this way the public may acquire a taste for beauty and real art, and the present deplorable and degenerate theater will vanish.

Just as Arnim was stimulated through Goethe's *Wilhelm Meister* to write the "echo," "Wunder über Wunder," he was also aroused by Goethe's monumental drama *Faust* to work up this material. He approached it, however, from a slightly different angle than Goethe. He called his version, a comedy, "Auch ein Faust." This work came to posterity as a fragment.[74] Arnim's undertaking was closely related to the studies on *Faust* which he had made in 1818, as an introduction to Wilhelm Müller's translation of Marlowe's *Doctor Faustus*. The translation and his introduction were sent to Goethe in March, 1818. In the accompanying letter Arnim touches on the question as to why Shakespeare, who had used so many old and historic themes, neglected Faustus. Was it because this drama was already too well-known and outgrown? Arnim believes that the old German popular play (*Volksschauspiel*) of Faust probably had its origin in Marlowe's *Faustus,* and that therefore Marlowe's drama does not strike one as foreign, even though it has a seriousness and grandeur lacking in the German Faust-play. Indeed it prepared the ground for Goethe's *Faust.*[75]

In his introduction Arnim makes a serious plea for more extensive studies and further poetic treatments of the theme. Not enough "Faustus" plays have been written as yet. He offers several rather far-fetched suggestions for possible treatments, such as the portrayal of Faust's fiendish urge to grasp the whole universe, including the infinite realm of the imagination and the soul, and to analyze it and tear it in pieces by scientific experiments; or the presentation of the tricks of criticism in their diabolical nature. Faust might be presented as a writer who sacrifices his soul and immortality to his work and is annihilated by it; or one might make use of the Faust story to show in general the disparity between intention and success, to demonstrate the

[74] This is an unpublished fragment of about ten pages. Many years earlier Brentano had mentioned to Arnim Tieck's idea of writing an "Anti-Faust," a comedy in which the devil is deceived by man. Arnim-Brentano, p. 97; Brentano's letter to Arnim, August 1803.

[75] *Schriften der Goethe Ges.,* XIV, 155.

questionable value of human merits and endeavors.[76]

Arnim knew, of course, only the first part of Goethe's *Faust*, as it appeared in 1808 with the publication of the twelve-volume edition of Goethe's works. Here he found already the full power of Goethe's all-embracing views and philosophy, for, as he says, Goethe has made here his own confession and also expressed the feelings and ideas of his age. In a masterly way Goethe has shown the struggles of Faust's soul and its fall, minimizing such superficialities as the pact with the devil and the devil's fetching away the soul, which was the chief scene of interest in the old popular play (*Volksschauspiel*).[77] Goethe has exposed the foibles and false beliefs of his age and driven home the danger of arrogant scientific speculation and experiment, by which the "scientist" or alchemist through delusions and occult practices thinks he can compel the powers of another world to interfere with natural events in our sphere.

Naturally, it was not Arnim's task in this introduction to discuss Goethe's *Faust*. He sought rather to show the relation of Marlowe's *Faustus* to Germany, and how it happened that the undeniably German subject matter found its way to England. It was not yet possible for Arnim to determine Marlowe's source, nor whether it reached the British Isles in the form of a story or a drama. He surmises that it most likely found its way through the mediation of the Netherlands, where one was engaged in active trade with England. The fact that the Grafschaft Emden and the Duke of Anhalt are mentioned by Marlowe might lead to this conclusion.[78] Arnim seems to have been well acquainted with the historic Faust legend, for his attempt in the introduction to trace the relationship between the old German story and Marlowe's *Faustus* is, on the whole, successful. After giving a biographical sketch of Marlowe, he points out that at the most Marlowe could have had access only to a German story, never to a drama. Even the best German historic dramas of those times were mere stories, since any dramatic development was impossible because of the

---

[76] Arnim's introduction to Wilhelm Müller's translation of Marlowe's *Dr. Faustus* (1818), p. XXIII.

[77] *Ibid.*, p. XXIV.   [78] *Ibid.*, p. XIX.

rigid rules concerning the rhyme imposed by the schools of the Meistersinger.[79]

In discussing *Faustus* and what the marionette play might have learned from it, Arnim also makes some general remarks about the German stage. He complains bitterly that at present every German theater manager lacks the ability to discover good dramatic material especially suitable to the times. In Marlowe's day, he continues, a theater manager would have noted immediately Goethe's early Faust fragments and adapted them to the stage. Even Maler Müller's *Faust* deserves to be performed.[80]

Goethe did not take any notice of his young friend's letter and Faust studies nor of the questions he raised in the introduction. Nor did he answer Arnim's letter of the following year (1819) which accompanied the transmission of his play *Die Gleichen*.[81] The conservative classicist and cosmopolitan, who in 1818 had coined the expression: "Everybody ought to be a Greek according to his own fashion, but a Greek he must be,"[82] could not be pleased with Arnim's latest creations. A few years later he said characteristically of Arnim: "He is like a barrel, where the cooper forgot to fasten the hoops. Thus it overflows."[83] On December 4, 1820, Arnim paid another call on Goethe. He was struck by his physical appearance and reported on it to Wilhelm Grimm: "He looks well in spite of his age, and yet it is sad to notice the change since I saw him last, nine years ago. His lips are sunken in, the fire of his eyes is gone, his posture reveals his age, and it seems that a habit of angry concentration has taken the place of the benevolent, pleasant expression he used to have."[84] In spite of Goethe's obliging manners, Arnim felt that the regrettable incident of 1811 had not been forgotten and that their friendship could not be renewed. Perhaps also Arnim, now approaching his fortieth year, was no longer the enthusiastic disciple, but had developed rather his own ideas and principles and become more critical of others. He wrote to the Grimm brothers a month later that Goethe had not lived up to an "essential requirement." His writings, with the exception

---

[79] *Ibid.*, p. XX.
[80] *Ibid.*, p. XX.
[81] *Schriften der Goethe Ges.*, XIV, 156.
[82] *Idem.*
[83] Goethe to Varnhagen, July 8, 1825.
[84] Bettina-Goethe, p. 237.

of the "Morphologische Hefte," lack harmonious unity and betray an irreligious soul; they strive too much for opposition and display. He adds that this lack is also apparent in many of Goethe's followers and has led them astray, particularly in matters of art.[85]

Now also publicly, in journals, Arnim begins to expose what he considers weaknesses in Goethe's personality and writings. When in 1822 the fifth part of Goethe's *Aus meinem Leben. Auch ich in der Champagne* appeared, Arnim reviewed it for Adolph Müllner's *Literatur-Blatt* in a frankly critical manner. In this review he discussed Goethe's work in connection with the memoirs of Casanova and Lauzun.[86] The first two pages of this comparison do not lack an ironical note, which is, however, touched with genial humor.

> The Italian allies himself with the German in disgust for everything political . . . the German through the dangers and privations of his military environment is stimulated to ponder on the laws of color (*Farbenlehre*). . . . It is unusual to find that the German in this book writes no tender and loving words, for it is he who has given to Germany for nearly a century the most attractive expressions of beautiful sensuality. . . .[87]

Arnim also points out that, unlike the Frenchman and Italian, Goethe is very discreet in relating his adventures, compromises nobody, is candid only about the dead, never about people still living, so that his memoirs actually appear less comprehensive than one would expect. One also gains the impression that although known and beloved by high and low, Goethe still keeps a wall around his inner self and the work that absorbs him. As was to be expected, the review, while supposedly dealing with all three men, tends to neglect Casanova and Lauzun in favor of Goethe.

Arnim was no longer the blind admirer. On the other hand, he

[85] Arnim-Grimm, p. 483.

[86] Arnim's review of Goethe, *Aus meinem Leben*, II, 5; of *Aus den Memoiren des Venezianers Casanova, Nach dem Manuskript bearbeitet von Wilh. von Schütz*, I. und II, Bd. (Leipzig, 1822), and of the Duke of Lauzun's Memoirs (2nd ed., Paris: Barrois, 1822), II. Vol., in the *Literatur-Blatt*, hrsg. von A. Müllner, 1822, pp. 262-3. This review led to disagreeable arguments with the editor, Müllner, and the publisher, Cotta, who objected to the disrespectful comparisons. Goethe ignored everything completely. Comp. *Goethe Jahrbuch*, XXI, 279-31.

[87] *Ibid.*, p. 262.

did not become spiteful and antagonistic, but sought to pay due tribute to Goethe's greatness as he saw it. He declares that he received this new book joyfully because here negations and inconsistencies are less apparent than in Goethe's later works. In fact, Arnim finds here only one instance of an unjustified attitude of negation, Goethe's disparagement of the art treasures at Treves. Among Goethe's inconsistencies Arnim counts his moody and irritating personal attitude, which he knew from his own experience. Only too often he would encourage, advise, and protect people, and then suddenly neglect them, as in the case of Plessing. In this particular instance Goethe gives a partial explanation when he says that he found Plessing's constant attentions and obtrusiveness too tiresome. But Arnim found contradictions not only in Goethe's personal relationships, which on some grounds are excusable, but also in his ideas. Thus he points out that in his *Westöstlicher Divan*[88] Goethe attacks the virtue of modesty, and on the contrary praises it highly in his "Morphologische Zeitschrift." Arnim wonders whether such inconsistencies have become habitual with Goethe as a result of peculiarities in his style which sometimes expresses unimportant things with great seriousness and emphasis.

Arnim takes this opportunity to set forth again his opinion of Goethe's studies in natural science. A year earlier he had stated that he found these studies more interesting than Goethe's poetical writings.[89] In the present review, his summary of Goethe's scientific achievements lacks the appreciative note. Speaking as a contemporary scientist, who is well acquainted with the controversies in question, he draws the general conclusion that with the exception of the mineralogists, none of the scientific scholars,

[88] *Ges.* (1819), pp. 801-7. Arnim's essay, "Otto Brüggeman, ein Beitrag zu Goethe's *Westöstlicher Divan*." Here Arnim protested against Goethe's denial of Brüggeman's definition of modesty, which reads, "Das Wenige, was der einzelne Mensch leistet, in seinem abhängigen Verhältnis gegen das große Weltleben zu erkennen und sich dessen nicht zu überheben." This essay on "Otto Brüggeman" (or Brughman, as Goethe wrote), who accompanied Olearius on his good-will trip to Russia and Persia, consists of anecdotes and adventures. Cf. Bettina-Goethe, p. 238.

[89] Bettina-Goethe, p. 238. Arnim wrote to the Grimm brothers, January, 1821: "Unter allen seinen jetzigen Arbeiten sind mir die 'Morphologischen Hefte' das Liebste, da ist er bei weitem weniger auf Schein and Opposition."

neither anatomists, botanists, nor physicists have much use for Goethe's contributions. The mineralogists recognize him because his work shows knowledge and a proper scientific humility before a vast field. The anatomists think that Goethe has given undue emphasis to certain details; the botanists consider his work *Die Metamorphose der Pflanzen* as unimportant. Above all the physicists are much annoyed by his controversy with Newton, and they find his *Farbenlehre* useless, obscure in theory, and unimaginative in the experimental part. If Goethe were not a master of rhetoric and an admirable poet carried away by the beauty and flow of words, his scientific writings might have been clearer, and he might have also given simple reports on questions arising and on doubtful experimental results, instead of omitting them. He might thus have made a really valuable contribution to science.[90]

In conclusion Arnim also discusses at length Goethe's description of the "Kanonenfieber" from which he suffered when he was at the front with the German army in 1793.

The review gives public utterance to Arnim's disgust with what he considered unattractive traits in Goethe's character and work. He makes it quite plain that not only his personal feelings had been deeply hurt, but that his opinions with regard to Goethe's rôle in Germany's cultural endeavors had undergone a fundamental change. One must admit, however, that this criticism can scarcely be called unbiased. He was more than doubtful of Goethe's fame as the greatest German poet of the present and future. He was now more eager to keep in touch with the Grimm brothers than with Goethe. He was doubtful of the merits of Goethe's works, for he himself got little enjoyment from reading them. This is his sincere reaction, even though ironically phrased, when Bet-

[90] *Literatur-Blatt,* hrsg. von A. Müllner, 1822, p. 262. Here Arnim writes: "Diesen Vorwurf einer seltsamen Dunkelheit über einfache Gegenstände möchte auch wohl das Schwerste sein, gegen welchen die Farbenlehre zu verteidigen; er möchte jedoch ganz schwinden, wenn Goethe aufrichtig das Ahndungsreiche, aber auch das ganz Schwankende, Unausgebildete seiner Anschauungen mitgeteilt hätte. Die Freude am Gelingen versteckt ihn aber, wo es nicht fort will, die Worte runden sich, alles scheint sich darin zu umfassen und zu beschließen, die Rhetorik wird Herr über den Gegenstand aber nicht der Verstand, geschichtliche Einsicht schmückt ihn und doch ist nichts geschichtlich verbunden und begründet."

tina writes him of her brief visit to Goethe in July 1824.[91]

Shortly before Arnim's death in January, 1831, Bettina visited Weimar twice, in the late summer and the fall of 1830, and tried to call on Goethe, but according to Goethe's diary, "Frau von Arnim's obtrusiveness was rejected."[92] Thus Arnim died unreconciled with the man whom he once considered his great master and rejecting him as Germany's spiritual leader. After Arnim's death the old bonds of friendship between Goethe and Bettina were not renewed. In 1832 she wrote him humbly: "Don't you know me any more? If you only knew how much your silence hurts me!"[93] However, Bettina had at least the satisfaction of knowing that Freimund, her son and Arnim's, was hospitably received by Goethe as the last visitor before his death.[94]

The other great poet in Weimar, Schiller, had died half a year before Arnim paid his first visit to Goethe in November, 1805. Reinhold Steig has emphasized that, unlike the early Romanticists, the Heidelberg circle, including the Grimm brothers, understood and appreciated Schiller. Jacob Grimm especially was full of admiration for Schiller's objective, aesthetic point of view. In young Arnim, however, one cannot discover much interest or understanding for Schiller's poetry and philosophy. On reading Schiller's *Wilhelm Tell* he wrote to Brentano: "Schiller's *Tell* is unworthy of both, Schiller and Tell; I feel a better 'Tell' striving for expression in myself."[95] In asking whether Schiller's chorus was received without applause in Weimar, he declares: "Such choruses are unsuitable to the present stage of musical development, and the ancients had never spoken choruses."[96]

Arnim's and Schiller's conceptions of poetry were indeed entirely different. Arnim wished to cultivate the simple natural

[91] Bettina-Goethe, pp. 263-4. We read here: "Von den Grimms schreibst Du wenig oder nichts, und doch hörte ich von ihnen lieber als von Goethe, von dessen künftiger Seligkeit bei mir nicht die Rede ist (er mag es sich wohl nur einbilden, daß sich die Leute darüber bekümmern), dessen jetzige ich aber schon lange bezweifle, seit mir selbst bei seinen Arbeiten nicht recht wohl wird."

[92] Bettina-Goethe, pp. 284-5.

[93] *Ibid.*, p. 286.   [94] *Ibid.*, p. 287.

[95] Arnim-Brentano, p. 115. Arnim's letter to Brentano, October 3, 1804. A critical reference to the *Braut von Messina* occurs in an earlier letter.

[96] *Ibid.*, p. 94.

poetry of the people (*Volkspoesie*), and he appreciated Goethe chiefly as the poet of popular songs (*Volkslieder*). Schiller, on the other hand, raised the people to an unreal poetic height and put words into the mouth of the masses which were unnatural and incompatible with their lives and surroundings. Whether peasant, burgher, or aristocrat, all spoke and acted on the same high aesthetic and poetic level. What applied to poetry, applied also to the theater; and this explains Arnim's criticism of Schiller's *Wilhelm Tell*. Schiller could never be a poet of the people (*Volksdichter*) and thus, in Arnim's eyes, merit the highest possible fame. It was only E. M. Arndt among contemporary poets who could, in his opinion, almost claim this distinction.

A few years after Schiller's death, however, there appeared in the *Zeitung für Einsiedler* a belated sign that Arnim had some appreciation for him. He published extracts from Schiller's letter to a young poetess,[97] praising them as excellent examples of constructive criticism, confidentially carried on between a master and a hopeful disciple. This publication, with Arnim's commentary, must be regarded as a rare admission by Arnim of Schiller's great rôle. Another, less emphatic, came a few years later in a review of Zacharias Werner's *Attila, König der Hunnen*. Here Arnim makes interesting comparisons between Werner's and Schiller's dramas, praising the latter. He calls attention to Schiller's diligence and precision. *Die Braut von Messina* he considers the best drama; in *Die Jungfrau von Orleans* the supernatural element is overdone.[98] Unfortunately Arnim did not follow Creuzer's suggestion to write a review of Schiller's "Theater" in the *Heidelbergische Jahrbücher*, though he took it under consideration.[99] A study of the correspondence between Goethe and Schiller which he began in 1829 remained also an unpublished fragment.[100]

About two other German classical writers, Lessing and Wieland, Arnim never wrote anything critical. Most likely their interests and personalities were still more foreign to him than Schiller's.

[97] *Tröst Einsamkeit,* pp. 196-9.
[98] HeidelbJbb., I, 1810, p. 11: "Doch sind die Ahndungen und höheren Empfängnisse in der 'Jungfrau von Orleans' zu stark überhäuft." Cf. p. 102.
[99] NHeidelbJbb., XI, (1902), pp. 195-6, 199, 204.
[100] Cf. Karl Henrici, "Auktions-Katalog," 149, Nr. 41, p. 7.

One is justified in the deduction that criticism in the wider and modern meaning of the term was not considered worth while by Arnim. He regarded it as his task to write critically only about such poets as he considered interesting, important, and constructive for him, and as furthering art for the people.

VII

NATIONALISM

Arnim's poetic life was nurtured in the ideas and activities of the Heidelberg circle. His interests as a critic were naturally very much concerned with all the writings of this group of friends. In this circle young Arnim held a distinctive position, on the one hand, because he enjoyed the special friendship of Goethe, and on the other, because he was the only North-German and aristocrat, and as such was able to take a broader view of affairs in Germany than, for instance, Brentano. Strong patriotic feelings drew him to participate actively in realistic political problems and the center for such activities was his native Berlin. Heidelberg remained the oasis of idealistic poetic pursuits.

At the beginning of the year 1809 Arnim returned again to Berlin, where people had just begun to breathe more freely after evacuation by the French army. With the return of the royal couple at Christmas, 1809, the metropolis was again the center of social and political activities. The founding of the university became the most important factor in the cultural life of the city. Men like Fichte, Adam Müller, and Savigny joined the faculty of this new institution, and the Prussian capital now became the meeting ground for all those who worked for the liberation of Prussia from the Napoleonic yoke. Arnim, too, was heart and soul for this cause. His political and national sympathies came into the foreground during this time until the tragic internal political situation of Prussia after the War of Liberation showed him the hopelessness of all further endeavors in the political field. The most productive period of his career encompassed these first years in Berlin; the same was true of Heinrich von Kleist, who was then his close associate.

As happens often in times of political restlessness, literature and literary journalism forsook the principle of art for art's sake and turned to the realistic questions of the day. In those days the questions foremost in the mind of intellectuals were such as these:

Should Prussia become permeated with the new spirit of the French Revolution, or should she pursue a policy of national development in which the historic state evolves organically? Should one adopt the political philosophies of Rousseau and Montesquieu or that of Edmund Burke? Finally, should Prussia open her gates to industrialization, following England's and France's example and the preachings of Adam Smith, or should every effort be made to have Prussia remain an agricultural country?

For the defence of tradition and a conservative policy Arnim founded the "Christlich-deutsche Tischgesellschaft," which counted among its members leading aristocrats, nationally minded intellectuals, poets, and scholars. Their voices were heard in the *Berliner Abendblätter*, the new journal founded by Kleist, devoted to a policy faithful to the king and Prussian tradition, and counting among its contributors Kleist himself, Adam Müller, Arnim, and Fouqué. The object of their attack was the policies and attitude of Chancellor Hardenberg. The sharp antagonism of the Kleist-Müller-Arnim group lasted through the entire period of Hardenberg's rule. As late as 1816 Arnim complained in a letter to Görres that with the beginning of the war of 1813, when he learned that Stein had not taken Hardenberg's place, he had immediately abandoned all hope for any permanent and thorough reforms within the state.[1] All documents of the "Christlich-deutsche Tischgesellschaft" that have come down to posterity, and likewise the topics discussed in the *Berliner Abendblätter*, attest this bitter struggle between the national conservative group and Hardenberg and his clique for supremacy in the cultural and political affairs of the state.

Arnim, well versed in all these controversial questions, a prolific reader, of quick perception and intelligence, now became in the field of economics and politics a valuable collaborator for both the *Berliner Abendblätter* and later the *Preussische Correspondent*. In these journals his witty, critical pen did valiant service for the development of a national program. One will search in vain for any strictly literary-historical criticism from Arnim's pen in either of these newspapers. None of the philosophers, poets, writers, or

---

[1] Josef von Görres, *Gesammelte Briefe*, hrsg. von Marie Görres, VII, 483; Arnim's letter to Görres, January, 1816.

artists who breathed the new political atmosphere in Prussia could escape the powerful currents of the time or fail to reflect political ideas in their writings. When Steig says, *"Des Knaben Wunder-horn* marks the beginning of this new Berlin movement," he does not exaggerate.[2] One might justly call Arnim the prophet of Prussia's national rise. This is shown by an examination of his program for *Der Preusse,* a weekly he had intended to publish in 1806, but the plans for which never materialized.[3] In his essay "Von Volksliedern," Arnim prophesied that "a time will come when tedious military service will become a source of great honor and joy."[4]

Nevertheless, history does not rank Arnim among the outstanding leaders of this period, such as Stein, Hardenberg, Fichte, Arndt, and Jahn. Among his contemporaries Fichte also lacked popular appeal, but his teachings and ideas began to meet with wide approval shortly before the War of Liberation.[5] On the other hand, Fouqué, a poet less know today, became very popular with the publication of his *Sigurd* in 1808. In spite of all Arnim's endeavors and the mission he felt called to undertake, namely, to speak the language of the people and to bring to them "their" poetry (*Volkspoesie*), he failed in popular appeal, partly because he lacked the opportunity, and partly because he could not surmount the barriers interposed by his aristocratic birth and thoroughly romantic character.

From 1809 till 1814 Arnim collaborated closely with most of the leading patriots. With greater maturity and confronted by different circumstances, he revised his earlier attitude toward Arndt and Fichte and his judgment of these men. They too had changed their outlook in accordance with the more urgent political needs and now believed that Prussia could play an important rôle in leading Germany to better days. A really close friendship grew up between Arnim and Heinrich von Kleist during the brief period before Kleist's suicide. Like Arnim, Kleist was an eccentric, ro-

---

[2] Reinhold Steig, *Heinrich von Kleists Berliner Kämpfe,* Berlin and Stuttgart, 1901, p. 3. Cited below as *Kleists Berliner Kämpfe.*

[3] The forthcoming publication of *Der Preusse* and Arnim's program as future editor for this weekly were announced in *Der Reichsanzeiger,* II, 1806, Sp. 3291-3293.

[4] DNL, CXLVI, 1, 67.

[5] *Kleists Berliner Kämpfe,* pp. 307-8.

mantic personality. He also lacked popular appeal and did not succeed in establishing any real contact with the masses.

Arnim's literary and patriotic influence first became noticeable in Berlin in the "Nordstern" circle, a group of young writers including Chamisso, Neumann, Varnhagen, and Bernardi. Fouqué also was connected with this group. These men regarded *Des Knaben Wunderhorn* as the realization of their own endeavors. On his arrival in Berlin in 1809, Arnim was enthusiastically received into this circle. Closer association, however, rather estranged him from it. Brentano even derided the "Nordstern" group.[6]

Neumann, Varnhagen, and Fouqué published jointly in 1808 the satirical novel, *Die Versuche und Hindernisse Karls,* which Arnim reviewed in the *Heidelbergische Jahrbücher* of 1810.[7] The critic had no very high opinion of the work nor of the circle from which it originated, as he plainly states in his review. An examination of the book shows that his attitude was abundantly justified. The satirical tone which marks it is, indeed, arrogant and mediocre. The authors not only ridiculed Johannes von Müller, Voss, and Jean Paul, but they also repeated the criticism of Goethe's *Wilhelm Meister* often heard in those days, namely, that all poetry is ruined in this novel. Naturally Arnim had to take issue sharply with this arrogant and satirical spirit, and impressed on the authors that they could learn much from *Wilhelm Meister,* its plot, style, etc. "The young men of the 'Nordstern' circle," he says, "should lay aside their supercilious attitude and desist from silly criticism of the work of so mature a writer as Goethe"; and he points out that the poetic element was not ruined when Wilhelm Meister entered real life and abandoned the career of an actor, as these young men had assumed. In short, Arnim had no use for a novel which was but a parody of other novels, and emphasized strongly that it was high time to begin to read original writers again instead of their critics and parodists. In comparison with *Wilhelm Meister,* he declares, *Die Versuche und Hindernisse Karls* is a novel that one can well shelve and forget, the sooner the better.

[6] Cf. *ibid.,* pp. 6-7.
[7] HeidelbJbb., 1810, pp. 347-9; Reinhold Steig in his *Heinrich von Kleists Berliner Kämpfe* does not mention this review of Arnim.

It is only for the chapters on war and military events, written by Fouqué, that Arnim has praise. These were permeated with a novel conception of the patriotic spirit and a new esteem for the soldier, which coincided with Arnim's ideals.[8]

The relationship between Arnim and the members of the "Nordstern" circle did not grow more intimate as the years passed. Their names did not appear in the list of the "Christlich-deutsche Tischgesellschaft" when its first meeting was called by Arnim on January 18, 1811. But among the members of the new organization was Heinrich von Kleist, who had become in the preceding year Arnim's closest collaborator and friend. It is most regrettable that these two idealists of early nationalism did not meet before and that fate terminated their association so soon. Even though they happened to be in Königsberg at the same time, in 1806 and 1807, there exists no evidence that they met before 1810 in Berlin.[9] From February 4, 1810, until his death on November 21, 1811, Kleist lived in Berlin; except for a brief trip to Frankfort-on-the-Oder. Strictly speaking, Kleist's and Arnim's acquaintanceship lasted only a year and a half, for Arnim and his young wife went on a trip to South Germany in August, 1811, and did not return till after Kleist's death. Kleist's regard for Arnim is expressed in a letter written in the summer of 1810. Here he remarks that of all his friends, Arnim is the one of whom he is most fond, although he has not seen Arnim so often since the latter's marriage.[10] Few documents except their joint journalistic productions remain to testify to this friendship. In the Heidelberg circle Kleist and his works found little mention. To be sure, Arnim had been asked by the *Heidelbergische Jahrbücher* to review Kleist's *Penthesilea,* but unfortunately for posterity, he did not comply with this request.[11] While the bonds between Kleist and Arnim grew closer, Brentano remained aloof. Jacob Grimm recognized Kleist as an outstanding poet; young Ferdinand Grimm exulted in him.[12]

[8] Cf. *Kleists Berliner Kämpfe*, p. 56.

[9] Reinhold Steig, *Neue Kunde zu Heinrich von Kleist*, pp. 37-8.

[10] *Ibid.*

[11] Alfred Kloss, *Die Heidelbergischen Jahrbücher der Literatur in den Jahren 1808-1816* (Leipzig, 1918), p. 55.

[12] Reinhold Steig, *Neue Kunde zu Heinrich von Kleist*, p. 122.

When he was editor of the *Zeitung für Einsiedler* Arnim had taken favorable notice of Kleist's *Phöbus*.[13] One is justified in assuming that the fairy tale *Das Märchen von der langen Nase*, published anonymously in the *Phöbus* (June, 1808) was a contribution of Arnim's to this periodical.[14] Arnim met Kleist soon after the latter's arrival in Berlin in February, 1810, and wrote in that month to Wilhelm Grimm of the newcomer as a very odd personality, of a sort that is apt to appear when talent breaks through the old Prussian forms. He characterizes Kleist as the most simple human being he has met in a long time, though he has, to be sure, an inclination toward cynicism. There is an uncertainty in his speech that approaches stammering, a reflection of which, Arnim declares, can be found in the constant erasures and corrections in Kleist's manuscripts. He leads a queer life, often stays in bed for days, smoking his pipe, in order to work undisturbed. His novel *Kohlhaas* Arnim regards as excellent.[15] In a letter to the Grimm brothers, September 3, 1810, Arnim calls Kleist the "best fellow," yet one who has talent to become a second Dante because he enjoys so much tormenting his poetical characters.[16]

In the same letter he announces the appearance and purpose of the *Berliner Abendblätter,* inviting the Grimms to send contributions. For the present the *Abendblätter* were to entertain the reader rather than be serious, or make attempts at instruction, or include literature. One can hardly take this statement of Arnim seriously, nor another, saying that he did not enjoy his collaboration on the *Berliner Abendblätter*. As a matter of fact, the journal was on a high level from the very beginning, containing serious discussions of political and literary events. It afforded Arnim an opportunity to criticize important personages and ministers, and this is his only reason, he states,[17] for continuing as an active collaborator. In spite of his pretended indifference to the *Abendblätter*, Arnim contributed no less than seventeen articles and reports,[18] and submitted ten others which did not pass the censorship.[19] This is certainly an impressive number for one writer, in view of the fact that the paper was published for only half a

[13] *Tröst Einsamkeit*, June 25, 1808; p. 35.
[14] Mallon, p. 35. [15] Arnim-Grimm, p. 84. [16] *Ibid.*, p. 70.
[17] Arnim-Grimm, p. 84. [18] Mallon, pp. 42 f., 48. [19] Arnim-Grimm, p. 96.

year, beginning October 1, 1810, and ending March 30, 1811.

Most of the articles written by Arnim were on political and economic topics. Those not passed by the censor are of greater interest because they touch upon local questions of literature and the theater. In these articles Arnim wanted to submit to the public and especially to Iffland the reforms and requirements for a new stage for the romantic drama, and thus pave the way for the production of Kleist's and Tieck's plays. The current discussions and quarrels about the theater Arnim raised to a more general and impersonal level. Apparently he was very optimistic of his rôle as a mediator, since he was on a better footing with Iffland, producer and director of the Berlin theater, than Kleist was.

Arnim demanded first of all a hearing for local playwrights. They have a greater right on the stage of their fatherland than foreign writers. It must be humiliating, he continues, for men like Kleist and Tieck as well as for the entire nation, to be neglected in favor of Contessa, Robert, and other similarly mediocre dramatists.[20] Of course, personal interest also motivated Arnim's efforts. For years he had studied and collected old German plays, and intended to edit them. He also hoped for a production of his drama *Halle und Jerusalem,* completed in 1810. His ideal was to have the old German and romantic plays dominate the German stage, and to continue and extend the Shakespeare revival, already begun by the early Romanticists.[21] However, Iffland did not react favorably to Arnim's endeavors as a mediator and made no concessions to the Berlin group of romantic playwrights. For this Iffland blamed the stubbornness and lack of cooperation of local poets.[22]

Arnim wrote to his friend Dorrow in April, 1811, about Kleist's and his own discouraging experiences: "Kleist with his *Abendblätter* had felt the severe pressure of the government. Half of the articles intended for publication had been suppressed by the censorship of the Berlin police. No free discussion of the local theater was permitted. Iffland and Hardenberg stuck together like grease to a wheel."[23]

[20] *Kleists Berliner Kämpfe,* p. 96.

[21] *Ibid.,* pp. 242-3.   [22] *Ibid.*

[23] Wilhelm Dorrow, *Reminiscenzen* (Leipzig, 1842), p. 457.

As stated above, Arnim was in Frankfort-on-the-Main at the time of Kleist's death. From here he wrote to the Grimm brothers, December 6, 1811, of his friend's suicide:

The poor fellow, I feel sorry for him. His stubbornness was not very pleasant, but he was honest in his work as few others. His short stories are good, and for his dramatic talents he only lacked a worthy stage which was interested in him. A series of unfortunate circumstances probably drove him to this unhappy act. There was the fiasco of the performance of his *Der zerbrochene Krug* in Weimar during Kleist's absence; the failure of his *Phöbus,* an excellent journal; the destruction of his *Berliner Abendblätter* by a government afraid of it, and finally poverty added to the strain.[24]

Kleist's tragic end caused considerable comment, but even now his opponents were not silenced. The attacks of the *Morgenblätter* assumed ugly personal forms, which made the indignant Arnim write to this paper in defence of Kleist. In this protest Arnim praises Kleist's exemplary life as an army officer and as a government official, the two callings he had abandoned in order to dedicate his life to poetry:

Perhaps only a few poets may boast of such sincerity of character and severity of standards in their work as the deceased. Instead of reproaching him for adherence to a new school, one should rather regret that he did not recognize any school and only in rare instances yielded to tradition and the judgment of his artist friends. With great stubbornness he rather gave way to the accidental, which may have misrepresented often the depth and beauty of his feelings. He ruled his destiny with a firm hand, and his persistence, increasing with the vicissitudes of his life, is explainable, for he carried his burden, realizing his inner powers.[25]

Throughout his life Arnim took Kleist's part, like a faithful friend. Brentano's comment that the poetic cloak of poor Kleist had been too scanty, he rebuked with the remark that that of Brentano was too ample and in the hurry had not received a good fitting, so that it covered his eyes.[26] In 1825 a poor performance

[24] Arnim-Grimm, p. 172.

[25] The *Morgenblätter* did not pay any attention to Arnim's protest, a copy of which is in the Varnhagen collection at the Staatsbibliothek in Berlin. Cf. *Kleists Berliner Kämpfe,* p. 684.

[26] *Ibid.;* Arnim-Brentano, p. 297, cf. Brentano's criticism of Kleist's *Penthesilea:* "Es ist doch in allen Arbeiten dieses unglücklichen, talentvollen Menschen eine ganz merkwürdige scharfe Rundung, eine so ängstliche Vollendung und wieder Armut, und es wird mir immer äußerst peinlich und doch macht es mir Freude, etwas von

of *Käthchen von Heilbronn* moved Arnim deeply and reminded him of all the noble talents that had been misunderstood in their time and killed by cold criticism. Then he wrote to Wilhelm Grimm that he was convinced Kleist would still be alive if he could have witnessed one performance of his play in Berlin, no matter how poorly done.[27] It is of interest that Arnim as a critic lavished praise on two men who were not appreciated by their contemporaries, and were equally tragic in their lives, Kleist and Hölderlin. Both were, in his opinion, great poets of the German people, and of the utmost sincerity in their poetic work.

Arnim's connections with nationalistic groups in Berlin were manifold. They brought an acquaintanceship with Ernst Moritz Arndt, who was secretly in Berlin from Christmas 1809, till Easter 1810. Speaking of this period in Berlin in his *Erinnerungen aus dem äußeren Leben,* Arndt says that he met there a number of men and youths who had bound themselves together in the interest of patriotic work, among whom was Arnim.[28] Arndt supported Arnim eagerly in his collection of folksongs for another volume of the *Wunderhorn*.[29] As mentioned earlier, Arndt's major book on national topics, *Geist der Zeit,* had not been received very favorably by Arnim. He objected to its general pessimistic outlook for Germany and the reproaches it voiced against Prussia. Seven years later, at the end of the great war year, in 1813, when he wrote his review of Arndt's *Das preussische Volk und Heer 1813,*[30] Arnim referred to the general impression which the book had made on him, recalling that the author evidently did not formerly have "a very high opinion of our people," that is, the Prussian people. However, Arndt had now changed his opinion and had made a study of Prussia and its army which led him to recognize the important rôle of Prussia in the war of 1813. In his review Arnim gives due credit to Arndt and now speaks of him

---

ihm zu lesen"; *ibid.,* p. 302. Cf. also Brentano's criticism of Kleist's *Hermann, ibid.,* p. 344.

[27] Arnim-Grimm, p. 544.

[28] *Ernst Moritz Arndts Werke,* hrsg. von Wilhelm Steffens, II, 88-00.

[29] Arndt wrote to Reimer on November 27, 1810: "Hier mein lieber Getreuer, sind einige Sächelchen, die meine Freunde gesammelt haben, wovon einiges vielleicht für das *Wunderhorn* dienen könnte. Du magst es Arnim geben." E. M. Arndt, *Ein Lebensbild in Briefen,* hrsg. von Meisner und Robert Geerds, 1898.

[30] *Der Preussische Correspondent,* December 25, 1813, p. 4.

as an honest writer who is filled with ardor for his ideas and a love of the subject.

Arndt's treatment of history interested Arnim very much. His method was to emphasize individual episodes in the history of nations, in this case the year 1813 in which he himself had participated, rather than to generalize and to pass historical judgments. He considered this method the only correct one, for it gave a realistic and truthful picture of events. The other was much too vague and difficult for a contemporary, and such a procedure should be left to future generations. Arnim also agreed with Arndt that it was solely the respect for spiritual freedom that had led Prussia to victory, and that therefore spiritual freedom, above all, should be preserved and treasured in the future. As a romanticist, historian, and collector, Arnim had still another wish at heart, namely the preservation of literary and historical documents and time-honored institutions. Thus, in the now abolished kingdom of Westphalia he wished to see preserved the old Germanic system of justice which had been reintroduced by Napoleon, and also all the historical documents relating to the seven years of the kingdom's existence.[31]

Of greater literary value is Arnim's review of Arndt's *Der Rhein, Teutschlands Strom, aber nicht Teutschlands Gränze*.[32] First, Arnim discussed here in detail Arndt's personality as a writer and politician, and secondly, the topic he had chosen for this book, which was one of a delicate political character. Arnim ranks Andt as one of the best contemporary writers, for Arndt's discussions of burning questions of his time reveal deep under-

[31] The passage is as follows: "Auch in dem untergegangenen Westfalen hatte sich bei aller Verderblichkeit und Fremdartigkeit des Ganzen im Einzelnen manches Gute entwickelt, was bewahrt zu werden verdiente. Manche Einrichtung wie die Friedensrichter und die Geschworenen, die vielleicht aus Deutschland stammen, nach weitem Umlaufe wieder als fremde Einrichtung dahin zurückkehrten, verdienten allgemeiner eingeführt zu werden, ebenso die mündliche kürzere Verhandlung, die Öffentlichkeit der Gerichte, usw. Eine Pflicht der Bibliothekare wäre es jetzt insbesondere alles, was auf jene unseligen sieben Jahr bezug hat, zu sammeln, da der allgemeine Haß gegen die Gewaltsamkeit jener Einrichtung auch den gedruckten Denkmalen so gefährlich ward. . . . *Der Westfälische Moniteur* wird künftig in der Geschichte eines der abenteuerlichsten Denkmale sein. Literarische Sammler werden aber unserer Zeit immer wesentlicher und leider immer seltener. . . ."

With regard to the Westphalian system of justice, cf. also Arnim's review of Jacob Grimm's *Deutsche Rechtsaltertümer*.

[32] *Der Preussische Correspondent*, January 28, 1814, p. 4.

standing and are marked by clarity of treatment. He has covered his field completely, and his manner of presentation does not lack appeal and energy. Arndt, indeed, comes close to being Arnim's ideal of a perfect writer, but he has one great defect:

> He has become a beloved poet of the people (*Volkschriftsteller*), yet not a genuine one. Whenever he tries to be really popular, he fails, for being popular (*volksmäßig*) is a talent and gift and does not depend upon the artist's endeavor. If it were possible to compare periods, one might liken him to Hutten—but our time does not have a Luther, of whom Hutten said, "Whatever comes from me is human and is bound to fail, but whatever comes from you is divine and will exist forever!" Luther as a political writer deserves the highest attention, but he has never received it, as far as we know.[33]

Men like Arndt and Hutten have the desire to present their opinion to the public, but Luther, like Frederick the Great, was driven by spiritual forces. Out of inner necessity such men say and do unconsciously what they must.

In this connection Arnim also expressed his opinion of Edmund Burke, then regarded by many as a great and fascinating political leader, like Luther in his age. Arnim disagreed with this view. He admitted that Burke was a political leader of great sagacity and of some prophetic foresight, but at the same time he was too rhetorical and affected, and lacked "unconscious divine directness."

With regard to the political topic of Arndt's book, the river Rhine and Germany, Arnim avoided statements regarding the contemporary situation and discussed the problem historically and in general terms. Arndt was concerned with the physical and cultural separation of the German-speaking people on both sides of the Rhine, and the question as to how, after Napoleon's defeat, they could be reunited. Arnim did not accept Arndt's rather romantic reasons for this separation; he also rejected geographic causes for it and differences in the character of the people, and ascribed it rather to the indifference of the population and mistakes in constitutions and in legislation. He believed that such a long historical separation could not be bridged over easily, and

[33] Arnim's review of Arndt's *Der Rhein, Teutschlands Strom, aber nicht Teutschlands Gränze*, in *Der Preussische Correspondent*, January 28, 1814.

preferred to build on the slogan: "Germany extends as far as the German language!" Arndt's idea of strengthening the German element by the formation of an order of knights, he rejected as artificial. He trusted that the future would solve the question of the political education of the population. If the people have high ideals, then education also will improve among them.

These reviews of Arndt's two books appeared in *Der Preussische Correspondent,* the outstanding patriotic political newspaper in Berlin during the War of Liberation. *Der Preussische Correspondent* had been founded by Niebuhr and supported by Scharnhorst. Its first issue appeared on April 2, 1813. The original intention was to enlarge it into a national journal. A number of outstanding men were its chief contributors: Niebuhr, Göschen, Schleiermacher, Arnim, Arndt, and Ludwig Jahn. Arnim served as editor from October 1, 1813, till January 31, 1814. His contributions to the *Correspondent* fall chiefly into this period and are very numerous. He notes in the farewell address to his readers of January 31, 1814:

I have written all articles, sketches, announcements, anecdotes, and poems, unless they are signed otherwise, or unless they are news dispatches by correspondents. . . . I have endeavored to add to all of my writings something of value for our people. This may have been disliked by the highly intellectual, but has pleased people of culture.[34]

Just as earlier in the case of the *Zeitung für Einsiedler,* Arnim tried to use the *Preussische Correspondent* as a means of serving the people and bringing national ideals before them in a popular form. From the literary point of view, the *Correspondent* falls behind both the *Zeitung für Einsiedler* and the *Berliner Abendblätter.* Arnim's contributions consisted mostly of short anecdotes and episodes from the battle-fields and from home. The only valuable literary reviews, besides those of Arndt's works noted above, are his discussion of Fouqué's poems, Zacharias Werner's *Die Weihe der Unkraft,* and of the anonymous publication *Der Frau von Staël Verbannung aus Frankreich.* To these must be added a eulogy on Fichte at the time of his death. During his editorship Arnim obtained the collaboration of the Grimm brothers and of

[34] Cf. DNL, CXLVI, 1, p. CXXI.

Brentano. These friends sent him anecdotes and news; Brentano from Vienna, Wilhelm Grimm from Cassel, and Jacob Grimm from France.[35]

Arnim's experience as a newspaper editor was only the short-lived adventure of a romanticist in the field of practical realities. Several reasons may be cited for his resignation. He himself attributed it to the annoying censorship: "Articles were cut to such an extent that finally only a lie remained".[36] Even in his farewell note to the reader, the following passage was eliminated by official direction:

> The restrictions are so severe that they suppress all desire to express even that which is permitted. Nations cannot learn any longer by mutual experience because they hear nothing truthful from each other.[37]

Differences of opinion between Niebuhr and Arnim may also have been a factor. Even though they were friends, their literary tastes differed, and they disagreed on some general policies.[38]

As noted above, one of Arnim's reviews in the *Correspondent* was that of Fouqué's poems.[39] Fouqué was a very prominent person in the literary and political circles of Berlin in those days. Arnim liked the poems because they were well written and incorporated the real war experiences of the poet. Arnim hoped, indeed, that the stirring days of the war would bring a revival in poetry:

> Time teaches and will do so more in the future, that poetry should bring not only tales of a lost paradise, but also prophecies of one to come, to which all heroic deeds point, so that this aspect of poetry will flourish again. Let us hope that the wealth of subject-matter during this year will arouse poets, for never in past decades has there been such an abundance of heroic material for German singers.[40]

Arnim's literary relationship with Fouqué had begun in 1809, when

[35] Cf. Arnim-Grimm, p. 288. The Grimm brothers originally intended to publish their own journal.

[36] Arnim-Brentano, p. 325; Arnim's letter to Reimer, November 18, 1813.

[37] *Ibid.*, p. 324.

[38] DNL, CXLVI, 1, p. CXX: Niebuhr's letter of January 11, 1814; also Arnim-Brentano, p. 334: "Die Ängstlichkeit der Censur, die Borniertheit und das Einreden von Niebuhr gestattete mir auch nur den kleinsten Teil des Möglichen. Sorgen und Besorgnis der eigenen Geschäfte raubte mir viel Zeit, die Verbindungen waren bei der allgemeinen Unruhe sehr schwer anzuknüpfen, ausländische Zeitungen fehlten."

[39] *Der Preussische Correspondent*, October 15, 1813, p. 4.

[40] *Ibid.*

Arnim returned to Berlin. As mentioned above, he reviewed in the *Heidelbergische Jahrbücher Die Versuche und Hindernisse Karls* by the "Nordstern" group of writers, among whom was Fouqué. On the appearance of *Sigurd, der Schlangentöter,* the work which made Fouqué famous, Arnim suggested to Wilhelm Grimm that they review it jointly, and in particular compare this new version with the original saga.[41] As it happened, Wilhelm wrote most of the review, which was published in the *Heidelbergische Jahrbücher* in 1809. Arnim added only a few words to soften Wilhelm's severe criticism, which had charged that Fouqué had been superficial in his treatment of old poetic treasures and had failed to reach a high poetic level in his version. As Arnim wrote to Wilhelm, Fouqué's chief mistake was that he alternated in a queer manner the unconscious mechanism of old poetry with that which had been evolved in modern poetry; in other words, that he put on the same string imaginary, unobtainable desires with actual fullfillment.[42]

While Arnim was in close contact with all circles of poets and writers of his day in Berlin as well as with many leading men in university and political circles, he did not seem to care for a closer acquaintanceship with the Berlin philosophers. His natural inclinations, his inherent romanticism, did not tend toward abstract philosophical thinking. In his youth he expressed strong disgust for speculative thought, he "despised all philosophy."[43] This may explain why his relations to Fichte and Schleiermacher in Berlin were rather superficial, even though both supported the "Christlich-deutsche Tischgesellschaft."

Fichte had taken a courageous position in his *Reden an die deutsche Nation* in the winter of 1807-8. Nevertheless, Arnim and the Berlin patriots remained rather cool. As a teacher at the university Fichte was not popular, a fact well known to Arnim, who repeated Fichte's words in a letter to Wilhelm Grimm: "Although I have lectured for fifteen years, students don't understand me."[44] In the *Phöbus,* Adam Müller said of Fichte that in spite of all good intentions, he could not attain any popularity because "he had no understanding for those (the students) who should under-

---

[41] Arnim-Grimm, pp. 30, 41. [42] *Ibid.,* p. 83.
[43] Arnim-Brentano, p. 53. [44] Arnim-Grimm, p. 83.

stand him."[45] Other reasons may have contributed to Fichte's un-popularity; the Berlin Romanticists would have preferred to see a professor of natural philosophy in the chair at the university, Arnim having in mind his old acquaintance Steffens.[46]

However, the beautiful eulogy which Arnim wrote at Fichte's death in 1814 corrects the impression we might derive from his earlier remarks on the philosopher. "In the morning of January 29," he writes, "our highly esteemed Fichte passed away. His death aroused something more than sadness, and compels us to meditate on how quickly the great spiritual leaders of Germany are vanishing, before the nation herself is rebuilt."[47] He goes on to praise Fichte's strength of character, his harmonious mentality, his determination, which almost might be called pride, his sincerity as a philosopher, his masterly power of polemic. As the greatest disciple of Kant, he created a new and very stimulating philo-sophical school of his own, without realizing it until Kant called attention to it. Arnim declares that he does not feel competent to pass judgment on Fichte's writings, but that the effects of Fichte's pen are obvious. In contrast with what had seemed to be the earlier opinion of himself and others regarding Fichte's popularity, he now calls Fichte "the sun on the students' heaven in Jena." Fichte did not give his students any formula or prescriptions, he gave his whole personality. He was worried often lest his students could not understand him, and this led him to attempt to express him-self in a more popular language and made him an even better writer. Arnim also extols Fichte's "insight into the corruption of his time". In public lectures he gave advice to all classes of the German people and set forth the severest admonitions in a pe-culiarly good-natured tone. With great courage he stigmatized French corruption in its influence on the German nation. Further-more, in 1813 he did not merely talk about the duties of a German, but volunteered for the Reserve Corps of the Army, in spite of ill health. In Arnim's opinion it would be a self-rewarding task to write a biography of this unusual man. The biographer must not overlook apparently insignificant events and utterances.

[45] Johannes Bobeth, *Die Zeitschriften der Romantik*, pp. 243-4.
[46] *Kleists Berliner Kämpfe*, pp. 307-8.
[47] *Der Preussische Correspondent*, January 31, 1814, pp. 1-2.

Fichte's manner of expression was "frank and uncouth, he did not shrink from the extraordinary, the shocking, and the ridiculous."

Like Fichte and Fouqué, Arnim volunteered to serve his native country in the army. However, his wish to go to the war-zone was never realized, for his Reserve Corps was dissolved early.[48] Perhaps if he had gone, we might have had from him at that time patriotic, lyrical poems, like those of Körner, Fouqué, and others. To fight as a journalist in Berlin, behind the front lines, brought him disappointment and humiliation, and too soon, as noted above, he resigned as editor of the *Preussische Correspondent*. He had hoped that with the war a new epoch for Germany would dawn, in which he himself might serve his fatherland in an important political position. So much the greater then was his disappointment over the prevalence of reactionary forces in Germany and Hardenberg's continued leadership. He had no choice but to retire to the quiet of his estate Wiepersdorf and to consecrate himself once more to his literary mission. Only the letters to his friends still spoke of his shattered aspirations and ideals. To Brentano he wrote in 1814:

Even though no important activity was allotted to me, I nevertheless sacrificed devotedly my time and thought, desires, and mentality to the serious call of this important year for our fatherland. But now I shall shake off all cares.[49]

Also in other letters to his romantic friends Arnim's disillusionment is noticeable, particularly those to Görres during the years 1814-1817 were written in this mood: "Almost by force a hand from above seems to push me away from all public life", he declares in 1816, "and at times intuition tells me that my love and ideals for the welfare of the nation are not appreciated now, but will be in a better, purer future, when greater mutual confidence reigns."[50]

[48] Arnim-Brentano, pp. 310-15.
[49] *Ibid.*, p. 337.
[50] Josef von Görres, *Gesammelte Briefe*, hrsg. von Marie Görres, VIII, 481-4; Arnim's letter of January 23, 1816. Cf. also Arnim's letter of June 4, 1814, p. 416.

VIII

THE DRIFT TOWARD REALISM

Arnim survived the War of Liberation by only a few years, dying in January 1831. The years following 1815 appear in the history of Germany as a period of general fatigue, of indefinite searching for something new. This feeling of emptiness and lassitude, especially in the political life of Prussia, was the result of Hardenberg's rule, and the élite of the time watched the developments with resignation. Unfortunately intellectual life did not escape the same fate. The German poets and writers of the postwar days were depressed and disgusted. A fear to speak freely, a dread of the unbelievably strict censorship made new creative work impossible. Of the powerful romantic intellectual and political life which had dominated Berlin about 1810, only a timid remnant had been rescued for the aesthetic salons of the metropolis.

Gradually, however, a change became perceptible. The year 1815 brought a new phase in the history of German civilization. Time was bringing about the collapse of the systems of the old world, the world of the rights of small sovereign states, the world of absolutism with its strong individualism and its romanticism. The younger generation of 1815 would no longer look on with resignation. It soon began to prepare the ground for the events of 1848.

Arnim's mind was divided between these tendencies. His previous training, his own inclinations, and whole personality made him adhere to the traditional and romantic outlook, but events, and in particular his personal circumstances, forced him to a change of attitude. But thirty-four years old in 1815, he still had an open mind, could perceive the new trends and experience transformations in his spiritual life. His writings during the years immediately following, especially his contributions to the daily papers, reveal a stronger tendency toward realism. Significant for this change of attitude is the termination at this time of his relationship to the *Heidelbergische Jahrbücher* and the *Preussische Correspondent,* as well as to Görres' *Rheinische Merkur.* He had to abandon his hope for closer collaboration with Görres. Instead of these typical romantic periodicals, he contributed now to *Der Gesellschafter oder Blätter für Geist und Herz;* to Brockhaus' publications, like the *Literarische Conversationsblatt* and the *Blätter für literarische Unterhaltung;* or to pseudo-romantic journals, like Fouqué's *Berlinische Blätter für deutsche Frauen;* and to Adolph Müllner's *Literatur-Blatt.* These are only a few of the more important periodicals for which Arnim wrote. To these must be added his numerous contributions to various "Almanacs," a type of periodical which reveals still more distinctly the transitory character of this literary period.

Toward the end of the war, out of necessity, he had to abandon his restless romantic wanderings and to settle down at his country estate Wiepersdorf to earn his daily bread as a farmer. Such a radical change in his life separated him from his restless friend Brentano. The romanticist had to become a realist if he wished to retain his family estate and support his family,[1] for the French occupation, war contributions, and high taxes had reduced his holdings considerably. Like Wilhelm Meister he had to resign from the great world of art and dedicate himself to the chores and routine of a gentleman-farmer. He did not fail in his new duties, but accepted the situation with admirable vigor and good humor. For the rest of his short life he carried himself like a typical "märkischer Junker," so much so that a youthful visitor to the "Literarische Mittwochsgesellschaft" in Berlin in 1824 was astonished when he was introduced to the romanticist Arnim and beheld a stout gentleman who was engaged in a discussion with Fouqué regarding wheat prizes, sheep-shearing, manure, etc.[2] He even came to like the rural solitude and the novel labor, as may be gathered from a letter to Wilhelm Grimm.[3]

[1] Arnim-Grimm, p. 327: ". . . aber so ist mein Verhältnis, daß ich gewissenlos gegen die Meinen würde, wenn ich meine Angelegenheiten nicht durchführte. So wird nun Lehmacker verteilt, Kohl, Salat und Selleri in Reihen gepflanzt statt Soldaten. . . ." Letter to Wilhelm Grimm, May, 1815.

[2] DNL, CXLVI, 1, p. CXXIV.

[3] Arnim-Grimm, p. 327: "Ein größeres öffentliches Leben war mir unerreichlich, ein kleines Mitlaufen gestattet meine Lage nicht, so ist mir die Einsamkeit will-

It is surprising that in spite of his manifold duties Arnim could continue his literary activities. However, he complained often that he could devote little time to poetry. As noted above, his changed circumstances brought a touch of realism into his writings. In the *Kronenwächter* in 1817 he showed far more respect for form and clarity than in previous works. Here he followed Goethe's example. The precise local and historical descriptions in the *Kronenwächter* foreshadow the historical novel as it evolved under other hands in the next decades. During this time also he turned more to the short story as a medium of expression, very much as Tieck was doing. In 1818 Arnim's *Der tolle Invalide* was published; in 1820, *Die Majoratsherren;* and in 1826 his collection of short stories entitled *Landhausleben*. These stories, like Tieck's, are purged of fantastic caprice and tend to bear the imprint of realism.

In his daily journalistic activities Arnim's changed outlook became still more apparent. The reason for this was that he now wrote chiefly for the pseudo-romantic literary circles in Berlin, the salons, aesthetic-tea societies, and Almanacs. He was attracted by the financial compensation offered by the Almanacs, and also enjoyed reporting realistically on the events of his time, contemporary situations in politics and economics. At first national political articles predominated in his contributions to the journals from Wiepersdorf, for the experiences of the war of 1813-15 were still fresh in his mind. During 1815 he was collaborator on the *Rheinischer Merkur,* for which he wrote eight articles, all more or less of a political nature, regarding the question of greater Germany and the constitutions of the single states. In 1817 he made political contributions to the *Deutscher Beobachter,*[4] of Hamburg, and to the Jena periodical *Nemesis*.[5] He displayed also keen interest in the outstanding personalities of Prussian political life, such as Hardenberg, Blücher, and Scharnhorst, and in what was

---

kommen und das mühevolle Erhalten dessen, worauf doch endlich das Ganze mitberuht, verliert von seiner Verdrießlichkeit."

[4] "Über Aushebung zum Kriegsdienst in Preußen," p. 522; "Über das Legen der Bauern," p. 543; cf. Otto Mallon, *Arnim-Bibliographie,* Nr. 92.

[5] "Betrachtungen über die Verfassung des vormaligen Königreichs Westfalen," pp. 441-467; cf. *ibid.,* Nr. 93.

written about them. In addition to this he liked to write about his travels, an interest in which he anticipated the *Jungdeutschland* group. In his "Memoirs of a Traveller" he wrote of a trip to Halle,[6] of the October festival in Munich in 1829,[7] of a visit to the "Teutoberg,"[8] of Prenzlau, Dresden,[9] Cologne, Bonn, Vienna, Antwerp.[10] These reports had little of romantic or fantastic color, but rather a modern, realistic tone. They must be conceived of as fragments of a greater book on travels on which Arnim was working just before his death.[11] That he was much interested in many kinds of political, administrative, and economic questions is shown in his numerous contributions to the *Gesellschafter* and the *Literaturblatt*. His reports of current art activities and exhibitions belong in a separate group. The *Blätter für literarische Unterhaltung* in 1830 alone contain five such articles.[12]

In comparison with these varied interests, Arnim's writings on purely literary questions fared rather badly. In his literary articles also realistic and factual-historical elements were dominant, such as one searches for in vain in his contributions to periodicals during the first decade of the century. It seems as if Arnim wanted to stem the tide of disgust and depression, to set up a countermovement to the censorship and the falsification of current events, the result of the strict censorship. His writings stand in strong contrast to the early *Biedermeyer* literature, the over-sentimental, aristocratic love-hero stories found in the Almanacs.

In this connection it may be mentioned that some of his unpublished literary productions in the years 1815 to 1831 relating to the Varnhagen group may have been destroyed by Varnhagen.

[6] *Literarisches Conversationsblatt*, pp. 117-18, Leipzig 1823; cf. *ibid.*, Nr. 124.

[7] *Blätter für literarische Unterhaltung*, pp. 157-9, Leipzig 1827; cf. *ibid.*, Nr. 141.

[8] *Berlinische Blätter für deutsche Frauen*, pp. 1-19, 107-138, Berlin 1829; cf. *ibid.*, Nr. 148.

[9] *Der Gesellschafter*, p. 719, Berlin 1817; cf. *ibid.*, Nr. 95.

[10] *Blätter für literarische Unterhaltung*, pp. 89-91, 93-94, Leipzig, 1831; cf. *ibid.*, Nr. 158.

[11] Joseph von Görres, *Briefe*, III, 361; Arnim's letter to Görres, October 7, 1829.

[12] "Ältere Nachricht vom Maler des Danziger Bildes"; "Ausstellung und Versammlung des Vereins der Kunstfreunde im preußischen Staat"; "Besprechung von A. Hirt, 'Kunstbemerkungen auf einer Reise' "; "Genrebilder, Staffage"; "Besprechung von T. H. Schuler, 'Beschreibung des Straßburger Münsters' "; cf. Otto Mallon, *Arnim-Bibliographie*, pp. 84-5.

According to Steig, Varnhagen did away with all of the letters of Arnim and Brentano in which he found disparaging remarks about the Varnhagen group and about Rahel in particular.[13] It is, however, to be emphasized, that Arnim and Brentano were on friendly terms with Rahel, due to Varnhagen's mediation. Between the widowed Bettina and Rahel a hearty and sincere bond of friendship existed. It was due to this that Bettina turned over to Varnhagen Arnim's unpublished papers for organization.

When Arnim formed his association with the *Gesellschafter*[14] he had at last found a paper for which he could write with enjoyment, for the *Gesellschafter* was, in Arnim's words, "not malicious and ignorant like most other papers, and only once in a while a little stupid, which one has to take for granted in this world."[15] The publisher, F. W. Gubitz, showed a full appreciation of his collaboration, and Arnim continued to write for the paper until his death in 1831. Altogether he made more than fifty contributions on subjects from all fields of human interest, using many forms of literary and poetic expression: reviews, essays, poems, and short stories. What flowed from the pen of the busy gentleman-farmer was indeed a variegated medley. That he was conscious of this is revealed by a letter to Görres in 1822,[16] where he expresses his chagrin that his writings have to suffer because of the diversity of his plans and the interruptions caused by business.

Gubitz called Arnim's work, "German from a varied panorama" (*Deutsches aus vielseitiger Umsicht*).[17] We have further information from Gubitz about Arnim's relationship to him and his paper. They were friends professionally and personally. A mutual confidence united them. They stimulated each other, although they had their quarrels and agreements.[18] Differences resulted only when Arnim submitted to the practically minded Gubitz romantic,

[13] *Kleists Berliner Kämpfe*, pp. 612, 623; Arnim-Brentano, p. 295.

[14] The history of the *Gesellschafter* or *Blätter für Geist und Herz* has not as yet been written. This periodical was not included by Houben and Walzel in their bibliography of Romantic periodicals, where it was supposed to appear in a later volume. Cf. p. XI of the introduction in Volume I of the *Die Zeitschriften der Romantik*. L. Geiger in his *Unbekannte Aufsätze A. v. Arnims* publishes twenty-seven of Arnim's fifty-seven contributions to the *Gesellschafter*.

[15] Joseph von Görres, *Briefe*, II, 520; Arnim's letter to Görres, October 21, 1817.

[16] *Ibid.*, III, 62 (1822).   [17] F. W. Gubitz, *Erlebnisse*.   [18] *Ibid.*, p. 104.

pseudo-scientific essays like that on Jung-Stilling's *Theorie der Geisterkunde* (cf. above). On the other hand, Gubitz had no objections to Arnim's political views; he found his essays always marked by clarity of thought and noble conviction. As the editor recalled in later years, Arnim presented his ideas in a definite, understandable manner, unprejudiced by class or social differences, with an impartiality and directness "which never left him when he traced the historical phenomena of the world" (*im Verfolg weltgeschichtlicher Erscheinungen*).[19]

Most of Arnim's critical writings which were published in the *Gesellschafter* have been discussed in the foregoing chapters. Here we shall confine ourselves to those which reveal best his critical attitude in later years and his relationship with the literary circles of Berlin in the days following the war. Thus in "Über eine Theater-Kritik" Arnim gives his opinion of Dorothea Schlegel's criticism of Oehlenschläger's *Ludlam-Höhle* and of the tasks of criticism in general. With bitterness he scourges the absurdity and vanity of this type of ignorant, destructive criticism, in which a number of his contemporaries indulged. These critics lack a genuine feeling for art, which Arnim defines as the "splendid intuitive knowledge how to grasp at once the essential, the inner urge of the artist, and to judge how far he succeeded."[20] They object to everything new and modern, and to everything traditional. Praise they consider superfluous, and in the end they discuss with great glee that which they can blame and deplore. The more such evil criticism increases, the more vanity and boredom will increase and the more hopeless and senile the state of society will become. Arnim closes his epistle with a poem entitled "Literargeschichte" on the theme, "Formerly people only talked and gossiped, but now most of them write, and writing promotes audacity, for one cannot contradict ink." The accord is given in the first two stanzas:

> Sassen sonst die alten Basen
> Bei dem Kaffee rings im Kreise,
> Dünkten sie sich auch schon weise,
> Und vergassen drein zu blasen;
> Doch wenn sie verbrannt die Zungen,

[19] *Ibid.*, p. 106.   [20] *Unbekannte Aufsätze*, p. 35.

Kam Vernunft im Widersprechen;
Rächte alle Mißhandlungen,
Sonst da blieb es noch beim Sprechen.

Statt Gesellschaft kommt jetzt Zeitung,
Wird beim Kaffee still gelesen
Und es stäubt der krit'sche Besen
Jede voll in der Verbreitung,
Bis nun jede eingesehen:
Daß sie dies auch könne leisten,
Ohne etwas zu verstehen,
Jetzt ach! schreiben schon die Meisten.[21]

Another attack on modern criticism was his review of Müllner's *Ährenlese neuerer Kritik*. Arnim entitled this discussion "Ährenlese auf dem Felde älterer Kritik,"[22] for he considered Müllner's attempt to collect abstracts of new criticism as unnecessary. It would be more important by far to collect critical writings from older periodicals, which cannot be found so easily in libraries and may completely disappear. Thus he called attention to the fact that Goethe in *Aus meinem Leben* had mentioned that he used to contribute to Schlosser's *Frankfurter Gelehrte Anzeigen* of the year 1772. It is, says Arnim, most important that these superior essays and reviews be saved for posterity, for they illustrate that criticism undergoes few changes throughout the ages and is always excellent whenever a great mind applies itself to it.[23] As examples he quotes from the *Frankfurter Anzeigen*, Goethe on "Klopstock's Oden"[24] and Goethe's opinion of translations.[25]

These two essays of Arnim, of the year 1818, "Über eine Theater-Kritik" and "Ährenlese auf dem Felde älterer Kritik," show

[21] *Ibid.*, pp. 35-7.
[22] *Ges.*, p. 335; 1818 (not in Geiger's collection).
[23] *Ibid.*, p. 335; 1818; "Ährenlese auf dem Felde älterer Kritik."
[24] *Idem,* and Goethe in the *Frankfurter Gelehrte Anzeigen*, p. 57 (1772): " 'Klopstocks Oden.' Bei einem Werke der Ewigkeit gilt weder Lob noch Tadel. Hier steht es! ist alles was der Liebhaber und Verehrer am Altare sagen kann. Weg also mit dem geschwätzigen Cicerone, der uns Gefühl an den Fingern herzählt und den Blitzstrahl des Genies mit der Hand greifen lehrt." Goethe's contributions to the *Gelehrte Anzeigen* have now been identified, and have been republished many times. Cf. Max Morris, *Der junge Goethe.*
[25] *Ibid.*, p. 766: "Es ist uns schon lange ein unerklärbares Phänomen gewesen, wie Leute, die so ganz ohne Geschmack die Alten lesen, sich einfallen lassen können, Übersetzungen davon zu machen."

that he had not abandoned his earlier views and principles in respect to criticism. In spite of the fact that he frequented the literary salons of the metropolis and contributed to many insignificant and second-rate journals and almanacs, he nevertheless did not lower his requirements or cease to raise a warning voice. He felt that the incongruities and excesses in criticism had taken on more dangerous forms and were more widely practised than a decade before, when he had struggled with the unhealthy conditions in criticism in his *Zeitung für Einsiedler*. His healthy realism now made him turn away from such literature as the *Theater-Kritik of Dorothea Schlegel* (cf. below), or the philistine literature Merkel was offering in his journal *Der Freimütige,* or the dramatic productions of Iffland and Ernst Raupach at the Royal Theater in Berlin. He left this branch of literature, which did not even attempt to ennoble and improve *belles lettres,* and delved more deeply into realistic topics, political and economic questions, short stories, travelogues, and biographical reviews.

The scope of his writings on literature for the *Gesellschafter* reflects very well the breadth of Arnim's interests in his later years. In one issue he published hitherto unknown letters of the Karschin, praising highly this poetess of the people and stating that many, like himself, wished that the first and original versions of her poems had been preserved rather than later ones which show the imprint of artificial improvements by her scholarly friends. Truly, he adds, natural poetry like hers is something rare in Germany.[26] In another number he discusses the willful and absurd destruction of valuable documents, such as happened, for example, around 1800 through the closing of the monasteries and their libraries: this at a time when people should have known better than to destroy such literary treasures.[27] Or again, he relates interesting incidents from Otto Brüggeman's life because it touched upon Goethe's *Westöstlicher Divan.*[28]

[26] *Unbekannte Aufsätze,* p. 56: "In einem Volke wie das unsere, wo diese Fertigkeit nicht, wie in Italien, künstlich anerzogen und ausgebildet wird, setzt es allerdings eine Eigentümlichkeit voraus, des Besten gerade auf diesem Wege, in dieser Art überraschender Begeisterung—als plötzlicher Einfall fertig ausgesprochen—sich bewußt zu werden."

[27] *Ibid.,* p. 95.   [28] *Ibid.,* p. 43.

Not until he began making contributions to the *Gesellschafter* did Arnim take cognizance of Sir Walter Scott in the form of essays and reviews. Henriette Schubart translated in 1817 the third volume of Scott's *Minstrelsy of the Scottish Border*. As early as July, 1803, while on his "grand tour" in England, Arnim had become acquainted with this collection, soon after its first publication.[29] It proved to be one of the stimulating influences which called forth the *Wunderhorn*.[30] Arnim now confirms this in his discussion of the Schubart translation. He goes on to say that in the revival of interest in poetry of the people it is to the credit of Scott that he made these old poems more intelligible by means of his historical introduction, and also brought them closer to his contemporaries by adding his own ballads from Scottish legendary material.[31] He speaks also of Shakespeare's relation to Scottish subject-matter and the similarities in art and spirit where the peoples of Europe touch each other, pointing out that the most tragic of Shakespeare's dramas, *Macbeth,* was based on Scottish history. He finds it surprising that Shakespeare did not write more Scottish tragedies, and also that he did not utilize more in his *Macbeth* the strong family inter-relationships and traditions prevalent in Scotland. The similarities in the spiritual and artistic life of the people of Europe (*Volksgesinnung*) could be revealed by a comparison of the German with the old Danish heroic legends made available in Grimm's translation. Kinship could also be traced with the modern-Greek robber tales, which had been collected by Freiherr von Haxthausen, though not yet published.[32] Arnim regarded Scott as the man who had given voice to the English-Scotch *Volksgesinnung,* who had therefore accomplished precisely the same as he, Arnim, had tried to do for the German *Volksgesinnung* with the publication of the *Wunderhorn.*

Scott's *Waverly* appeared in 1814 and the first part of Arnim's *Kronenwächter* in 1817. In its well-rounded, realistic portrayals, this work shows that Arnim was not Scott's, but rather Goethe's apprentice. This he emphasized in a notation to his short story *Die Ehrenschmiede. Novelle aus den Denkwürdigkeiten eines Naturforschers.* Here he states that as a poet he had stepped on the

---

[29] Arnim-Brentano, p. 95; Arnim's letter to Brentano, July 5, 1803.
[30] *Unbekannte Aufsätze*, p. 80.   [31] *Ibid.*   [32] *Ibid.*

fertile soil of natural poetry before Scott discovered the Scottish Highlands.[33]

In 1822 Arnim wrote an extensive review of a series of Scott's publications.[34] They included translations of Scott's *Waverly* (Leipzig, 1822) and *The Pirate* (three translations, Berlin, Leipzig, Berlin, 1822), the original *The Pirate* (Edinburgh, 1822), and a novel by K. H. L. Reinhardt, *Die Circe von Glas-Llyn. Ein Roman nach Walter Scott,* which was one of the numerous contemporary imitations of Walter Scott in subject-matter and style. This discussion differs from all of Arnim's previous reviews in its precision, severity, and its approach to modern, critical standards. It is surprising to note how carefully Arnim discusses details of these translations, and with what assurance he appraises the endeavors, successes, and failures of the translators,[35] revealing an intimate knowledge of the English language and of Sir Walter Scott. Whereas he has nothing but praise for Scott the lyric poet, he criticizes him vigorously as a writer of prose.[36] He compares his work with Goethe's and condemns Scott for wordiness and for repetition in the construction of plots. Arnim finds that his later novels are devoid of new themes and that they lack suspense. This applies in particular to the *Pirate.* Here Arnim finds no confirmation of Virgil's "Nova progenies caelo demittitur alto,' for several characters in *The Pirate* are reminiscent of similar ones in *Waverly* and *Kenilworth.* The plot is neither novel nor interesting, and the whole is successful only in its portrayal of local *mores.* To be sure, *Kenilworth* is also unduly long, but it is full of interest, has suspense in the plot, and an interesting character-development, all of which *The Pirate* lacks. In *Die Circe von Glas-Llyn; Ein Roman nach Walter Scott,* the author, K. H. L. Reinhardt, has caught nothing worth while from the Scottish master. It lacks style and suspense, it is not romantic but obscure, and is much like a mediocre play acted by ordinary comedians.

Arnim's lively interest in English literature continued. We have

[33] Werke, II, 3.

[34] *Literatur-Blatt,* hrsg. von Adolph Müllner 1822, pp. 250-2.

[35] *Ibid.;* Arnim reproached severely the translator of *Waverly* for inexcusable mistakes in his mother tongue; but he praised all three translations of *The Pirate,* that by Spiker being perhaps the best because he preserved very carefully the style and explained unknown words and objects.

[36] *Ibid.;* cf. also Arnim's *Landhausleben; Werke,* XIX, 11-12.

evidence of this in 1829, in a study *Hamlet und Jacob*,[37] published in Fouqué's *Berlinische Blätter für deutsche Frauen*. This journal affords a typical picture of the decline of Romanticism. Its name and still more the articles it contains suggest that one treads here the slippery ground of aesthetic rodomontades (*ästhetisierendes Geflunker*).[38] Arnim's article is, however, a notable exception. His other contributions to this journal consisted of travelogues.[39]

In this study our critic attempts to show that Shakespeare's motivation in writing *Hamlet* lay in the English political problems of his time. The question of succession to the English throne after the death of Queen Elizabeth was uppermost in everybody's mind. The queen herself gave the solution during the last days of her life. According to Arnim's interpretation, this painful question, which dominated for years the political life of English as a "to be or not to be," as well as the doubts which tore at the soul of James I and his sinister fate, made a great impression on Shakespeare. The duty to avenge his mother and father created a severer problem for James than was Hamlet's. The theory that *Hamlet* was an acute, timely problem explains in Arnim's opinion why this great tragedy is so unusual and so entirely different from all others by Shakespeare. The poet has given expression here to all the anxiety for England's future under the reign of a doubtful successor like James I, as well as to the ease of mind that followed many years of watchful waiting, when the successor turned out to be better than his reputation. At the same time, Shakespeare voices the apprehension that an ill fate may trouble this successor, who is given to contemplation rather than action at a time when ruthless action was demanded of a ruler. Thus the Danish fable was but the core around which Shakespeare built the greatest of his dramas.[40]

This theory about the origin of *Hamlet* had suggested itself to

[37] *Berlinische Blätter für deutsche Frauen*, I, 1-12. This study is not found in Mallon's *Arnim-Bibliographie*, but it is assigned to Arnim by Houben and Walzel in *Zeitschriften der Romantik*, Vol. I.

[38] Houben and Walzel, *Zeitschriften der Romantik*, I, p. XIII.

[39] *Berlinische Blätter für deutsche Frauen*, IX, 1-19, 107-138.

[40] *Ibid.*, pp. 1-12: "Die dänische Fabel ist ein Schiff, Shakespeare ist der Steuermann, aber der Sturm, der es treibt, gehört weder den Dänen, noch dem Shakespeare, sondern der englisch-schottischen Geschichte."

Arnim during his studies of Mary of Scotland. He wanted to write a drama *Maria Stuart;* but, unlike Schiller's, it was to include not only the last events of her fateful life, but also all the earlier ones, such as the death of Rizzio and her husband Darnley, the murder of Bothwell, the strange life of her son James, his knowledge of the plot of Essex, the death of Elizabeth, and James' coronation in London. Now, however, after discovering and studying *Hamlet,* Arnim abandons his plan, for it would, he says, be "like writing the Iliad after Homer."[41]

Like Goethe, Arnim recognized Hamlet's complicated character. He was a highly gifted youth who was not at the mercy of his strong emotions, but rather examined and weighed them before reaching a decision. When two equally strong motives and waves of feeling pulled him in opposite directions, he might delay action, but was not weak-willed. In passing, Arnim also mentions that Shakespeare possibly portrayed other contemporaries in *Hamlet,* Essex perhaps as Laertes. This, however, he regards as unimportant. It is not his intention to analyze *Hamlet* by tearing it to pieces, but rather add to its interpretation and understanding by showing its close relationship to the age of the poet.

A year earlier, in 1828, Arnim had published in the *Monatliche Beiträge zur Geschichte dramatischer Kunst und Literatur* a somewhat similar study, an attempt to investigate the relationship between the stage and the courts or ruling houses of Germany and to determine how far the latter influenced the German stage. It was his intention to show the effect of the much admired foreign art on German stage life during the Eighteenth Century, and how the stage was "Germanized" under Frederick the Great. He called this extensive study "Sammlungen zur Theatergeschichte"[42] and wrote to Wilhelm Grimm that he had labored hard on it. He had had to look through many business papers of his father, the late "directeur des spectacles" in Berlin. The study had been received

[41] *Ibid.,* "Ein unbequemes Gefühl, als ob ich mich schon in einem bekannten Theaterstück befände, das ich nur halb vergessen, störte mich bei der Ausführung, bis mir endlich Jakob, wie ich ihn mir dachte, wie er geleibt und gelebt, als Hamlet im schwarzen Kleide erschien."

[42] *Monatliche Beiträge zur Geschichte dramatischer Kunst und Literatur,* hrsg. von Holtei, 1828, pp. 1-42.

by the public with great curiosity and interest, for he had given
a picture of Frederick the Great as it evolved from the documents,
not simply a generalization.[43] This study, indeed, reveals Arnim
in a new role, as historian of the Berlin stage at the time of
Frederick the Great. The work is also noteworthy as a romanticist's criticism of the stage and its management.

A decade earlier, in 1818, German stage management had been
criticized by Arnim and Brentano in a series of notes, "Briefe
über das neue Theater,"[44] in which they attacked the theater of
Iffland and Kotzebue. Arnim's "Sammlungen zur Theatergeschichte" in its critical aspects must be regarded as an outgrowth
and continuation of these fragmentary "Briefe." He took great
pains to analyze and emphasize the importance of proper stage
management, in which, he says, the German stage had failed completely in the past. The evil was not completely remedied on the
contemporary stage. The fault lay with the stage manager, in so
far as this poorly defined office demanded the impossible or that
which only a genius could fulfill. Hence there were few or no good
stage managers in Germany.

A three-fold task was demanded of this individual. First, he
must serve art and therefore be artistic and imaginative, must possess "den freiesten Kunstaufschwung des Geistes." Secondly, he
must be a business manager and therefore be economical and
practical. Third, too often he must be a polite courtier who has
to pretend compliance and still carry through artistic plans of a
high order. Naturally such a "dreiartiger, dreieiniger and dreibei-
niger Musenvorsteher"[45] is seldom found, and for this reason too
often the princes were their own stage managers, which proved
to be a "happy" solution, for now the stage manager no longer
needed to be a courtier! Even the second requirement could be
dispensed with, for the prince was wealthy. Only the first, artistic
talent, was necessary. Arnim goes on to show ironically how under
these circumstances criticism is silenced, for everybody feels in
duty bound to display enthusiasm; the decline of the theater is cer-

[43] Arnim-Grimm, p. 574.
[44] *Wünschelrute*, hrsg. von H. Straube und F. P. von Holmthal, Göttingen, 1818,
pp. 80-90, 93, 123, 128, 134-135.
[45] *Monatliche Beiträge zur Geschichte dramatischer Kunst und Literatur*, p. 12.

tain, even if the whimsical prince does not throw aside his "stage duties" like a tiresome toy. With indignation Arnim asks whether the theater has now to remain in a subordinated position, like a whist party, like a barrel-organ.[46] To this must be added another deplorable factor, namely, that there was a lack of good German plays during the Eighteenth Century. There was no poetic freedom, and nothing novel ever arose to create a furor. Nobody thought of encouraging the development of national talent, but the theatrically inclined princes resorted to foreign plays and called on French actors and Italian singers, not realizing that the foreign examples might smother native art and talent,[47] native taste and language. Arnim admits, however, that foreign artists are not always detrimental to native art, and as examples mentions that Gluck and Mozart had raised French and Italian opera to a higher level. One may assume, therefore, that Arnim had the feeling that real genius is not smothered by "foreign influences" and that art is mutually stimulated.

Frederick the Great, Arnim continues, like other German princely sponsors of the theater, gave his support only to the foreign stage. But the wars and victories during his reign and the internal governmental policies of this great Prussian king awakened national feeling among the Prussians in their own worth, and this in turn wakened an interest in native art and opposition to the French theater. These forces grew silently in spite of the fact that Frederick continued to support only the French theater in Berlin. Several stage managers put on German plays, disregarding financial sacrifices. Friendly criticism encouraged them and called attention to weaknesses in the French stage and praised the English drama. Only the fact that the public, of its own inclination and initiative, began to frequent the German theater more and more, can explain that the latter in 1775 in Berlin became more of a financial success than the French theater, which had

---

[46] *Monatliche Beiträge*, p. 23: "Soll nun ein Schauspiel etwas Untergeordnetes sein und bleiben wie eine Whistpartie, soll es wie eine Spieluhr das Wohlbekannte ableiern, ohne durch neue Strebungen Herz und Geist zu beunruhigen?"

[47] *Ibid.*, p. 33: "Daß jene fremde Richtung eigenen Geschmack und Sprache verderben, großen Talenten den Raum zu ihrer Entwicklung verschließen konnte, war jener Zeit fremd, jene Fürsten meinten wohlwollend, gute Vorbilder zu eigener Entwicklung aufgestellt zu haben."

the support of Frederick the great and the large French colony.[48]
Yet, in spite of this victorious power of national interest on the
part of the common people, the Prussian king did not change his
personal attitude towards the German theater, as Arnim notes
with some embitterment, yes, he even declared all its actors
incompetent. On the other hand, during these years the king very
rarely visited the very excellent French theater. Arnim doubted
that the reason was solely disgust with the petty quarrels among
actors and actresses; he thought rather that the king must have
felt an unconscious weariness of the French theater.

Providence spoke the last word. The Bavarian war of succession in 1778 threatened to become dangerous for Prussia. Expenses had to be retrenched and Frederick decided to cut considerably the allotment for the French theater in the budget. This
had a slow but deadly effect. Eight years later the German theater,
by that time a state-sponsored enterprise, was able to move into
the new royal opera house. In the end, Arnim concludes, providence and fate, or rather the will of the people decided, and
Frederick the Great, who was but a tool, had to carry out his
predetermined mission.[49] Not out of love for the German stage
did he send away the foreigners, but because he had become tired
of the expenses and monotony. Thus "Sans Souci," the name of
Frederick's favorite palace, applies here also: we can be without
care, for the German theater will live, Arnim concludes optimistically.

When one looks back over the writings discussed in this chapter,
one notices above all the increased attention which Arnim pays
to facts and minute details. He is no longer the roaming romanticist who can afford to disregard reality. In the Walter Scott
review he even pointed out minor mistakes in translation, some-

[48] *Ibid.*, p. 37: "Während das deutsche Theater über 21,000 Rthlr. jährlich ein-
nimmt und viel mehr noch einnehmen könnte, wenn das Haus Raum gewährte, sinkt
die Einnahme im neuen französischen Schauspielhause von 17,000 Rthlr. auf 11,000
Rthlr., und doch muß jeder eingestehen, daß es nie so wohl besetzt mit ausge-
zeichneten Talenten, so dekoriert, so bekleidet erschienen sei."

[49] *Ibid.*, p. 41: "Über Friedrich dem Großen als Stifter und als Vernichter des
französischen Theaters waltete der gute Genius seines Volkes wie über alle großen
Führer der Völker, er aber mußte hier wie in so vielen Fällen tun und erfüllen, wozu
er bestimmt war, ohne diese seine Bestimmung zu kennen."

thing a romanticist would not bother about, one can rest assured. Again, in the essay last discussed he furnishes figures and data about the theaters in Berlin which he has collected, and he incorporates documents of his father, the "directeur des spectacles," all of which goes to prove that here a romanticist's path leads at history and literature from an entirely different angle. Arnim had been interested in recording historic events concerning the arts, but his approach had been a different one. In his *Zeitung für Einsiedler* and in *Halle und Jerusalem,* for instance, he looked at history and literature from an entirely different angle, Arnim now feels that the censored literature and press of the day could not be regarded as historically reliable, and that it was therefore his task to give a more faithful—and thus more realistic—treatment of the past. Repeatedly he emphasized this point in the reviews of Blücher and Scharnhorst to be discussed below.

Prior to the politically restless days of 1830, literary societies and aesthetic-tea circles, the "discutier et debatier cliques," gained great popularity. Such a "Biedermeyer" group had gathered around Varnhagen von Ense. Arnim and Bettina were occasional guests there. While Arnim, the Prussian aristocrat, and Bettina with her background of Frankfort and Italy, already showed marked differences in personality, Arnim and the strict, pedantic Varnhagen, and even more the restless, extravagant Rahel, were opposite poles. Yet all four came to know each other very well during the last years of Arnim's life, and later, the widowed Bettina and Rahel, the two most prominent women of the intellectual society of Berlin, became close friends, so close indeed, that Bettina, as we have seen, asked Varnhagen to organize Arnim's literary remains. Varnhagen's opinion of Arnim in his memoirs must be taken with a grain of salt, however, for he was biased in favor of Rahel and did not do justice to Arnim and Bettina. Varnhagen was a very prolific writer, yet without originality or poetic imagination; he was a typical representative of the insipid, lifeless literature in Berlin after the Wars of Liberation. To write biographies was his predilection. Most of them were published in a series of *Biographische Denkmäler.*

Arnim, his friend, was also interested in biographical works and reviewed three of Varnhagen's sketches.[50] These reviews are not of particular value as literary documents because Arnim, in most cases, only summarizes the contents, emphasizing the historical importance of the hero and neglecting all questions relating to the literary value of the book in question.

His first review, "Fürst Blücher von Wahlstadt," could still be published in the *Gesellschafter*. Here he voices in the very first lines his strong indignation at the censorship of the press in Germany, which distorts history, and he points to England as the only ideal country, where everything that is published in newspapers and current journals is true and can serve future generations as reliable documents.[51] Varnhagen's biography of Blücher Arnim finds incomplete because of the censorship, and he hopes that some day a biography of Blücher will be written which will become a valuable folkbook, like that of the knights of King Arthur's table, and which will expose freely all the sins of politics and the forces which brought so much suffering to Europe and tried to destroy the brave, freedom-loving German nation. Blücher, as Varnhagen in his introduction has emphasized, was the hero of the people, in whom the demoniacal forces of the masses found expression at that crucial moment when the fate of whole nations was at stake and civilization grasped desperately at blind forces of nature for salvation.[52]

In his review he elaborates this conception of Blücher. He calls attention to the fact that the biographer, perhaps because of the censorship, has told too little of the discontent of Blücher's soul in later years, discontent that the noble hopes of the titanic age were not fully realized after the victory of arms. Outwardly the

[50] *Ges.*, 1826, pp. 144-148: L. A. von Arnim, Besprechung von K. A. Varnhagen von Ense, *Biographische Denkmäler* III, Fürst Blücher von Wahlstadt. *Blätter für literarische Unterhaltung*, Nr. 197, 785-6. 1830: L. A. v. Arnim, Besprechung von K. A. Varnhagen von Ense, *Denkwürdigkeiten des Philosophen und Arztes Johann Benjamin Erhard*, Stuttgart, 1830. *Ibid.*, Nr. 213, 849-851. 1830: L. A. v. Arnim, Besprechung von Varnhagen von Ense, *Biographische Denkmäler* V, *Leben des Grafen von Zinzendorf*, Berlin, 1830.

[51] *Ges.*, 1826, pp. 144-8: "In England mag es leicht genug sein, über Zeitgenossen zu schreiben, denn alles Bedeutende, von allen freundlichen und feindlichen Gestirnen beleuchtet, stellt sich in seinen frischen Schöpfungen unverhüllt dar; die Zeitschriften sind die Jahrbücher der Weltgeschichte."

[52] Karl August Varnhagen von Ense, *Biographische Denkmäler*, III. Fürst Blücher von Wahlstadt. Einleitung, 3.

hero was very reserved, severe and abrupt, but this coldness covered a highly sensitive, emotional, and religious soul. He was very intelligent, and knew how to handle people. Arnim felt called upon to add a few personal observations to Varnhagen's excellent description (page 588) of the hero's external appearances. Thus, for instance, he read in Blücher's face, in the expression of his eyes, an unusual, secretive attraction which arrested the attention of everybody, even of those who did not know him. It was as if his eyes knew of the final victory.[53] This expression was entirely different from the abysmal, desperate depth noted in Napoleon's eyes, even at a time when no one could yet surmise his final fate. Perhaps it was strange also that Blücher's whole external appearance was so singular. Nobody resembled him in the slightest, as if, Arnim says, nature had created such a man only once and then broke the mould.

Arnim's other reviews of Varnhagen's biographies were published, as noted above, in Brockhaus' *Blätter für literarische Unterhaltung*. This periodical was a typical "Biedermeier" product. In fear of censorship, practically all articles and reports were printed anonymously under *chiffres*. The collaborators are today considered rather mediocre. Arnim began to contribute to the periodical after 1826, when he had become convinced of the intellectual impartiality of the editorial board.[54] Recently Mallon's researches have established the total number of his contributions to this journal[55] as thirty-one. It had been founded by Kotzebue in Weimar as the *Literarisches Wochenblatt*. After his death the publisher, W. Hoffmann, became editor. With the sixth volume it was acquired by the publisher Friedrich A. Brockhaus in Leipsic, and continued to be issued by that firm until 1900. Soon after this transfer to Leipsic difficulties arose with the censor and the journal was prohibited in Prussia, but shortly thereafter it was permitted again under a new title, *Literarisches Conversations-*

[53] *Ges.*, 1826, pp. 144-8. "Es erschien uns nämlich in seinem Antlitz ein geheimnisvoller Reiz, wie eine Ahnung, daß diese mächtigen bedeutsamen Augen durchaus nicht im gemeinsamen Laufe der Dinge untergehen könnten."

[54] Arnim-Grimm, p. 544; Arnim's letter to Wilhelm Grimm, January 16, 1825.

[55] Otto Mallon, "A. v. Arnim's Beiträge zum 'Literarisches Conversations-Blatt,' und zu den 'Blättern für literarische Unterhaltung' (1823-31)," *Preuss. Jahrb.*, 1931, Bd. I, 44-68.

blatt. A second conflict with the censorship in 1826 brought still another and final title, *Blätter für literarische Unterhaltung.*

Arnim reviewed for this periodical the biography of another Prussian hero, Scharnhorst,[56] of anonymous authorship. As in the Blücher review, the critic deplores the evils of the censorship, which alone is responsible in this case for the anonymous biographer's giving only a very general picture of the unusual Scharnhorst. He has touched only very briefly on Scharnhorst's relationship to other generals and contemporaries and to the unhappy events of the year 1806. Hardly anything is included of Scharnhorst's notes, diaries, letters, or concerning the motives which would explain his personality and influence.

Another more extensive review of Varnhagen which Arnim wrote for the *Blätter für literarische Unterhaltung* is that of the biography of Graf Zinzendorf.[57] This review is rather interesting, because here Arnim makes his own observations on Zinzendorf as educator and on the literary and cultural activities of his religious sect and community, the Herrenhuter Gemeinde, which had been founded by Zinzendorf. Arnim praises Varnhagen's biography as a valuable addition to existing books about Zinzendorf, because it describes him very admirably as a statesman. Varnhagen had compared Zinzendorf as a religious personality with Lavater and Stilling. Arnim in turn draws a parallel with Pestalozzi, with regard to education, and emphasizes that Zinzendorf started a new, milder, and more humane movement, which no longer looked on learning as the only aim.[58] He discusses a few more characteristics of this unusual man. Zinzendorf was always a great philanthropist, in spite of the fact that he did not possess great wealth. Perhaps it was because he gave people faith and self confidence, Arnim thinks.

Like his contemporaries, the critic also found it extraordinay that Zinzendorf after his visit to America renounced all his titles and privileges. This does not appear to meet with Arnim's approval. Even though he recognizes the noble religious motive, the brotherhood of mankind, similar to the equality of men that had

---

[56] *Blätter für literarische Unterhaltung,* Nr. 303-4, 1830, 1209-10, 113-14.
[57] *Ibid.,* Nr. 213, 1830, 849-851.
[58] *Ibid.,* p. 849.

been fought for in revolutions, Arnim thinks that both, Zinzendorf and the political revolutionist, lost sight of the past in the dream of a future which can never be brought to reality. Examining the literary and cultural activities of the Herrenhuter community, the critic comes to the conclusion that of the many good hymns which originated there, none is really excellent, and that the community has thus far made no really original contribution to art and literature. Only the dissolved communities which settled in the Wetterau have made a remarkable approach to poetry with their emotional hymns, an outgrowth of Zinzendorf's "Morgenländische Spielerei mit Lieblingsliedern des Glaubens."[59]

The last review which was published before Arnim's death was that of Houwald's *Seeräuber*.[60] As if he had a premonition that the days of his own life were numbered, Arnim in this review takes account of the failures and successes of Houwald's life, and perhaps of a poet's life in general, including his own. Here he comes to dwell on the bitter fact that the world always denies the recognition due to greatness.

What he has to say about *Die Seeräuber* may be briefly mentioned first. The subject-matter of Houwald's tragedy abounds in highly dramatic moments and theatrical effects, such as stealing of the brides, the fire and seizure of the pirate's castle, the return of the brides, the excitement of the masses at the death sentences, and so on. But Houwald did not make use of these dramatic moments; they are not enacted on the stage, but only described in monologues and otherwise. One asks why? Because the discouraged Houwald knew that he probably would not be able to find a producer; he therefore adapted this dramatic material only for the reading public. The dictators of the stage resort almost exclusively to translations; foreign plays with foreign customs and ideas, foreign characters and foreign riots, are performed. Arnim mentions still another point in explaining why the dramatic moments are not more fully exploited. The author in this play shows a certain tendency towards moralizing and generalizing (*moralische Casuistik*) in emotional scenes. This philosophizing is, how-

[59] *Ibid.*, p. 851.
[60] *Blätter für literarische Unterhaltung*, 1830, Nr. 361, pp. 1441-3. *Die Seeräuber. Ein Trauerspiel in 5 Aufzügen von Ernst von Houwald* (Leipzig: Göschen, 1830).

ever, a natural outgrowth of the plot and action; he did not set out deliberately to write a moralizing play.

Houwald's fate as a poet had been a very unhappy one, sadder than Arnim's, who as we have seen, after the War of Liberation had to retreat to the country in order to earn a livelihood. When, therefore, in this review the writer with bitter irony arraigns the world and Germany in particular for injustice to its poets, he is most likely voicing resentment at his own disappointments. Embittered complaints like the following recall those of the "Jungdeutschen":

> While in France it has become customary only since the Revolution, in Germany it is an old custom that poets are exploited for labors which others could do. To give examples: Wieland had to become a tutor for princes; Lessing, a librarian in a small town; Goethe, a minister of state; Schiller, a teacher of history".[61]

Arnim complains that there is always money for superfluous buildings, fashions, acrobats, singers, etc., but never for poets; poetry is a breadless art. There may be some truth in the argument that the material cannot affect the spiritual, that there must be "art for art's sake," and that the poet finds his own satisfactions independent of the world, as Houwald expresses it so effectively:

> Die Rose will nur blühen,
> Der Vogel singt nur sich,
> Drum blühe du und singe,
> Ist's auch allein für dich![62]

But Arnim warns that indifference towards the poets will have a detrimental effect on the nation as a whole. There is dire need that publications and copyrights be better protected so that literary creations may remain the poet's and the people's own; that the stage do something to encourage native talent, so that most playwrights may not have to adapt their plays for only a *reading public*. Should there not be room for every talent and capacity in a well ordered human society, Arnim asks, so that it may drive roots and bear fruit?

[61] *Ibid.,* p. 1441
[62] *Ibid.,* p. 1442, cf. also *Berliner Musenalmanach,* 1831.

Arnim had not found such a well ordered human society among his contemporaries. His best years he had spent performing the duties of a farmer, which left him little time for concentration on poetic and literary subjects. Yet his spirit was unbroken and in the numerous essays, reviews, and literary notes of his spare time he continued to preach on his old text: Back to an intuitive approach to art, and art based on the historical and national wealth of the people. Now, a few days before his death, still in a challenging mood, he concluded this, his last review, with Houwald's bold words:

> Ich brauche kein Gebet von fremder Lippe,
> Denn mein Gedank' ist schon Gebet, ich brauche
> Den Priester nicht, denn ich bin selbst dein Priester,
> Mein Will' ist rein! Du hast ihn, Herr, geläutert.
> Und im Vertraun, daß ich dich ganz verstanden,
> Weshalb du mich die dunkle Bahn geführt,
> Glaub' ich, er muß dir wohlgefällig sein![63]

[63] *Blätter für literarische Unterhaltung,* 1930, p. 1443.

ARNIM'S POSITION IN THE HISTORY OF CRITICISM

Literary critics may be divided into two groups. The members of one of these, through their vast range of information in the historical field, their clear and logical reasoning, and their brilliant style, have been able to guide contemporary poets and prose writers into new paths and to make important contributions to the theory of literary genres and the methodology of criticism. Such were Lessing and August Wilhelm Schlegel, who formulated successively the ideas of rationalism and romanticism in Germany. It is in another direction that we must seek the importance of the second group of critics. This includes many writers whose chief importance was in the creative rather than the judicial office. Such critics are idealists and their attitude is an outgrowth of genius ruled by emotion. Their opinions on literature have their greatest value as interpretations of the writers' personalities and of their contributions in other fields of production. As idealists they project their view of life into their discussions of literature, thus making a fuller revelation of themselves and of the struggles and aspirations of the generation to which they belong.

Goethe and Herder were outstanding representatives of this type of critic and it is to this group that Achim von Arnim must be assigned. His impulsive, idealistic *Weltanschauung,* which found expression in a long series of productions in the field of romantic poetry and fiction, could not adapt itself to processes of analytical reasoning and logical categorizing which are necessary for the establishment of theories of general validity. Arnim was first and foremost a *Dichter* and his judgment of literary sources and achievements flowed from the same fountain of intuitive genius as his *Dichtung.* His critical style, even in the later, more realistic years, bears everywhere the stamp of romantic imagination. This makes his work at times difficult to understand, and it may be added, none too easy to translate into English. Often his meaning must be *felt,* and certainly a part of the importance of his contribution lies in the enthusiastic and fanciful manner in which his ideas are presented.

Nevertheless, Arnim has a significant place in the history of German criticism. A younger son of the great idealistic generation, he came very early under the influence of Goethe and Herder, with whose work he became well acquainted as a student, through the comradeship of Clements Brentano, and while on his "grand tour." How strong the influence of Goethe's personality and writings was, has been shown in the foregoing pages. While we have abundant evidence of this dependence on Goethe, specific references to Herder are almost entirely lacking. Nevertheless, like others of the younger romantic group, he was strongly affected by the ideas of this great philosopher of the humanistic age. It can hardly be denied that the conceptions which guided the editorial work of young Arnim on *Des Knaben Wunderhorn* and his critical attitude throughout life were deeply rooted in Herder's spiritual and historical approach to literature.

In his early critical writing Arnim shows himself a progressive. This appears first in his essays on physical science, where we have seen him to be a protagonist of a dynamic, monistic view of nature's processes. Later, it reveals itself in his attitude toward art. Here he supports the Schlegel brothers and Tieck in the fight against the wretched state of contemporary criticism, the same struggle against cliquish narrowness, pedantry, and shallow gossip that had been waged a little earlier by Schiller and Goethe in their *Xenienkampf*. Arnim's concepts of art, then, developed, as we have seen, under the influence of the political events of the first decade of the new century. His national feeling was fanned into flame when Prussia's glory was annihilated at Jena and Germany lay prostrate under Napoleon's heel.

This enthusiasm becomes outspoken with the establishment of the *Zeitung für Einsiedler* in 1808. Here he voices emphatically the idea that art must be an expression of the creative genius of a people, for only that literature is truly great which is imbued with a national, popular spirit. Arnim is now firmly convinced that literary schools, such as classicism and romanticism, have outlived their day and that the need now arises for a literature that voices a unified German spirit. Imitation of Hellenistic culture must cease, for Germany can attain to the artistic heights of the ancients only if she becomes conscious of the native resources in her glorious past. Arnim now assigns to literary criticism the task of making the reader acquainted with the best creations of this popular spirit, of unearthing and making known the treasures of a mighty past, of re-creating the "remote and unknown." Only when the critics shall have fulfilled this great mission can Germans expect a great national literature.

This is the doctrine that underlies the critical work of Arnim in the years that followed. While these ideas were in the main those of the younger generation of romanticists, Arnim has nevertheless a peculiar and striking position. To be sure, certain similarities with his romantic contemporaries are obvious. In family background and the force of the national ideal one may group him most closely with Heinrich von Kleist. With Tieck he shared the romantic idealization of the German past. He has much in common with Görres and Brentano, but stands apart from these, his personal friends, in his North German militant Protestantism and Pan-Germanism, which were an organic outgrowth from the experiences and ideals of the race of Brandenburg aristocrats from which he sprang. Undoubtedly he learned much from the Schlegels, and he confesses it. He certainly uses a very similar method of approach to literature to that which marks A. W. Schlegel's general critical procedure, especially in the latter's famous series of Berlin lectures, *Über schöne Literatur und Kunst,* 1801-1803, a programmatic criticism which seems to foster new ideas by means of a critical evaluation of a work of *belles lettres.* However, he differed from Schlegel in important respects. Arnim's criticism is programmatic, but for him the "program" is not an exact system or a set of dogmatic rules. It is rather an enthusiasm and a hopeful vision of an ideal artistic future.

This serves Arnim as a basis for a highly emotional approach. He scarcely ever analyzes single traits and features, but reacts to the work as a whole. His programmatic spirit prefers to select for consideration works which are in conformity with its conception of the purpose of literature and makes these constructive for

the world of art as the critic envisions it. Thus, it is noteworthy
that Arnim rarely writes about works that do not interest him
personally. The writings of the physicist Ritter, the poems and
dramas of the Schlegels, and other productions of romantic spirits,
formed, as we have seen, welcome material for the exposition
of his own ideas on nature and art.

As was noted in the introduction, many of the most interesting
views of Arnim respecting poetry found expression in his correspondence with friends like Brentano, Goethe, and the Grimms.
Here he is intensely serious in pressing his point, and although
informal in style, his remarks are put in a form that is worthy
of the dignified subject-matter. His reviews and critical essays,
published and unpublished, are very uneven in quality. As is the
case with his stories and plays, brilliant productions are at times
succeeded by those that are hasty and superficial. In its entirety,
however, the material that we have traversed is of much greater
value to the student of literature for a knowledge of Arnim's
spiritual personality than could have been supposed. It is surprising both in quality and quantity, and might well be supple-
mented by an examination of his writings on painting, sculpture,
history and social questions, themes which did not fall within
the range of this investigation.

Judged by quality of content and vigor of style, the contributions to the *Berliner Abendblätter* and the *Preussischer Correspondent* rate lowest among the material that has been examined.
Of highest rank are the reviews in the *Heidelbergische Jahrbücher*.
Here we see Arnim, the critic, at his very best. He was writing
primarily for two groups—the romantic sympathizers, for whom
his ideas, as he hoped, would become a stimulus and a program
for the development of national poetry; and his opponents, such
as Johann Heinrich Voss, to whom he and his romantic associates
were anathema and who, he felt, must now recognize the strength
and beauty of the new literary garb which was to replace the
outworn garment of dry classicism. After 1815 we have noted
a change in Arnim's critical style. The drift toward realism brings
an increasing clarity of ideas and a more careful and finished form.

Finally, it must be stressed again that the literary-critical writings of Arnim are the expression of a thoroughly poetic soul. Bettina likened them to a *fermata* in a musical composition, the prolonging of a tone or measure from the work itself.[1] In Arnim's case this prolongation of the tone of the work under consideration is often better than the original. All of the diverse and scattered writings that have been brought together for our examination flow organically from one unique personality. His literary criticism, even more than his correspondence, reveals the noble idealist.

[1] Arnim-Bettina, p. 380.

BIBLIOGRAPHY

Reviews, essays, and notes by Arnim are not listed in this bibliography. With a very few exceptions Arnim's published writings are given in their chronological order in Otto Mallon's *Arnim-Bibliographie* (Berlin, 1925). Details regarding them will be found in the footnotes. Some of the unpublished material discussed is listed in Karl Ernst Henrici's *Auktions-Katalog* 148 *(Bettine von Arnim)* and in *Auktions-Katalog* 149 *(Arnim und Brentano Des Knaben Wunderhorn)*. Unpublished material in the Goethe-Museum in Frankfort, to which references are made in the present work, is to appear in the *Jahrbuch des Freien Deutschen Hochstifts*.

Arnim's Works

Ludwig Achim's v. Arnim sämtliche Werke. XXI Bde. Neue Ausgabe. Berlin, v. Arnim's Verlag, 1857.

L. A. von Arnim, Unbekannte Aufsätze und Gedichte. Hrsg. von Ludwig Geiger, Berlin, 1892.

Arnims Tröst Einsamkeit. Hrsg. von Fridrich Pfaff, Freiburg i.B. und Tübingen, 1883 *(Zeitung für Einsiedler)*.

Arnim's Letters

Görres, Josef von. Gesammelte Schriften, Vol. VIII-IX. Hrsg. von Marie Görres, München, 1874 (twenty-seven letters of Arnim).

Holtei, Karl von. Briefe an Ludwig Tieck. Breslau, 1864 (three of Arnim's letters).

Schüddekopf & Walzel. Goethe und die Romantik. Weimar, 1898 (nineteen of Arnim's letters).

Steig, Reinhold. Achim von Arnim und die ihm nahe standen, 3 Bde. Stuttgart, 1894-1913 (Arnim's letters to Clemens Brentano, Bettina Brentano, Jacob und Wilhelm Grimm).

Steig, Reinhold. Zeugnisse zur Pflege der deutschen Literatur in den Heidelberger Jahrbüchern. *Neue Heidelberger Jahrbücher*, 1902 (ten of Arnim's letters).

General

L. Achim von Arnim

Becker, Hermann. A. von Arnim in den wissenschaftlichen und politischen Strömungen seiner Zeit. Leipzig, 1912.

Bottermann, Walther. Die Beziehungen des Dramatikers Achim von

Arnim zur altdeutschen Literatur. Diss., Göttingen, 1895.

Darmstaedter, Ernest, "A. v. Arnim und die Naturwissenschaft." *Euphorion,* Vol. XXXII, 1931.

Geiger, Ludwig. "A. v. Arnims Beiträge zum Literaturblatt." *Zeitschrift für vergleichende Literaturgeschichte,* Vol. XII, pp. 209-29, 1898.

Gundolf, Friedrich. Romantiker. Bd. II, Berlin-Wilmersdorf, 1930.

Kayser, Rudolf. Arnims und Brentanos Stellung zur Bühne. Berlin, 1912.

Koch, Max. Arnim, Klemens und Bettina Brentano, J. Görres. "Deutsche National-Literatur," CXLVI.

Mallon, Otto. Arnim-Bibliographie. Berlin, 1925.

Mallon, Otto. "A. v. Arnims Beiträge" zum 'Literarischen Conversations-Blatt' und zu den 'Blättern für literarische Unterhaltung' 1823-31." *Preussische Jahrbücher,* 1931.

Müller, Johann, Ed. Arnims und Brentanos romantische Volksliedforschungen; ein Beitrag zur Geschichte und Kritik des "Wunderhorns." Hamburg, 1906.

Rieser, Ferdinand. "Des Knaben Wunderhorn" und seine Quellen; ein Beitrag zur Geschichte des deutschen Volksliedes und der Romantik. Dortmund, 1908.

Rudolf, Wilhelm. Achim von Arnim als Lyriker. Straßburg, 1914.

Schönemann, Friedrich. L. Achim von Arnims geistige Entwicklung an seinem Drama "Halle und Jerusalem" erläutert. Leipzig, 1912.

Schulze, Friedrich. Die Gräfin Dolores: Ein Beitrag zur Geschichte des deutschen Geisteslebens zur Zeit der Romantik. Leipzig, 1904.

Romanticism

Arnim, Bettina v. Sämtliche Werke. Hrsg. v. Waldemar Oehlke, Berlin, 1920.

Blochmann, E. "Die deutsche Volksdichtungsbewegung in Sturm und Drang der Romantik." *Deutsche Vierteljahresschrift,* H.3, 1923.

Bobeth, Johannes. Die Zeitschriften der Romantik. Leipzig, 1908.

Borries, Kurt. Die Romantik und die Geschichte, Studien zur romantischen Lebensform. Berlin, 1925.

Czygan, Paul. Zur Geschichte der Tagesliteratur während der Freiheitskriege. Berlin, 1911.

Eichendorff, J. von. Geschichte der poetischen Literatur Deutschlands. Bd. II, Paderborn, 1857.

Gubitz, F. W. Erlebnisse. Berlin, 1868. Berlin, 1922.

Gundolf, Friedrich. Shakespeare und der deutsche Geist. Berlin, 1920.

Gundolf, Friedrich. "Schleiermachers Romantik." *Deutsche Vierteljahresschrift,* H.3, 1924.

Houben & Walzel. Zeitschriften der Romantik, Bibliographisches Repertorium, I. Berlin, 1904.

Houben, Heinrich, Hubert. Verbotene Literatur von der klassischen Zeit bis zur Gegenwart; ein kritisch-historisches Lexikon über verbotene Bücher, Zeitschriften und Theaterstücke, Schriftsteller und Verleger. Berlin, 1924-8.

Kloss, Alfred. Die Heidelbergischen Jahrbücher der Literatur. Leipzig, 1918.

Lettow-Vorbeck, M. von. Zur Geschichte des Preussischen Correspondenten von 1813-14. Berlin, 1911.

Levin, Herbert. Die Heidelberger Romantik. München, 1922.

Meinecke, Friedrich. Das Zeitalter der deutschen Erhebung, 1795-1815. Bielefeld, 1906.

Nadler, J. Die Berliner Romantik, 1800-14. Berlin, 1921.

Poetzsch, Albert. Studien zur frühromantischen Politik und Geschichtsauffassung. Leipzig, 1907.

Steig, Reinhold. Heinrich von Kleist's Berliner Kämpfe. Berlin, 1901.

Steig, Reinhold. Neue Kunde zu Heinrich von Kleist. Berlin, 1902.

Steig, Reinhold. Clemens Brentano und die Brüder Grimm. Stuttgart, 1914.

Steig, Reinhold. Bettinas Briefwechsel mit Goethe. Berlin, 1922.

Steig, Reinhold. "Goethesche Handschriften erhalten durch Bettina and Achim von Arnim." *Jahrbuch des Freien Deutschen Hochstiftes*, 1910.

Stephan, Heinz. Die Entstehung der Rheinromantik. Köln 1922.

Stockmann, A. Die deutsche Romantik, ihre Wesenszüge und ihre ersten Vertreter. Freiburg, 1921.

Varnhagen von Ense, K. A. Denkwürdigkeiten und vermischte Schriften. Leipzig, 1843-59.

Weiss, Alfred. Die Entwicklung des Fühlens und Denkens der Romantik auf Grund der romantischen Zeitschriften. Leipzig, 1912.

Literary criticism

Bran, F. A. Herder und die deutsche Kulturanschauung. Berlin, 1932.

Elkuss, Siegbert. Zur Beurteilung der Romantik und zur Kritik ihrer Erforschung. Diss. Straßburg, 1918.

Günther, Hans. Romantische Kritik und Satire bei Ludwig Tieck. Leipzig, 1907.

Haack, F. Die Deutschromantiker in der bildenden Kunst des 19. Jahrhunderts. Erlangen, 1901.

Harnack, Otto. Die klassische Ästhetik der Deutschen; Würdigung der kunsttheoretischen Arbeiten Schillers, Goethes und ihrer Freunde. Leipzig, 1892.

Kircher, Erwin. Philosophie der Romantik. Jena, 1906.

Körner, Josef. Nibelungenforschungen der deutschen Romantik. Leipzig, 1911.

Lempicki, S. von. Geschichte der deutschen Literaturwissenschaft bis zum Ende des 18. Jahrhunderts. Göttingen, 1920.

Lempicki, S. von. "Über literarische Kritik und die Probleme ihrer Erforschung." *Euphorion*, XXV, 1924.

Lempicki, S. von. "Bücherwelt und wirkliche Welt. Ein Beitrag zur Wesenserfassung der Romantik." *Deutsche Vierteljahresschrift*, 1925.

Lichtenstein, E. "Die Idee der Naturpoesie bei den Brüdern Grimm und ihr Verhältnis zu Herder." *Deutsche Vierteljahresschrift*, H.3, 1928.

Matthias, Theodor. Der deutsche Gedanke bei Jacob Grimm. Leipzig, 1915.

Möller, E. von. "Die Entstehung des Dogmas vom Ursprung des Rechtes aus dem Volksgeist." *Mitteilungen der Zeitschrift für österreichische Geschichte*, Vol. XXX.

Müller, G. "Zur Bestimmung des Begriffes 'altdeutsche Mystik'." *Deutsche Vierteljahresschrift*, H.1, 1926.

Neumann, F. "Das Nibelungenlied in der gegenwärtigen Forschung." *Deutsche Vierteljahresschrift*, H.1, 1927.

Wolf, H. "Die Genielehre des jungen Herder." *Deutsche Vierteljahresschrift*, H.3, 1925.

Rothacker, Erich. Einleitung in die Geisteswissenschaft. Berlin, 1930.

Schlegel, A.W. Kritische Schriften. Berlin, 1828.

Unger, R. "Vom Sturm und Drang zur Romantik. Eine Problem- und Literaturschau." *Deutsche Vierteljahresschrift*, H.3, 1924; H.1-2, 1928.

Unger, R. Hamann und die Aufklärung. Halle, 1925.

INDEX

VITA

Herbert R. Liedke was born April 8, 1905, at Heiligenbeil, Germany. He received his secondary education at the Gymnasium in Oranienburg, Germany. From 1925 till 1929 he studied at the University of Berlin, and the following year he taught secondary school in Halle, Germany. In 1931 he entered the Graduate School of Columbia University, studying Germanics. At the same time he taught at the College of the City of New York, holding the position of tutor until 1934 when he was appointed instructor.